Children, Families and Leisure

This book aims to further academic debate within the leisure and tourism studies community about the role of 'families' in contemporary life and the experiences of families and their children in the leisure environment. It is based on the recognition of the diverse nature of the family in the contemporary era and the position of children in families and society in general as active and knowing social agents rather than as passive objects. The family is, on the one hand, our first community with its own special kind of human attachment and, on the other, a little world on which the larger society is modelled. Families form the closest and most important emotional bond in humans. This relationship is what drives humanity and society, and positions families at the centre of leisure activities. This international and multi-disciplinary compilation of recent research into children and families examines progress made and challenges ahead for leisure studies. It extends the academic discourse to a wider understanding of what families, children and their leisure behaviour mean in today's societies. This book was originally published as two special issues of *Annals of Leisure Research*.

Heike Schänzel is a Senior Lecturer in International Tourism Management at Auckland University of Technology, New Zealand. Her research interests include tourist behaviour and experiences, children and family in tourism, sociality in tourism, and theory development in tourism and hospitality.

Neil Carr is an Associate Professor and Head of the Department of Tourism at the University of Otago, Dunedin, New Zealand, as well as the Editor of *Annals of Leisure Research*. His research focuses on understanding behaviour within tourism and leisure experiences; with a particular emphasis on animals, children and families, and sex.

Children, Families and Leisure

Edited by
Heike Schänzel and Neil Carr

LONDON AND NEW YORK

First published 2016
by Routledge

2 Park Square, Milton Park, Abingdon, Oxfordshire OX14 4RN
711 Third Avenue, New York, NY 10017

Routledge is an imprint of the Taylor & Francis Group, an informa business

First issued in paperback 2017

British Library Cataloguing in Publication Data
A catalogue record for this book is available from the British Library

ISBN 13: 978-1-138-64385-7 (hbk)
ISBN 13: 978-1-138-30922-7 (pbk)

Typeset in Times
by diacriTech, Chennai

Publisher's Note
The publisher accepts responsibility for any inconsistencies that may have arisen during the conversion of this book from journal articles to book chapters, namely the possible inclusion of journal terminology.

Disclaimer
Every effort has been made to contact copyright holders for their permission to reprint material in this book. The publishers would be grateful to hear from any copyright holder who is not here acknowledged and will undertake to rectify any errors or omissions in future editions of this book.

Contents

CONTENTS

Citation Information

The following chapters were originally published in the *Annals of Leisure Research*, volume 18, issue 2 (August 2015). When citing this material, please use the original page numbering for each article, as follows:

Chapter 7

'We have not seen the kids for hours': the case of family holidays and free-range children
Marie Vestergaard Mikkelsen and Bodil Stilling Blichfeldt
Annals of Leisure Research, volume 18, issue 2 (August 2015) pp. 252–271

Chapter 8

A review of gay and lesbian parented families' travel motivations and destination choices: gaps in research and future directions
Rodrigo Lucena, Nigel Jarvis and Clare Weeden
Annals of Leisure Research, volume 18, issue 2 (August 2015) pp. 272–289

The following chapters were originally published in the *Annals of Leisure Research*, volume 18, issue 3 (October 2015). When citing this material, please use the original page numbering for each article, as follows:

Chapter 9

Intersection of family, work and leisure during academic training
Stephanie Chesser
Annals of Leisure Research, volume 18, issue 3 (October 2015) pp. 308–322

Chapter 10

Family leisure and the coming out process for LGB young people and their parents
Dawn E. Trussell, Trisha M.K. Xing and Austin G. Oswald
Annals of Leisure Research, volume 18, issue 3 (October 2015) pp. 323–341

Chapter 11

Family experiences of visitor attractions in New Zealand: differing opportunities for 'family time' and 'own time'
Joanna Fountain, Heike Schänzel, Emma Stewart and Nora Körner
Annals of Leisure Research, volume 18, issue 3 (October 2015) pp. 342–358

Chapter 12

Understanding ambivalence in family leisure among three-generation families: 'It's all part of the package'
Shannon Hebblethwaite
Annals of Leisure Research, volume 18, issue 3 (October 2015) pp. 359–376

Chapter 13

Families in the forest: guilt trips, bonding moments and potential springboards
Alice Goodenough, Sue Waite and Jade Bartlett
Annals of Leisure Research, volume 18, issue 3 (October 2015) pp. 377–396

Chapter 14

Celebrating the family abroad: the wedding tourism experience
Giovanna Bertella
Annals of Leisure Research, volume 18, issue 3 (October 2015) pp. 397–413

Chapter 15

More than putting on a performance in commercial homes: merging family practices and critical hospitality studies
Julie Seymour
Annals of Leisure Research, volume 18, issue 3 (October 2015) pp. 414–430

For any permission-related enquiries please visit:
http://www.tandfonline.com/page/help/permissions

INTRODUCTION[1]
Special Issue on children, families and leisure

Heike Schänzel[a] and Neil Carr[b]

[a]School of Hospitality & Tourism, Auckland University of Technology, Auckland, New Zealand; [b]Department of Tourism, University of Otago, Dunedin, New Zealand

This special issue of *Annals of Leisure Research* aims to further academic debate within the leisure studies community about the role of 'families' in contemporary life and the experiences of families and their children in the leisure environment. It is based on the recognition of the diverse nature of the family in the contemporary era and the position of children in families and society in general as active and knowing social agents rather than passive objects. The family is, on the one hand, our first community with its own special kind of human attachment, and on the other, a little world on which the larger society is modelled. Families form the closest and most important emotional bond in humans. This relationship is what drives humanity and society, and positions families at the centre of leisure activities.

In recent years, there has been a greater focus on the leisure and tourist experiences of children and families (i.e. Carr 2011; Reis, Thompson-Carr, & Lovelock 2012; Schänzel & Smith 2014; Shaw 2010). Despite this, there is arguably much left to do in order to fully understand the position and experiences of children and families. Much of the current discourse is based on 'Western', 'middle class' and more 'traditional families', which does not reflect the increased diversity among families in terms of cultural and educational background and family composition. As a result, little research has been conducted on gay and lesbian parents and/or children's family leisure. Consequently, this special issue seeks to extend the existing literature to provide a wider understanding of what families, children and their leisure experiences are and mean today.

There was a high response to our call for contributions and the quality of the work submitted, leading to 13 papers being published, thus demonstrating how family leisure is gaining momentum and becoming mainstream for leisure researchers. Overall, this special issue seeks to expand upon what we already know of family and children's leisure by providing a cohesive forum for new research and emergent conceptualisations to provide a window into previously unstudied or understudied aspects of family leisure.

As Freysinger (1997) pointed out for a special issue on family leisure almost two decades ago, 'how we think about and what we know about leisure and families' is situated in cultural and societal contexts and 'our definitions or conceptualisations of family and leisure are constantly reconstructed' (p. 3). Since then, family leisure scholarship has progressed considerably and several global developments and changes have shaped, constrained and enriched family interactions and practices inside and outside of the home. These include increased mobility, family diversity, technological connectivity and shifts towards a much closer approximation of gender equality. These have themselves been shaped by changes in demography and parenting ideologies leading to greater democratisation within families.

Another significant change occurring and reflected in more recent conceptualisations and methodologies used for families is the more active involvement of children in family research. This reflects the reality that children have more say within families today and are increasingly becoming active agents within families. No longer is family leisure research conducted solely through parents/guardians. No longer either is it mothers' voices that predominate. Increasingly children get their own voice, either independent of others or through a more inclusive whole family approach to research. The active agency of children in leisure research is demonstrated by several contributions to this special issue, including a conversation between a father and his teenage son.

Three decades ago Holman and Epperson (1984) made recommendations for the need to theorise research on family leisure. It is then encouraging to see how studies in this special issue reveal significant progress made in this area. As readers will see theory is not only guiding research but also research is resulting in new theorisations. It is note-worthy that all the empirical papers in this special issue use innovative methods which are predominantly qualitative in orientation. The papers presented here suggest that we have become more sophisticated in our approaches to knowledge production. This is not to suggest that more traditional research approaches are without value but rather to recognise the potential value of stepping beyond them.

Within leisure research there is much ideological emphasis on the benefits of bonding and strengthening of relationships through family leisure participation, such as family outings. Much of this centres on time together or the idea of family time but with increasing theorisations the focus also falls on the need to explore time alone or own time (see Schänzel & Smith 2014). Parents who negotiate time away from their children during family holidays to pursue their own interests in climbing, the teenager who escapes into the world of gaming, or the children who happily entertain themselves away from their parents on caravanning holidays – all of these are representations of more nuanced understandings of what sociality within the family means in the new millennium. Leisure is full of inherent contradictions and negotiations of time within diverse family groups and this allows much scope for new insights into family leisure.

The founding principle for this special issue sought to broaden our theoretical and conceptual understandings of children and family leisure based on current research, high-lighting progress made and identifying gaps in need of attention. Despite this, most of the contributions in this issue are based on nuclear, Western families. Traditional family models still make up the majority of family households but there continues to be a noticeable absence of research on single parents, although a review of gay and lesbian family leisure and the coming out of young members of the gay and lesbian communities are included in this issue. Other voices rarely heard in the scholarship on leisure and family are families who are poor or extremely wealthy, or who come from non-Western countries. It is then encouraging to offer in this issue two studies that are inclusive of working-class families: one on urban family outings and the other on caravanning holidays.

There is a global spread of research presented here, incorporating North America, Europe, Australia and New Zealand but contributions from Asia, Africa and South America are still missing. This issue then covers new ground and answered the call for more inclusion of children and gender representations in family leisure research. However, it also alerts us to not be complacent and further extend work into previously unexplored areas of children's and family leisure. If family leisure lies at the heart of how families engage with each other and families are the heart of society then much can be gained from further research and increased understandings of what makes intergenerational kinship ties tick. Families are complex and diverse and unravelling that complexity and diversity and the constraints and negotiations surrounding their leisure behaviour is not only a worthy endeavour but, we would argue, essential to understanding human life (and even non-human life if we extend traditional definitions of the family to incorporate the myriad domesticated animals that now intimately share our leisure lives).

As the papers presented here demonstrate, research into children, families and leisure is a field of intense activity that is reflective of the healthy state of research in leisure studies more generally. Recognition of this is long overdue. For far too long leisure studies academics have stood and cried at the edge of the imagined grave into which leisure studies has been widely reported as having fallen (Rowe 2015). There is no denying that far too many leisure studies departments at universities around the world have disappeared into the mists of time or been merged with others, yet this does not mean that leisure studies has died. Rather, it thrives in the melting pot of interdisciplinarity into which it was born and arguably belongs. Evidence for this is presented in the rich diversity of departments in which the authors of the papers in this special issue are to be found. This diversity encompasses education, management, culture and global studies, a medical school, social and behaviour sciences, and applied human sciences, as well as areas traditionally thought of as being more akin to the study of leisure, such as recreation, sport and tourism. Leisure studies, as evidenced throughout this special issue not only thrives on this diverse diet but offers a vibrant arena in which to explore the lives and social experiences of children and families. In this way, leisure is seen not to be a distinct segment of life but an integral part of it. As all the papers attest, there is a strong recognition that any boundary between leisure and non-leisure is a falsehood. Rather, anything that happens in a leisure experience influences the nature of the family and childhood and the experiences of parents and children outside of this context, and vice versa. What this demonstrates is that the significance of leisure as an arena for understanding family relations and experiences is increasing in the twenty-first century.

We are in the fortunate position to have Scott McCabe providing a critical commentary for this special issue and thank him for his insightful comments on the state of research with regards to children and family leisure. Scott and his fellow researchers have in recent years brought attention to the phenomenon of social tourism or the benefits of leisure for underprivileged families. This is something we all need to remember, that enjoyable family leisure is mostly the prerogative of the most privileged families, as evidenced by the findings on urban family outings in this issue.

Keri Schwab opens this special issue with a simplified model of optimal family leisure functioning that is concerned with better understanding the group dynamics within families. This paper acknowledges that within the complexities of family groups there is a need to decrease constraints and fragmented interactions in order to increase quality family leisure interactions. Schwab's study provides a representation of the social and relational aspects of family leisure, or what can be termed as family time important for bonding and strengthening of relationships. Presenting such a model based on empirical research is a laudable effort to synthesise different family leisure behaviours and add to the theorisation of the field.

For the second paper, Lia Karsten and Naomi Felder conducted research on parents' and children's consumption of the city through family outings. Like Schwab's paper this one is concerned with family time but the focus here is wholly on an urban environment. This contribution is notable for its methodology and the variety of families included in the study. Not only does this paper cut across social class but also employs mixed methods and innovative ways to engage children in the process, such as neighbourhood walks with the children and weekly diaries. Such approaches highlight that family leisure research requires special considerations to better understand the interactions between children and parents within families from different educational and social backgrounds.

The contribution by Stephen Wearing on leisure in a world of computer games represents a father and son conversation. It illustrates some conceptual links within consumer culture, and between adolescent leisure and gaming, through an interview with a young gamer. It argues that gaming for the teenager provides an escape, or his own time away from his parents and consumer society. To this extent, this paper offers a critical reflection on gaming culture and represents a father's way to understand his son's construction of identity in the new world of computer games. Wearing in his study provides an innovative engagement with his teenage son and through giving him a voice comes to appreciate the personal development taking place in a different forum. This contribution succeeds in opening the door to a teenage world and the ways that young people grapple with self-identity, which remains a mystery to most parents and academics. It also airs the issue of parents' conducting research through and with their children, a contentious issue but one that has significant potential to enrich social understandings of children and families at the same time as doing so at the individual parental and family level (Carr 2011).

Moving on from adolescenthood to parenthood, Ben Clayton and Emily Coates researched how parents negotiate the activity of climbing in the family. They depict this work through a fictional representation of climbing that discusses gendered parenting and the morality of time. Again this paper is concerned with the negotiation of time within the family, in this case the time used by parents to pursue their own interests and differences in gender representations. Creative fictional techniques and Foucaultian analysis are employed to provide more innovative ways to engage with the contradictory and gendered nature of the discourses experienced by the climbers. The paper illustrates that despite increased equality in society gender is still central and critical to our experiences of life and leisure in the family.

The contribution by Marie Mikkelsen and Bodil Stilling Blichfeldt explores what 'children having a good time' means on caravanning holidays. This paper relies on theorisation of family time and children's own time and delves deeper into what children happily entertaining themselves means to the sociality of family life on holiday. Parents seem to have a good holiday when the children are having a good time, which in this case includes children not being seen for hours by the parents. This study underlines the point that it is not the quantity of time that the family spends together on holiday but the quality of family time, interspersed between the freedom to pursue their own interests for parents and children alike. A successful holiday then provides freedom from family commitments to allow all the family members to enjoy their holidays both together and apart.

We then arrive at the review of gay and lesbian parented families' travel motivations and destination choices by Rodrigo Lucena, Nigel Jarvis and Clare Weeden. This paper examines a different reality to the traditional 'mother-father-children' triadic and offers much needed insights into same-sex parented family tourism as a new form of tourism representing the increased diversity of families. Empirically little is known about gay and lesbian parented family travel as most leisure research is based on heterosexual families. Progress then has been made but there are still many avenues open to further understandings of leisure behaviour with other different-to-norm families.

Stephanie Chesser provides an insightful discussion of the process of balancing life across a number of competing demands. The focus of this paper is on the lives of PhD students and those in Post-Doctorate positions as they deal with the demands of their work and their position as parents of young children. The paper is intimately bound up with discussions of the position and importance of leisure in the life of the individual and the role that children often play in the well-being of their parents. This is a strong conceptual paper which has much to add to current debates about the health of the university system and academics in general, and particularly the early career ones who inhabit it.

The remaining five papers are all, in various ways, focused around discussions and analysis of the stresses and strains associated with family leisure and how these experiences can be enriching and rewarding for all those involved. The first of these papers, by Dawn Trussell, deals with the emotive issue of how families deal with the coming out of their young as members of the gay and lesbian communities. The paper focuses discussion on how this journey often shapes the leisure experiences of all involved, neatly showing how leisure is an integral part of our lives. The paper stands out as a prime example of the richness of material that can be garnered through qualitative methods, enabling an analytical story to be told that has the potential to move academic and social understandings and appreciations forward.

Following on from Dawn's work is the paper by Joanna Fountain, Heike Schänzel, Nora Körner and Emma Stewart. These authors explore what can at first look like an inherent contradiction: namely parental perspectives of 'family time' and 'own time' in family leisure. The findings speak of gendered differences between mothers and fathers; something that is inherently bound up with social constructions of 'good parents' (Carr 2011).

Shannon Hebblethwaite's paper continues the examination of the potential stresses that can inhabit the world of family leisure, focusing on 'ambivalence'. The potential presence of ambivalence in family leisure, and how participants seek to manage it in search of positive leisure experiences, is explored in detail by Shannon. From this flows an analysis of the implications for family cohesion in and beyond the leisure experience. Shannon's paper is innovative, as she rightly notes, in that it extends definitions of family to include three generations (grandparents, parents and adult grandchildren).

The paper by Alice Goodenough, Sue Waite and Jade Bartlett looks at the potential of leisure experiences to deliver family bonding opportunities and enable the construction of positive parental identities amongst participating parents. This paper is a good example of what can and should be achieved between academic researchers and those working in the wider society. To use the lexicon of the academic world, it is an example of community engagement. Yet the term is irrelevant; rather it is the meeting of minds, academic and non-academic, that is important. This is a promising trend that is starting to occur in diverse areas of leisure studies (this paper and a chapter by Winter and Young [2015] looking at the brutal realities of horse racing are examples) and is one that is well overdue. Still, rather than berating ourselves over what is now past, it is better to look forward in the hope that similar work to that undertaken by Alice and her colleagues, is a sign of good things to come.

The last paper in this group of five is by Giovanna Bertella and it focuses on the wedding tourism experience. This paper speaks to the social construction of weddings and how the family in all its complexity is woven into both the wedding and the leisure experience that surrounds it and the wedding tourism experience more broadly.

The final paper takes the reader in a new direction by exploring the position and experiences of the families and children of commercial accommodation providers. Written by Julie Seymour this paper provides a window through which we are given a view of the leisure experiences of families and children who perform as hosts/workers in the tourism experiences of their guests. At the same time, the paper gives the reader an insight into how these workers/hosts live their non-leisured family lives in a world of constructed leisure experiences.

The majority of the papers in this special issue have overtly focused on leisure while several have focused on tourism. The paper by Seymour is the only one set in hospitality. One perspective of the ongoing debate about what constitutes leisure studies might suggest that tourism and hospitality situated papers have no place in a leisure journal. However, a different perspective would argue that they are actually ideally placed in a journal such as this one since leisure is the umbrella under which these various areas of study should all be housed. The *Annals of Leisure Research* itself would support such a standpoint, noting as it does in its aims and scope that it 'seeks theoretical or applied articles which cover any topic within the broad area of leisure studies, including recreation, tourism, hospitality, the arts, outdoor recreation, events, entertainment, sport, culture and play'. This position is based in the belief that all of these areas share conceptual roots that are grounded in leisure, which gives academics working in each field the potential to access the rich history and tapestry of theoretical and conceptual work on leisure and its meaning that has been undertaken over millennia.

So as we come to the end of the construction of this special issue dedicated to families, children and leisure, it is time to reflect not just on the wealth and diversity of work that is currently being undertaken in this arena but to think about what still needs to be done. Indeed, this is vital if the potential of the special issue is not to be wasted. It is not sufficient to simply place on record what work is being done and to pat our collective selves on the back for placing it in the academic press. A challenge for the future, and the now, is to see that this work finds its way into the wider society and that academics and practitioners engage one another in a productive manner that benefits the well-being of the family, in all its diversity, and the children that exist within it. This is not a call for shallow consulting work but for a true meeting of minds where the rich conceptual academic work can be utilised in a productive manner by society and in the process be further informed and enriched by it.

More specifically, this raises an important question. What remains to be done? The work by Hebblethwaite identifies a rich area for further research; namely the multi-generational family. This is arguably increasingly important as we see people living longer, making the multi-generational family a more prominent feature in the lives of people. In addition, alongside an increasingly internationally mobile segment of the global population that stresses the bonds between disparate generations of individual families, we are witnessing a growth in multi-generational households in Western nations, where the nuclear family household was previously the norm. This has the potential to place a different variety of stressors on families. The position of leisure in the lives of these multi-generational families and its ability to act as a counterweight to stresses is in need of further investigation.

It has been very positive across this issue to see homosexuality in the family being discussed and dealt with. This may be seen as part of a wider social awakening to the realities of the position of homosexuals in society more generally, gay rights and the importance of well-being. The latest pinnacle in this shift is arguably the decision of the United States in 2015 to recognise the rights of gay people to marry. Yet, the war (for a war is exactly what it is) for equal rights, irrespective of who you are, is an ongoing one, and its battles are often fought in the leisure environment and in a family context. It is in this context that there is still much work for academics to do to look at the position of the rest of the lesbian, gay, bisexual and transgender (LGBT) community within family and children's leisure.

The diversity of the family in the contemporary era has been attested to in this special issue and those working in the field need to explore this further to understand the leisure experiences of different types of family and how they not only differ from one another but also the extent to which they share similarities. A trick that academics need to learn, which to be fair a few are beginning to, is to look not just at the new and different (from the perceived norm) but also at the mundane. In the context of family leisure, this can be constructed as the 'nuclear family', the 'middle class' and the 'heterosexual'. With the new critical lens that has been and continues to be developed by exploring the 'other' there is a need to re-engage with this mundane side of the family (Scott 2015). There is also a need to look not just at the disadvantaged 'other' but also hyper-privileged families and their children, those of the social elite segments of society. This examination needs to be undertaken with open eyes that appreciate the 'privileged' life for what it really is, one that is often restricted and constrained in its own ways.

Finally, despite the richness of the work that makes up this special issue and the geographical diversity of the universities where the authors are based, there remains a dearth of work, published here or elsewhere, that examines family and/or children's leisure outside of a Western-centric context. The leisure experiences of families and children living in Asia, Africa, the Middle East and Latin America remain under-explored. It would be naive and simply wrong to assume that ideas based on Western premises can be extrapolated to non-Western contexts. Rather, research is needed to understand the leisure experiences of non-Western families and their children. Recognising the increasing cultural diversity of national populations, there is also arguably the need to examine the diversity of family and children's leisure experiences in any one space where the population is multi-cultural/ethnically diverse. Doing all of this will arguably not only increase academic understandings of family and children's leisure but also help to resolve conflict and misunderstandings in society in general and the leisure environment in particular. This speaks of the potential leisure studies has to help society with real-world problems that threaten peace and harmony at a societal, family and ultimately individual level.

Have we managed to mention everything that could or should be looked at in relation to families and children's leisure moving into the future? Undoubtedly not, and it would be presumptuous to claim otherwise.

Note

1. The original special issue was published in two parts in the *Annals of Leisure Research*. Consequently, this represents an amalgam of the introductions to the two parts rather than a completely new introduction.

References

Carr, N. (2011). *Children's and Families' Holiday Experiences*. London, UK, and New York, NY: Routledge.

Freysinger, V. J. (1997). Special issue introduction: Redefining family, redefining leisure: Progress made and challenges ahead in research on leisure and families. *Journal of Leisure Research*, 29(1), 1–4.

Holman, T. B. & Epperson, A. (1984). Family and leisure: A review of the literature with research recommendations. *Journal of Leisure Research*, 16(4), 277–294.

Reis, A. C., Thompson-Carr, A., & Lovelock, B. (2012). Parks and families: Addressing management facilitators and constraints to outdoor recreation participation. *Annals of Leisure Research*, 15(4), 315–334. doi:10.1080/11745398.2012.737299

Rowe, D. (2015). Complexity and the leisure complex. *Annals of Leisure Research*. doi:10.1080/11745398.2015.1028949

Schänzel, H. A. & Smith, K. A. (2014). The socialization of families away from home: Group dynamics and family functioning on holiday. *Leisure Sciences: An Interdisciplinary Journal*, 36(2), 126–143. doi:10.1080/01490400.2013.857624

Scott, D. G. (2015). The practice of everyday life performed away from home: A reflexive ethnography of a group tour (Thesis, Doctor of Philosophy). Dunedin, New Zealand: University of Otago.

Shaw, S. M. (2010). Diversity and ideology: Changes in Canadian family life and implications for leisure. *World Leisure Journal*, 52(1), 4–13.

Winter, C. & Young, W. (2015). Fatalities and fascinators: A new perspective on thoroughbred racing. N. Carr (ed.). *Domestic Animals and Leisure*. Basingstoke, UK: Palgrave Macmillan. pp. 241–258.

CRITICAL COMMENTARY
Family leisure, opening a window on the meaning of family

Scott McCabe

Nottingham University Business School, Nottingham, UK

Introduction

The concept of *family* is something that everyone can instantly relate to as being identifiable and comprehensible. And yet it is also confounding in its nebulousness and is subjectively constructed. Therefore, the idea of family leisure as being something that is intrinsic to the establishment and maintenance of functioning family life, and I use the work 'functioning' purposely in this context, is both critically important to leisure studies and also capable of transcending the discipline to speak to wider contemporary social life and social relations. Family leisure can be thought of in terms of 'doings', accomplishments, activities and also in terms of temporality, the time we give to pleasurable experiences. But it also opens up a wider set of questions about the meanings attached to these activities in space and time, the implications of these questions having the potential to reverberate on individual's and their sense of identity as well as society as a whole. Family life, and specifically the practices that make up leisure within the context of family life, is subject to powerful social norms and regulation at the micro level of individual family 'units' and the macro level of society, government and the media. Thus, family leisure provides an interesting frame to examine meanings and practices of 'family'. For the purposes of this critical commentary, I want to discuss a number of areas that I believe leisure studies research could develop to add to the richness of the field, but these are by no means exhaustive and in many ways reflect my own research interests and agendas. The commentary begins with a brief resume of the main approaches to family leisure that have been taken in the field, before moving on to highlight three potential areas of intersection between family leisure and meanings of the family: moral panics, technology and the marketization of family leisure.

A very brief tour around family leisure

Shaw has produced an excellent review of family leisure that maps out the major debates and critical research issues in this broad area of interest (1997). Shaw recognizes that family leisure is a widely used concept in everyday language (albeit from a Western European and North American social context) and one that has gained significant traction in the academic field. Family leisure can be defined as time spent together as a family in free time or recreational activities. Much, although not all leisure (and in no way intending to underplay the importance of leisure which is undertaken for intrinsic motivations, goals and pleasurable outcomes), is not an isolated and individualistic aspect of life, but is interweaved within a social context and embedded within innate social relations. These factors make family leisure an area of sustained interest to leisure researchers, and yet there have been a number of controversies which have led to significant debates within the field. Shaw synthesizes these in three types: first is the difficulty on establishing how to define families. The notional model of family that comprises two heterosexual adults and a child(ren) living at home has been challenged in recognition of the increasing diversity of family structures that exist in modern society. There is an increasing acknowledgement in the literature of the wide range in diversity of family structures including gay and lesbian families, blended and non-custodial families, but of huge importance in terms of volume of people, are single parent families or families consisting of a broader range of extended relationship structures.

Secondly, Shaw identifies that researchers face the difficulty of defining the concept of leisure within the family. Here, the main issues surround the experience of family activities *as* leisure for different members of the family. Should family leisure imply that shared participation in leisure activities is subjectively experienced by all members of the family equally as leisure? Some family leisure activities might involve 'emotional labour', particularly for women in conventional models of heterosexual family relationships. Additionally, family leisure might also imply 'relational leisure' (Shaw 1997, 99), where the focus is on social interactions, rather than intrinsically motivated, immersive activities, often associated with leisure definitions. Some family leisure may be perceived as obligated, role-bound, dutiful activities. We might associate this type of subjective experience with a perceived set of social norms and obligations around 'good parenting' for example. The third area of controversy identified by Shaw is the issue of outcomes of family leisure activities. Shaw argues that much research on family leisure focuses on beneficial outcomes, including an increase in the quality of family relationships, improved communications and enhanced cohesiveness amongst families. This is contrasted with a strand of research which has noted the negative outcomes that can arise from family leisure such as increased stress, conflict and the fact that family leisure can place constraints on individuals' ability to engage in autonomous, immersive leisure.

Shaw argues that two broad paradigms are commonly applied in family leisure research: the social psychological approach, which has driven research on the interactions within families and the positive outcomes arising out of family leisure. This is contrasted with the sociological approach, which is characterized by an emphasis on the broad scale societal gender relations that have cast doubt on the universality of the categorization of family leisure experiences. Shaw recommends a blended approach through her review to advance future research in this area. I agree with Shaw, but argue that we can use the family leisure lens to explore the meaning of social life, and in the rest of this commentary I focus on two examples, moral panics, the impact of technology on family life, and on the marketization of family leisure as offering potential for future research.

Moral panics in family life

One area of potential interest is in the exploration of the meanings and values attached to family leisure. A number of researchers have recently argued for the need for much more detailed focus on the different voices of children, and adults in the field of family leisure tourism experiences (Mikkelsen and Blichfelt 2015). Carr (2011) and Schänzel, Yeoman, and Backer (2012) and others point to an absence of research on the family per se and individual perspectives on goals, experiences and outcomes of family leisure, specifically holidays. Holidays are important as they provide a context where idealizations of family life can be created (Mikkelsen and Blitchfielt 2015). Obrador argues that the 'thick' sociality of family life, as played out by the pool, can be a source of stress and tension as well as happiness (2012). There is an increasing sense that families can sometimes struggle to live up to the expectations set by society, their peers and themselves (Mikkelsen and Blitchfield summarize these debates 2015). This is suggestive of a type of moral panic. Perceived time poverty and a culture where all adults in a family need or feel the need to work, places pressure on work–life balance, family time and has the potential to incite a range of mixed feelings such as guilt, pride, anger and anxiety (Brown and Warner-Smith 2005). Do we place too much emphasis on material wealth gain at the expense of family leisure? Do we spend enough time at simple play with our children? Is the quality of family leisure time and quality and quantity of activities adequate? As parents, are we too tired and stressed to really engage in leisure fully together? How have the changes in the socio-economic environment, specifically the global economic recession brought on by the banking crisis in 2007, affected family leisure?

These are the types of questions that are intrinsic to the modern parenting experience. Yet we rarely place these contemporary concerns within an historical context. As a father of two sons, looking back to my own childhood experiences of family life I believe (albeit from an anecdotal white, middle class and male perspective) that the number and quality of interactions between me and my sons is dramatically better than it used to be. In the 1960s and 1970s of my youth, family leisure comprised of occasional evenings playing board games, and Sunday afternoons out. These were complimented by the annual family holiday, almost exclusively consisting of a week or 10 days camping in Devon or West Wales. In contrast, many of my contemporaries spend much more time within the family, doing family activities and leisure. Therefore, although it is recognized that gender stereotypes that structure relationships within families remain entrenched, further research is needed on the dynamics within and between family members in terms of the inputs into leisure activities and time, and outcomes in terms of satisfaction, communication and bonding. Much of the research in the leisure literature has come from a gender perspective, and rightly so, necessarily focusing on the gendered nature of leisure, and particularly the emotional labour and 'work' that characterize the experience of family leisure for women. However, there is a need to compliment this with further research on the perspectives of all family members (Schänzel and Smith 2011), dynamics and interactions between family members, intergenerational perspectives on leisure experiences, and on the patterns of family leisure within the explicit reference point of interactions and relationships. This is just a type of moral panic shaping contemporary family relationships. Other examples might include the level of surveillance over children and their activities, perceptions of risks associated with children having the freedom to roam and play without adult supervision and diet, health and education, all having the potential to influence family leisure research.

The impact of technology on family leisure

In some ways, we can consider the issues brought about by technological adoption as a type of moral panic. Many adults brought up in the 'pre-digital' era might consider that technology use amongst children has fundamentally altered the ways in which families experience leisure, disrupting social interactions between family members, shifting leisure from the social to the solitary, from active to sedentary and so on. We are often anxious about our children who are 'born digital'. Mums are dissatisfied with the level of quality time they have with their children, identifying technology as a barrier to communication. Digital native children are able to swipe screens before they can hold a crayon and have a digital presence by the age of two years old which can (cf. www.mobicip.com) cause concerns for modern families (Turkle 2011 reminds us that technology can lead to fundamental shifts in relationships and even identities). Technology allows us to be connected constantly, so we can use technology to spend more time with each other when we are apart, but also from a negative perspective, leads us to the problem of 'co-presence', being physically present but immersed in our individual screens. O'Keeffe, Clarke-Pearson, and Council on Communications and Media (2011) point out the many benefits that accrue to adolescents and young people from engagement with social media technology as enhancing communication, social connection and technical skills. This suggests that the negative connotations of technology on human relations may receive greater attention than the benefits. However, O'Keeffe et al. also acknowledge the risks for children such as cyberbullying, privacy issues and sexual experimentation through 'sexting', internet addiction and sleep deprivation (2011, 800).

The area in which the impact of technology on family relationships is most acutely relevant is in leisure life. On the one hand, mobile digital technologies offer us opportunities to expand shared leisure experiences from the physical into the virtual realm negating the need for co-presence in the experience. This could include participation in online games together, or sharing and socializing online through social networking sites. This could add a significant value to family leisure outcomes. On the other hand, absorption in digital and online media could negatively affect the perceived value of family leisure. The intricacies of conversation are potentially lost in the truncated and mediated online world, seriously affecting our orientations to social relations both within and beyond the family realm (Turkle 2011). Not only do modern parents worry a lot about the amount of time that children spend interacting with technology and screens in particular, but also about the types of content they interact with, either in terms of the internet or gaming. But we have little knowledge of the consequences of technology on family leisure, either as a mediator or as a constraining factor. Family leisure research has the potential to add significant new understandings to our knowledge of the effects of technology on social relations and family life.

The marketization of family leisure

A final consideration for this commentator relates to the ways that family leisure has become marketized, alongside many other areas of social life. This also has a number of dimensions including the 'outsourcing' of family leisure in an attempt to manage modern dual parent working roles and commitments (Cullen 2015). This goes beyond hiring child minders in conventional caring roles to the wide-scale provision of services designed to cater for family leisure needs (e.g. birthday party organization, family days out and so on). Since traditionally the organization of activities together could have been perceived as an intrinsic part of the sociality of the activities themselves, the marketization of these practices may influence the ways in which family leisure activities are experienced. A related issue involves the ways families are presented in the media and advertising of leisure. Advertising can shape patterns and trends of behaviour and idealize family leisure norms, yet there is little understanding of how representations affect leisure practices. There is a need to ensure that constructive images of families appear in the context of advertising for leisure activities and that visitor attractions promote healthy and positive outcomes associated with them. Images and other representations of family life and values need to be carefully presented in order to reflect the different structures and patterns of family relationships as identified earlier. Zink and Kane (2015) recently found that images of families were virtually absent from magazine and news advertising in the context of outdoor recreation. They reiterated that the media plays such a powerful role not only in representing reality but in shaping and framing reality through the reinforcement of existing power relations. Advertising and media practices can be analysed to help us understand social practices and issues of the power of the market over family leisure. Family leisure provides excellent potential as a lens to explore human social relations and we must grasp the opportunities to develop inter-disciplinary research to maximize this potential.

Notes on contributor

Scott McCabe is Professor of Marketing and Tourism at the University of Nottingham. His research interests are in tourist and leisure experience, particularly for vulnerable consumers. He is particularly interested in the impact of holidays on quality of family life.

References

Brown, P., and P. Warner-Smith. 2005. "The Taylorisation of Family Time: An Effective Strategy in the Struggle to 'Manage' Work and Life?" *Annals of Leisure Research* 8 (2): 75–90.

Carr, N. 2011. *Children's and Families' Holiday Experience*. London: Taylor & Francis.

Cullen, J. 2015. "Parenting, Work and the Marketization of Family Life." *Work, Employment and Society*. doi:10.1177/0950017015581768.

Mikkelsen, M. V., and B. S. Blichfeldt. 2015. "We Have Not Seen the Kids for Hours: The Case of Family Holidays and Freerange Children." *Annals of Leisure Research*. doi:10.1080/11745398.2014.999342.

Mobicip. www.mobicip.com/'Parenting in the Digital Era'. http://content.mobicip.com/content/parenting-digital-era

Obrador, P. 2012. "The Place of the Family in Tourism Research: Domesticity and Thick Sociality by the Pool." *Annals of Tourism Research* 39: 401–420.

O'Keeffe, G. S., K. Clarke-Pearson, and Council on Communications and Media. 2011. "Clinical Report – The Impact of Social Media on Children, Adolescents, and Families." *Pediatrics* 127 (4): 800–804.

Schänzel, H. A., and K. A. Smith. 2011. "The Absence of Fatherhood: Achieving True Gender Scholarship in Family Tourism Research." *Annals of Leisure Research* 14 (2–3): 143–154.

Schänzel, H. A., I. Yeoman, and E. Backer, eds. 2012. *Family Tourism: Multidisciplinary Perspectives*. Bristol: Channel View.

Shaw, S. S. 1997. "Controversies and Contradictions in Family Leisure: An Analysis of Conflicting Paradigms." *Journal of Leisure Research* 29 (1): 98–112.

Turkle, S. 2011. *Alone Together: Why We Expect More from Technology and Less from Each Other*. New York: Basic Books.

Zink, R., and M. Kane. 2015. "Not in the Picture: Images of Participation in New Zealand's Outdoor Recreation Media." *Annals of Leisure Research* 18 (1): 65–82.

Towards a model of optimal family leisure

Keri A. Schwab[a] and Daniel L. Dustin[b]

[a]Recreation, Parks, & Tourism Administration Department, California Polytechnic State University, San Luis Obispo, CA, USA; [b]Department of Parks, Recreation, and Tourism, University of Utah, Salt Lake City, UT, USA

Leisure is an important component of family life, yet many families struggle to focus on or participate in family leisure. This study examined the structural characteristics of family life that can impede or promote family leisure. Employing a systems perspective, a literature-based model of family leisure was created, and in-depth interview data were gathered from three families to compare to the model. Results indicated that while the content of the families' leisure varied, their leisure shared similar organizational properties; the need to negotiate constraints, increase focused interactions and decrease fragmented interactions to achieve higher-quality family leisure. The paper concludes with a discussion of the study's relevance to the existing family leisure literature, a description of a simplified model of optimal family leisure functioning based on the study's findings, implications for its application and suggestions for future research.

Introduction

Family leisure is an important component of family life and is often considered vital to the growth and socialization of children and overall family cohesion. Decades of research support the idea that family leisure contributes to strong parent–child relationships (Barnett 1991; Shaw 1999), cohesion, adaptability, communication (Zabriskie and McCormick 2001), overall family functioning (Freeman and Zabriskie 2003; Zabriskie and Freeman 2004) and satisfaction with family life (Zabriskie and McCormick 2003). Leisure time spent interacting with family members can also build an individual's overall sense of competence (Bronfenbrenner 1979), enhance communication and bonding (Shaw and Dawson 2001; Smith, Freeman, and Zabriskie 2009) and create a sense of equity (Orthner and Mancini 1991). In addition, many parents report the importance of family leisure for socializing children to family values or teaching them about health and fitness (Kleiber 1999; Shaw and Dawson 2001). Multiple studies also indicate a relationship between core and balance leisure activities and family life satisfaction and family functioning (Hornberger, Zabriskie, and Freeman 2010; Smith, Freeman, and Zabriskie 2009; Zabriskie and McCormick 2003; Freeman and Zabriskie 2003). The Core and Balance Model of Family Leisure Functioning (Agate et al. 2009) suggests that core or everyday leisure activities are important for family bonding, while balance or novel and unique activities provide opportunities for challenge and adaptability.

14

Given family leisure's benefits, it is unfortunate that many families struggle to find time to participate in, or focus on, family leisure (Gillis 2001; Jacobs and Gerson 2004). Not engaging in quality family leisure appears to stem from multiple causes, including increased social pressures regarding parenting, a lack of time for family leisure and general multitasking and disengagement during leisure activities (Bianchi, Robinson, and Milkie 2006; Jacobs and Gerson 2004). Rushed or fragmented leisure may decrease the quality of leisure interactions or contribute to contradictory leisure experiences for family members, as parents and children put much effort into completing work, household chores, self-care and otherwise trying to fit family leisure into their harried lives.

A perceived lack of time and an increase in work-related obligations are increasingly commonplace in modern families (Bianchi 2011). The nature and structure of family life has shifted greatly in the past several decades with notable increases in single parent (Hornberger, Zabriskie, and Freeman 2010) as well as dual earner families (Jacobs & Gerson, 2004). Seldom is someone home to provide childcare, carry out domestic chores or help in general, which leads to an increased perception of too much to do and not enough time to do it. This feeling is especially pronounced among women working outside the home, who are still largely responsible for the bulk of household chores (Jacobs and Gerson 2004; Lareau 2003; Lee, Zvonkovic, and Crawford 2014). Women, who often do the hidden work of family leisure organization (Shaw 1992; Trussell and Shaw 2012), report feeling overworked, stressed, sleep deprived and unable to accomplish everything required of them (Bianchi 2011).

The absence of quality family leisure may also stem from increased social expectations and pressure on adults to be "good" parents by being highly visible, active and involved in their children's lives (Coakley 2006; Shaw 2008; Trussell and Shaw 2012). Families invent domestic rituals such as dinner time, bed time or play time to increase family interactions, yet ironically they increase the perception of not having enough time to complete the acts (Grimes 2000). Still other research suggests that family leisure has been "respaced" and "despaced". Respacialization means family leisure occurs in non-household settings such as the car, vacation homes or family-friendly resorts. Despacialization means family leisure can occur digitally through cell phones or electronic communications (Daly 1996), increasing access to family time, yet also changing the pace and nature of these interactions. In addition, recent research suggests that parents with non-traditional work hours – such as those who work varying shifts, or on the weekend – also experience respaced, or simply less, leisure time with their children (Craig and Brown 2014).

Attempts to create more family leisure opportunities have thus led to the unintended consequence of less perceived leisure time. Technology meant to increase leisure time often serves to speed up interactions and expectations for change. Family members, including children, frequently feel rushed during the day (Gillis 2001), and the ability to multitask only adds to a sense that life is speeding up rather than slowing down. Family leisure researchers have noted that in a busy society, "optimal contexts for family communication to regularly occur appear to be increasingly limited" (Smith, Freeman, and Zabriskie 2009, 81).

In sum, modern families spend more time in paid employment, experience less support at home, feel increased pressure to meet or exceed social expectations of "good" parenting and experience family time in respaced and despaced ways. These lifestyle changes have contributed to the perception of time famine and a decline in the quality of family interactions. Family leisure, once touted as "one of the few experiences that bring family members together for any significant amount of time" (Zabriskie and McCormick 2001, 287), now occurs in ways and environments that feel rushed, fragmented and distracted conditions that may not be conducive to the quality interactions needed to realize the full benefits of family leisure.

A family systems perspective

To date, research on family leisure has focused largely on individuals in family settings and has examined less often the family unit as a whole. This reductionist approach has created knowledge gaps regarding family leisure interactions. This is not entirely surprising given the methodological difficulties of studying complex systems in their totality. Family time, writes Gillis (2001), is "notoriously difficult to measure … because it has a qualitative as well as quantitative dimension" (24). For example, previous research has focused on the relationship between leisure and individual reports of family satisfaction (Poff, Zabriskie, and Townsend 2010; Zabriskie and McCormick 2003), perceptions of constraints and social support (Brown et al. 2001) and mothers' experiences in family leisure (Shannon and Shaw 2008; Irving and Giles 2011), or has relied on individual census data or self-reports to gauge daily leisure time experiences (Robinson and Godbey 1999). These approaches have sought to measure or understand an individual's experiences, or have isolated variables, rather than examining whole family functioning and the role leisure plays in such functioning. For example, the Core and Balance Model of Family Leisure Functioning analyses data points independently. While Poff et al. (2010) have examined large data sets through advanced statistical methods, they have also acknowledged that this approach has limitations, and that "alternate analytical methods would allow for family level analysis and provide better use of the rich interdependent family data collected" (Poff, Zabriskie, and Townsend 2010, 388).

Additionally, studies that focus on individual experiences of leisure within a family context have frequently been conducted using a definition of leisure as an individual experience. When viewed this way, leisure is understood as something a person participates in for individual reasons, and from which individual benefits are derived. Furthermore, leisure is seen to occur when an individual is free from obligation, intrinsically motivated to participate and finds the experience personally pleasing or satisfying for its own sake (Kelly 1983; Neulinger 1974). In a family, however, traditional individual-focused leisure constructs like intrinsic motivation, obligation and personal pleasure may be filtered through one's roles or responsibilities within the family unit (Buswell et al. 2012; Coakley 2006; Kelly 1983; Shannon and Shaw 2008). These roles and responsibilities are often played out in family leisure, thus changing the nature of the experience. Leisure may no longer be participated in for individual reasons or benefits, but rather for reasons and benefits associated with the family as a whole. For example, a mother may organize a family leisure activity not because she enjoys the activity, but because she values the final outcome for the whole family (Schwab 2011). Put differently, leisure is experienced relative to one's role in the family system. Breaking down the family in a way that isolates experiences, outcomes or variables may thus not be the best way to understand family leisure.

A more holistic approach, one that focuses on the overall functioning of a family, including interactions, reciprocity, patterns and feedback, may be better suited for understanding the whole of family leisure. If family leisure is contextual, relational and social, one way to examine it is through the lens of Family Systems Theory (Zabriskie and McCormick 2001). A derivative of General Systems Theory, Family Systems Theory is often used by therapists and counsellors to better understand the interactions, behaviours and beliefs of all family members within the context of the family unit

(O'Brien 2005). General Systems Theory posits that a system is more than the sum of its individual parts and that to know anything about the system, the interactions among the parts must be understood in their totality rather than by isolating each part for observation (Fingerman and Bermann 2000). Family Systems Theory also assumes that families are mutually influential and reciprocal in their interactions, and that there is circularity to family interactions rather than linear cause and effect relationships. These reciprocal and interconnected influences shape the family system into a unique whole (Fingerman and Bermann 2000; Mactavish and Schleien 2004) and can be studied as such.

The study on which this paper is based aimed to extend previous research by applying systems thinking to create a literature-based model of family leisure and then testing the model's usefulness by examining three families' leisure functioning relative to the model. Proceeding from the assumption that the content of the three families' leisure pursuits could vary substantially, our approach focused on the identification of common organizational properties shared by the three families that might be useful for better understanding, planning and programming for family leisure.

Methodology

The research reported here emphasizes the interactions among important elements that occur during family leisure. First, guided by an extensive review of the relevant literature, the most important elements that typically characterize family leisure were identified. Second, a literature-based model of family leisure was created to represent the interactions among those elements. Third, in-depth interviews were conducted with three different types of families to test the model's usefulness. Fourth, based on an analysis of the interviews, the literature-based model was pared down to its most essential parts, suggesting a more simplified model of optimal family leisure (MOFL).

A literature-based model of family leisure

The first stage of the study involved creating a literature-based model to graphically represent important elements, interactions and feedback loops characterizing family leisure. In model building the goal is to find an "economical set of interrelated assumptions and principles that can account for both the patterned behavior of family members and the variations in these patterns across and within families over time" (Broderick 1993, 59). Based on an extensive review of the family systems literature concerning itself with leisure behaviour, the most common structural characteristics evident in family leisure were employed to create a literature-based model of family leisure. These common characteristics shared a similar order of occurrence, including antecedents to leisure, the leisure experience and outcomes. The common characteristics included motivation; social role constraints and obligations; work or effort in the antecedent subsystem; focused and fragmented interactions; conflict, communication, adaptability and support in the experience subsystem; and education, shared values, family cohesion and identity salience in the outcome subsystem. Finally, the literature reviewed suggested many relationships among the characteristics, and those most frequently suggested were then incorporated into the model. For example, the leisure constraints literature suggests that social obligations can increase motivation to negotiate constraints. This is indicated in the model by linking social role obligation to increasing motivation. As another example, the family leisure literature indicates that parents experience greater identity salience from quality family leisure, or that of focused leisure interactions, in which they have a chance to enact their desired parent identity (Shaw and Dawson 2001). This link is illustrated in the model as a line from focused interaction to increasing identity salience.

Once the model's elements were chosen and relationships outlined, the next step was to create a graphical representation with the aid of a computer software program (see Figure 1). The program, called Stella™ software, made it possible to draw, move and connect elements in various ways, as well as to simulate the influences of elements on one another. Stella offers several building blocks for creating a visual representation of a

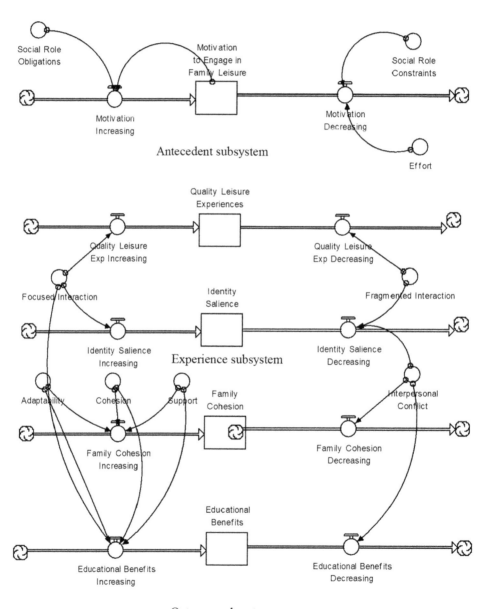

Figure 1. Literature-based model of family leisure.

system; namely, stocks, flows, converters and connectors (Richmond 2001). These are the internal pieces that enable the system to operate. Stocks, or reservoirs, are collections of resources and are represented by a square. In this study, one stock was the motivation to engage in leisure. Like a reservoir, stocks can fill up or drain down depending on how much of something flows into or out of it. The flow is the process of resources moving into or out of a stock, and is represented by a valve-like piece on a line running into the stock. An example from this study is the flow controlling how social role obligation flows through motivation. Another piece, a converter, is used to regulate the flow of something into the reservoir, thus causing the level in that reservoir to increase or decrease, such as the line between social role obligation and motivation. Finally, connectors represent links among all the elements of a system (Richmond 2001). For example, support might flow through a cohesion converter, which results in an increase in the stock of family cohesion.

In essence, the literature-based model is a hypothesized "mental map" of family leisure based on ideas found in the family leisure literature. It is one way to think about how the important elements that occur during family leisure interact with one another and influence the desired outcomes from family leisure experiences.

Data collection for model comparison

After creating the literature-based model of family leisure, the next step was to gather information from different kinds of families to provide data by which to compare the elements and interactions in the literature-based model. This information was gathered through a single, afternoon-length interview and observation with each of three families during late 2010 and early 2011 in the USA. Each family was first interviewed about its family leisure behaviour, then the family was asked to plan and engage in a leisure activity and then after, the members were again interviewed to discuss and reflect on their experience. The researcher video recorded all parts to preserve the audio and video for later data analysis. The audio portions were transcribed verbatim and became the qualitative data for this study. The video recordings were a potential second data source, but the dialogue provided by each family was much more informative data than the video recordings, and the video was ultimately not used. During each interview, the researcher asked the family open-ended questions, and at first let responses flow as the family might naturally talk. But, if a member did not respond to two questions in a row, the researcher would specifically ask that person for thoughts on both previous questions, to ensure that all voices were included. The findings of these interviews were then used to compare the leisure functioning of each to the literature-based model. Because each of the families' leisure functioning ended up differing substantially from the literature-based model, three individual family leisure models were then created to compare all organizational properties. Finally, based on the discovery of shared organizational properties among the families and the study's overall outcomes, the literature-based model was simplified to provide a more general overview of family leisure functioning.

Sample characteristics and procedures

Three families were recruited for the study using purposive sampling. Because of the study's exploratory nature, three families was deemed to be a sufficient number for revealing pronounced organizational similarities or differences. The families were of different socio-economic status, age and educational backgrounds. Each family included two heterosexual parents and at least one child between the ages of 10 and 17. Families were asked to participate in one video-taped family interview and one leisure activity of their choice, with a researcher present. The Reynolds family (all names are fictional) was an affluent family with two children aged 10 and 13, and the parents were in their late 40s. The family lived in a large home in a mountain town, with access to many natural resources, as well as the time and money to purchase equipment to recreate together. The Perry family was a low-income family that lived in a small townhouse in a downtown, urban area. The parents were 28 and 29 years old and their daughter was 11 years old. Neither parent completed high school or had a job. The third family, Greg, Emma and Abe, consisted of an unmarried couple raising the father's son from a previous marriage. The parents were in their mid-30s and Abe was 11 years old. Both parents had college degrees and worked as artists, careers that brought in varying amounts of income each month.

The mothers from each family were contacted to set up an interview. They were told that the study was about family leisure, and that they would be asked to discuss and participate in a family leisure experience of their own choosing. The interviews, including videotaping, lasted approximately three hours, took place in each family's home, and each family was compensated US$100 for its time. The interview questions were designed to explore family members' ideas about antecedents, experiences and outcomes from their family leisure in general. In each interview, members were asked to discuss leisure activities they participated in most often, and to describe one activity they had completed recently. As the family talked, the researcher asked follow-up questions to probe further into each topic, such as why the family chose an activity, what they hoped to gain from it, and what went into planning the activity.

Next, each family was asked to choose and plan a leisure activity they could complete during the data collection process. The researcher recorded their conversations, and once they decided on an activity, the researcher asked follow-up questions about their choice. The questions were intended to explore the family's antecedent motivations and expected outcomes from their experience. Questions included why the family chose the activity, what they hoped to gain from it, and how they would prepare for it.

After the antecedent portion of the interview, the family completed the activity and then discussed it. Interview questions following the activity were intended to explore the family's actual experience as well as their reflections on the experience and desired outcomes. Questions included asking the family to describe how others influenced their participation during the activity, why the activity "worked" or did not "work" for them, and any positive or negative outcomes. During each interview, the researcher provided clarification on questions as needed, and at times asked for additional information.

The researcher chose to interview the family members as a unit rather than interviewing them separately. While acknowledging that individual family members might have been hesitant to be completely forthcoming about their feelings regarding their family leisure experiences because of other family members' presence during the interviews, to break down the family unit into its individual parts for the interviews could have obscured what transpired as a family unit. It is important to remember that systems theory suggests the total family experience is more than the sum of its parts (Fingerman and Bermann 2000; Zabriskie and McCormick 2001), and of interest in this study was the family in its totality.

Data analysis

Content analysis was used to interpret the data, and identify themes, patterns and insights within the data (Patton 2002). This method consisted of developing a coding scheme, coding and classifying data into themes while looking for convergence and divergence, organizing themes into a useful framework and interpreting themes. Following Patton's (2002) recommendation, the study moved back and forth between induction and deduction, using both opened-ended and hypothetico-deductive approaches to examine hypotheses or solidify ideas that emerged, sometimes even manipulating elements.

Prior to data analysis, the researcher created an *a priori* coding scheme for labelling and categorizing themes and for noting which themes were most important for each family and which themes should be included in later analyses and modelling. The *a priori* codes were based on the literature-based model of family leisure as well as other themes present in the family leisure literature.

To prepare for coding, the researcher watched all the videos and divided each into 2- to 3-minute segments, befitting the flow of conversation. Two coders were selected for their relevant educational background, experience working with families in social work settings and knowledge of family dynamics, interaction patterns and parenting styles. Before coding the data, coders were given a sheet that listed all the codes and a brief definition of each. The coders and researcher reviewed all the codes and definitions, discussing and clarifying differences among codes. The research group then watched, coded and discussed five short practice videos to make sure everyone understood the codes. Once trained, the trio coded the family interviews by watching them in predetermined 2- or 3-minute intervals, then coding and discussing each segment until they reached agreement on the codes that best fit the interactions. New codes were added and defined (coders added bonding, shared memories, happiness and variety), while other codes were relabelled to more accurately describe what the family expressed (e.g., intensive parenting became concerted cultivation; effort was clarified as constraint negotiation). When a new code was added, the group discussed what it looked like in the video, what it meant and how it differed from an existing code. In total, 10 codes were added, indicating that some aspects of family leisure experiences were not well-represented in the initial literature-based model. This systematic observation of behaviour and coding was an effective way to identify and label themes and relationships present for each family and as related to the topic. Finally, coders were asked to pause after every two or three video segments to draw connecting lines (via the codes) of any themes that influenced another.

Using the data analysis provided by the coders, the researcher wrote a narrative for each family. The narratives provided an overview of each family's demographics and described what went on during their interviews. Each narrative included quotations used by family members that illustrated the major themes discussed during the interview and evidenced during the activity. While writing the narrative, the researcher hand-sketched causal fragments (Miles and Huberman 1984) of the antecedent, experience and outcomes experienced by each family. These fragments included the major themes identified during the coding process, and looked similar in structure to the individual subsystems presented in the literature-based model. The fragments were the beginning of the eventual models created to illustrate each family leisure system. The researcher created many causal fragments, trying out various combinations of elements, stocks and flows before finally combining fragments into one model for each family. This process was iterative and, like coding and categorizing data, went through many revisions. The final individual models illustrated the major themes present, and connections among them, for each family. Overall, the process of spending additional time with the interview data, videos, codes, quotations and model drafts helped the researcher gain deeper insight into the most important themes for each family, and the connections among them.

Finally, the literature-based model of family leisure was compared to the three individual models of family leisure to identify organizational similarities and differences, of which there were many, and this led to the development of a new MOFL. This model better fit the more general structure of family leisure functioning exhibited by all three families in the study.

Results

First, the qualitative interview data for each family's leisure experience are summarized, along with the main themes reflected in those experiences. Then, the individual family leisure models constructed for each family are described, illustrating their common organizational properties – properties that led to the development of an MOFL.

The Reynolds family

The Reynolds family consisted of four members: Maria and John, the parents, and two children, Ashley, aged 10, and David, aged 13. The family lived in a large house in an affluent neighbourhood with access to many nearby recreational activities, such as hiking and biking trails, ski resorts and local parks. Both parents had college degrees and the father worked full-time operating a successful small business. The mother assisted with her husband's business and cared for their children, who attended a nearby public school.

The Reynolds family was highly motivated to participate in family leisure. During the interview, all members expressed several reasons why they liked family leisure, specific activities they enjoyed and activities they would like to try again. As the family chose their leisure activity for the interview, they discussed their leisure repertoire, reviewing varying skills and interests, challenges related to certain activities and how much they liked or disliked activities.

For their activity, the family decided to play Frisbee in a nearby park. This choice built on prior experience, that of walking to the park together, but the addition of Frisbee was new to them, and they all agreed it was not one of their strengths. There was a strong sense of *family* throughout their conversation, as each member always considered or included the others in their memories or ideas about family leisure.

What emerged from this conversation was a dominant theme of the family engaging in leisure for the long-term outcome of building and reinforcing their family and individual identities. This idea came up again in their conversation after the activity. In looking at specific antecedents to leisure, their conversation touched on several motivators to engage in family leisure, specifically having and creating shared memories, concerted cultivation, challenge, bonding and, as a de-motivator, constraints to leisure.

The primary antecedents that motivated the Reynolds family included shared memories, concerted cultivation, challenge, bonding and minimal constraints. The main themes during their activity included a high level of focused interactions, which were fuelled by shared learning experiences and support. Focused interactions were those that took place without any distractions, when the primary activity was the only activity going on. For this family, within their focused interactions, two main themes noted included shared learning experiences and support.

After playing Frisbee, the family returned home to discuss their experience. They were asked to review what they did, their interactions with one another, what they learned about each other and their overall reactions. Each theme expressed in the final stage of the interview was related to teaching and sharing values. The themes that helped support the transmission of values included bonding, having fun, education and being outdoors. During this portion of the interview, the family talked in general terms about their leisure, rather than about specific activities.

Each member of the Reynolds family appeared to enjoy family leisure activities. The family worked well together, sharing stories, ideas and learning. Family members were supportive of one another, even when frustrated. The parents put much time and effort into their family leisure, and the children seemed to appreciate their opportunities. Their family leisure appeared to most often consist of easy, positive, focused interactions that increased their shared family values.

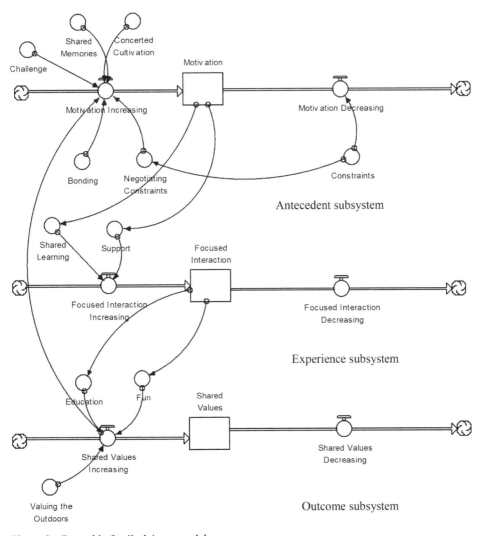

Figure 2. Reynolds family leisure model.

Reynolds family leisure model

Based on the interview data and themes described in the vignettes, the Reynolds family's themes were organized into a basic model (see Figure 2). The model is a mental map of what occurred during the family's leisure and how the elements interacted to influence outcomes or stocks. The model followed the structure of the initial literature-based family leisure model, with an antecedent, experience, and outcome subsystem. Each subsystem consisted of elements that flowed into or out of the three main stocks, filling up or draining that resource.

The Reynolds family offered many reasons why they were motivated to participate together in family leisure. Those reasons are part of the antecedent subsystem flowing into and building up their stock of motivation to leisure. Elements flowing into that stock included challenge, shared memories, concerted cultivation, bonding and negotiating constraints. The only elements flowing out of the stock were interpersonal constraints (which were in the experience subsystem in the literature-based model), such as recreating with different skill levels. In this subsystem, elements flowing into motivation were of greater importance to the family than reasons not to recreate together, likely increasing this stock at a greater rate.

The only element draining the stock, interpersonal constraints, was also linked to negotiating constraints on the left side, indicating that the family realized their constraints, and could usually find strategies to successfully negotiate around them. Overall, this first subsystem had many elements increasing the stock of motivation.

In the experience subsystem, shared learning and support flowed into the stock of focused interactions, while nothing flowed out of it. The stock of motivation also flowed into support and shared learning, helping to increase focused interactions. It is clear that this family had more elements flowing into their subsystems than out of them. In their interview, the family talked more about reasons for participating and their positive experiences in family leisure than they did about anything taking away from their experiences. This is reflected in the model.

Finally, the stock of focused interactions flowed into the elements of education and fun, both of which, along with valuing the outdoors, flowed into the stock of shared values. Nothing flowed out of it. Increasing shared values also flowed back up to motivation increasing, creating a feedback loop for the entire system.

The Perry family

The Perry family consisted of three members: Paula, the mother; Steven, the father; and Abby, their daughter. Abby was 11 years old, and Paula and Steven were in their late 20s. The family lived in a low-income housing unit in the downtown area of a midsized city. Their townhouse was one of four in a row, with another row directly behind them and a long, narrow common area between rows.

The family identified itself as poor, and Paula and Steven attributed that to their lack of education and poor choices as teenagers. They both dropped out of high school and neither returned to complete a degree. Paula gave birth to Abby when she was 16, and spent most of her life caring for Abby, and occasionally for Steven's mother, who had a mental disability. Steven was at one point employed as a construction worker, but lost his job six months prior to the interview. At the time of the interview, he spent much of his time at home with Paula, or working odd jobs.

When asked about their family leisure experiences, Paula and Steven talked mostly about their lack of income and how that dictated what they could and could not do. They also said that because they were unemployed, they had ample free time to participate in family leisure, but little income or resources with which to do so. They talked about trying to provide as many educational leisure experiences for Abby as they could because they wanted her to have more opportunities and a better life than they had. From the first portion of the interview, the major antecedents to their family leisure included constraints to leisure, free choice, constraints negotiation and educational opportunities, all of which led to or took away from their motivation to engage in family leisure.

The Perry family decided to play ball and Frisbee for their leisure activity. They wanted their family to be happy, safe, have ongoing educational opportunities and understand their shared family values and choices. They spoke about sharing their values with Abby through direct conversations and by modelling behaviours, both of which they noted could happen during family leisure. From this final interview portion, the main themes were the importance of leisure for providing variety or a change in routine, for facilitating communication to share values, and for bonding. These themes seemed to lead to their final desired outcome of family leisure, happiness.

Overall, the Perry family did their best to find free leisure activities that provided education and a sense of variety in their daily life. While their leisure interactions were often fragmented, they continued to put much effort into seeking out opportunities for family leisure.

Perry family leisure model

Based on the Perry family narrative, the themes presented were organized into a model of family leisure (see Figure 3). This model is a simplified picture of the most notable interactions that occurred during their family leisure and influenced their desired outcomes. The Perry family had a simple life, restrained by lack of income, yet with ample free time. The family also placed great value on education. This simplicity is reflected in their family leisure model, and its stocks of motivation, quality interactions and happiness.

In the antecedent subsystem, education and constraint negotiation flowed into and increased the stock of motivation, while constraints decreased motivation. The family members made it clear that education was a strong motivator for family leisure activities. A desire to find educational and no-cost activities increased their motivation to leisure and was part of their constraint negotiation process. However, the family could not always find free or nearby activities, and these constraints seemed to drain their motivation.

Somewhat disconnected from their antecedent subsystem and stock of motivation was their experience subsystem. Their desired experience stock was quality interaction, which was fed by the parents' sense of role obligation. Fragmented interactions drained their quality leisure experience and were prevalent during the leisure activity. Overall, the family's experience was choppy and their interactions did not link very well to their desired outcomes. When discussed, their experience seemed to stand alone with little connection to the antecedents or outcomes they had talked about. Looking at these two systems together, there is not a strong connection between motivation and experience. While the family was highly motivated to do activities, and found no-cost leisure on a regular basis, this did not translate to focused or quality interactions. Motivation to leisure moved them to action, but did not help with leisure quality.

The outcome subsystem contained the stock of happiness. During their interview, they said they wanted a happy life with positive outcomes, such as fun and happy times together. The family drew from their quality leisure interactions to support elements they

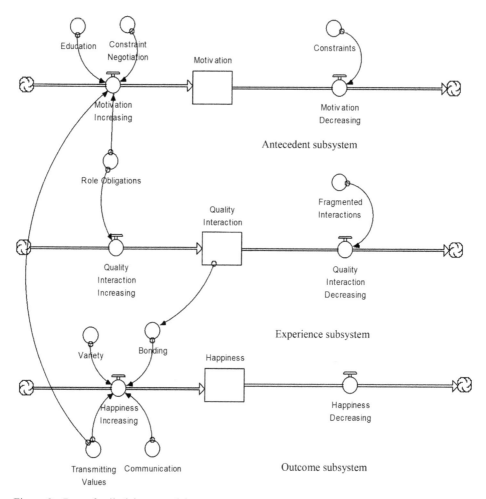

Figure 3. Perry family leisure model.

thought would create more happiness. These elements included trying to find a variety of leisure activities, communication, transmitting values and bonding. Each element had a specific way it could add to the stock of happiness. Variety provided a needed change in routine, communication allowed the parents to teach their daughter life lessons and the parents felt teaching values would improve chances of lifelong happiness. Bonding flowed directly from quality interactions, as these experiences could help the family increase their sense of emotional closeness. On the right side of the model, nothing was discussed as decreasing happiness, seemingly as the family had so little to work with to get to the leisure experience, little else could be taken away. Transmitting values was discussed as an outcome and a motivator for their family leisure and linked the outcome subsystem to the antecedent subsystem.

Greg, Emma and Abe

Greg, Emma and Abe were a blended family. Abe was Greg's 11-year-old son from a first marriage. Greg and Emma had been dating for four years and the trio had lived together for three of those years.

The dominant theme from this interview was about the process of becoming a family, and the role family leisure could play in that process. Throughout the interview, Greg, Emma and Abe talked about family leisure as a potential way to help them learn about one another, adapt to living together and bond. They also talked about the challenges in their family leisure as they went through the process of becoming a family. The main themes articulated during their interview included a level of high motivation to engage in family leisure. During their leisure, the experience was influenced by constraints and their ability to negotiate them, as well as by their focused and fragmented interactions. Finally, the desired outcome for their family leisure had to do with increasing overall bonding, and was influenced by a desire to learn, grow and create shared memories.

For their activity, the family decided to play a new version of *Clue*.[1] They had played it together once before and found it confusing, but were interested in trying again. Emma and Abe were especially interested in playing, and in using a text message feature with the game. While they were trying to create a quality leisure experience, their interactions overall were characterized by segments of total focus by all members, and segments of fragmented interaction, especially caused by Greg. This was likely due to their differing levels of interest in the game. *Clue* took several minutes to set up, and Emma and Abe focused on reading the rules while Greg cleared dinner dishes.

The main desired outcome noted during their interview was that Greg, Emma and Abe wanted to engage in family leisure in order to bond as a family, and that quality leisure experiences might help them do this. In their conversation afterwards, they talked about how quality family leisure experiences created a space for them to learn about one another, grow into their new family roles and build memories, all of which could increase family bonding. But, as noted in the antecedent section, the family members did not have many similar interests, and sometimes experienced conflict because of this, which actually served to further fragment their leisure.

Greg, Emma and Abe family leisure model

After completing the vignette for this family, the themes were organized into a model that provided a simplified picture of what occurred during this family's leisure (see Figure 4).

In this model, the first subsystem was motivation to participate in leisure. This family's main reason for participating in leisure was to create a way to spend time together, whether directly interacting or not. Being together for this family often meant being in the same room together but doing separate activities. Wanting to be together increased their motivation to participate in family leisure. However, their interpersonal constraints of a lack of shared activities served to deplete their stock of motivation. The family was in the process of learning to negotiate constraints via compromises to find activities they could all enjoy.

In the experience subsystem, both interpersonal constraints and negotiating constraints flowed into the stock of quality leisure experiences. As indicated in the interview, both elements influenced the family's ability to have quality experiences, or those in which the only activity occurring was the leisure activity, and the family was focused on that activity. Interpersonal constraints often prevented quality leisure from occurring, while negotiating constraints did the opposite and helped the family find ways to have quality experiences. However, their interview data indicated that these two elements flowed into and out of quality leisure experiences at different rates, preventing that stock from ever filling completely.

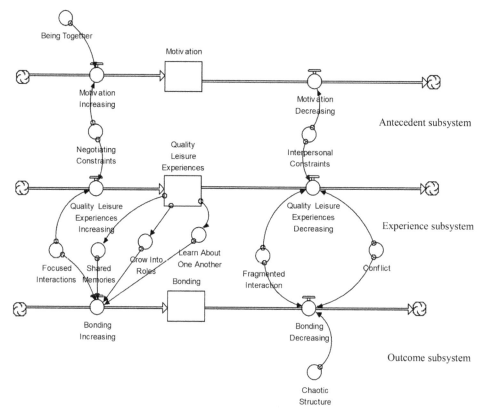

Figure 4. Greg, Emma and Abe family leisure model.

As all the systems in this model were connected, the stock of quality leisure was also affected by the elements between it and the outcome subsystem. Focused interactions contributed to quality leisure increasing, while conflict and fragmented interactions contributed to it decreasing. Finally, in the outcome subsystem, many elements are present. When this family had a quality leisure experience, it appeared to pique their interest in learning about one another, sharing experiences and practising their new roles together. These processes fed into their stock of bonding as they shared these elements of emotional closeness through their leisure. Keeping in mind that this family came together about four years ago, it made sense that these elements were part of the outcome of their family leisure. Focused interactions also helped increase bonding, and fed back up into quality leisure experiences. On the right side of the outcome subsystem, fragmented interactions, conflict and a chaotic structure decreased their level of bonding. There is nothing linking the outcome subsystem back to motivation, or the antecedent subsystem, which could cause further delays in increasing motivation.

Discussion

Overall, the results of this study reinforce the growing conviction that family leisure is an increasingly important part of healthy family functioning (Poff, Zabriskie, and Townsend 2010; Shaw 2008; Shaw, Havitz, and Delamere 2008; Taylor et al. 2012; Ward and Zabriskie 2011). All three families, while very different, seemed to understand leisure's potential for strengthening family values and enhancing family cohesion. In a similar fashion, the study's results reinforce the significance of "core" leisure experiences in promoting family satisfaction (Buswell et al. 2012). The opportunity for everyday family-focused enjoyment was in reach of all three families, regardless of their social or economic status.

Of more particular note, systems modelling was used to organize complex family leisure interactions to gain an overview of family leisure functioning. The initial literature-based model of family leisure was only partially supported, as the three individual family models shared some stocks and elements, but not others. Based on those shared organizational properties, a more simplified MOFL is proposed, including its potential usefulness for better understanding, planning and programming for family leisure.

Towards a model of optimal family leisure

General Systems Theory suggests there are models or principles that can be applied across systems to help explain the relationships and interactions among elements within those systems (Bertalanffy 1968). But a model that is too specific will lose its meaning, and if too general, will have no content. The challenge is to find an "optimum degree of generality" (Boulding 1956, 197). In this study, the three families appeared to have similar stocks each wanted to fill. Supported by the idea of equifinality (Becvar and Becvar 1999), it could be said that the families tried to arrive at these outcomes through their family leisure, but each family reached them by different paths. These different paths were paved with specific content that made up each individual family model. While the content gathered for each family model was not helpful for creating a general model of family leisure, the more general stocks, converters, connectors and flows shared by the families revealed a set of interactions that may typify family leisure experiences, and thus proved useful for creating a pared down model of family leisure.

An MOFL integrates similarities between the literature-based model and the three individual family models into one pared down model (see Figure 5). The model provides essential stocks, converters, connectors and flows and offers one way to understand the most important interactions that occur during family leisure. The MOFL suggests an organizational path families might take en route to leisure outcomes, regardless of the individual content of their leisure. It provides an organizational framework that family therapists, researchers and recreation practitioners might find useful when thinking about creating or facilitating family leisure opportunities.

In the MOFL, the antecedent subsystem contains motivation as the stock, with constraints depleting it and constraint negotiation filling it. It was evident in all three family models that an ability to negotiate constraints impacted motivation. This differs from the literature-based model of family leisure which included effort as an element that decreased motivation. The term "effort" was taken from the family leisure literature and indicated the effort, or work, parents put into planning, organizing and executing family leisure, and that can be draining or de-motivating for parents. However, data gathered from the family interviews indicated that, for two of the families, effort required to arrange family leisure became a motivator as members discovered ways to negotiate constraints so they could participate. As previous literature notes, the activation of negotiation strategies can be motivating (Hubbard and Mannell 2001) and may be more motivating for families than previously thought. Further, negotiating constraints may require family members to compromise and problem-solve, listen and consider various opinions, interests, strengths and weaknesses. These efforts, as indicated in the MOFL, could lead to increased focused interactions and ultimately increased bonding.

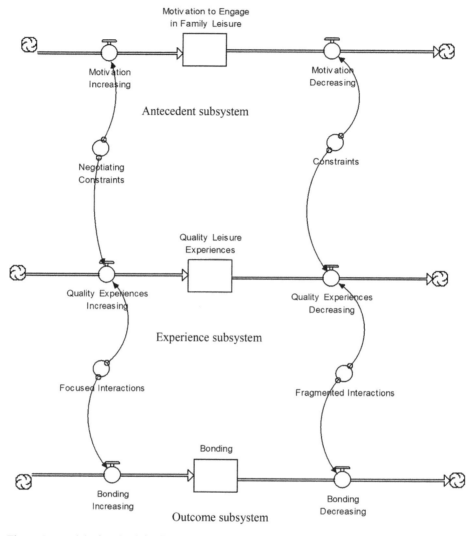

Figure 5. Model of optimal family leisure.

Constraints are also included in the motivation subsystem, as each family talked about personal and structural constraints that influenced motivation to participate. The leisure literature has many examples of constraints as stalling or changing leisure choices, and families in this study were no different. Constraints in the initial literature-based model were specifically social role constraints, indicating that constraints were more likely to be of an inter- or intrapersonal nature (as related to beliefs about self, role and others' perceptions of the parenting role). In the interviews, families talked about all types of constraints, so the MOFL contains only the element of constraints, recognizing that the specific content of those constraints will be unique to each family.

The experience subsystem contains the stock of quality leisure experience with focused interactions increasing it and fragmented interactions decreasing it. The initial literature-based model contained quality leisure experiences as the stock, and information from the families somewhat supported this as being a desired outcome. A quality leisure experience is hard to define, but from this study, it appears to be made up of focused leisure interactions, in which only one leisure activity is engaged in and nothing else is going on in the background. Such quality interactions supported bonding, sharing memories, learning about one another and growing into roles. The content of the goals may differ from family to family, but in the end a quality leisure experience will be focused and aid a family in attaining desired leisure outcomes. In contrast, fragmented interactions occur when more than one activity is going on, and the main activity is often interrupted or disrupted by other events or people (Beck and Arnold 2009). Fragmented leisure often feels more rushed and less satisfying as it is made up of many, short, disconnected leisure moments (Bittman and Wajcman 2000). This idea has been supported in the literature as well. For example, a study of adolescent well-being found that joint family leisure (such as enjoying a meal together) was positively associated with teens' emotional well-being (Offer 2013).

It should also be noted that activity choice may influence focused or fragmented interactions. In this study, not every family member was interested in the family-chosen leisure activity all the time, and this contributed to that person being distracted, or distracting others, from the main activity. In a family, it can be very difficult to find an activity of interest to everyone, but to the extent that each member can maintain a certain level of focus and remove distractions, the family may have a better chance to achieve a quality leisure experience.

The antecedent and experience subsystems are connected through constraints, negotiated successfully or otherwise. As previously noted, the presence of constraints can activate negotiation strategies, which can lead to more focused interactions among family members. The model of optimal leisure suggests that if families have to work together to overcome constraints, they may be more focused on their leisure experience. On the other hand, if constraints persist, the family may experience fragmented leisure as they struggle to find a shared activity.

The outcome subsystem of the MOFL features bonding as the desired outcome. During the family interviews, members used different terms to express ideas of gaining emotional closeness to one another, but most often they used the term bonding. Each family also had many elements flowing into their final outcome, as well as similar elements flowing into their antecedent stock. Almost all elements flowing into their final outcome stock and, in turn, into their new antecedent stock, could be considered desired goals for family leisure. Based on this study, the elements flowing into or out of bonding vary depending on the family, their values, history and place in the family life cycle. In the MOFL, the stock of bonding is filled or depleted by focused or fragmented interactions. If bonding is made up of emotional closeness, and emotional closeness is more likely to occur through focused interactions, then focused interactions are necessary to support bonding. Similarly, fragmented interactions will detract from the quality of the experience, and the family's ability to bond during a leisure experience.

Finally, the MOFL contains a feedback loop from bonding to motivation to engage in family leisure. During the post-activity interviews, each family expressed the idea that a positive leisure experience with increased bonding would motivate them to participate in the activity again. Similarly, a leisure experience comprised of fragmented interactions and less bonding would likely decrease motivation to participate again. Overall, the MOFL provides an organizational framework within which to fill in individual family elements. The model could be useful for better understanding the challenges families face as they attempt to achieve their family leisure goals.

Implications for theory and practice

The results of this work have numerous implications for theory and practice. They can best be discussed in the contexts of motivation, freedom and constraints.

Motivation

One of the main findings of this study was the impact of multiple motivations on family leisure. The decision to engage in a particular leisure pursuit often appeared to be secondary to concerns for doing something that would enhance educational opportunities for children, bring the family together for some quality time or bond the family as a unit. This indicates that in a social context desired outcomes for self and others may be more important and a greater source of motivation than the activity itself. This finding is reminiscent of Samdahl and Jekubovich's (1997) assertion that leisure activity itself can be secondary to what is valued in social relationships. If being together matters most, then what families do when they are together may matter less, and this has research and programming implications. This study's findings also support Henderson's (1997) observation that "being with a partner or others is activity" (457), and that a broader definition of activity may be called for so leisure service providers can "understand better what people do and what's important to them" (Henderson 1997). For practitioners, then, this suggests it is more important to consider how an activity is designed and experienced by family members, rather than what the activity is. While activities must attract a family of participants, what should be given more consideration by the programmer are the opportunities for family members to interact with one another in a meaningful and focused manner. This means considering and removing as many barriers to participation as possible, and creating an environment in which family members are encouraged to talk and recreate together, as a unit.

Family member motivation to recreate together is also impacted by a variety of sources, and this was one of the primary lessons learned from studying family leisure from a systems perspective. Motivation ebbs and flows as multiple forces affect it, and the motivational determinants of leisure behaviour are highly nuanced. Engaging in a particular leisure activity is determined by a variety of social considerations, some of which have little to do with the activity itself. Understanding that it is the individual in relationship to others that may be the most influential aspect of leisure involvement has important implications for a profession that has traditionally focused on the provision of activity for activity's sake without fully appreciating the social embeddedness of the constituency it serves. For practitioners, it is important to be aware that parents are likely motivated to engage in an activity not because they enjoy it, but because of their desire to fulfil their relational role of parent, or to meet perceived social expectations of what it looks like to be a "good" parent. Providing parents with specific ways to engage with their children during an activity, such as having a specific task to complete, or taking turns with their child may help increase their satisfaction with themselves, their role fulfilment and ultimately increase their motivation to engage in a family activity again.

Freedom

In the same way that studying family leisure from a systems perspective alters the way in which we might think about motivation, it also changes the way in which we might think about freedom. The freedom to pick and choose our individual leisure pursuits has been viewed as sacrosanct, but when examined in the context of family leisure, freedom, too, becomes a much more nuanced construct. Rather than seeing freedom as the unobstructed pursuit of intrinsically rewarding experiences, freedom in family leisure tends to be tempered by concern for others. Freedom becomes obligation as well as opportunity (Brightbill 1960). This represents a shift in focus from a more psychologized view of leisure, a shift that necessarily comes about when we acknowledge that aspect of ourselves that is connected to others.

In this family leisure study, the parents in general, and the mothers in particular, chose to limit their freedom out of a social concern for others. They put their own individual preferences on hold out of an interest in doing something that would benefit the family system as a whole. Oftentimes this meant considering what was best for the children, spouse, partner or the whole unit. The emphasis was on the family as a whole and on nurturing a sense of family and strengthening family ties. Moreover, singular leisure engagements, rather than being treated as discrete events, were treated as part of an unfolding pattern of familial interactions that could be sustained over time and that could lead to a much stronger and harmonious family unit.

This study also illustrated that it was more difficult for the fathers and husbands to limit their freedom than the mothers and wives, resulting in a lower-quality leisure experience for the fathers and husbands. The kinds of "focused interactions" that were required to work through competing motivations to engage in family leisure and to work through the leisure engagements themselves were more difficult for the fathers and husbands to effect. The fathers were more often characterized as having "fragmented interactions", which means they were harder pressed to do what was necessary to achieve a quality family leisure experience. They were more scattered in their attention and in their commitment to ensuring successful family leisure outcomes. By not imposing limits on their own freedoms, fathers had too much choice and were not able to concentrate on the activity or people around them. This study thus supports the seemingly counterintuitive notion that limits to freedom may in fact help create smaller social or interactive spaces, thus freeing people to choose from the few rather than feeling overwhelmed by the many. As McGuire and Norman (2005) suggested, such restraints may actually help set individuals free. The degree to which mothers and wives are more accultured into such sacrifices, or self-imposed limits to freedom, for the sake of family welfare vis-a-vis fathers and husbands remains an important topic for research, discussion and debate. For professionals and recreation programmers, this means that offering specific programmes with simple, clear goals and limited choices may actually benefit family leisure, and fathers in particular. Too many choices or too little structure, such as "open-gym" time or free play at the swimming pool or on the playground, may offer too many options, allowing family members to each choose a different activity, switch between activities or participate in one activity while watching another, thus leading to fragmented interactions.

Constraints

Throughout the leisure literature, constraints are considered to be something that creates a barrier to, or prevents an individual from, doing what he or she would like (Jackson 2005). Constraints are most often portrayed in a negative light with research focusing on how constraints limit individual freedom and choice, and then discussing how constraints can be mitigated, negotiated or avoided so individuals can maximize their full range of leisure choices.

However, when viewed from the perspective of family leisure or in a larger social or environmental context, constraints may be seen as more than mere limitations on individual freedoms. They may be seen as acknowledgements of our social existence. People do not live solitary lives. They are in constant interaction with one another and the environment around them. People exist in a complex web of social and ecological interrelationships, and when we recognize this interconnectedness, we can see that our actions are not ours alone. They frequently have far-ranging impacts. When we acknowledge our social selves as well as our individual selves, we understand that we live in relationship to family members, friends, neighbours, communities, and the larger living world. This reality is seldom acknowledged in cultures that champion individual freedom and prize individual effort, but it is a fundamental assumption underlying systems thinking. When we consider the influence we have on one another, both good and bad, we can more easily appreciate that there are times when we should constrain our behaviour for the sake of others. Such constraints, when self-imposed through ethical consideration, are not to be negotiated, avoided or surmounted. They are to be embraced and lived with. They are the accommodations we make in recognition of our social obligations to others (Samdahl and Jekubovich 1997).

In the context of family leisure, such a "constraint" is most evident in a mother's "ethic of care" (Noddings 1984). An ethic of care is a type of moral development oriented towards intimacy, caring, concern and relationships with others (Gilligan 1982). It is considered specific to females and suggests that a woman's moral compass directs her to place care and concern for others before herself. Putting others first clearly creates a constraint on a woman's behaviour, yet many women report that in doing so they gain greater satisfaction from their behaviour than if they act only out of self-interest (Schwab 2011). An ethic of care can thus be considered a constraint on one's behaviour or it can be embraced as a condition of living a social life.

Finally, and again in the context of family leisure, when an individual enters into a partnership, such as a marriage or child-rearing relationship, the individual may choose to limit her or his behaviour based on what is good or bad for the other person(s), the relationship or for oneself. By choosing to limit one's own behaviours, the individual is not really choosing to limit freedoms or choices, but rather to behave in ways that might better serve the relationship in its totality. Under these circumstances, "constrained" individual behaviour may improve relations and open up possibilities for the family as a whole to prosper. When parents, for example, choose activities that are of interest to their children rather than to themselves, they are placing limits on their own freedom, yet they accept these limitations because they understand the social benefits for the family unit. The "constraint" is really an acknowledgement of a greater social duty.

Optimal family leisure, in sum, is likely the result of successful negotiations among family members about what leisure pursuits can be engaged in that benefit the family as a whole. Satisfying individual preferences is less of a concern. "Optimal", then, does not mean recreation programming that ensures everyone gets to do what he or she wants. "Optimal" means recreation programming that serves a family's common interests. Group activities more so than individual activities take centre stage. Social concerns trump individual concerns. Family bonding, growth and development require engaging in leisure pastimes together.

Recommendations for future research

The research reported here is based on a systems view of family leisure that proceeds from the assumption that while the specific content of family leisure may vary, general family leisure functioning may share similar organizational properties, and by better understanding those shared organizational properties, researchers and practitioners might be better positioned to understand and plan for family leisure experiences. Testing the utility of the proposed MOFL would be a logical first step.

Focusing on constraint negotiation in family leisure as well as the role of focused and fragmented interactions in contributing to quality family leisure are also promising areas for future research. The results of this study suggest that an ability to negotiate constraints may be helpful in increasing motivation to engage in family leisure. There is already a large body of leisure research that examines constraints at both theoretical and practical levels (e.g., Crawford, Jackson, and Godbey 1991; Hubbard and Mannell 2001), but more work is warranted that focuses on how or by whom constraints are negotiated in a family. Understanding constraints can help practitioners and policy-makers work towards removing barriers to participation. Furthermore, this study demonstrated that constraints can activate a desire to negotiate them. Negotiating constraints requires problem-solving and compromising skills, which, when done successfully, can help family members hone valuable life skills, learn about one another and bond as a family. Future research might consider the unique constraints experienced by families, how these constraints impact their leisure experiences and how negotiating these constraints can enhance family bonding.

This study also found support for the proposition that quality leisure experiences can be adversely affected by fragmented interactions. This finding suggests two questions for future research. First, researchers must agree on what defines a quality leisure experience. One example comes from Bittman and Wajcman (2000), who defined it as uninterrupted or unobligated time, or time in which only one activity occurs. A second question for future research concerns how fragmented interactions specifically detract from family leisure and overall family functioning.

Conclusion

The findings from this study illustrate the utility of systems thinking for better understanding family leisure functioning. General Systems Theory has proven useful for understanding systems' organizational properties that are invariant to change even as the content changes continuously from system to system and within systems over time. This study has demonstrated the usefulness of thinking of family leisure functioning in terms of stocks, flows, connectors and converters that represent the social and relational aspects of family leisure. The study ascertained that while it may not be possible to create a highly detailed model of family leisure, a simplified model may still be useful for better understanding the dynamics of family leisure. Leisure professionals might employ the MOFL to improve constraint negotiation through focused interactions, while also decreasing constraints and fragmented interactions. Together, these actions might help families increase problem-solving skills, learn to compromise, increase their undivided attention, appreciate one another and increase bonding through family leisure. These would be important steps towards improving overall family functioning and well-being.

Note

1. *Clue* is a board game in which players try to gather evidence and solve a murder mystery.

Notes on contributors

Keri A. Schwab, Ph.D., is an Assistant Professor in the Recreation, Parks, and Tourism Administration Department at California Polytechnic University, San Luis Obispo, California,

USA. She earned her undergraduate degree in Journalism from James Madison University, and a Masters and Ph.D. from the University of Utah in Salt Lake City, Utah, USA. Her research interests include youth development, community recreation, and family leisure. She currently teaches core undergraduate classes and is currently working on a research project to examine how social media can be used to motivate youth to recreate outdoors. She is co-editor of several books including A Career with Meaning and Just Leisure: Things that we Believe In.

Daniel L. Dustin is a Professor in the Department of Parks, Recreation, and Tourism in the College of Health at the University of Utah, Salt Lake City, Utah, USA. He holds a bachelor's degree in geography and a master's degree in resource planning and conservation from the University of Michigan, and a Ph.D. in education with an emphasis in recreation and park administration from the University of Minnesota. Among his recent works as an author and editor are *Stewards of Access-Custodians of Choice: a Philosophical Foundation for Parks, Recreation, and Tourism; Speaking Up and Speaking Out: Working for Social and Environmental Justice through Parks, Recreation, and Leisure; Service Living: Building Community through Public Parks and Recreation; The Wilderness Within: Reflections on Leisure and Life; Making a Difference in Academic Life: a Handbook for Park, Recreation, and Tourism Educators and Graduate Students; and Nature and the Human Spirit: Toward an Expanded Land Management Ethic.*

References

Agate, J., R. Zabriskie, S. Agate, and R. Poff. 2009. "Family Leisure Satisfaction and Satisfaction with Family Life." *Journal of Leisure Research* 41 (2): 205–223.

Barnett, L. 1991. "Characterizing Playfulness: Correlates with Individual Attributes and Personality Traits." *Play and Culture* 4 (4): 371–393.

Beck, M., and J. Arnold. 2009. "Gendered Time Use at Home: An Ethnographic Examination of Leisure Time in Middle-class Families." *Leisure Studies* 28 (2): 121–142.

Becvar, D., and R. Becvar. 1999. *Systems Theory and Family Therapy.* Lanham, MD: University of American Press.

Bertalanffy, L. 1968. *General System Theory; Foundations, Development, Applications.* New York: G. Braziller.

Bianchi, S. M. 2011. "Family Change and Time Allocation in American Families." *The ANNALS of the American Academy of Political and Social Science* 638 (1): 21–44. doi:10.1177/0002716 211413731.

Bianchi, S., J. Robinson, and M. Milkie. 2006. *Changing Rhythms of American Family Life.* New York: Russell Sage Foundation.

Bittman, M., and J. Wajcman. 2000. "The Rush Hour: The Character of Leisure Time and Gender Equity." *Social Forces* 79 (1): 165–189.

Boulding, K. E. 1956. "General Systems Theory: The Skeleton of Science." *Management Science* 2 (3): 197–208. doi:10.1287/mnsc.2.3.197.

Brightbill, C. 1960. *The Challenge of Leisure.* Englewood Cliffs, NJ: Prentice-Hall.

Broderick, C. 1993. *Understanding Family Process: Basics of Family Systems Theory.* Thousand Oaks, CA: Sage.

Bronfenbrenner, U. 1979. *The Ecology of Human Development: Experiments by Nature and Design.* Cambridge, MA: Harvard University Press.

Brown, P. R., W. J. Brown, Y. D. Miller, and V. Hansen. 2001. "Perceived Constraints and Social Support for Active Leisure among Mothers with Young Children." *Leisure Sciences* 23 (3): 131–144. doi:10.1080/014904001316896837.

Buswell, L., R. Zabriskie, N. Lundberg, and A. Hawkins. 2012. "The Relationship between Father Involvement in Family Leisure and Family Functioning: The Importance of Daily Family Leisure." *Leisure Sciences* 32: 143–161.

Coakley, J. 2006. "The Good Father: Parental Expectations and Youth Sports." *Leisure Studies* 25 (2): 153–163. doi:10.1080/02614360500467735.

Craig, L., and J. E. Brown. 2014. "Weekend Work and Leisure Time with Family and Friends: Who Misses Out?" *Journal of Marriage and Family* 76 (4): 710–727. doi:10.1111/jomf.12127.

Crawford, D. W., E. L. Jackson, and G. Godbey. 1991. "A Hierarchical Model of Leisure Constraints." *Leisure Sciences* 13 (4): 309–320. doi:10.1080/01490409109513147.

Daly, K. 1996. *Families and Time: Keeping Pace in a Hurried Culture.* Thousand Oaks, CA: Sage.

Fingerman, K., and E. Bermann. 2000. "Applications of Family Systems Theory to the Study of Adulthood." *International Journal of Aging and Human Development* 51: 5–29.

Freeman, P., and R. Zabriskie. 2003. "Leisure and Family Functioning in Adoptive Families: Implications for Therapeutic Recreation." *Therapeutic Recreation Journal* 37 (1): 73–93.

Gilligan, C. 1982. *In a Different Voice: Psychological Theory and Women's Development*. Cambridge, MA: Harvard University Press.

Gillis, J. 2001. "Never Enough Time: Some Paradoxes of Modern Family Time(s)." In *Minding the Time in Family Experience*, edited by K. Daly, 19–36. Kidlington: Elsevier Science.

Grimes, R. 2000. *Deeply into the Bone: Re-inventing Rites of Passage*. Berkeley: University of California Press.

Henderson, K. 1997. "A Critique of Constraints Theory: A Response." *Journal of Leisure Research* 29 (4): 453–457.

Hornberger, L. B., R. B. Zabriskie, and P. Freeman. 2010. "Contributions of Family Leisure to Family Functioning among Single-parent Families." *Leisure Sciences* 32 (2): 143–161. doi:10.1080/01490400903547153.

Hubbard, J., and R. C. Mannell. 2001. "Testing Competing Models of the Leisure Constraint Negotiation Process in a Corporate Employee Recreation Setting." *Leisure Sciences* 23 (3): 145–163. doi:10.1080/014904001316896846.

Irving, H., and A. R. Giles. 2011. "Examining the Child's Impacts on Single Mothers' Leisure." *Leisure Studies* 30 (3): 365–373. doi:10.1080/02614361003716974.

Jackson, E., ed. 2005. *Constraints to Leisure*. State College, PA: Venture.

Jacobs, J., and K. Gerson. 2004. *The Time Divide: Work, Family, and Gender Inequality*. Cambridge, MA: Harvard University Press.

Kelly, J. 1983. *Leisure Identities and Interactions*. London: George Allen & Unwin.

Kleiber, D. 1999. *Leisure Experience and Human Development*. New York: Basic Books.

Lareau, A. 2003. *Unequal Childhoods: Class, Race, and Family Life*. Berkeley: University of California Press.

Lee, N., A. M. Zvonkovic, and D. C. Crawford. 2014. "The Impact of Work-family Conflict on Facilitation of Women's Perceptions of Role Balance." *Family Issues* 35 (9): 1252–1274.

Mactavish, J., and S. Schleien. 2004. "Re-injecting Spontaneity and Balance in Family Life: Parents' Perspective on Recreation in Families that Include Children with Developmental Disability." *Journal of Intellectual Disability Research* 48 (2): 123–141.

McGuire, F., and W. Norman. 2005. "The Role of Constraints in Successful Aging: Inhibiting or Enabling." In *Constraints to leisure*, edited by E. Jackson, 89–101. State College, PA: Venture.

Miles, M., and A. Huberman. 1984. *Qualitative Data Analysis: A Source Book of New Methods*. Thousand Oaks, CA: Sage.

Neulinger, J. 1974. *The Psychology of Leisure: Research Approaches to the Study of Leisure*. Springfield, IL: Charles C. Thomas.

Noddings, N. 1984. *Caring: A Feminist Approach to Ethics and Moral Education*. Berkeley: University of California Press.

O'Brien, M. 2005. "Studying Individual and Family Development: Linking Theory and Research." *Journal of Marriage & Family* 67 (4): 880–890. doi:10.1111/j.1741-3737.2005.00181.x.

Offer, S. 2013. "Family Time Activities and Adolescents' Emotional Well-being." *Journal of Marriage and Family* 75 (1): 26–41. doi:10.1111/j.1741-3737.2012.01025.x.

Orthner, D., and J. Mancini. 1991. "Benefits of Leisure for Family Bonding." In *Benefits of Leisure*, edited by B. Driver, P. Brown, and G. Peterson, 215–301. State College, PA: Venture.

Patton, M. 2002. *Qualitative Research & Evaluation Methods*. Thousand Oaks, CA: Sage.

Poff, R. A., R. B. Zabriskie, and J. A. Townsend. 2010. "Australian Family Leisure: Modelling Parent and Youth Data." *Annals of Leisure Research* 13 (3): 420–438. doi:10.1080/11745398. 2010.9686856.

Richmond, B. 2001. *The "Thinking" in Systems Thinking*. Waltham, MA: Pegasus Communications.

Robinson, J., and G. Godbey. 1999. *Time for Life: The Surprising Ways People Use Their Time*. University Park: The Pennsylvania State University Press.

Samdahl, D., and N. Jekubovich. 1997. "A Critique of Leisure Constraints: Comparative Analyses and Understandings." *Journal of Leisure Research* 29 (4): 430–452.

Schwab, K. 2011. "A Mother's Leisure?" In *Speaking Up and Speaking Out: Working for Social and Environmental Justice through Parks, Recreation, and Leisure*, edited by K. Paisley and D. Dustin, 53–62. Urbana, IL: Sagamore Publishing LLC.

Shannon, C. S., and S. M. Shaw. 2008. "Mothers and Daughters: Teaching and Learning about Leisure." *Leisure Sciences* 30 (1): 1–16. doi:10.1080/01490400701544659.

Shaw, S. 1992. "Dereifying Family Leisure: An Examination of Women's and Men's Everyday Experiences and Perceptions of Family Time." *Leisure Sciences* 14 (3): 271–286.

Shaw, S. 1999. "Purposive Leisure: Examining Parental Discourses on Family Activities." In *Symposium on Leisure Research*, edited by W. Stewart and D. Samdahl, 7. Ashburn, VA: National Park and Recreation Association.

Shaw, S. 2008. "Family Leisure and Changing Ideologies of Parenthood." *Sociology Compass* 2: 1–16.

Shaw, S. M., and D. Dawson. 2001. "Purposive Leisure: Examining Parental Discourses on Family Activities." *Leisure Sciences* 23 (4): 217–231. doi:10.1080/01490400152809098.

Shaw, S., M. Havitz, and F. Delamere. 2008. "'I Decided to Invest in My Kids' Memories': Family Vacations, Memories, and the Social Construction of Family." *Tourism, Culture & Communication* 8 (1): 13–26.

Smith, K. M., P. A. Freeman, and R. B. Zabriskie. 2009. "An Examination of Family Communication within the Core and Balance Model of Family Leisure Functioning." *Family Relations* 58 (1): 79–90. doi:10.1111/j.1741-3729.2008.00536.x.

Taylor, S. M., P. Ward, R. Zabriskie, B. Hill, and C. Hanson. 2012. "Influences on Active Family Leisure and a Healthy Lifestyle among Adolescents." *Leisure Sciences* 34 (4): 332–349. doi:10.1080/01490400.2012.687643.

Trussell, D. E., and S. M. Shaw. 2012. "Organized Youth Sport and Parenting in Public and Private Spaces." *Leisure Sciences* 34 (5): 377–394. doi:10.1080/01490400.2012.714699.

Ward, P., and R. Zabriskie. 2011. "Recreation as a Developmental Experience." *New Directions for Youth Development* 130: 29–42.

Zabriskie, R. B., and P. Freeman. 2004. "Contributions of Family Leisure to Family Functioning among Transracial Adoptive Families." *Adoption Quarterly* 7 (3): 49–77. doi:10.1300/J145v07n03_03.

Zabriskie, R. B., and B. P. McCormick. 2001. "The Influences of Family Leisure Patterns on Perceptions of Family Functioning." *Family Relations: Interdisciplinary Journal of Applied Family Studies* 50 (3): 281–289. doi:10.1111/j.1741-3729.2001.00281.x.

Zabriskie, R., and B. McCormick. 2003. "Parent and Child Perspectives of Family Leisure Involvement and Satisfaction with Family Life." *Journal of Leisure Research* 33 (2): 163–189.

Parents and children consuming the city: geographies of family outings across class

Lia Karsten[a] and Naomi Felder[b]

[a]Department of Urban Geographies, AISSR, University of Amsterdam, Amsterdam, the Netherlands; [b]Bureau Feld, Amsterdam, the Netherlands

Cities are generally described as urban jungles for everyday family life. This is mainly based on poor facilities for outdoor play. But children's everyday life consists of many more leisure activities. In this paper, we focus on family outings: the various ways children and parents consume the city. It is argued that family outings are important building blocks for growing up and cementing family ties. They can be grouped under the umbrella of consuming the city and as such their growth fits perfectly into the new position of cities as consumption landscapes. Empirical data are drawn from a case study in Amsterdam and Rotterdam, the Netherlands, among families of different classes with young children ($N = 42$) living in inner city districts. The main conclusion of this study is that social risers and upper-middle classes enjoy the city for family outings much more than the lower class families, even when they live in the same neighbourhoods (as is the case in this study) and even when we focus on free to enter public spaces. The discussion part of this paper reflects on the issue of the urban jungle as opposed to the rural idyll for growing up and family life.

Introduction

Urban childhood can easily be considered to be deteriorating over generations with its decrease in outdoor play and the heavy restrictions on children's freedom of movement. Urban public space has developed into an adult space in which children are either not welcome or are welcome only when they are supervised by adults (Valentine 2004). Compared to previous generations, children are under seemingly constant parental control. For children, the city is often described as an urban jungle and is contrasted with the rural idyll where children have full opportunities for spontaneous play without adult interference. In the literature focus on children's independent play as the best representation of an idyllic childhood, large parts of city children's everyday life, however, are ignored and may be undervalued. A considerable portion of children's after-school and weekend time is indeed spent within parents' company, but this can be seen positively as cementing family ties (Morgan 2011; Shaw and Dawson 2001). In this paper, we focus on one such type of children–parent time-sharing activity: family outings (DeVault 2000).

Family outings point to the various ways parents and children consume the city together and 'spontaneously'. Spontaneously refers here to activities that can be distinguished from activities that are fixed in time and space such as is the case with club-membership activities that repeatedly occur. But we have written spontaneously between commas because, in an urban setting, every step outdoors with young children is a complicated one. Family outings are always a result of significant efforts and organization in terms of time, space, mobility and often financial investments as well. They include a range of urban experiences, from a family picnic in the city park to a visit to the zoo or a recently opened mall. These urban experiences are difficult to define but are important building blocks of growing up urban. They can be grouped under the umbrella of consuming the city, and as such, they fit perfectly into the new position of gentrifying cities as consumption landscapes (Zukin 1995).

Gentrification processes contribute to better housing conditions and also to a wider supply of facilities that make cities more attractive to live in. Gentrified neighbourhoods attract more middle class households, including young families (Boterman, Karsten, and Musterd 2010). But at the same time, it becomes more difficult for lower class families to remain living in those gentrifying neighbourhoods, let alone to profit from upgraded consumption infrastructure. In the study reported in this paper, practices of family outings have been analysed as class informed activities. By locating our case study in gentrifying neighbourhoods, we are able to cover class differences in one and the same spatial context. We used the method of time diary research to obtain an overview of all the activities of children during 1 week, including family outings. This resulted in a long list with remarkable differences among families and across classes.

The aim of this paper is to contribute to the knowledge of new – parentally supervised – urban childhoods of different classes and to redress the balance in the literature from unsupervised play and club-based enrichment activities towards family outings. Empirical findings are drawn from research in inner city neighbourhoods in Amsterdam and Rotterdam, the Netherlands among 42 families with young (aged 4–12) children.

Literature

The rise of family outings (McKendrick, Bradford, and Fielder 2000; DeVault 2000; Clarke 2007) can be understood in the context of gentrifying cities and the increase in parental time spent on children. Cities and children have always had ambivalent relationships, and that is very much related to the generally poor opportunities for outdoor play in cities (Chawla 2002; Karsten 2005). This shortcoming has been acknowledged in urban planning although never in a fully satisfying way. Urban public space has become adult space (Valentine 2004). Over the twentieth century, children's playgrounds were established as age-specific domains for the youngest citizens away from the unsafe and unhealthy street (Verstrate and Karsten 2011). From the 1970s onwards, the growth of privately initiated children's domains has been mapped. The new children's domains can be considered the result of both the emancipation of children (they are recognized as little consumers) and the ignorance of children, who are denied access to the ordinary space of the street. This development is further intensified by gentrification processes and the arrival of the new urban middle classes who decided to remain in the city after the birth of their children (Boterman, Karsten, and Musterd 2010; Butler 2003; Lilius 2014). Along with the growing number of urban middle class families, various adult spaces such as pubs and restaurants have transformed into family spaces (Karsten, Kamphuis, and Remeijnse 2015). In their everyday use, children's domains and family spaces are comparable: both welcome children and parents alike. Today, cities publish calendars with activities for children, which are part of the branding of cities as family welcoming. The supply of family outings is becoming an important target in the urban leisure industry (Carr 2011).

Family outings are a time-consuming activity that involves choosing, travelling to and engaging in activities and spaces. Parents and children spend more time together than they used to, and this even applies for working parents (Craig and Mullan 2012; Sociaal en Cultureel Planbureau 2011). The close parental supervision in children's leisure time has evoked criticism from scholars in the field of children's studies, including the authors of this paper (Hillman, Adams, and Whitelegg 1990; Karsten 2005; Freeman and Tranter 2011). However, although the worries about city children's constantly supervised lives are valid, as researchers, we have the task of exploring not only what has been lost but also what has become new practice (Holloway and Pimlott-Wilson 2014). What has sometimes been overlooked is that family outings can be a means for both children and parents to construct a family. Family is not a pre-given but something that has to be constructed continually in everyday practices (Morgan 2011). The new family- and children-welcoming urban consumption spaces offer opportunities for 'doing family' (Van der Burgt and Gustafson 2013). Sharing time and space is seen as cementing social ties. Family outings enable parents to establish an identity as an involved parent (Finch 2007).

Parental choices about family outings are class-informed and can be analysed as ways of reproducing class status. Following Lareau (2003), middle class children's leisure activities are very much orchestrated by parents, whereas lower class children are allowed to enjoy hanging around with contemporaries and kin. The first group follows a childrearing approach of concerted cultivation with a broad range of enrichment activities, whereas the latter group is directed to a more general accomplishment of natural growth, without many specific after-school activities. Vincent and Ball (2007) and many other authors have affirmed the strong cultivation of institutionalized leisure participation by young middle class children (Karsten 2005; Holloway and Pimlott-Wilson 2014). Van der Burgt and Gustafson (2013) place this new development in the context of the densification of cities and their adult-directed design. They relate the rise of the 'agenda' middle class child to the urban environment and its lack of outdoor play space. Attractive places to play are even more vital for urban lower class children, who generally do not have many alternative ways of spending after school time (Power 2007; Karsten 2005). Several studies show that many lower class parents either keep their children at home or put several social and spatial restrictions on their involvement in out of home leisure (Pinkster and Droogleever Fortuijn 2009; Galster and Santiago 2006). Most studies on the urban lower class, however, are located in inner city disadvantaged neighbourhoods. In the case study reported here, we focus on middle and lower class families living in the same neighbourhoods transforming from disadvantaged to gentrifying. Does the living in an upgrading neighbourhood contribute to a less sharp divide between the classes?

The sharp contrast in raising children between middle and lower class families has been contested by some authors. Irwin and Elley (2011) conclude in their UK research that the differences in class in parental values about children's education must not be overestimated. Holloway and Pimlott-Wilson (2014) argue that it is not so much the differences in attitudes between lower and middle class parents – both groups value enrichment activities – but differences in resources that cause middle class children to have longer lists of after-school activities. The inability to pay for leisure activities restricts the participation of lower class children.

While children's institutionalized leisure activities have been researched to some extent, family outings have not been the focus of much research, with some exceptions (e.g. McKendrick, Bradford, and Fielder 2000; DeVault 2000; Karsten, Kamphuis, and Remeijnse 2015). Family outings and enrichment activities are similar in their adult-led character, but family outings are unique in their parent–child meeting without the interference of a specialist/teacher. It is only family who are engaged. In addition, family outings do not have a planned schedule over a period of time; they are not about having an activity with obligations every Tuesday or Saturday. However, as with children's enrichment activities, family outings are not without effort. Family outings must be organized: they involve creating time, choosing space, organizing mobility and often spending money. Following Hagerstrand (1970), family outings are about making space–time bundles as a family, creating out-of-home places and after-school/work times where and when family members meet. Within the context of cities with large distances, motorized traffic and unsafe routes and the busy agendas of both parents and children, the creation of family outings can be considered to be a complex task.

With this paper, we want to fill two niches in the literature. First, we want to shed light on family outings as an indication of a changing urban childhood with children and parents spending considerably more time together than they used to. We focus on the emergence of new urban childhoods beyond children's unsupervised outdoor play and children's enrichment activities. We intend to explore different types of family outings, the way they are organized in time and space and the choices families make. Family outings are the outcomes of negotiations between children and parents, and choices are class-informed. The focus in the literature is mostly on middle class childhood with some denial of lower class children being engaged in family outings. Our second aim is to analyse the relationship between family outings and families' class position within the same spatial context: the residential environment of the gentrifying neighbourhood. Class is considered to affect family outings, and family outings are considered to constitute family class. Class is not just there; it is also enacted in daily practices (Vincent, Ball, and Braun 2008).

A mixed method study

Our research population consisted of 42 families with children between 4 and 12 years of age living in inner city neighbourhoods in Amsterdam and Rotterdam, the Netherlands.

Neighbourhoods

This study has to be understood in the context of gentrifying European cities with inner city districts growing in popularity as places to live (Boterman, Karsten, and Musterd 2010; Authier and Lehman-Frisch 2013; Butler 2003; Lilius 2014). The inner city neighbourhoods studied were built between roughly 1920 and 1960 in the first ring around the city centre. They are all high-density mixed use neighbourhoods with both social housing and owner occupied apartments. Streets are full of parked cars and sidewalks are full of bikes; outdoor space to play is limited. Most neighbourhoods have parks nearby, but they generally are difficult to reach safely by young children. Some of the neighbourhoods have very recently started to gentrify, and others have already made some progress in that direction. None of the neighbourhoods can be firmly defined as gentrified, and the mixes of classes and ethnicities are a key feature of all neighbourhoods studied.

Social class

The 42 families of this study have been classified into 9 lower class, 11 lower-middle class and 22 upper-middle class families. Class has been defined as a combination of education level and position in the labour market. Lower class families have education levels two times (in the case of two parents) below the mid-level vocational training (The Netherlands Middelbaar Beroeps Onderwijs [MBO]) and no or only one (part-time) job per family. The 11 lower-middle class families have higher education levels (MBO plus) and a higher number of working hours per household than the lower classes. However, none of them combines two-times Hoger Beroeps Onderwijs (HBO) academic level with two paid jobs, which is classified as upper-middle class. Within the upper-middle class of this study, both parents have been educated at the highest level and work as professionals (except for two parents who describe themselves as in-between jobs). With this definition of class, we tried to avoid a one-dimensional approach of income level and focus instead on both economic and cultural capital (Bourdieu 1984). In their combined status as professional and parent, the upper-middle class families belong to the category of young urban professional parents: Yupps (Karsten 2014b).

With the distinction of three social classes, we wanted to get away from the dichotomously defined class concept (Vincent, Ball, and Braun 2008) and to better reflect the specific status of social class for the Dutch context of this study. In the Netherlands, lower class and upper-middle class families are relatively easy to demarcate. The lower-middle class is characterized by in-between levels of education and paid work. Families of the lower-middle classes are neither rich nor poor. They have limited to medium resources in terms of education (cultural capital) and of income (economic capital). In the UK context, Allen et al. (2007) call them marginal middle classes who may have been hampered in their careers somewhere. Across generations, the lower-middle classes may build, however, cultural and economic capital, and as such, they symbolize the upward mobility of social risers (Van der Zwaard 1999). In the Netherlands, social risers are frequently found among the so-called second-generation immigrants, who make more progress in life than their first-generation parents. They cannot yet claim a fully arrived middle class status, but they do not describe themselves as lower class anymore (see also Vincent, Ball, and Braun 2008). As Table 1 illustrates, the social risers in this study have their immigrant background in common with the lower class families, but they have shown upward mobility in terms of education and jobs. The generational upward mobility of migrant families justifies the concept of social riser rather than marginal middle class.

Immigrant status is diverse, and it ranges from Turkish, Moroccan and Surinamese (the three biggest groups in the Netherlands) to various African and Asian backgrounds. While almost all lower class families and social risers families belong to an ethnic minority, the studied upper-middle class families almost all have a native background.

Table 1. Interviewed families by class and immigrant status.

	Both parents have an immigrant background	One parent has an immigrant background	Both parents have a native background	Total
Lower class	8	1		9
Social risers	8	1	2	11
Upper-middle class	1	3	18	22
Total	17	5	20	42

Among both the lower class families and the social risers were three single mothers. The upper-middle class families were all two-parent households. All lower class families live in social housing, as do eight of the social risers. All but three upper-middle class families live in owner-occupied housing. Both lower class and social riser families have a car in approximately half of the cases (4/9 and 6/11, respectively). Almost all of the upper-middle class families have a car (20/22). Eight families out of the entire sample have some form of a second home (including an allotment garden, a boat or a family home abroad).

Methods

Families were first invited to make a diary of one child (the eldest under 12) with all activities carried out during the week before the interview took place, including locations of the activities, mobilities (travel mode used to reach the locations) and companies (with whom they did the activity). Filling in the diaries according to strict time schedules turned out to be difficult for most parents. That is why in the results of this study we handle activities in terms of frequencies rather than exact time durations. Activities were grouped afterwards in a database with the following categories: indoor play at home, outdoor play (within easy reach of the home, both supervised and unsupervised), school, clubs (membership), after-school care, after-school visits with playmates (without the parents staying) and family outings. Family outings are defined as children's out-of-home activities beyond their own street/block that are supervised by one or both parents. They have been be grouped into five sub-categories: public outdoor outings (e.g. going to parks, specific playgrounds or squares), commercial outings (e.g. going to restaurants, the zoo or a swimming pool), shopping (e.g. going to specific shops and/or shopping streets), social outings (e.g. visiting family and friends) and other outings (e.g. visit a public library, a church or a mosque). It should be mentioned that categories were defined after the fieldwork had taken place and the interviews had been analysed and by the researchers themselves.

The week diaries were followed by a questionnaire, a parental interview and a neighbourhood walk with the child. Most interviews were held with the mothers focusing on the daily lives of 17 boys and 25 girls. The interview started with a reflection on the week and how it had been scheduled in time and space. Over half of the interviews were held in the company of both a parent and a child, and children were invited to respond to questions, as well. In most of the cases, however, children participated in the interviews only marginally; the younger ones particularly preferred to play around. The neighbourhood walks showed a contrasting picture with children playing the main role. The fieldwork thus resulted in transcribed interviews with parents; transcribed conversations during walks with children, sometimes including photographs; the week diaries with precise activities, locations, company and mobilities; and a database with personal and household variables. This paper focuses mainly on children's week diaries and the interviews with the parents. In so doing, this paper combines quantitative and qualitative data on family outings, be it mainly from a parental point of view.

Practices of family outings

The week diaries show that family outings occur quite often: 178 times or a mean of around four times a week per child. The variety between the classes is large, but it is a little different than expected (Table 2).

Table 2. The frequencies of outings per child/class/week.

Class/outing	Public	Commercial	Shopping	Social	Other	Total/N
Lower class	3	2	7	10	3	25/9
Social riser	16	6	25	15	5	67/11
Upper-middle class	21	19	22	20	4	86/22
Total	40	27	54	45	12	178/42

It is not the upper-middle class but the social risers who are most active with family outings (over six times a week), whereas the lower class families are the least involved. Looking at the different types of outings, social outings do not differentiate much between the classes: all families participate more or less once a week. Shopping outings are done most by the social risers and not particularly by the families with the highest incomes. Differential access to financial resources, however, is evidently clear with the commercial family outings, which included buying tickets for the zoo, the museum, etc., and spending money on services such as having lunch outdoors. The involvement of money makes the differences between the classes understandable. For the lower classes, these types of activities are simply too expensive and thus less common; as a lower class mother declares, 'Yes sometimes when it's a school holiday, we go to the zoo or we go surfing at Hoek van Holland'. The zoo requires an entrance fee, and for surfing, you need to rent a surfboard; such activities are only rarely engaged in. However, public family outings that cost no money, such as going to the park or to a children's farm, are also not frequently conducted by the urban lower class. It is social risers who are the most active in exploring the public domain of the city.

Distinctions between the types of family outings can be made for analytical reasons but must not be overestimated. Interviews reveal that all types of family outings often contain elements of play. Many family outings have a hybrid character with both functional and playful elements included that symbolize a compromise between adults' and children's interests. Social family outings, for example, are not only about visiting friends but also about meeting potential playmates; public family outings, such as going to the park, often include visiting a playground and commercial family outings often take children and their need to play seriously. Even shopping with children may result in playful activities, as this Rotterdam upper-middle class mother describes: 'When we are at the Bijenkorf [a big department store] and he likes the escalator, yes, then we go five times'.

Parental narratives reveal that family outings often come up when the weather is bad and children are struggling with boredom. Such conditions stimulate the search for alternatives, as is explained by this single mother (social riser):

> However, if it is really raining outside, then also the garden is not an option; that is no fun either. And looking back at last year, we had, in my perception, quite a rainy year. So they played a lot inside … and then we took the kids to Ballorig [a commercial indoor play operation].

It is obvious in many interviews that parents feel it is their responsibility to help the children through periods of boredom, and this feeling creates an extra parenting task in urban environments where children cannot be sent outdoors without adult supervision: 'There is a lot to do in the neighbourhood. That is very nice. The only down point is that you always have to go with them. You can't just send them outside on their own' (social riser).

Thus, family outings require some effort from the parents, and they have to be scheduled for a certain time and place. Planning is considered to be a complicated task by all families regardless of class. Across class, the urban outdoors is considered by all families to be a space where adult supervision is needed, and that takes time. Because of its time-consuming character, family outings are organized mostly for the weekends, when children are free from school and parents do not have to work: 'On the weekend, we often go to a different playground', an Amsterdam upper-middle class mother said. By 'different', she means not the one around the corner. On the weekend, they go as a family, and then they want to make something special out of it by choosing a 'special' playground with better facilities. For lower class families, the special character of the weekend family outing is often embedded in a meeting with aunts and uncles, nephews and nieces: 'Yes, we always go on Saturday to Bos en Lommerplein to the market with lots of relatives'.

Going to special places not around the corner would suggest that most outings are done by car. However, that is not the case. Only a minority of the outings were car driven (44/178), and these are mostly social outings: '…Usually I don't use my car in the city when I'm with the children, only when visiting family'. The preference for alternative transportation is related to the strict parking rules in both Amsterdam and Rotterdam – 'Yeah, you know you won't find a parking space for your car' – applies to all classes, including the upper-middle classes. In the context of Dutch cities, bikes are used for family outings much more often than cars. Not being able to cycle is another explanation for the low number of family outings in lower class families. Almost all of these families have origins outside of the Netherlands, and parents were not raised with bikes. As a group, the lower class families have the lowest number of bikes per family.

Exploring the city

Family outings of urban households are very much about exploring the city where they live. Sometimes this must be taken very literally, as this mother explains:

> Then, he will climb on and under everything and jumps over benches and stuff. That is a type of playing field for him. The city is really fun because there are many strange attributes on the route. You have to allow that. And, you must have the patience for that.

However, the focus of this upper-middle class mother on enjoying the urban experiences is not generally shared. The narratives of lower class families reveal another story with more fear than fun when discussing the urban outdoors.

A lower class Amsterdam mother who is not satisfied with the playgrounds in her neighbourhood wants her son (10 years of age) to play within sight in the square in front of the house: 'Yes, I constantly look out of the window. Then, I look to see where he is. And then I shout from the window in case he turns the corner'. She lacks the time and the energy to search for better options elsewhere. Another lower class mother answers the question of where she likes her 10-year-old daughter to play: 'At home. I want to see my daughter all the time'. In the category of lower class families, urban fear goes hand in hand with a lack of knowledge about attractive spaces elsewhere. They lack a clear idea about the layout of the city and how to reach specific places. Mothers are not used to travelling on their own, and most do not have a bicycle or a driver's license. Some explore the city with the support of friends, but that does not always result in building personal knowledge of specific locations. On the question of what places she likes to visit with her children, a lower class African Amsterdam mother remembered a children's farm she visited some time ago with her children and a Dutch friend. She would like to go there another time, but 'Last summer we went there, but I don't know any more exactly where it is. Somewhere near the Dam? We always go with her car'. The interviews make clear that a lack of knowledge among lower class families hinders them from exploring the urban outdoors, including activities that do not cost any money.

Social risers are the top of the urban explorers in regard to public outings (Table 2). They frequently visit different parks, playgrounds and squares of the city. In the interviews, parents demonstrate their knowledge of different family-welcoming public spaces:

> Well, at the arches, the railroad, there is quite an extensive playground with soccer fields and more. We also sometimes go there. Especially on the weekend. He likes going there to play soccer with his dad. And at Koninginnestraat, there is also a play square where you can play soccer. However, we also sometimes, on the weekend, go to a park of some type. The Kralingse Woods, where we have been just lately, or Plaswijckpark or the Zoo, or at Schiebroek, there is also a park with a pond that is also really nice. I find it important to now and then go out of the city with the four of us, to experience a nice green environment together.

Another mother explains that she and her daughters explore 'all' the playgrounds of the city by bike. That is something she thinks is necessary when you live in the city with children: 'You have to actively look for sites to do things. If you find a playground for the children, it is always good, and that doesn't have to be expensive'. The social riser families explicitly favour the city for its public attractiveness without financial repercussions. They know many spaces and activities in the city that are free to enter.

Upper-middle class families are similar to social risers in their exploration of the fun of the city, but their orientation is slightly different. Their focus is relatively often on commercial (cultural and food) family outings both in the city where they live and elsewhere in the Netherlands. One Amsterdam family diary showed a museum visit in Leiden and a family dining out in Utrecht within the same week. Another Rotterdam family visited the summer parade (cultural manifestation) in Amsterdam and visited a pub and a restaurant with the children. The cultural qualities of the city are considered to create a positive learning environment for children, as a Rotterdam higher-educated mother explains: 'Well, he is a minimum of once every two weeks either at the NAI (museum) or at Plaswijckpark, or …. So, those types of things, they are also instructional'.

In choosing specific spaces (and neglecting others), parents are critical consumers. The interviews reveal that critical comments made by the lower class families easily result in not going outdoors as a family. They define the urban outdoors as unattractive or unsafe and feel obliged to supervise their child all the time. Social risers and upper-middle class families feel the same need of supervising their child but seem to be more able to avoid negative spaces and look for better opportunities elsewhere. They share with the lower class families that they are not always happy with the burden of supervising 'all the time', but within this restriction, they try to make the best of it by choosing attractive spaces for outings. In the interviews, they compare at length urban public spaces and their unique qualities for family outings. Answering the question of why she visited a specific playground some distance from their house, one mother (a social riser) answers: 'Well, the fact that it has all been made out of natural materials. All tree trunks with high grass around it, you can play hide and seek in it. It is simply a rugged playground'. Another playground nearby, in contrast, is described by this mother as 'very clinical'; she does not visit that one.

Social riser families and upper-middle class families make perfectly clear that family outings need to be attractive for both children and parents. Family outings are not chosen only because of their qualities for children; the outings must also correspond to the parents' needs and taste:

> What I miss a little bit is a place where the children can play and where there is a restaurant or coffee. At the Erasmuspark and Westerpark that all is realised, but at the Rembrandtpark, there is nothing at all. That is why we almost never go there because you cannot buy a cup of coffee anywhere. Woeste Westen is okay; there, you can first go get a cup of coffee at the Espressofabriek and then go to the playground. However, a bit closer to home there are fewer such possibilities ... Yes, when they just opened the playground at the Willem de Zwijgerlaan, we went there a lot, but everybody started to complain about the absence of a coffee place. They should just place a mobile coffee cart of some kind!

This social riser mother looks for a green space that can be used to play in while coffee is served. Her opinion is shared by another parent, an Amsterdam upper-middle class father who focuses both on the supply of consumptions and facilities for children's play. One of his favourite family outings is at a restaurant in a former industrial district with abundant sandy space around: 'Its sea sand, so you might find interesting things there such as sea stars and all types of other things that are in the sand'. His daughter adds that 'Behind it, there is also a big area with mainly earth and a few grass bits, and then there is a giant foreland with rocks, and there I play a lot; I do many things there'. Her father concludes: 'So, that place [the restaurant and its outdoors] is also a playground; of course, somebody should accompany her. We sit there and they can play around freely'.

Escaping the city

Children's play is found to be an important element of family outings. However, enthusiastic many parents are about specific family spaces, not everybody are satisfied with the opportunities for play in the city. Some families try to find other places where their children can 'really' play: the countryside and other green environments. In their search for additional play spaces, families of different classes rely on different solutions. As has been demonstrated above, lower class families frequently complain about the play facilities for their children in the neighbourhood. They do not know many good options elsewhere in the city where they live, but some of them know some alternatives outside the city where they have kin living; for instance, this Rotterdam mother who regularly goes to visit her sister who lives in Barendrecht explains that her child does not play outdoors very often because there are some problems with the neighbouring children. When the interviewer asks 'I saw in the diary that you visited family this weekend; do you do this more often?' she answers: 'Yes, almost once every week. We go by train to Barendrecht. The children love it. My sister lives there'. She and her children enjoy the small town atmosphere of Barendrecht where the children can move around freely.

Eight of the interviewed families have some type of 'second home' outside the big city where they live. One lower class family has a family home in Turkey they visit once a year. Three social riser families and four upper-middle class families have a modest space where they like to go on the weekends: an allotment garden, a permanent place on a camping site, a caravan or a little boat. Those spaces are seen as good additional spaces to raise children. Parents speak enthusiastically about their second homes as a possibility for offering their children 'real play'. When the interviewer asks 'Why does your family have a caravan in Bakkum?', the Amsterdam mother of three answers:

> Well, because I think it is important that they also have earth under their feet – that I find really important – and also because there they can …. I find the social context very important. Children learn to grow up free because, in Bakkum, they learn how to ride a bike really well or they learn how it is to go to the shop on their own to get some buns. That is all possible there, and here [Amsterdam], I find that, well, uh … less transparent, and there I dare let them do that. If they can do it there, then they might also do it here at some point. So that is very nice. And, the children love playing outside. They always have friends around.

She continues:

> and it is a place where we don't have to constantly go out with them; you can read a book yourself there and the kids have fun around you. And, in the city, you always have to organise things. That's the main difference. It is mostly relaxing, both for parents and children.

From this quote, it is clear that however popular the urban family outings are, parents still see the value of children's exploration of their environment on their own, not least of all because it is much more relaxing for themselves. The families with a 'second home' make a clear distinction between the city and the rural setting, whereas the city offers merely play, the countryside (or camping site/allotment garden) offers 'real play'; unsupervised opportunities in green environments. This 'real play' affords extra freedom for parents: they do not have to accompany their children, and they can enjoy their own leisure time. As such, urban family outings are considered to be second, compared to children's independent nature-directed play.

Conclusion and discussion

Family outings are a substantial part of children's and parents' urban lives that we do not yet know much about. In this small-scale study, we have tried to offer some insight into families' class specific engagements in different types of family outings in the two largest cities of the Netherlands.

The city, as the provider of family outings, is not generally appreciated by all urban families. All families see their child as primarily vulnerable, and good parenthood is considered to involve taking care of your child in terms of supervising them in the outdoors. This shared attitude results, however, in unequal outcomes (Holloway and Pimlott-Wilson 2014). The main conclusion of this study is that social risers and upper-middle classes enjoy the city for family outings much more than the lower class families, even when they live in the same neighbourhoods (as is the case in this study) and even when we focus on free to enter public spaces. Lower class families struggle to cope with daily life and feel disappointed about the quality of family spaces nearby. They consider the outdoors to be unsafe for children, but they lack the time, money, knowledge and mobility to explore the city with their children. The result is that family outings in urban public spaces are only rarely conducted by lower class families compared to more resourceful families living in the same inner city environment. Family outings reinforce class divisions. This is a sad conclusion in an era in which many Western European cities are in a process of upgrading with nicer parks, well-maintained squares and new playgrounds. These newly created facilities are mostly free to enter, but with the results of this study, we have to fear that they will not reach the urban lower class families and their children.

Social risers and upper-middle class families also complain about unattractive and unsafe urban spaces and all the efforts needed to create nice family outings. However, they have the economic and cultural resources required to engage in urban consumption. For them, good parenthood means that you invite your child to explore the urban outdoors in a supervised way. Those families do not want to refrain from visiting places, as the lower class families feel forced to do. The social risers and the upper-middle classes describe themselves as both burdened by a city that demands they accompany their children at every moment outdoors and blessed by a city that has such a broad supply of family-welcoming places. With their ample resources, they are able to consume the urban setting. Although social risers do not have abundant economic resources, they demonstrate the knowledge (cultural resources) and have the mobility to really benefit from the city and everything that is for free. They enthusiastically speak about their explorations of the best parts of the city that are publicly accessible and can be reached by bike. The upper-middle classes, with limited time but sufficient money, are most focused on the new family consumption spaces where financial resources are required. Both categories are focused on spaces that combine services for children (e.g. play) and adults (e.g. coffee) and stress the learning experiences the city offers.

We want to end with two reflections that can be considered to be avenues for further research. The first one is on the changing character of urban childhood. This study on family outings shows that children's and parents' lives are very much interrelated in time and space. Traditional children's spaces such as playgrounds have developed into family spaces with supervising parents all around (Valentine 2004), and former adult spaces such as cafes are developing into family-welcoming spaces that are open to children (McKendrick, Bradford, and Fielder 2000; Karsten et al. 2015). Parents and children spend more time together than has ever been the case, and this is surely an important change in the nature of urban childhood. We share worries about the decrease in children's freedom of movement and independent outdoor play. However, this study shows that family outings are focused on children's wishes and include play. Are family outings compensating for the decrease in children's outdoor play? A serious limitation of this study is that we did not systematically assess children's views on family outings. To what extent are urban children satisfied with the playful dimension of family outings? The answering of this question should be the topic of new research.

Our second reflection refers to the discourse on the urban jungle as opposed to the rural idyll for growing up. This study concludes that it is mainly the families with middle to higher education and income who are able to selectively explore the positive attributes of the city for their children. They discover urban spaces, including green spots, nice shops and restaurants that they and their children enjoy, and they believe in the learning experience of the city for their children. Some resource-rich families feel the limits of this urban exploration and are glad to have access to a countryside alternative with its 'real play' opportunities. However, even they are not only negative about the urban environment for their children and very few consider the option to leave the city for the countryside. In contrast, the lower class families experience the city as an urban jungle in which they find it difficult to find their way. They resemble the city survivors without many alternatives to explore (Power 2007). Are urban parents constructing a new urban idyll for children (Karsten 2014a) and is that idyll exclusively for the better off? This question also requires further research.

Acknowledgements

We would like to thank Monique van Benthem, Charlotte Kemmeren, Corien Remijnse, Hanna Tak and Tim Tensen for their participation in the field work of this research.

Funding

This research was funded by Stimuleringsfonds voor de Aarchtitectuur, the Netherlands [Q11/021.RPS].

Notes on contributor

Lia Karsten is an Associate Professor of Urban Studies at the University of Amsterdam. Her research focus is on children's and families' geographies, including leisure and consumption issues. In 2013, she received an honorary doctorate from Uppsala University, Sweden. www.uva.nl/profile/c.j.m.karsten

Naomi Felder is an Architect fascinated by cities, it's streets and it's inhabitants. After working for a decade for renowned architectural firms, she started her own office, bureau Feld, specialized in research and design at all scales. www.bureaufeld.nl

Karsten and Feld work together on a research and design project called families in cities. www.gezinindestad.nl

References

Allen, C., R. Powell, R. Casey, and S. Coward. 2007. "Ordinary the Same as Anywhere Else': Notes on the Spoiled Identity in 'Marginal' Middle-class Neighbourhoods." *Sociology* 41 (2): 239–258.

Authier, J., and S. Lehman-Frisch. 2013. "Le gout des autres: Gentrification told by Children." *Urban Studies* 50: 994–1010. doi:10.1177/0042098012465127.

Boterman, W., L. Karsten, and S. Musterd. 2010. "Gentrifiers Settling Down? Patterns and Trends of Residential Location of Middle-class Families in Amsterdam." *Housing Studies* 21 (1): 83–98.

Bourdieu, P. 1984. *Distinction*. London: Routledge.

Butler, T. 2003. *London Calling. The Middle-class and the Re-making of Inner London*. Oxford: Berg.

Carr, N. 2011. *Children's and Families' Holiday Experiences*. London: Routledge.

Clarke, A. 2007. "Consuming Children and Making Mothers: Birthday Parties, Gifts and the Pursuit of Sameness." *Horizontes Antropologicos* [Anthropological Horizons] 13: 263–287.

Chawla, L., ed. 2002. *Growing up in an Urbanizing World*. London: Earthscan Publications.

Craig, L., and K. Mullan. 2012. "Shared Parent-child Leisure Time in Four Countries." *Leisure Studies* 31 (2): 211–229.

DeVault, M. L. 2000. "Producing Family Time: Practices of Leisure Activity beyond the Home." *Qualitative Sociology* 23: 485–503. doi:10.1023/A:1005582926577.

Finch, J. 2007. "Displaying Families." *Sociology* 4 (1): 65–81.

Freeman, C., and P. Tranter. 2011. *Children and their Urban Environment*. London: Earthscan.

Galster, G., and A. Santiago. 2006. "What's Hood Got to Do with it? Parental Perceptions about How Neighbourhood Mechanisms Affect Their Children." *Journal of Urban Affairs* 28 (3): 201–226.

Hagerstrand, T. 1970. "What about People in Regional Sciences?" *9th European Congress of Regional Science Association* 24: 7–21.

Hillman, M., J. Adams, and J. Whitelegg. 1991. *One False Move. A Study of Children's Independent Mobility*. London: Policy Study Institute.

Holloway, S., and H. Pimlott-Wilson. 2014. "Enriching Children, Institutionalizing Childhood? Geographies of Play, Extracurricular Activities, and Parenting in England." *Annals of the Association of American Geographers* 104: 613–627.

Irwin, S., and S. Elley. 2011. "Concerted Cultivation? Parenting Values, Education and Class Diversity." *Sociology* 45: 480–495.

Karsten, L. 2005. "It All Used to be Better? Different Generations on Continuity and Change in Urban Children's Daily Use of Space." *Children's Geographies* 3: 275–290.

Karsten, L. 2014a. "Middle-class Childhood and Parenting Culture in High-rise Hong Kong: On Scheduled Lives, the School Trap and a New Urban Idyll." *Children's Geographies*. doi:10.1080/14733285.2014.915288.

Karsten, L. 2014b. "From Yuppies to Yupps: Family Gentrifiers Consuming Spaces and Re-inventing Cities." *Tijdschrift voor economische en sociale geografie* [Journal of Economic and Social Geography] 105 (2): 175–188. doi:10.1111/tesg.12055.

Karsten, L., A. Kamphuis, and C. Remeijnse. 2015. "Time out with the Family: The Shaping of Family Leisure in the New Urban Consumption Spaces of Cafes, Bars and Restaurants." *Leisure Studies* 34 (2): 166–181. doi:10.1080/02614367.2013.845241.

Lareau, M. 2003. *Unequal Childhoods: Class, Race and Family Life*. Berkeley, CA: University of California Press.

Lilius, J. 2014. "Is There Room for Families in the Inner City: Life-stage Blenders Challenging Planning." *Housing Studies* 29 (6): 843–861. doi:10.1080/02673037.2014.905673.

McKendrick, J., M. Bradford, and A. Fielder. 2000. "Kid customer? Commercialization of play space and the commodification of childhood." *Childhood* 7: 295–314.

Morgan, D. H. J. 2011. *Rethinking Family Practices*. Basingstoke: Palgrave MacMillan. doi:10.1057/9780230304680.

Power, A. 2007. *City Survivors. Bringing up Children in Disadvantaged Neighbourhoods*. Bristol: The Policy Press.

Pinkster, F., and J. Droogleever Fortuijn. 2009. "Watch Out for the Neighborhood Trap! A Case Study on Parental Perceptions of and Strategies to Counter Risks for Children in a Disadvantaged Neighborhood." *Children's Geographies* 7: 323–337.

Shaw, S., and D. Dawson. 2001. "Purposive Leisure: Examining Parental Discourses on Family Activities." *Leisure Sciences* 23: 217–231.

Sociaal en Cultureel Planbureau. 2011. *Gezinsrapport 2011*. Den Haag: SCP.

Valentine, G. 2004. *Public Space and the Culture of Childhood*. Aldershot: Ashgate.

Van der Burgt, D., and K. Gustafson. 2013. "'Doing Time' and 'Creating Space': A Case Study of Children's Outdoor Play and Institutionalized Leisure in an Urban Family." *Children, Youth and Environment* 23: 24–42.

Van der Zwaard, J. 1999. *Met hulp van vriendinnen. Moeders uit lage inkomensgroepen over rondkomen en vooruitkomen*. Amsterdam: SWP.

Verstrate, L., and L. Karsten. 2011. "The Creation of Play Spaces in Twentieth-century Amsterdam: From an Intervention of Civil Actors to a Public Policy." *Landscape Research* 36 (1): 85–109. doi:10.1080/01426397.2010.536205.

Vincent, C., and S. Ball. 2007. "'Making Up' the Middle-class Child: Families Activities and Class Dispositions." *Sociology* 4: 1061–1077.

Vincent, C., S. J. Ball, and A. Braun. 2008. "'It's like Saying "Coloured"': Understanding and Analysing the Urban Working Classes 'It's like Saying "Coloured."'" *The sociological Review* 56 (1): 61–77. doi:10.1111/j.1467-954X.2008.00777.x.

Zukin, S. 1995. *The Cultures of Cities*. Oxford: Blackwell.

Leisure in a world of 'com-pu-pu-pu-pu-pu-pu-pu-pu-pu-pu-puter-puter, puter games': a father and son conversation

Stephen L. Wearing[a], Jamie Wearing[a], Matthew McDonald[b] and Michael Wearing[c]

[a]Management Discipline Group, University of Technology Sydney, Sydney, Australia; [b]Department of Management, RMIT University Vietnam, Vietnam; [c]School of Social Sciences, University of New South Wales, Sydney, Australia

This article is a conversation between an academic and his 14-year-old son and investigates the links between leisure and computer games. It focuses specifically on the son as an adolescent in the context of Western consumer society. It is interested in how he explores his leisure in relation to the computer game 'League of Legends' and how this indicates his adolescent self, which is a self that is increasingly targeted, marketed, packaged and purchased. This analysis illustrates how the consumer packaging of the adolescent self through commodified leisure creates in a neoliberal society the negotiated realities of youth experience and social identity. The paper argues that consumer culture manufactures a world of escape, particularly for adolescent boys. It allows him (J) to transform his world into one he has more control over, separate from his parents' imposed regime and in a way that resists other forms of market-based influence. This is achieved through the adoption of identities that are offered in the games (a choice) that appear to challenge authority, albeit produced within youth culture and marketing, purchased and consumed in the belief that it is resistance. There is also a sense of friendship and shared identity with others in forming teams online to play the game. In these games, forms of adolescent deviance, resistance and control are normalised as challenging, exciting and risky while providing associations with power, self-fulfilment and a degree of online celebrity and identity exchange. In the final analysis, the paper explores some possibilities for parents to enter this world and understand the children and their constructions of self-identity in Western consumer society.

Introduction

This paper argues that the struggle for self-identity in adolescence[1] is a struggle that is neither tied to roles or socialisation in the traditional theories of youth culture and deviance nor as a fluid unregulated multiplicity of selves as described by postmodern theories and that until we untie ourselves from the restrictions of this past we will not understand the complexities surrounding the youth of today (McDonald 1999, 207; see also Wearing, McDonald, and Wearing 2013). In neoliberal regimes characterised by fluid, mobile and cosmopolitan cultures, the adolescent can mobilise a self or several selves in discursive 'fields structured by competition or rules of innovation and conformity' (McDonald 1999, 205). Online gaming offers a way of shaping social identity that includes virtual friendships and socialising using up hours of leisure time. Access to such leisure experience is reliant upon socio-economic resources and stratified across family life for primarily the demographic of 'gamers' (i.e. reasonably well-off middle-class adolescent boys and young men). There is in this sense a thin building of social capital beyond place for young people, notably boys who can afford such practice within familial economies. We are also deeply concerned with the nature of corporate marketing through the media of the 'virtual realism' of computer games products and their potential benefits and harm for the consciousness and vulnerable social minds of adolescence (Beder 2009).

In this social terrain, adolescent experience and action can also create resistance to commodifying processes as subverting dominant adult modes of self. Many adolescent self-identities are constructed in neoliberal regimes to challenge the social order and to liberate adolescents from societal norms (e.g. Rietveld 1998). Within such fields, there is also a counter-discourse, a debate we take up in this case study of father and son interactions over computer gaming. However, in many instances these self-identities feed off the signifiers and coding of mass consumption and are incorporated into the commercialisation of adolescence by neoliberal capitalism (e.g. Nixon 1998). Does gaming create a virtual space for self-identify and exchange that also extends social interaction and friendship and possibly builds social capital? While we cannot definitively answer such questions, there is a suggestion that we will follow-up in further research that young people find and define their own social and cultural benefits from online gaming. It is within this context that we wish to examine the development of the relationship between parent and child, in this case the relationship of Stephen (55-year-old academic) and his son Jamie[2] (14-year-old son) through J's account of his leisure activity of gaming and more specifically the game 'League of Legends', a PC online game.

In setting out the parameters of this analysis, we argue that to understand the adolescent computer gamer it is important to rethink how leisure consumption is experienced by adolescents. The analysis presented here builds on previous work (McDonald and Wearing 2013; McDonald, Wearing, and Ponting 2008; Wearing, McDonald, and Wearing 2013) by linking consumer culture with adolescent behaviour, enabling us to better understand, in this case J's insights into his computer gaming. We draw on conceptual perspectives from social psychology, leisure studies and critical theory to frame the conversation. The discussion that follows is largely schematic and involves a degree of exploration and reflexivity. As Cohen (2013, 333) suggests, leisure researchers have come some way in addressing issues of reflexivity in their own research, this effort towards engaging with positionality has lagged approximately 10 years behind when the broader social sciences confronted the 'reflexive turn'. For a more detailed look into the methods used in this paper, see Forsey (2010) and Dupuis (2010). In this approach, we attempt to account for the various factors and issues that link three main concepts – 'consumer culture', 'adolescent leisure' and 'computer gaming', in particular online gaming. We see this analysis making a contribution to future empirical and cultural research that will help to better understand modern adolescent identities, corporate marketing and the impact of gaming.

The data from this research come from an ongoing conversation and negotiation between a father and son about computer gaming. The data come from a transcribed interview (a conversation), a review of that interview by the son and a number of years of exchanges between the father and son who share a home office. The third and fourth authors of this paper had no access to the son in the data-gathering process for this study.

Both parents and the son gave consent for the data to be collected, and in the interests of family equity, the son is included as an author on the paper. No formal ethics approval was sort beyond the consent of the son and the other parent as it was deemed unnecessary for this research. The research falls within the general area of 'family' (Carr 2011, 181) and the son was given the option to opt out of the research at any time he so wished. The UN document 'Ethical Research Involving Children' (Graham et al. 2013) was used to guide this research. It required that J could opt out of the research at any time and that the transcript would only be made available to the two other researchers involved in this research (the two co-authors on this paper). The final approval of the paper's contents and quotes would be the son's. The transcript was stored on the three researcher's computers only, all of which are protected by passwords. No incentives were used to encourage participation in this research. The process for the data gathering recognises that the exchange is an active and ongoing interview. It was a collaborative interaction between the father and son and all knowledge was co-constructed (Cohen 2013). The research follows on from the traditions in leisure research dating back to work such as Dupuis (2010) and fitting within Cohen's (2013) more recent work. Its research framework also acknowledges Forsey's (2010) work on active listening, which has been a part of the father's discussions over the many years of sharing a home office space with his son.

Computer games

Since the days of the invention of space invaders (released in 1978 and one of the first global video games), the concern for many parents and leisure policy makers has been the amount of time that boy's in particular spend playing these games. Although the games have changed, it appears the concerns have not (Chai, Chen, and Khoo 2001). Some of the time-use data show that boys engage more than girls in physically active leisure and games, while girls are more actively involved in what is sometimes labelled 'bedroom culture'. As adolescents grow up, they are more involved in social leisure, spend less time at home and more with peers. Seventy-two percent of adolescents report that they are in very good health. These teenagers spend less time on computers, surfing the net and hobbies. They are less alone and spend more time in the company of others (Glorieux, Stevens, and Vandeweyer 2005). Further evidence suggests that home computer game playing appears to be one of the social and leisure phenomena of the 1990s and the new millennium (Wawrzak-Chodaczek 2011), yet there is still little known about the acquisition, development and maintenance of computer game playing among children and adolescents (Baer, Bogusz, and Green 2011; Ferguson 2009). A survey of 147 eleven-year-old computer game players attending a summer camp revealed that their main reasons for playing were for fun, for a challenge, because there was nothing else to do and because their friends did it. Boys played computer games significantly more regularly than girls and were significantly more likely to play sports simulation games and violent games. Girls were found to play platform games and puzzlers significantly more than boys. Importantly, it is suggested that computer game playing for most children is a fairly absorbing and harmless activity but that, for a small minority of children, it may be problematic (Durkin and Barber 2002; Griffiths 1997; Wei 2007).

Research suggests that although Australian teenagers in the late 1990s were spending less time working and more time at leisure, the type of activities they were spending their free time on (watching television and playing computer games) may have a negative impact on their health and well-being (Lui, Szeto, and Jones 2011; Soupourmas 2005). The computer game is now a common way of using leisure time, and therefore, it is worth examining its impact on and relationship to the self, given how much time adolescents devote to them. Additionally, from a research and educational point of view, it is important to understand what kind of games young people play and what functions computer games play in their lives (Carbonaro et al. 2008). Content analysis of games available on the market shows that most of them (about 80%–85%) involve acts of extreme violence and cruelty (Wawrzak-Chodaczek 2011) and this appears to be a major concern for many parents and policy makers.

Our analysis makes use of existing notions of adolescent leisure to suggest that our understanding of computer gaming needs to explore the areas of leisure experience in its analysis (Flammer and Schaffner 2003; Verma and Larson 2003; Wearing and Wearing 1996, 2000). For example, computer gaming is linked to deviation, being labelled, reified, stereotyped and commonly stigmatised by social actors such as the media, family, school teachers, the police, religious groups and politicians (Rojek 2000; Stebbins 1997; Stebbins, Rojek, and Sullivan 2006; Williams 2009). Does the concept of deviant leisure through our reading of consumer culture and social psychological definitions offer some further insight into the computer game experience of the adolescent?

It is suggested that adolescents build up defence mechanisms against the continual barrage they receive to their senses through consumer culture (particularly through the mass media and advertising) and that one area of life where they might be able to escape is in the use of leisure time and spaces, in this instance the computer game. In these games they can seek some sense of individual purpose for themselves free from the constraining influence of authority figures.

S: Do you have enough freedom in your life and lifestyle? Do you feel constrained?

J: Yes, I definitely feel constrained a lot of the time. I couldn't put a finger on what I like but I definitely feel like my life is very controlled. Sometimes I don't mind so much I suppose.

However, with the sophistication of consumer marketing, media and advertising can be manipulated to provide a mechanism to repackage feelings of constraint and to resell it to those same adolescents; the outcome being a leisure that is commodified. We suggest that this makes the computer gaming phenomena as a leisure experience for these adolescents both precarious and ambivalent, in that its potential for the enhancement of self-identity is narrowed by its repackaging where it produces tendencies that relate to behaviour that is concerning.

We see gaming in the context of the shift from a producer society and its associated institutions, which have gradually faded away (e.g. family, community, religious observances, job security, trade unions) to be replaced by a consumer society that has altered the experience of self-identity, so that life choices, images, symbols and lifestyles are now increasingly filtered through abstract systems like computers and commodification (Bauman 1988, 2000, 2005; Beck 1992; Giddens 1991; Langer 2004). This allows the market, through highly targeted forms of marketing, media and advertising, to create a *desire* for expressive individualism, norm violations, rebelliousness, celebrity, wealth and beauty. The result is a narcissistic self-identity, constructed via the manipulation of the signs and symbols of consumer culture, which is offered as a form of self-actualisation and a defence against the ontological insecurity characteristic of post-traditional society (Hebdige 1979; Baudrillard 1970/1998; Baumeister 1987; Featherstone 2007; Giddens 1991; Lasch 1979). Adolescent gamers then walk a fine line between gaming as a form of defiance, resistance and escape from various forms of societal control, to one of adopting the value sets imposed by the games themselves (both as consumer products and the internal values within the games themselves, see for example 'How to Read Donald Duck' [Dorfman 1991]).

The game played by J in this paper is 'League of Legends', which is a multiplayer online battle arena video game. Sheer (2014) suggests that, over 67 million people in 2014 play this game per month, 27 million per day and over 7.5 million concurrently during peak hours. J talks about the game as:

> J - I like playing it because it playing with other people online and it's a challenge – because you're playing against people and so it's always different. It's a new style of game – recently developed brings in concepts and ideas that makes it more interesting than other types. Online five people vs five people the aim of the game is to destroy the enemy nexus (which is a building) the viewpoint is bird's eye and you play as one of those five characters and you destroy objectives and enemy characters in the attempt to get to the enemy nexus and destroy it. It is a very complex game people have been playing it for five years and never master it, its versatile and always changing and being updated. In this game there are three lanes they are named top middle and bottom – one person goes top one person goes middle and 2 people go bottom with one person playing in the jungle which is the area in-between lanes. Each lane has different characters that are suited to it – the top lane generally has champion with high health that soak up damage for the team. Mid lane generally has champions that deal ability power damage such as a mage bot lane has two people in it one a support who plays champions who back up the team and helps heal them and generally helping the entire team but does not deal much damage. The other person in the bot lane is the opposite they are called the attack damage carry or ADC – this champions role is to dish out the damage for the team – the rest of the team backs the champion up and makes sure they don't die. Finally there is the jungle role – this role does not have set champions as such but mainly focus around people with lots of health points who can engage on an enemy.

The next section provides some analysis of the conversation between father and son.

Computer games, consumer culture and commodified leisure

> S: And gaming as a part of your life?

> J: Well at the moment it's a big part of it, it's a lot of my social life, it's a lot of my leisure time. It's a lot of who I base myself as being and who I express myself as being to other people. In the future I hope it carries on, I hope I'm playing games for a long time. I'd like to see where gaming goes in the future; I'd like to see how it progresses. At the moment, in my life it's a large part of my life and I like it.

> S: How do you feel about you in current society? Are you happy with the society around you? Or do you have any issues?

> J: By society or friends at school?

> S: Yeah, your friends, yourself your identity, freedom in society?

> J: You're meaning social status?

> S: Yes

> J: I think its fine; I don't really care too much about what people think about me. I think it's easy that way. If I go around caring so much then I'm not going to really enjoy much at all. I tried to learn not to care too much. I think I'm pretty happy how I am with friends and stuff.

Most social commentators now agree that modern Western societies have become consumer societies, indicating they arc 'increasingly organised around the consumption (of goods and leisure), rather than the production of materials and services' and the fluid production of identity especially amongst the middle class and their offspring (Marshall 1998, 112–113; see also Bauman 2005, 23–42). This in turn has created a *consumer culture* – habits, customs, language, dress and forms of social interaction that stem from marketing, mass media and advertising-driven constructions of the world (Beder 2009). Featherstone (2001) proposes that consumer culture refers to the 'culture' of consumer society. 'It suggests that the representation (signs and images) and values of contemporary societies revolve around consumption: the purchase and enjoyment of goods for the construction of lifestyle' (Featherstone 2001, 2262).

> J: Ok, sorry. So when you play a character there's two things you can spend money on in the game. Skins and champions. So you can buy the actual champion. There's a lot of them as I said before and you can buy skins of various looks for that champion that make them look different. Like someone who might have been a guy with a shotgun suddenly turns into a guy wearing flippers with a water gun. It changes the look; it changes their body as well. They have four abilities in the game. It really customises that entire champion.

> S: So you're saying it's like your sister going and buying a dress? And you prefer to be in the game doing those things?

> J: Yeah, shopping takes time. It's not something I'm very interested in. I just wear clothes that. I just wear all black all the time, just very simple.

Consumer culture, according to Baudrillard (1970/1998) is a process in which the purchaser of an item is actively engaged in trying to create and maintain a sense of identity through the display of purchased goods. Mainstream commercial discourse constructs self-identities that are not only compatible with the neoliberal emphasis on consumption but also enable the reproduction of such relations of power and imagery in social and cultural life. Adults, adolescents and children are subject to a varying intensity and recognition of self-identity within these relations. Some adolescents are duped into thinking that individuality, uniqueness and distinction might be satisfied in consumption, however, commodities are almost always mass produced, mass marketed, mass sold and mass consumed (Ewen 1988; Klien 2001). Thus, much leisure in consumer cultures is neither liberating nor self-enhancing. Aligned with this lack of self-identity comes a need to resist and break away from the shackles of authority and conservatism – taking the form of deviant leisure. Deviance, however, is not always to be seen in a pejorative way. It can be creative, refreshing and fun. It pushes and redraws boundaries, often has its own language and particular meanings for common expressions, and sometimes strengthens human connections and spirituality (Williams 2009, 212; see also Rietveld 1998). Nonetheless, deviance is a set of constructed freedoms that ultimately return to the incorporation of hedonistic and expressive individualism, and consumer resistance by adolescents, back into the dominant and formalised cultures.

The basic mechanism that drives consumer society is the consumption of goods and services. It therefore relies on leisure that can be purchased and is easily accessible (Sassatelli 2007, 164–170). The merging of consumption with leisure was finally consummated in the earlier twentieth century when business leaders and politicians realised that mass production would not survive without a corresponding mass consumption (Ewen 1976/2001). In order to achieve this aim, corporate public relations advocated for shorter working hours and higher rates of pay so that workers would have enough free time and money to consume. Rather than allowing workers the freedom to control the means of production, business leaders and politicians devised for workers a narcissistic form of self-actualisation that would take place 'among the uncontestable fruits of the new industrial cornucopia' (Ewen 1976/2001, 27). As production mechanisms changed, work became increasingly routinised and monotonous, 'consumer culture presented itself as the realm within which gratification and excitement might be had – an alternative to more radical and anti-authoritarian prescriptions' (Ewen 1976/ 2001, 189; see also Curtis 2002). This contributes to the view and to a certain extent modernity's myth, that family and home (bedroom) cultures are more informal and resistant to economic globalisation and commodification.

The general shift away from family/community-based forms of leisure, to leisure organised around consumption has now become a normative expression. For example, adolescents use sites of consumption such as shopping malls and arcades, franchised fast-food outlets and cinema complexes as places to socialise in safety, recreate, compare, contrast, try out and purchase goods and services (Watt and Stenson 1998). Shopping malls and precincts have become significant for adolescents because they function as spaces for social interaction, identity experimentation, resistance and deviance. Critical theory argues that many large corporations researched, packaged and sold deviant ideologies and behaviours in order to capture the growing adolescent market (Brake 1979; McDonald 1999, Beder 2009). In pursuit of this market, every anti-establishment cultural innovation (e.g. rock music, rap music, surfing, skateboarding) and emotions and attitudes like rebellion are targeted by marketers who turn attempts to escape convention and social norms into their exact opposite (Hamilton and Denniss 2005). Examples include the use of rappers like The Fat Boys and Run-DMC to endorse products such as wrist watches (Swatch) and sporting clothing (Adidas) (Charnas 2010). Or the marketing and advertising of Diesel jeans as the uniform of the anti-globalisation movement, the commercial appropriation of Che Guevara's image as an emblem of youthful rebellion, or the clothing brand FCUK.

> The marketing experts developed a strategy of appealing to young people by deliberately offending staider members of the community. Buying and wearing the brand (FCUK) would mean giving the finger to conventional society, as if uttering a profanity in public is an assertion of independence. This is the sort of tame 'rebellion' modern consumerism thrives on. (Hamilton and Denniss 2005, 45–46)

The market offers signs and symbols in the form of brands, products and activities that establish real and imagined difference, at both the group and individual level (e.g. Konig 2008; Waerdahl 2005). Consumer products, branding, advertising, film, print media and television celebrate rebellious individualism, a character type frequently played by film actors like Bruce Willis, Vin Diesel, Daniel Craig and Jason Statham. These actors typically play characters that do not play by the rules and win, because they are not weighed down by entanglements and responsibilities to other people. In consumer cultures, the 'heroes of production' – the self-made men, corporate founders, tycoons, pioneers, explorers, entrepreneurs and colonisers – have given way to the 'heroes of consumption' - film, music, celebrity and sporting stars – whose self-absorbed entitled lifestyles are voyeuristically analysed and celebrated by the media (Baudrillard 1970/1998). This creates a desire in adolescents to live in some way like the rich and famous who make their own rules and are seen to behave in self-centred narcissistic ways.

So where does the gamer fall within this analysis:

> S: You're not into anything else? Do you like to go shopping?

> J: No, If I do go shopping I generally go to 'EB Games' and then I don't buy anything because I'm not actually interested in any other games other than 'League of Legends'.

> S: So why would you go to EB Games?

> J: Just to look at games. I wouldn't go to EB Games just to go to EB Games but if I have to go shopping with my Mum and my sister that would be where I would spend my time because there's nothing better to do.

J appears to negate the consumption model that is suggested and falls back on the focus he has on gaming, his desire is only to make shopping an extension of his gaming – however he is also able to purchase particular items in the game League of Legends that assist in making the game more sophisticated and enjoyable.

> J: Yeah, you can buy in-game purchases which I guess adds a fair bit of money onto it but I don't mind at all.

> S: Ok so you think its value for money?

> J: Yeah, you pay money for visual things that are never going to help your life at all but I suppose if someone goes and buys…. if my sister goes and buys another dress I suppose it might help her social life and make her feel good but in the end it doesn't matter that much. When I buy a skin for my champion that makes it look cool I suppose I get social status within the game which makes me feel good so it's exactly the same as going and buying an item of clothing or something that doesn't actually help you but it's just fun to get.

> S: So you get status in the game by being able to buy things in the game?

> J: Not really, I don't think anyone really cares if someone has skins or not but it does… if you have a really cool skin people comment and that's always nice. Otherwise it's just fun, having skins is just a working part of the game.

Where is gaming as deviant leisure and resistance?

Often pleasure, escape, release, excitement, relaxation, socialisation, social status and challenge are the most common reasons for adolescents to participate in leisure. J appears to resist my strong sense of non-violence and opposition to first-hand shooting games by playing them despite my objections, he sees them as fun and exciting. Here I think is a strong link to explore the ideas of deviant leisure and the theoretical construct of resistance. So does gaming involve this idea of deviant leisure, which is participated in for pleasure, excitement and escape? Is there a fit in J's activities around resistance to parents but also the ability to explore being deviant even if it is based around feelings that are a direct result of the market-created computer game?

> J: No I can see some people might (see) it that way. I don't play because my parents might not like me doing this. I don't think 'this is so good, I'm such a rebel', no, I just do it because I find it fun and I find it enjoyable. I don't do it to resist anything … society … go against anyone. No.

So J's central desire appears to revolve around the fun of leisure while generally we find that deviant leisure creates a means for adolescents, to violate and resist certain rules and norms, experiment and play with identities and to test the boundaries of independence through risk-taking behaviours, breaking rules and pushing the limits of societal norms. As we lack any significant research that informs us of motivations to game we turn here to the general literature to explore this. Research suggests that adolescents are seeking to oppose rules and regulation, monotony, boredom, anxiety and the constraints of contemporary society, which prescribes education, productivity, capital accumulation and consumption, in line with agreed forms of thinking, emotional expression and behaviour (Fromm 1956; Hall, Winlow, and Ancrum 2008; Rojek 2000). Adolescence is locked into an intersectional struggle over deviant identity that cuts across and through social class, gender, ethnicity and geo-territorial boundaries (Wearing 2011). There is also a building of 'thin' social capital in shaping revised social identities for these adolescents that builds on virtual friendships and team play when online gaming. We suggest that this is thin or superficial in that such friendships are usually temporary in order to compete as a team in such games. In some cases real-life friends also participate in the same online games. Of course, such marketing and design strategies are now requisite within the selling of these games. They are positioned in neoliberalism to consume goods and services and to pursue status-defining products provided by global multinational companies. So we suggest that the addictive and enchanting qualities of personal computer gaming technology for adolescent boys, in particular those provided by large multinational companies such as Nintendo, Microsoft (Xbox) or Sony (Play Station) (Langer 2004; Anderson, Gentile, and Buckley 2007; Rice 2009; Wilson 2010) are targeted to the ideas that surround deviant leisure and resistance but this is not how J constructs it and so further research might be needed.

It is of interest here to make the link between computer pirating of films and music and computer game playing, the first being counter to the rules of intellectual and artistic property – but if it can be controlled, it can be commodified by its repackaging and sale as sexist and violent games such as *Grand Theft Auto, 50 Cent: Bulletproof* and *Call of Duty: Modern Warfare*. While both activities might be considered adolescent-deviant leisure, the repackaging of the latter for consumption is alegitimatising process that sanctions deviance through its targeting of leisure in the home (Nixon 1998). The adolescent gamer then becomes the prefect market even if not seen as such by the adolescent target market.

We see deviant leisure existing 'in the shadows of conventional morality' (Lynch and Veal 1996, 291), outside or on the margins of the 'centre'. The centre, or 'common ground', according to Rojek (1995) normalises certain values and morals and excludes others as a result of the designation of existing power relations. The central authority and adjudicator of that authority in the home is the parent/guardian. Their application of power comes from the communication of a dominant discourse within society (Shaw 2001; Aitchison 2001; Weedon 1997). And so where power is exercised, there is often resistance. Often this resistance comes from counter or new knowledge (Shaw 2001), disorderly discourses and the struggle against subjectification, submission and exploitation (Foucault 1984). Therefore, adolescent-deviant leisure is seen as those activities that lie on the margins of morality or opposing those in power (e.g. Jaimangal-Jones, Pritchard, and Morgan 2010). For example, parents have the potential to exercise significant power over the gamer in the home and this might be considered essential for the stability of the home environment. Regimes imposed on the gamer such as time restrictions are often resisted or ignored, and thus, the gamer takes on the role of resisting when the gamer defies things like time restrictions or the types of games allowed and this may be classified as resistance or theoretically on the outside or margins of the centre.

The previous point made on power is strengthened by the explanations of deviance by Foucault (1981) and Becker (1963). Becker (1963, 18) states that, 'the label of deviance is not the quality of the act itself but a question of the rules and sanctions applied by others'. In this case, both the overt and not-overt power parents exercise to sanction the various elements of computer gaming. So the contested area of first-hand shooters with J or how old he has to be to play games that are rated higher than his age group are frequent topics of arguments. Foucault (1981) identifies power relations as the crux to understanding deviance. He suggests where there is power there will be resistance but consequently, this resistance is never in a position of exteriority in relation to power. Foucault (1981) describes this inherent possibility of resistance as locatable within tactical reversal or in the re-appropriation of local conflicts, which, according to the rule of 'double-conditioning', can have effects beyond the merely local and thus within the strategic (Thompson 2003, 113; see also Hartmann 2003). Jary and Jary (2000) pose a fundamental question that corresponds to Foucault's (1981) understanding of deviance and Rojek's (2000) suggestion of power: what or who within society determines deviance?

So we might say that in J's case his focus on gaming is more on it as an enjoyable activity rather than offering resistance to any specific authority figure(s) or influences.

S: It's just a leisure activity?

J: It's not influenced by any third parties I don't think. I just choose to spend my leisure time doing it.

S as a parent observes, however, that when the time to play is shortened by other family activities there is resistance to participating, particularly if it involves losing access to the game for long periods of time. This is resistance from his point of view. So the resistance is not in the playing of the game but in the threat in not being able to access it for periods of time. The withdrawing from family activities or continual requests to be able to go and play form that resistance.

It is interesting then to explore the motivations for J who frames his participating in computer gaming from a leisure perspective. It is generally thought that the motivation for leisure in contemporary society has shifted from the acquisition of status through displays of wealth (Veblen 1899), to the active creation of self-identity through associations with consumer products, brands, services and experiences (Bauman 2007; Baudrillard 1970/1998; Featherstone 2007; Giddens 1991; Hamilton 2003). A phenomenon Slater (1997, 91) refers to as the 'cult of the self'. For adolescents, leisure functions as an escape from the pressures and expectations of parents, teachers and other forms of authority. The psycho-cultural dimensions of leisure is based in both self-affirming strategies of the narcissistic 'mirror self' and those identities largely constructed by market forces through for-profit firms. Youth cultures, Lury (1996) and Miles (2000) argue, are cultures of leisure and consumption organised around peer groups, where solidarity, differentiation and status are expressed through consumer products. For adolescents the activity of consumption is often mixed with the need for difference and a desire to express both peer group and individual self-identity through activities of resistance. It is often hard for adolescents to take part in leisure in consumer cultures that do not involve some form of consumption. This situation is made even more difficult for young people from poor, disadvantaged or impoverished backgrounds where, 'common remedies against boredom are not accessible to the poor' (Bauman 2005, 40). J regularly plays League of Legends with friends and uses Skype to have contact with them while playing:

> J: I talk about the game with friends from school that's always fun. You can Skype each other during the game and playing with them. I know a lot of people that only play with their friends…. Along with this social element with peers comes the status from level of achievement in the game – J … I suppose I get social status within the game which makes me feel good.

J's gaming activities fit well into the concepts provided to us in the literature on leisure.

Resisting market-based self-identity

In spite of leisure's commodification and potential for ideological control and conformity, it does have the potential to act as a source for the enhancement of self-identity. For although the commodification of leisure merely tempts the individual to more and more consumerism in an attempt to find the romance of self-fulfilment without necessarily solving practical needs, we believe that the preciousness of leisure and the need for resistance and deviance in adolescents are important elements of constructing a viable self-identity.

> J: (Gaming) It's about the only thing I spend money on. I don't really buy anything else and considering I only play one game I've actually got a lot of money saved up so it's kind of nice in that way. Yeah but as a consumer, gaming is the entirety of my consumerism.

Research that focuses on leisure experiences for the individual and the policies which provide opportunities for this provide insights into spatial resistance for alternative adolescent identities. Roberts (1978, 6) suggests: 'amid all … limitations on pure free will, individuals can feel that they possess scope for choice and this is one of the definitive features (of leisure)'. Foucault's analysis (cited in Rojek 1995) suggests that leisure activities are bound up with a complex division of power and discipline, which permeates society in many ways. He shows that leisure should be conceptualised as simultaneously freedom and control. However, within our analysis, the precariousness of this balance has been tipped by consumer culture in favour of subjectification through the commodification of self-identity and deviance and its resale to youth culture. Where then might adolescents find their own liberation to provide a balance? J's identification of skins is of interest here – he suggests:

> J: So when you play a character there's two things you can spend money on in the game. Skins and champions. So you can buy the actual champion. There are a lot of them as I said before and you can buy skins of various looks for that champion that make them look different.

So he finds he can purchase a 'skin' in the game, which provides him with an identity of his choosing even though it is constructed by the provider of the game. He has found choice and also a mechanism to resist being who his parents wish him to be while also still conforming to the purchasing regime of contemporary society.

Other prominent ways that today's youth resist, we suggest, can come in the form of countercultural resistance arising in Generation Y, suggesting such activities as taking a

Gap Year and travelling that incorporates some form of volunteering where young people, visiting other cultures, promote alternative values in parts of developing countries – these potential spaces that are not so dominated by the consumer culture of advanced capitalist countries and where individual motivations have a more altruistic and personal development focus (Wearing 2001). The growth of leisure activities like this provides encouragement for the future. In this sense, for Gap Year travellers, tourism (or travel as leisure) is a 'heterotopia', a personal space for resistance to domination, a space where there is room for choice (other than consumer choice) and for self-identity to expand beyond what it is told it should be by authority figures. Travel becomes a space where the 'I' can resist and move beyond the societal input, which constructs the 'me' of the self as a counterforce to retreating into personal space (e.g. the home), which has now been commodified. For the Gamer, it can just become an extension of their activity thus extending the Gaming beyond the home into their travel.

> J: Yeah, if I had a gap year I'd probably just go around and follow the competitors in Leagues of Legends because I suppose in your gap year you do something that's interesting to you. Some people might tour around and see some soccer games and I would see that as no different to that. Just touring, watching that, maybe with some friends. I wouldn't do it by myself, I'd take friends with me. That would be a very fun experience for me.

Conclusion

According to J's account this leisure gaming is a form of self-expression providing many things to his identity including a space in which to get away from parental supervision and control. From J's own subjectivity about his gaming elements of his identity are exposed, often transformed and incorporated into mainstream consumer culture under the marketised guise of difference and packaged hedonistic rebellion. Much of J's gaming is packaged, incorporated and sold by the marketing, mass media and advertising industry and presented to adolescents in the form of rebellious computer games. Nonetheless, J takes from his online gaming a raft of other things. These other 'things' may have unforeseen benefits in his future work identity or over his life span such as skills and consciousness in forming working team friendships, 'sustained concentration' and cognitive processing, which are extremely important in post-industrial work cultures (i.e. a social training in the e-based virtuality of the modern world) and as part of social capital building. Further, they may enable his self-identity to understand from a young age and resist from below, transform and reshape his consciousness in and against the rise of corporate technologies and cultures and multinational hegemony over our 'private worlds'. Our analysis extends Langer's (2004) thesis that children and adolescents are both ready targets for the commodification of self-identity, but we maintain that within this experience the social interaction that J experiences is a useful form of personal development that has been overlooked in the discussions about gaming.

In undertaking gaming as an activity, there is a level of self-gratification for adolescents such as J. This gratification seeks to create meaning in one's life, for example, not only should the leisure activity result in enjoyment, it must also signify a break from normal rules and regulations. Even though this leisure is to a degree pre-packaged in various ways, with some games deliberately marketed as deviant, it does provide J with a social identity that he uses to build and maintain relationships with others.

S: And what role does your gaming have in your day to day school life?

J: Um.... most of my conversations would be based around gaming. I use that as part of my social identity. I use that as a way to make conversation. I use that as a way I make friends. It makes up a very large part.

J as an adolescent is the target of this marketised self-identity formation and the resistance to the normal rules and regulation is found in the product that is purchased so the activity takes on a depthless superficial element. It is important to note that he sees this just as gaming activity and is solely interested in his motivation behind participating in the leisure activity as a young consumer while I as a parent and academic reconstruct this in various ways.

Finally, this paper seeks to contribute by illustrating some of the conceptual links between consumer culture, adolescent leisure and gaming, through an interview with a young gamer. We have argued that most forms of leisure are readily open to control and manipulation by the market and as such gaming has evolved in the same way. This is particularly striking in the manipulation of the gamer to purchase games, which are often represented as deviance and for the adolescent this leisure allows for self-expression and also resistance even where the game is a product that has been commodified and repackaged for consumption. We have argued that adolescence and, in particular, adolescent leisure is now heavily influenced by consumer discourses, which promote hedonism and narcissism. Needless to say the marketing of computer games and capture of adolescent minds in a global market economy is undertaken by multinational electronic companies and their benefactors for profit and economic gain. At one level, we have argued that young people are much more vulnerable and more easily manipulated (than adults, though adults are the targets of multinationals 'nag marketing' – see YouTube the 2008 documentary *The Corporation* and also parents are usually the providers of their children's computers and their gaming software [Big Picture Media Corporation 2003]) by an economic system that seeks to commodify rather than validate young people's experience of the world. At another level, there is a resistant social dynamic which means these youth can work within the existing societal parameters, albeit in limited ways in building virtual friendships, strategic resistance to global leisure technologies and in limited forms of social capital, the imposition by markets of such technological commodities to engage and facilitate their developmental, intellectual and emotional growth.

Notes

1. We define adolescence as the period between the onset of puberty and adulthood. Typically, this period ranges from age 13 to 21. However, in late modern societies the period of time that young people spend in adolescence is often extended from the beginning of puberty up until young people leave formal education and the care of their parents, which for some might extend to the age of 27 (Scott and Marshall 2009).
2. For ease of reading and to ensure the focus for the reader is on the ideas not the specific people, the names are shortened to the letters S for Stephen and J for Jamie.

Notes on contributors

Stephen Wearing is an Associate Professor at the University of Technology, Sydney (UTS). He has conducted numerous projects and lectures worldwide and is the author of 13 books and over 100 articles dealing with issues surrounding leisure and sustainable tourism.

Jamie Wearing is a year 10 student at Oxford Falls Grammar School, Oxford Falls in Sydney.

Matthew McDonald is a Lecturer at Department of Management RMIT University Vietnam, Vietnam.

Michael Wearing is a Senior Lecturer in the School of Social Sciences at the University of New South Wales, Sydney Australia.

References

Aitchison, C. 2001. "Gender and Leisure Research: The 'Codification of Knowledge'." *Leisure Sciences* 23 (1): 1–19. doi:10.1080/01490400150502216.

Anderson, C. A., D. A. Gentile, and K. E. Buckley. 2007. *Violent Video Game Effects on Children and Adolescents.* Oxford: Oxford University Press. doi:10.1093/acprof:oso/9780195309836.001.0001.

Baer, S., E. Bogusz, and D. A. Green. 2011. "Stuck on Screens: Patterns of Computer and Gaming Station Use in Youth Seen in a Psychiatric Clinic." *Journal of the Canadian Academy of Child and Adolescent Psychiatry* 20 (2): 86–94.

Baudrillard, J. 1970/1998. *The Consumer Society: Myths & Structures* (C. Turner, Trans.). Thousand Oaks, CA: Sage.

Bauman, Z. 1988. *Freedom.* Milton Keynes: Open University Press.

Bauman, Z. 2000. *Liquid Modernity.* Cambridge: Polity Press.

Bauman, Z. 2005. *Work, Consumerism and the New Poor.* 2nd ed. Buckingham: Open University Press.

Bauman, Z. 2007. *Consuming Life.* Cambridge: Polity Press.

Baumeister, R. F. 1987. "How the Self Became a Problem: A Psychological Review of Historical Research." *Journal of Personality and Social Psychology* 52 (1): 163–176. doi:10.1037/0022-3514.52.1.163.

Beck, U. 1992. *Risk Society: Towards a New Modernity.* London: Sage.

Becker, H. 1963. *Outsiders.* New York: Free Press.

Beder, S. 2009. *This Little Kiddy Went to Market: The Corporate Capture of Childhood.* Sydney: UNSW Press. Big Picture Media Corporation. 2003. "The Corporation." Accessed June 10, 2010. http://www.filmsforaction.org/watch/the_corporation/.

Brake, M. 1979. *The Sociology of Youth Sub-cultures and Youth.* London: Routledge Kegan Paul.

Carr, N. 2011. *Children's and Families Holidays Experience.* London: Routledge.

Carbonaro, M., M. Cutumisu, H. Duff, S. Gillis, C. Onuczko, J. Siegel, J. Schaefferb, A. Schumacherb, D. Szafron, and K. Waugh. 2008. "Interactive Story Authoring: A Viable Form of Creative Expression for the Classroom." *Computers and Education* 51 (2): 687–707. doi:10.1016/j.compedu.2007.07.007.

Chai, S. L., V. H. H. Chen, and A. Khoo. 2011. "Social Relationships of Gamers and Their Parents." Paper presented at the 2nd World Conference on Psychology, Counselling and Guidance, WCPCG-2011, Antalya.

Charnas, D. 2010. *The Big Payback: The History of the Business of Hip-hop.* New York: New American Library.

Cohen, S. A. 2013. "Reflections on Reflexivity in Leisure and Tourism Studies." *Leisure Studies* 32 (3): 333–337. doi:10.1080/02614367.2012.662522.

Curtis, A. (Writer). 2002. *The Century of the Self* [DVD]. London: BBC Four.

Dorfman, A., And A. Mattelart. 1991. *How to Read Donald Duck: Imperialist Ideology in the Disney Comic.* New York: International General.

Dupuis, S. L. 2010. "Naked Truths: Towards a Reflexive Methodology in Leisure Research." *Leisure Sciences* 21 (1): 43–64. doi:10.1080/014904099273282.

Durkin, K., and B. Barber. 2002. "Not so Doomed: Computer Game Play and Positive Adolescent Development." *Journal of Applied Developmental Psychology* 23 (4): 373–392. doi:10.1016/S0193-3973(02)00124-7.

Ewen, S. 1976/2001. *Captains of Consciousness: Advertising and the Social Roots of Consumer Culture.* Rev. ed. New York: Basic Books.

Ewen, S. 1988. *All Consuming Images: The Politics of Style in Contemporary Culture.* New York: Basic Books.

Featherstone, M. 2001. Consumer Culture. In *International Encyclopaedia of the Social & Behavioral Sciences*, edited by N. J. Smelser and P. B. Baltes, 2662–2669. Amsterdam: Elsevier.

Featherstone, M. 2007. *Consumer Culture and Postmodernism*. 2nd ed. London: Sage.

Ferguson, H. 2009. *The Science of Pleasure: Cosmos and Psyche in the Bourgeois World View*. New York: Routledge.

Flammer, A., and Schaffner, B. 2003. "Adolescent Leisure across European Nations." *New Directions for Child and Adolescent Development* 99: 65–78. doi:10.1002/cd.67.

Forsey, M. G. 2010. "Ethnography as Participant Listening." *Ethnography* 11 (4): 558–572. doi:10.1177/1466138110372587.

Foucault, M. 1981. *Power/Knowledge: Selected Interviews and Other Writings, 1972-77*. London: Harvester.

Foucault, M. 1984. "Space, Knowledge and Power." In *The Foucault Reader*, edited by P. Rabinow, 239–256. Harmondsworth: Penguin.

Fromm, E. 1956. *The Sane Society*. London: Routledge.

Giddens, A. 1991. *Modernity and Self-identity: Self and Society in the Late Modern Age*. Stanford, CA: Stanford University Press.

Glorieux, I., F. Stevens, and J. Vandeweyer. 2005. "Time Use and Well-being of Belgian Adolescents: Research Findings and Time Use Evidence." *LoisiretSociété / Society and Leisure*) 28 (2): 481–510. doi:10.1080/07053436.2005.10707692.

Graham, A., M. Powell, N. Taylor, D. Anderson, and R. Fitzgerald. 2013. *Ethical Research Involving Children*. Florence: UNICEF Office of Research.

Griffiths, M. 1997. "Computer Game Playing in Early Adolescence." *Youth and Society*, 29 (2): 223–237. doi:10.1177/0044118X97029002004.

Hall, S., S. Winlow, and Ancrum, C. 2008. *Criminal Identities and Consumer Culture: Crime, Exclusion and the New Culture of Narcissism*. Abingdon: Willan.

Hamilton, C. 2003. *Growth Fetish*. Sydney: Allen & Unwin.

Hamilton, C., and R. Denniss. 2005. *Affluenza: When too Much Is Never Enough*. Sydney: Allen & Unwin.

Hartmann, J. 2003. "Power and Resistance in the Later Foucault." 3rd Annual Meeting of the Foucault Circle, John Carroll University, Cleveland, OH, February 28 to March 2.

Hebdige, D. 1979. *Subculture: The Meaning of Style*. London: Menthuen.

Jaimangal-Jones, D., A, Pritchard, and N. Morgan. 2010. "Going the Distance: Locating Journey, Liminality and Rites of Passage in Dance Music Experiences." *Leisure Studies* 29 (3): 253–268. doi:10.1080/02614361003749793.

Jary, D., and J. Jary. 2000. *Collins Dictionary of Sociology*. 3rd ed. Glasgow: Harper Collins.

Klien, M. 2001. *No Logo*. London: Flamingo.

Konig, A. 2008. "Which Clothes Suit Me? The Presentation of the Juvenile Self." *Childhood* 15 (2): 225–237. doi:10.1177/0907568207088424.

Langer, B. 2004. "The Business of Branded Enchantment: Ambivalence and Disjuncture in the Global Children's Culture Industry." *Journal of Consumer Culture* 4 (2): 251–277. doi:10.1177/1469540504043685.

Lasch, C. 1979. *The Culture of Narcissism: American Life in an Age of Diminishing Expectations*. New York: W.W. Norton.

Lury, C. 1996. *Consumer Culture*. Cambridge: Polity Press.

Lynch, R., and A. J. Veal. 1996. *Australian Leisure*. Sydney: Longman.

Lui, D. P. Y., G. P. Y. Szeto, and A. Y. M. Jones. 2011. "The Pattern of Electronic Game Use and Related Bodily Discomfort in Hong Kong Primary School Children." *Computers and Education* 57 (2): 1665–1674. doi:10.1016/j.compedu.2011.03.008.

Marshall, G. 1998. *Oxford Dictionary of Sociology*. 2nd ed. Oxford: Oxford University Press.

McDonald, K. 1999. *Struggles for Subjectivity: Identity, Action and Youth Experience*. Melbourne: Cambridge University Press.

McDonald, M., and S. L. Wearing. 2013. *Social Psychology and Theories of Consumer Culture: A Political Economy Perspective*. London: Routledge.

McDonald, M., S. Wearing, and J. Ponting. 2008. "Narcissism and Neo-liberalism: Work, Leisure and Alienation in an Era of Consumption." *LoisiretSociete (Society and Leisure)* 30 (1): 489–510.

Miles, S. 2000. *Youth Lifestyles in a Changing World*. Buckingham: Open University Press.

Nixon, H. 1998. "Fun and Games Are Serious Business." In *Digital Diversions: Youth Culture in the Age of Multimedia*, edited by J. Sefton-Green. London: University College London Press.

Putnam, R. D. 2001. *Bowling Alone: The Collapse and Revival of American Community.* New York: Simon & Schuster/Touchstone.

Rietveld, H. 1998. "Repetitive Beats: Free Parties and the Politics of Contemporary DiY Dance Culture in Britain." In *DiY Culture: Party and Protest in Nineties Britain*, edited by G. McKay, 243–267. London: Verso.

Roberts, K. 1978. *Contemporary Society and the Growth of Leisure.* London: Longman.

Rojek, C. 1995. *Decentring Leisure.* London: Sage.

Rojek, C. 2000. *Leisure and Culture.* Hampshire: Palgrave.

Rice, J. 2009. "Educational Games Research: Video Games Addiction: Fact or Fiction." http://edugamesblog.wordpress.com/2009/04/27/video-game-addiction-fact-or-fiction.

Sassatelli, R. 2007. *Consumer Culture: History, Theory and Politics.* London: Sage.

Scott, J., and G. Marshall, eds. 2009. *Dictionary of Sociology.* 3rd ed. Oxford: Oxford University Press.

Shaw, S. 2001. Conceptualizing Resistance: Women's Leisure as Political Practice. *Journal of Leisure Research* 33 (2): 143–159.

Sheer. 2014. "Player Tally for 'League of Legends' Surges." http://www.wsj.co.

Slater, D. 1997. *Consumer Culture and Modernity.* Cambridge: Polity Press.

Soupourmas, F. 2005. "Work, Rest and Leisure – Trends in Late Adolescent Time Use in Australia in the 1990s." *LoisiretSociété/Society and Leisure* 28 (2): 571–589. doi:10.1080/07053436.2005.10707696.

Stebbins, R. A. 1997. "Casual Leisure: A Conceptual Statement." *Leisure Studies* 16 (1): 17–25. doi:10.1080/026143697375485.

Stebbins, R. A., C. Rojek, and A. -M. Sullivan. 2006. "Editorial: Deviant Leisure." *Leisure/Loisir* 30 (1): 3–5. doi:10.1080/14927713.2006.9651338.

Thompson, K. 2003. "Forms of Resistance: Foucault on Tactical Reversal and Self-formation." *Continental Philosophy Review* 36 (2): 113–138. doi:10.1023/A:1026072000125.

Veblen, T. 1899. *The Theory of the Leisure Class: An Economic Study of Institutions.* New York: Penguin.

Verma, S. and R. W. Larson., eds. 2003. *Examining Adolescent Leisure Time across Cultures: Developmental Opportunities and Risks.* New York: John Wiley.

Waerdahl, R. 2005. "'May be I'll Need a Pair of Levi's Before Junior High?': Child to Youth Trajectories and Anticipatory Socialization." *Childhood* 12 (2): 201–219. doi:10.1177/0907568205051904.

Watt, P., and K. Stenson. 1998. 'It's a Bit Dodgy around There': Safety, Danger, Ethnicity and Young People's Use of Public Space." In *Cool Places: Geographies of Youth Cultures*, edited by T. Skelton and G. Valentine, 249–265. London: Routledge.

Wawrzak-Chodaczek, M. 2011. "Place of Computer Games in the Leisure Time of Polish Youth in Their Adolescence." *New Educational Review* 26 (4): 143–157.

Wearing, B., and S. Wearing. 1996. Refocussing the Tourist Experience: The Flaneur and the Choraster." *Leisure Studies* 15 (4): 229–243. doi:10.1080/026143696375530.

Wearing, M. 2011. "Strengthening Youth Citizenship and Social Inclusion Practice – The Australian Case: Towards Rights based and Inclusive Practice in Services for Marginalized Young People." *Child and Youth Services Review* 41 (4): 15–21.

Wearing, S. 2001. "Volunteer Tourism: Experiences That Make a Difference." Wallingford, UK: CABI.

Wearing, S., and B. Wearing. 2000. "Smoking as a Fashion Accessory in the 90s: Conspicuous Consumption, Identity and Adolescent Women's Leisure Choices." *Leisure Studies* 19 (1): 45–58. doi:10.1080/026143600374833.

Wearing, S. L., M. McDonald, and M. Wearing. 2013. "Consumer Culture, the Mobilisation of the Narcissistic Self, and Adolescent Deviant Leisure." *Leisure Studies* 32 (4): 367–381.

Weedon, C. 1997. *Feminist Practice and Poststructuralist Theory.* 2nd ed. Oxford: Blackwell.

Wei, R. 2007. "Effects of Playing Violent Videogames on Chinese Adolescents' Pro-violence Attitudes, Attitudes toward Others, and Aggressive Behavior." *Cyberpsychology and Behavior* 10 (3): 371–380. doi:10.1089/cpb.2006.9942.

Williams, D. J. 2009. "Deviant Leisure: Rethinking 'The Good, the Bad, and the Ugly'." *Leisure Sciences* 31 (2): 207–213. doi:10.1080/01490400802686110.

Wilson, J. 2010. "The Parent Report: Video Game Addiction and Video game Violence." http://www.theparentreport.com/resources/ages/preteen/kidsculture/130.html.

Negotiating the climb: a fictional representation of climbing, gendered parenting and the morality of time

Ben Clayton and Emily Coates

Institute for Sport, Exercise, Recreation and Well-being, Buckinghamshire New University, High Wycombe, Buckinghamshire, UK

This paper employs fictional techniques to convey the competing discourses of parenting and 'serious' climbing in relation to time and risk as they are experienced by heterosexual couples with at least one child and a history of commitment to traditional climbing. The resultant story is constructed from data produced by topical life-history interviews with seven white-British, middle-class couples and is interrupted, but not overlaid, by a late-modern and Foucauldian analytic thread through which we posit that the parents must negotiate a number of discourses of modernity in their pursuit of an authentic identity. The story, however, is intended more as dais for sociological dialogue, to allow the situated reader to inhabit the lifeworld and respond to its imagery. The story replicates the parents' leisure time and space on a typical weekend and shows the contradictory and gendered nature of the discourses experienced by these climbers.

Prologue

While recognizing Kay's (2000) call to broaden empirical research to reflect the growth of non-traditional family forms and acknowledging those attempts to answer such a call in leisure and sport studies (e.g. Bagley, Salmon, and Crawford 2006; Dagkas and Stathi 2007; Quarmby and Dagkas 2010), we also recognize a residual gap in the existing literature about leisure patterns and experiences in the traditional, dual-parent family. Much of the research on family leisure has considered the impact that parenting has had on mothers' time and access to leisure, taking a critical feminist approach to analyse the sacrifice of time that mothers make, in part, by putting their children first (Bittman and Wajcman 2000; Brown et al. 2001; Kimmel and Connelly 2007). More recently, the literature has expanded to consider fathers who support their children's involvement in sport (Coakley 2006; Kay 2007). However, there has been a general lack of consideration, particularly within the adventure sport literature, of how parents maintain their involvement in sport or leisure following conception and the birth of their child(ren) (for some notable exceptions see Robinson 2008; Spowart, Hughson, and Shaw 2008; Spowart, Burrows, and Shaw 2010; Summers 2007; Wheaton and Tomlinson 1998).

This paper employs the creative non-fiction tradition to explore the experiences of heterosexual dual-parents who rock climb and their negotiation of competing leisure discourses and demands at the weekend, primarily the Saturday. From the outset, we take the position that the weekend is the prime space for 'family leisure' and, moreover, a space in which one's identity is not fixed or separate from other spheres, for example, as a father/mother/husband/wife and climber (Lupton and Barclay 1997) and that 'these subject positions might stand in complete contradiction to each other' (Helstein 2007, 85). In this sense, we acknowledge that our 'story' originated as part of a broadly Foucauldian agenda. It is especially infiltrated by Foucault's (1972) central ideas of discourse as language as a source of thought and as a relativized a-priori constraint placed, in any given time and space, on how people think and subsequently act. In other words, discourse provides the 'conditions of possibility' for thought, which are contingent on the particular historical situation (Foucault 1970). Because such conditions are relative, not only do discourses change but also multiple discourses shape human life (Markula and Pringle 2006) and alternative discourses compete for attention. However, a strict Foucauldian reading of the lifeworld of parents who climb is not our primary concern in this paper (for such a reading see Coates 2012) and we also draw on ideas about the reflexivity of late-modernity and the move beyond the binaries of modern social thought towards an incorporation of uncertainty and contingency (see Heaphy 2007). What we really seek is an authentic representation that might provide a platform for debate about gendered, moral parenting and serious leisure discourses. That is to say, while our analytic lens and written account are coloured, but not saturated by a Foucauldian and late-modern thesis, this is intended to be neither hidden nor obtrusive and we note it here only as a pre-story and epistemological confession of sorts.

Stories of parents who climb: methods and fictional representation

The use of a variety of fictional techniques has become a common feature of studies examining diverse phenomena particularly in sport-related research (see for example, Bruce 2000; Clayton 2010, 2013; Douglas and Carless 2010; Grenfell and Rinehart 2003; Jones 2006; Rowe 2000; Sparkes 1996; see also Denison and Markula 2003). Scholars that employ or support the use of fictional representation regularly purport, as their first 'defence', an ethical imperative to disguise the identity of participants where fictive text can assure greater anonymity (Angrosino 1998 cited in Sparkes 2002, 150; Coffey and Atkinson 1996). However, fictional techniques can also provide authors with the tools to write more inclusive representations that do not obscure possible alternative readings and effectively present 'the inconvenient truth of [a story] that [has] been unheard' (Frank 2000a, 363). Such a story may provide a greater sense of 'reality' where the lived-experience is complex and perhaps not possible to convey using theoretical explication alone (Frank 2000b), thus offering something 'more ethical, less constraining [and allowing for] more balanced representations [of people and phenomena], complexities, contradictions, contingencies and all' (Clayton 2013, 216).

It is these sentiments that have drawn us towards the creative non-fiction tradition to convey a 'typical weekend' (albeit the story concentrates on the Saturday) for parents who climb. The story that follows is the product of one of the authors' doctoral research (see Coates 2012), which examined the process of negotiation of competing discourses of climbing and parenting faced by seven heterosexual couples. It became apparent early in the analysis that the lived-experiences of these couples were complex and multifaceted and could not be done justice in a 'realist tale' (see Sparkes 2002; Van Maanen 1988). Instead, we adopt Richardson's (1994) view that the written account is not simply a way of 'telling', but can (and should) be a way of 'knowing' and 'showing' a reality for a proactive reader (see Sparkes 2002). While we are grounded by our own analytic conventions and conceptual signposts, we reject a foundationalist stance in favour of dialogue and a communicative and pragmatic concept of validity (Lincoln and Guba 2003) and submit our story for 'unremitting reflection' (Clayton 2013, 207) where the 'truth' is to be found in the reader's response – a 'storied response to a story heard' (Smith and Sparkes 2011, 39). As a consequence, we consciously omit a traditional literature review as a textual staging or vestibule for subsequent empirical post-mortem, but acknowledge our association with the literature by way of an irregular, concomitant narrative and an 'epilogue' that summarizes the main themes as we see them in a more general way via some of the conceptual and empirical literature that resonates with our story.

Like all fictional representations, the story is the result of 'being there' (Sparkes 2002), where data were collected by way of traditional qualitative methods. The seven couples were selected using purposive and snowball strategies and had at least one child and both parents had pursued climbing, in some form, as serious, hobbyist leisure for a number of years prior to the conception and birth of their children. With the exception of one of the mothers, all the parents in the sample were still climbing at the time of the research and had been climbing for at least 11 years. All participants were white-British with ages ranging from 32 years to 62 years and the age of their children was from 6 months to 27 years, with one couple expecting their second child. Only one couple had grown-up children at the time of the research and were asked to recall their experiences of when their children were young. While we were not immediately disposed to use the experiences of this couple to inform the story, we found that there was more continuity than change in the couples' experiences of parenting. All participants were university educated, including five doctorates and a further five post-graduates, and all worked as professionals in the service industry. As a consequence, while socio-economic position was not an intended feature of this or the original research – and the coincidental sample might suggest something about the relationships of social class and climbing as a leisure pursuit and social class and traditional family structures – we recognize that the story below may only be representative of, and garner an empathetic response from, a fairly exclusive section of the leisure community. Participants were interviewed individually in the couples' own homes, with each parent in a couple interviewed consecutively following a topical, life-history narrative approach (see Wengraf 2001). Interviews were supported by a sustained period of observations at climbing walls and crags and in the participants' homes. The data were produced principally in the year between autumn 2010 and autumn 2011 in the Peak District National Park region of the UK, in central England.

Our focus in this paper is the multiple and competing discourses of parenting and climbing that are encountered at the weekend. Therefore, this paper has concentrated on data concerned with family activities and climbing experiences specifically at the weekend, or data that alludes to 'family time', where neither parent is at (paid) work. Part of the 'fiction' of the story is that the events depicted transcend time and space and therefore while the story aims to represent a typical weekend scenario, raw data were not necessarily concerned with any one weekend. The story contains no 'pure' fiction but is a partial account derived from empirical data sometimes using untainted duplications of witnessed actions or naturally occurring talk, or responses taken from interview, explicitly relayed or paraphrased and woven into the story as words from the mouths of actors, or as internal thoughts of actors, or as the narrative that ties the story. The actors themselves are not facsimiles of participants and, rather, the experiences of all of the couples are condensed into the single experience of the story's primary couple, Liz and Jack, and the supporting actors they encounter through the story. The story then, using fictional techniques, attempts to 'capture a sense of the subjects' world' (Markula and Denison 2005, 168) not by reporting the 'reality' but by 'replicat[ing] the sense of experience' (Rinehart 1998, 204) and allowing the reader to viscerally inhabit the lifeworld in order to create a better sense of reality. As Smith and Sparkes (2011) suggest, one reading of the story will compete for attention with others and the reality is to be found in the situated reader's response to it.

Friday evening

Darkness descends over the Nottingham suburb. Jack swings his bike from the road, the beam of his mounted cycle lamp momentarily slicing across the rose bushes and the front of his house before saturating the garage door with an eerie glow. He glides to a near-stop and expertly dismounts and, one hand on the rear of the saddle, pushes his bike through the gate, the back garden and into the shed. The light from the kitchen and upstairs bedroom tumbles across the lawn, providing just enough visibility for Jack to secure the padlock on the shed door and dodge the strewn plastic toys as he makes his way to the house. On entering, he contentedly inhales the roving aroma of tomato, garlic and onion that is escaping the pan on the stove.

'Liz? Sam?'

'Up here'.

'Be up in a minute'. Jack jangles his keys and drops them to the table where a messy spread of fresh finger-paintings near covers the somewhat congested calendar. Appointments, meetings, work event, Sam's nursery, Sam's play date. Saturday: Sam's friend's birthday party, recently struck through with red pen and 'CHICKENPOX' written boldly underneath. 'Good!' Thinks Jack to himself with only a momentary sense of remorse. Sunday: Sam's swimming class, only an hour but slap-bang in the middle of the day! 'Out for a climb Saturday then'.

Jack lazily kicks off his shoes and gropes his way through the dimly lit hall, nearly knocking the vase of assorted roses and lilies from the small, decorative table near the front door. He ascends the stairs on his toes, remembering to lunge over that squeaky step – fourth from the top – which so often has been his downfall late at night. He brushes against the wall adjacent to the bathroom door and smiles broadly as he listens to Sam splashing in the bath and talking about his day at nursery.

'And then I coloured in a wabbit and, um, mummy, in playtime I have been going woar at the girls like this ... WOAR!'

'Boo!' Jack jumps two-footed into the doorway. Sam's arms fly upwards out of the bathwater, soaking Liz on her perch at the side of the bath.

'Thank you, daddy', she says sardonically, scooping the bubbles from her blouse and flicking them back into the bath.

'DAddddddyyy!' Sam shouts.

'Just at the girls, hey?' Jack winks at Liz. 'Hello, wife'.

'Hello, husband'. Liz retorts.

Jack leans in and kisses her, and at the same time reaches over and tickles Sam, being careful to avoid the splashes. 'How was your day, beautiful? Did you sort things out with that student?'

'Not much was resolved but I'll tell you about it over dinner', Liz sighs.

'Look at me, look at me'. Sam shrieks frenziedly, with a layer of white bubbles over his top lip. 'I've got um m-m-mustard just like gran-pops'.

Liz smiles. 'It's moustache, Sam. You try and sound it out after me. M-u-st-o-sh'. Sam repeats it slowly, getting it right the second time ... more or less. 'Clever boy! Right, I think you must be very clean now, so how about you put the toys in the basket and we get you ready for bed?'

'Oh, but mummy' Sam begins to argue.

'Sam'. Jack's firm tone provides enough impetus for Sam to reluctantly begin putting his toys away.

'All done'. Sam grins, standing up and putting his arms out.

'Well done Spam, aren't you a good boy?' Jack wraps a towel around him and lifts him out of the bath. He turns to Liz, 'So are we climbing tomorrow?'

'Yes, absolutely. We must get out. Sam's party has been cancelled'.

'Yes, so I saw'. The same guilty smile comes across Jack's face.

'Don't be so mean', Liz chastises him, albeit with a mischievous smile of her own. 'Poor Harrison. It was awful when Sam had chickenpox. Anyway, I've already spoken to Emma so we're set for tomorrow'.

'Great', Jack grins. 'I did text Mike and Lee but wasn't sure then if we were out. Mike did suggest Millstone. He wants a re-match on London Wall. What do you think?'

'Hmm, I would like to do Great North Road but it might be better for later in the year. The forecast looks like it might be quite windy and cold. So maybe we should go somewhere more sheltered. Maybe bouldering that we can all do? Sam could do a bit of climbing then too?'

'Okay, fair enough. I'm sure Lee and Caroline would prefer it if we're bouldering anyway, although I think they can only get out for a bit in the afternoon'

'Let's just see what it's like tomorrow'. Liz finally manages to get a wriggling Sam into his bed-time nappy and pyjamas. 'Right, I think its sleepy babies time for you. Who's reading the first story tonight?'

'Um … mummy!' Sam jumps up in the air. 'Then daddy, then mummy again, then daddy'.

For Jack and Liz, like Featherstone (2009) says, the weekend is an important time for the reaffirming of family life. While they work at their thoroughly middle-class jobs, Sam is placed in nursery and outside of nursery hours ad hoc arrangements are made. They draw, as they always have, on discourses of individualism; the same discourses that have given them their thoroughly middle-class existence and provided for their son, which included high-quality childcare. But with their son came a shrinking of individual freedoms and a simultaneous acceleration of time. In a political culture that extols both the ethic of work and the ethic of care (Gerson 2009), time is both a political and a moral issue. Family time is tied-up with family values, the latter of which may often be equated to a hostile response to changes in family life and sexual behaviour (Weeks 1995), part of a steadfastly hegemonized morality. Foucault (1972) may argue that morality is a normative behaviour with the power to discipline Jack and Liz, but equally no form of morality can be acceptable to all and they have learned to negotiate the omnipresent menace of discourses of 'good parenting' and the moral pluralism of late-modern times. They are climbers, for as long as either of them can remember, guided by discourses of a commitment to authenticity (Rinehart and Sydnor 2003; Wheaton 2004) and voluntary risk-taking (Heywood 2006; Lewis 2004; McNamee 2007). Now they are parents, for as long as either of them cares to remember, guided by an overwhelming and confusing plethora of parenting discourses even the most alternative of which appears risk adverse and governed by the ideology of intensive parenting (Furedi 2008). Their negotiations of these discourses lead them to what at first they perceive to be a space for both them and Sam, a space where 'being with' Sam supersedes without prohibiting 'being there' for him (Such 2006, 2009). This space is family leisure or a family climb. That the space is formed and sustained more by Jack and Liz's self-interested, individualized identities as climbers is a moral wrangling that can be offset and legitimized even amidst discourses of intensive parenting by the fact that it remains family leisure and that it remains lower in the hierarchy of time than Sam's leisure. That is to say, it fills the gaps in Sam's leisure lifeworld.

Saturday

6:30 am

'MUUUMMMY!' The human alarm tears across the landing and ricochets around the house, waking Liz from her dreams. She rolls from the bed as the pitter-patter of feet grows louder and two blue eyes peer through the crack in the door. Jack groans and turns on his side.

'Don't worry, I'll go', Liz whispers, perching on the bed and rubbing her eyes. She slides her feet into her slippers and drags herself up and through the door.

7:30 am

Jack turns off the shower tap and emerges through the cloud of steam, vigorously towelling his deep brown hair. He wraps the towel around his waist, lodges a toothbrush into his cheek and walks back to the bedroom. He peeks through the curtains to reveal an unwelcoming dull grey and then riffles through his drawers and wardrobe in search of his thermals, khaki trousers and fleece.
'What do you think? Somewhere with bouldering options?' He calls down the stairs. 'Maybe Stanage Plantation? Car park at ten?'
'Yeah, that's maybe a better idea', comes a delayed response. 'It's looking too cold for Sam to be sitting around all day, but the wind is low so we could do some routes first. I'll text Emma'.
Jack grabs his phone from the bedside table and slumps on the bed. He puffs out his cheeks and with a purposeful, rapid exhale pulls up Mike's number. 'Mike will understand', Jack thinks to himself. 'Plans change when you have kids. Mike knows that'.
He hurriedly texts the new plan and throws down his phone on the pillow and trots downstairs. Sam is on the kitchen floor pulling a train around an unsoundly and illogically designed wooden track while Liz slices sandwiches into neat triangles, wraps them and places them methodically into the lunch-bag. Jack fumbles through various drawers and cupboards and lines-up the day's supplies on the table: gear, rope, harnesses, climbing shoes, chalk bags, finger-tape, first-aid kit, baby wipes, spare nappies, toy cars and picture books. Bouldering mats are already in the car.

Foucault (1984) and others, such as Bauman (1993), may write that it is indicative of post-modernity – or perhaps a postmodern turn to the late-modern – that we take a more considered and eminently flexible approach to ethics and to morality itself. As Jack and Liz demonstrate, the morality of time for parents is negotiated in context (see Smart and Neale 1998), and where the increasingly questioned power-knowledge threatens to rupture self-identity, the subject must surely become 'undisciplined' in order to reconstitute the self (cf. Heaphy 2007). However, inscribed selfhood may be more difficult to reconstitute than the context that calls for the reconstitution. The contestation in Jack's and Liz's identities as both parents and climbers provided the tools and motivation to reconstitute time and space, rather than the self, so that both family and self might benefit. It is a balance of individual choice and family responsibility (Ribbens McCarthy, Edwards, and Gillies 2000) where serious, hobbyist time becomes family time and the crag the space for family leisure. A sacrifice is of course made but who, we may ask, might sacrifice the most? For Jack, or so *he* might have us believe, the identity imperatives at stake here are greater than for Liz where climbing has been a site for the (re)production of hetero-normative masculinities and homosociality (Robinson 2008). The limited versions of masculinity prescribed by modernity constrain women's leisure relative to their male partners (Such 2009), but the democratization of gender of late-modernity renders any idea of the male self far less certain. In turn, fatherhood and indeed husbandhood become equally tinged with uncertainty calling for a reconstitution of these identities and a concomitant readdressing of homosocial relations. Femininities have arguably remained more constant and motherhood, Guendouzi (2006, 902) finds, is 'a product of both hegemonic institutional discourse and discourse expressed by women' themselves. This is in part, perhaps, because of the 'network of medicalisation' (Foucault 1984) that has forefronted the biological aspects of motherhood (growing, carrying, giving birth, breast-feeding) for maternal and, accordingly, feminine identity (Lee 2008) as part of a gendered and child-centred parenting ideology (Faircloth 2009; Knaak 2005). As such, we postulate, Liz's sacrifice is greater though perhaps less painful to rationalize.

10.00 am – Stanage Plantation

Emma and Bill's mud-streaked Fiesta swings into the nearly full car park at the popular end of Stanage. Sam – wrapped in so many layers to be almost spherical – waddles quickly towards them as they exit the car. They had watched over Sam a number of times since Liz met them at a local climbing club shortly after Sam was born. Emma was as bubbly as Bill was quiet. Neither was a serious climber and instead preferred kayaking, but they loved the gritstone and were always keen to get out and were flexible on time and destination, which was just what Liz and Jack needed these days.
'Hello you three', Emma greets Sam with open arms. 'So nice to be getting out at last', she says, sweeping her long brown hair into a ponytail.
'Oh, I know', Liz agrees. The rain and snow over the winter had led to many long hours and money spent at indoor bouldering walls around the Peak.
The group begins the walk up the path to the crag. Sam at a half run doesn't take long to stumble and fall. He begins to cry.
'It's alright, little man, you're okay', Jack helps him to his feet. 'Just watch where you are going. Daddy will walk a bit slower'. He engulfs his son's small hand and leads him slowly to the crag where Mike is warming up at the Goliath area,
'Are you sleeping at the crag now?' Jack shouts from a distance.
'I've only got this morning before I'm on double-trouble duty, so no wasting time for me', Mike replies.
'Didn't fancy bringing the twins out today then?'
'You must be joking, they're a nightmare at the crag, not like your young man here' Mike ruffles Sam's hair as he and Jack shake hands. 'They get bored and start wandering about and then neither of us get any climbing done. Anyway, they're at another bloody birthday party this morning, but Becky might join us once she's dropped them'.
'Believe me, Sam has his moments too', Liz interrupts, leaning in to kiss Mike on the cheek. 'Not that that stops my husband from climbing, of course'.
'I don't know what you mean', Jack raises his arms in mock protest. 'But if that's how you feel, my darling, perhaps you would like to climb first with Emma and Bill can climb with Mike. If that's okay with everyone? And Mike, we could get a top rope on Indian Summer after?'
'Like your thinking. Right Bill, we'll go have a look at a couple of the E1's and 2's up here'. Mike is clearly itching to get back to climbing as he and Bill gather their bags and move along the rock face.
'Ready, Liz? You get first lead', Emma retrieves a tatty guidebook and flicks through the well-read, yellowed pages. 'Oh, how about Goliath's Groove? HVS 5a? Or do you want to warm up first?'
'No, best just jump straight in. It's not like I'll have time for a second route', Liz smiles as she watches Sam pushing his toy cars around the stones on the path. She takes a deep breath and exhales brusquely. 'Right, let's do this before I talk myself out of it. It's been a while'.

Liz looks the route up and down, preparing herself with a number of short, sharp pants. 'Loads of friends in the first crack, you can do E1 5a, Liz. How hard can it be?' She persuades herself. 'Right, love you. Keep Sam warm'.

'Of course. Have fun', Jack tells her.

Liz walks tentatively to the base of the route. She checks her harness, ties onto the rope, and pulls on her helmet and rock-shoes.

'You're on belay, so whenever you're ready, Liz', Emma says.

'Ready? Right, here we go, I'm climbing'. Liz smiles broadly at Emma whilst simultaneously taking in a very deep breath. She dips her hands in her chalk bag and with one last pant starts gingerly up the face, struggling to get very far before wedging a foot in a crack. 'Well, this is pretty desperate', she mutters to herself, putting her free hand to her forehead and smearing chalk dust down her cheek.

'Mummy, hello', Sam's voice reverberates around the enclosed landscape. Liz tries to block him out. 'I need a wee-wee, Mummy'.

'Okay, darling', Liz calls back, trying to disguise her exasperation. 'Jack, do you think you could sort him out?'

'No!' Sam begins to cry. 'Mummy takes me'.

'Don't be silly, Sam. You can see mummy's up there', Jack says firmly.

Liz closes her eyes and pushes her forehead to the rock face. 'Go with daddy, Sam. Mummy will be done very soon', she says. 'Look at that boulder, Sam. After your wee, why don't you do what mummy's doing? Climb the rock like mummy, yes?'

1.15 pm

'Lunch is ready, Sam', Liz calls. Sam slips down the few inches from the rock he is clambering on to the ground and runs hurriedly toward the picnic blanket. Jack unwraps a cheese sandwich, hands Sam a triangle and peals the plastic lid from a container of strawberries and places it down on the blanket.

'Daddy's going to go for a climb with Uncle Mike now. Okay, Sam?' Jack asks. Sam gives a pronounced nod, his cheeks near bursting as he chews. 'And later you and me can do some climbing together while mummy does another route. That'll be good, won't it, Sam?'

Sam immediately stops chewing. His jaw drops to reveal a soggy ball of masticated bread and cheese lodged between his tongue and teeth. His eyes well. 'No! Mummy climbs with me', Sam wails. Jack rolls his eyes and looks to Liz.

'It's okay, Sam. Mummy's not going anywhere'. She hugs him and turns to Jack. 'It was a nice thought, thank you'.

Indeed, the sacrifice of time is undoubtedly gendered. Feminist research has shown us how women in employment effectively take a double-shift; paid work followed by the majority of domestic responsibilities, making a commitment to personal leisure that much harder than for a male partner (Hays 1996; Hochschild 1989; Pfister 2001). In socio-history, leisure, and especially sport, has had greater significance for men, associated as it is with masculine identity (cf. Messner 1992; Messner and Sabo 1990), making a commitment to the personal leisure identity imperative. Such discourses remain strong, but late-modernity has tainted them with uncertainty and necessitated a number of contingencies, such as the discourses of compromise and balance, which may produce an involved, flexible father (Such 2009), who's sense of self is established by performing a moral responsibility. Jack certainly experiences a degree of guilt about taking time for himself and has found that he is not alone in this as the changing construction of fatherhood causes his peers also to increasingly worry and strive to meet ideals of the selfless and caring father (Henwood and Procter 2003). Jack consciously reduces his climbing time to ensure he meets those requirements of late-modern family life, which ultimately allows him to enjoy – guilt-free – personal leisure and maintain a serious hobbyist identity. So, the gesture is not entirely selfless, we argue, and moreover the medicalization of motherhood in many ways makes any such gesture rather futile. For Liz, discourses of the 'good mother' began with conception and she struggled with the competing discourses of the committed, voluntary risk-taking climber and risk adversity when pregnant (for full discussion see Coates 2012). Now, years later, while Sam is largely unscathed by Jack's temporary absence, the attachment he has to Liz has far greater ramifications for her personal leisure. Despite a strong desire to maintain a commitment to climbing and a degree of reflexive self-making, maintaining multiple versions of the self, Liz continues to draw on 'conventions of selflessness' (Miller 2007), engaging in the moral project to marginalize all 'other' identities and centre motherhood. Being on the margins is hard and has affected her confidence and in turn her ability to climb. Sam cannot climb with her, which then requires a decentring of motherhood, and that he is present, watching does not in itself create the space for family leisure. The 'being with' that Such (2006, 2009) speaks of requires a sharing of more than just physical space; there must be a sharing of the leisure experience. But when the experience is climbing, all new competing discourses may be tapped into.

3.40 pm

'Hey, how are you?' Liz embraces Caroline. 'No Lee?'

'Yeah, he's here. I gave him a pass and let him go off for a bit. It means I get to spend some time with Connor'.

'You're not climbing?'

'Not today'. Caroline looks to her feet and pushes her jaw to one side. 'I've struggled with it a bit since Connor came along. I have other things now'

Liz perches on a rock and dumps her equipment at her feet. She reaches back and massages her tight shoulder. Caroline sits next to her and they watch Sam and Connor play. 'What time did you get here?' Liz asks.

'Oh, a little while ago. Connor had his football this morning but we wanted to get out for most of the day. How was your climb with Emma?'

'Tough'. Liz says with a smile. 'And knackering. But felt great'.

Connor chases Sam along the winding path through the shrubs and back onto the main track, both screaming with excitement. 'Boys, be careful'. Liz warns. 'Don't trip'.

The boys continue their wild game, oblivious to Liz's words. Jack walks the track towards them, equipment weighing heavy in his arms. Sam runs to Jack butting him in the groin and wrapping his arms around his legs.

'Ugh', Jack crumples from the middle, half jokingly, and drops his gear to the ground. He embraces Sam and then ruffles Connor's hair. 'Right, come on you two, fancy a bit of climb?'

'Are you sure?' Caroline interjects. 'I don't know about … well, if Connor would'.

'I'm so sorry, Caroline', replies Jack with sudden realisation and penitence. 'I just assumed you guys allowed Connor to have a go. Just bouldering, of course, and only the small ones. We'll be there the whole time'.

'He doesn't have to'. Liz stands and places her hand on Jack's shoulder to offer support. 'It's just that now Sam is a bit bigger he sometimes likes to clamber a bit, nothing more than that really'.

Caroline smiles. 'I'm being silly, I know. Lee always says we should get Connor climbing but I don't like to push'.

'No pushing', Jack replies grabbing his gear again and slinging it over his shoulder. 'It's no different to what they do anyway when playing around the rocks, except that I can help a bit and stick the mats down so it's even safer, really. Lee already at the boulders?'

'Yes, he's been working on some problem since we got here. Not having much luck though'. Caroline chuckles. The three begin to wander leisurely down to the boulders. Sam and Connor charge ahead, skipping over the bracken and talking noisily.

'We felt the same as you for a long time', Liz says to Caroline as they stroll down the path. 'But Jack's friend, Aaron, got his kids going from an early age and then we kind of thought that "they're here anyway, why not have a go?"'

'Aaron's eldest is getting good'. Jack adds. 'She's gonna be one to watch. Only six now I think, but real technical. Systematic in her approach, you know?'

'Boys, please be careful'. Caroline shouts. 'And don't go too far ahead'.

No-one, Foucault would argue, is free from moral dilemmas or able to conjure a new morality that would relieve them of concerns, but some may invent practices that defraud the binaries of, for example, the natural and the perverse, domination and subordination, freedom and constraint (Weeks 1995). It would seem reasonable as well to suggest that some may be better at this – more able or disposed – than others. Liz and Caroline, one might argue, lived their lives in parallel until the conception of their children but Liz, for reasons perhaps beyond the scope of this paper, was able to reflect more critically, to juggle competing discourses without, as we have seen, rejecting one to conform to another (cf. Foucault 1984). She is not alone here. Pedersen (2001) and Little (2002) have demonstrated in their respective case studies how women athletes often strive for a status outside of motherhood after the birth of children, becoming more focused on performing than ever before or at least focused on improving steadily. The same can be said of Jack. A sacrifice of time for climbing has been made, but for Jack and Liz this does not correspond to a sacrifice of commitment, a rejection of discourses of improvement or 'climbing hard'. Rather, they have deconstructed these discourses and invented practices that allow them to reconstruct a climbing identity. Lee, too, has managed to do this, but his wife, Caroline's, identity is arguably far less fluid. The morality of time, those discourses of motherhood, the normalizing and medicalizing of a commitment to one's child, has had a more profound effect here; its intended, disciplinary effect. The discourses carry further messages about risk where parents are expected to virtually remove any possibility of risk or harm to children (James, Jenks, and Prout 1998; Lee 2008) under the panoptic gaze of the police, schools and social workers. Discourses of responsibility ensure that risk is gendered (Donnelly 2004; Laurendeau 2008) and fathers are far less prone to accusations of irresponsibility when partaking in precarious leisure (Summers 2007). Liz, however, is more defiant, or reflexive, in the face of discourses of modernity that, as Giddens (1992) may remark, would overwhelm us if it were not for the late-modern quest for authentic self-identity. The concept of authenticity is used here in a Foucauldian sense that rejects a fixed way of being and 'turns back to the idea that we have to be ourselves – to be truly our true self' (McNay 1992, 171 cited in Weeks 1995, 67). Jack and Liz, we argue, sought and continue to seek authenticity by prioritizing the life and leisure of Sam but at the same time not de-prioritizing climbing's discourses of voluntary risk and commitment.

Epilogue

The depreciation of personal leisure time is inevitable with the conception and birth of children and is notoriously gendered, related as it is to both the historical primacy given to the maternal care of children (Davis 2008; Hollway 2006; Richardson 1993) and the gendering of sport and leisure spaces (Clarke and Humberstone 1997; Hargreaves 1994; Wearing 1998). As Draper (2000) notes, the mothering identity is clearly structured by expert, medical, legal and popular discourses, and this identity has been powerful in conveying that motherhood is a natural part of being a woman (Faircloth 2009; Gillespie 2001; Littunen 2002) and that a mother's leisure time is enduringly relational and for the consumption of others (Odih 1999, 2003), notably for partners and children (see also Wimbush 1988). Individuals become the bearers of discourse, internalizing and acting out ideals of behaviour and so an awareness of self as mother has meant that mothers often express a sense of guilt at sacrificing time with their children to make time for themselves (Shaw 1994, 1997), including those mothers involved in outdoor or alternative sports (e.g. Spowart, Hughson, and Shaw 2008) and particularly in climbing (e.g. Coates 2012; Loomis 2005; Stirling 2009). All the mothers depicted in our story expressed such sentiments. In the same way that discourses of intensive parenting felt and embodied by mothers are tied-up with dominant discourses of femininity (see for example Littunen 2002), discourses of fathering are regularly masculinized and involve shared time with children predominantly through play, sport and other leisure pursuits (Brandth and Kvande 1998; Brannen and Nilsen 2006; Dermott 2008; Kay 2006). As a consequence, changes to men's leisure in the transition to parenthood do not necessarily mean a depreciation of leisure time, although upon fatherhood leisure becomes less individualized and more child-centred (Such 2009). Certainly, our story has shown how the fathers had more opportunity to climb and were more able to close out the fathering identity for a time, but also that they took an active role in encouraging their children to participate and to ensure that their partners had time and space to climb.

Indeed, in dual-working parent families, Nentwich (2007) suggests couples regularly work together to balance paid and domestic work and childcare, 'blurring the gender lines' (222) and allowing both mothers and fathers to more easily develop a self-identity outside of their parenting role. However, as our story has shown, such a view might be idealistic at best not only because of the medicalization of motherhood but also, Quirke (2006) argues, because parents tend to overcompensate for time spent at work with an intensification of the parenting role, an obligation to provide a number of labour intensive activities for children that dominate family life (Lareau 2002). While our story has focused on the parents' leisure, it is also made clear that such occasions were a rarity and needed to be actively created by a reflexive Jack and Liz, intent on finding some kind of authenticity. Indeed, the family calendar was dominated by Sam's leisure. Furthermore, there appears to be a general agreement that it remains the mother, more so than the father that feels the full force of the obligation of children's activities (Green, Hebron, and Woodward 1990; Lareau 2002; Mattingly and Sayer 2006). Arguably, it is because of these competing discourses of intensive parenting and personal investment in leisure that leads parents like Jack and Liz, and the others depicted in our story, to sharing, or often pushing, their own leisure preferences as legitimate activities for children. While a few warnings about the perils of parental *coercion* exist in the field (e.g. Hellstedt 1987; Trussell 2009), the sharing of leisure and sport experiences is largely taken to be a positive action for children's longitudinal involvement and achievement in physical activity (Cote 1999; Hellstedt 1995; Lareau 2002; Woolger and Power 1993) and for family relations more generally (Gillis and Gass 1993; Harrington 2006). However, where those experiences are of forms of risk recreation, such as climbing, discourses of risk and risk management compete further with those of parenting and the related discourse of risk aversion (Maynard 2007; Robinson 2008). Coffey (2003, 2005) suggests that the risks taken in mountaineering (a particularly 'extreme' form of climbing) are often unquestioned within the climbing world – despite prominence in the national media and adventure sports literature (see Donnelly 2003; Laurendeau 2008; Palmer 2004;

Summers 2007) – ignoring the potential costs of those risks, not to the climber but to his or her family and friends. As Robinson (2008) shows, climbers often take deliberate steps to circumvent the competing discourses of individual risk and responsibilities to dependents and others by avoiding forming close relationships and especially avoiding having children. Of course, our purposive sample may skew the reality here, but the traditional climbers in our story certainly did not avoid relationships with others but they were caught between a number of competing discourses, including those of the necessary and even celebrated discourses of risk-taking (see Dougherty 2007; Ebert and Robinson 2007; Lewis 2004; Stranger 1999) and commitment to the activity (Rinehart and Sydnor 2003; Wheaton 2004; Wheaton and Beal 2003), and those of shared time and shared leisure with children (see Agate et al. 2009; Freeman and Zabrieskie 2002; Harrington 2006), and protecting children from risk and harm both directly (see James, Jenks, and Prout 1998; Lee 2008) and indirectly as a result of harm to the parent (see Coffey 2003; Furedi 1997; Olivier 2006). For parents who climb, then, a weekend of leisure is potentially fraught with the dangers of ostracism, experiences of guilt and contention around a lost leisure identity. The parents in our story, perhaps with the exception of Caroline, were critical of the legitimacy of such feelings of guilt and keen not to lose touch with their climbing selves. They juggled the competing discourses in a search for authenticity, whether they found it is matter for further dialogue.

Acknowledgement

We would like to thank Dr Ina Stan and Prof. Barbara Humberstone and the two anonymous reviewers for their insightful feedback on an earlier version of this paper.

Notes on contributors

Ben Clayton is a Senior Lecturer for socio-cultural issues in sport at Buckinghamshire New University. He has published widely on the broad topic of gendered sport and has a particular interest in the use of fictional forms of representation to show experiences of sport participation.

Emily Coates is a keen climber and recently a parent. She earned her Ph.D. at Buckinghamshire New University examining the experiences of traditional climbers with young children. Emily remains an associate member of the Institute for Sport, Exercise, Recreation and Well-being at Buckinghamshire New University.

References

Agate, J., R. Zabriskie, S. Agate, and R. Poff. 2009. "Family Leisure Satisfaction and Satisfaction with Family Life." *Journal of Leisure Research* 41 (2): 205–223.
Angrosino, M. 1998. *Opportunity House.* London: Altamira Press.
Bagley, S., J. Salmon, and D. Crawford. 2006. "Family Structure and Children's Television Viewing and Physical Activity." *Medicine and Science in Sports and Exercise* 38 (5): 910–918. doi:10.1249/01.mss.0000218132.68268.f4.
Bauman, Z. 1993. *Postmodern Ethics.* Oxford: Blackwell.
Bittman, M., and J. Wajcman. 2000. "The Rush Hour: The Character of Leisure Time and Gender Equity." *Social Forces* 79 (1): 165–189. doi:10.1093/sf/79.1.165.
Brandth, B., and E. Kvande. 1998. "Masculinity and Child Care: The Reconstruction of Fathering." *Sociological Review* 46 (2): 293–313. doi:10.1111/1467-954X.00120.
Brannen, J., and A. Nilsen. 2006. "From Fatherhood to Fathering: Transmission and Change among British Fathers in Four-generation Families." *Sociology* 40 (2): 335–352. doi:10.1177/0038038506062036.
Brown, P., W. Brown, Y. Miller, and V. Hansen. 2001. "Perceived Constraints and Social Support for Active Leisure among Mothers with Young Children." *Leisure Sciences* 23 (3): 131–144. doi:10.1080/014904001316896837.

Bruce, T. 2000. "Never Let the Bastards See You Cry." *Sociology of Sport Journal* 17 (1): 69–74.

Clarke, G., and B. Humberstone, eds. 1997. *Researching Women in Sport*. Basingstoke: Palgrave MacMillan.

Clayton, B. 2010. "Ten Minutes with the Boys, the Thoroughly Academic Task and the Semi-naked Celebrity: Football Masculinities in the Classroom or Pursuing Security in a 'Liquid' World?" *Qualitative Research in Sport and Exercise* 2 (3): 371–384. doi:10.1080/19398441.2010. 517043.

Clayton, B. 2013. "Initiate: Constructing the 'Reality' of Male Team Sport Initiation Rituals." *International Review for the Sociology of Sport* 48 (2): 204–219. doi:10.1177/1012690211 432659.

Coakley, J. 2006. "The Good Father: Parental Expectations and Youth Sports." *Leisure Studies* 25 (2): 153–163. doi:10.1080/02614360500467735.

Coates, E. 2012. "A Fine Balance: Stories of Parents Who Climb." PhD diss., Brunel University.

Coffey, A., and P. Atkinson. 1996. *Making Sense of Qualitative Data*. London: SAGE.

Coffey, M. 2003. *Fragile Edge: A Portrait of Loss on Everest*. Huddersfield: Arrow.

Coffey, M. 2005. *Where the Mountain Casts its Shadow: The Dark Side of Extreme Adventure*. New York: St, Martin's Griffin.

Cote, J. 1999. "The Influence of the Family in the Development of Talent in Sport." *The Sport Psychologist* 13 (3): 395–417.

Dagkas, S., and A. Stathi. 2007. "Exploring Social and Environmental Factors Affecting Adolescents' Participation in Physical Activity." *European Physical Education Review* 13 (3): 369–384. doi:10.1177/1356336X07081800.

Davis, K. 2008. "'Here's Your Baby, on You Go': Kinship and Expert Advice amongst Mothers in Scotland." PhD diss., Monash University.

Denison, J., and P. Markula, eds. 2003. *Moving Writing: Crafting Movement in Sport Research*. New York: Peter Lang.

Dermott, E. 2008. *Intimate Fathering: A Sociological Analysis*. London: Routledge.

Donnelly, P. 2003. "Sport Climbing vs. Adventure Climbing." In *To the Extreme: Alternative Sports, Inside and Out*, edited by R. Rinehart and S. Sydnor, 291–306. Albany: State University of New York Press.

Donnelly, P. 2004. "Sport and Risk Culture." In *Sporting Bodies, Damaged Selves: Sociological Studies of Sports-Related Injury*, edited by K. Young, 29–58. Oxford: Elsevier.

Dougherty, A. 2007. "Aesthetic and Ethical Issues Concerning Sport in Wilder Places." In *Philosophy, Risk and Adventure Sports*, edited by M. McNamee, 94–105. London: Routledge.

Douglas, K., and D. Carless. 2010. "Restoring Connections in Physical Activity and Mental Health Research and Practice: A Confessional Tale." *Qualitative Research in Sport and Exercise* 2 (3): 336–353. doi:10.1080/19398441.2010.517039.

Draper, J. 2000. "Fathers in the Making: Men, Bodies and Babies." PhD diss., University of Hull.

Ebert, P., and S. Robinson. 2007. "Adventure, Climbing Excellence and the Practice of 'Bolting'." In *Philosophy, Risk and Adventure Sports*, edited by M. McNamee, 56–70. London: Routledge.

Faircloth, C. 2009. "Mothering as Identity-work: Long-term Breastfeeding and Intensive Mother-hood." *Anthropology News* 50 (2): 15–17. doi:10.1111/j.1556-3502.2009.50215.x.

Featherstone, B. 2009. *Contemporary Fathering: Theory, Policy and Practice*. Bristol: The Policy Press.

Foucault, M. 1970. *The Order of Things: An Archaeology of the Human Sciences*. London: Tavistock.

Foucault, M. 1972. *The Archaeology of Knowledge*. London: Routledge.

Foucault, M. 1984. "On the Genealogy of Ethics: An Overview of a Work in Progress." In *The Foucault Reader*, edited by P. Rabinow, 340–372. New York: Pantheon.

Frank, A. W. 2000a. "The Standpoint of Storyteller." *Qualitative Health Research* 10 (3): 354–365. doi:10.1177/104973200129118499.

Frank, K. 2000b. "'The Management of Hunger': Using Fiction in Writing Anthropology." *Qualitative Inquiry* 6 (4): 474–488. doi:10.1177/107780040000600404.

Freeman, P. A., and R. B. Zabrieskie. 2002. "The Role of Outdoor Recreation in Family Enrichment." *Journal of Adventure Education and Outdoor Learning* 2 (2): 131–145. doi:10.1080/14729670285200241.

Furedi, F. 1997. *Culture of Fear: Risk-taking and the Morality of Low Expectation*. London: Cassell.

Furedi, F. 2008. *Paranoid Parenting: Why Ignoring the Experts May be Best for Your Child.* London: Continuum.

Gerson, K. 2009. *The Unfinished Revolution: Coming of Age in a New Era of Gender, Work and Family.* New York: Oxford University Press.

Giddens, A. 1992. *Modernity and Self-Identity.* Cambridge: Polity.

Gillespie, R. 2001. "Contextualizing Voluntary Childlessness within a Postmodern Model of Reproduction: Implications for Health and Social Needs." *Critical Social Policy* 21 (2): 139–159. doi:10.1177/026101830102100201.

Gillis, H., and M. Gass. 1993. "Bringing Adventure into Marriage and Family Therapy: An Innovative Experiential Approach." *Journal of Marriage and Family Therapy* 19 (3): 273–286. doi:10.1111/j.1752-0606.1993.tb00988.x.

Green, E., S. Hebron, and D. Woodward. 1990. *Women's Leisure: What Leisure?* Basingstoke: MacMillan.

Grenfell, C. C., and R. Rinehart. 2003. "Skating on Thin Ice: Human Rights in Youth Figure Skating." *International Review for the Sociology of Sport* 38 (1): 79–97. doi:10.1177/1012690203038001729.

Guendouzi, J. 2006. "'The Guilt Thing': Balancing Domestic and Professional Roles." *Journal of Marriage and Family* 68 (4): 901–909. doi:10.1111/j.1741-3737.2006.00303.x.

Hargreaves, J. 1994. *Sporting Females: Critical Issues in the History and Sociology of Women's Sport.* London: Routledge.

Harrington, M. 2006. "Family Leisure." In *A Handbook of Leisure Studies*, edited by C. Rojek, S. Shaw, and A. Veal, 417–432. Basingstoke: MacMillan.

Hays, S. 1996. *The Cultural Contradictions of Motherhood.* New Haven, CT: Yale University Press.

Heaphy, B. 2007. *Late Modernity and Social Change: Reconstructing Social and Personal Life.* London: Routledge.

Hellstedt, J. 1987. "The Coach/Parent/Athlete Relationship." *The Sport Psychologist* 1 (1): 151–160.

Hellstedt, J. 1995. "Invisible Players: A Family System Model." In *Sport Psychology Interventions*, edited by S. Murphy, 117–146. Champaign, IL: Human Kinetics.

Helstein, M. 2007. "Seeing your Sporting Body: Identity, Subjectivity, and Misrecognition." *Sociology of Sport Journal* 24 (1): 78–103.

Henwood, K., and J. Procter. 2003. "The 'Good Father': Reading Men's Accounts of Paternal Involvement during the Transition to First-time Fatherhood." *British Journal of Social Psychology* 42 (3): 337–355. doi:10.1348/014466603322438198.

Heywood, I. 2006. "Climbing Monsters: Excess and Restraint in Contemporary Rock Climbing." *Leisure Studies* 25 (4): 455–467. doi:10.1080/02614360500333911.

Hochschild, A. 1989. *The Second Shift: Working Parents and the Revolution at Home.* New York: Penguin.

Hollway, W. 2006. *The Capacity to Care: Gender and Ethical Subjectivity.* London: Routledge.

James, A., C. Jenks, and A. Prout, eds. 1998. *Theorising Childhood.* Cambridge: Polity.

Jones, R. 2006. "Dilemmas, Maintaining 'Face', and Paranoia: An Average Coaching Life." *Qualitative Inquiry* 12 (5): 1012–1021. doi:10.1177/1077800406288614.

Kay, T. 2000. "Leisure, Gender and Family: The Influence of Social Policy." *Leisure Studies* 19 (4): 247–265. doi:10.1080/02614360050118823.

Kay, T. 2006. "Where's Dad? Fatherhood in Leisure Studies." In *Fathering through Leisure*, edited by T. Kay, 133–152. Eastbourne: Leisure Studies Association.

Kay, T. 2007. "Fathering through Sport." *World Leisure Journal* 49 (2): 69–82. doi:10.1080/04419057.2007.9674487.

Kimmel, J., and R. Connelly. 2007. "Mothers' Time Choices: Caregiving, Leisure, Home Production and Paid Work." *Journal of Human Resources* 42 (3): 643–681.

Knaak, S. 2005. "Breast-feeding, Bottle-feeding and Dr. Spock: The Shifting Context of Choice." *Canadian Review of Sociology* 42 (2): 197–216. doi:10.1111/j.1755-618X.2005.tb02461.x.

Lareau, A. 2002. "Invisible Inequality: Social Class and Childrearing in Black Families and White Families." *American Sociological Review* 67 (5): 747–776. doi:10.2307/3088916.

Laurendeau, J. 2008. "'Gendered Risk Regimes': A Theoretical Consideration of Edgework and Gender." *Sociology of Sport Journal* 25 (3): 293–309.

Lee, E. J. 2008. "Living with Risk in the Age of 'Intensive Motherhood': Maternal Identity and Infant Feeding." *Health, Risk and Society* 10 (5): 467–477. doi:10.1080/13698570802383432.

Lewis, N. 2004. "Sustainable Adventure: Embodied Experiences and Ecological Practices within British Climbing." In *Understanding Lifestyle Sports: Consumption, Identity and Difference*, edited by B. Wheaton, 70–93. London: Routledge.

Lincoln, Y., and E. Guba. 2003. "Paradigmatic Controversies, Contradictions and Emerging Confluences." In *The Landscape of Qualitative Research: Theories and Issues*. 2nd ed., edited by N. Denzin and Y. Lincoln, 253–291. Thousand Oaks, CA: SAGE.

Little, D. 2002. "Women and Adventure Recreation: Reconstructing Leisure Constraints and Adventure Experiences to Negotiate Continuing Participation." *Journal of Leisure Research* 34 (1): 157–177.

Littunen, S. 2002. "Gender Equality or Primacy of Mothers? Ambivalent Descriptions of Good Parents." *Journal of Marriage and Family* 69 (2): 341–351. doi:10.1111/j.1741-3737.2007.00369.x.

Loomis, M. 2005. "Going Manless." *The American Alpine Journal* 47 (79): 98–115.

Lupton, D., and L. Barclay. 1997. *Constructing Fatherhood: Discourses and Experiences*. London: SAGE.

Markula, P., and J. Denison. 2005. "Sport and the Personal Narrative." In *Qualitative Methods in Sports Studies*, edited by D. Andrews, D. Mason, and M. Silk, 165–184. Oxford: Berg.

Markula, P., and R. Pringle. 2006. *Foucault, Sport and Exercise: Power, Knowledge and Transforming the Self*. New York: Routledge.

Mattingly, M. J., and L. C. Sayer. 2006. "Under Pressure: Gender Differences in the Relationship between Free Time and Feeling Rushed." *Journal of Marriage and Family* 68 (1): 205–221. doi:10.1111/j.1741-3737.2006.00242.x.

Maynard, T. 2007. "Encounters with Forest School and Foucault: A Risky Business?" *International Journal of Primary, Elementary and Early Years Education* 35 (4): 379–391.

McNamee, M., ed. 2007. *Philosophy, Risk and Adventure Sports*. London: Routledge.

McNay, L. 1992. *Foucault and Feminism*. Cambridge: Polity.

Messner, M. 1992. *Power at Play: Sports and the Problem of Masculinity*. Boston, MA: Beacon Press.

Messner, M., and D. Sabo, eds. 1990. *Sport, Men and the Gender Order: Critical Feminist Perspectives*. Champaign, IL: Human Kinetics.

Miller, T. 2007. "'Is This What Motherhood Is All About?': Weaving Experiences and Discourse through Transition to First-time Motherhood." *Gender and Society* 21 (3): 337–358. doi:10.1177/0891243207300561.

Nentwich, J. 2007. "New Fathers and New Mothers are Gender Troublemakers? Exploring Discursive Constructions of Heterosexual Parenthood and their Subversive Potential." *Feminism and Psychology* 18 (2): 207–230. doi:10.1177/0959353507088591.

Odih, P. 1999. "Gendered Time in the Age of Deconstruction." *Time and Society* 8 (1): 9–38. doi:10.1177/0961463X99008001002.

Odih, P. 2003. "Gender, Work and Organization in the Time/Space Economy of 'Just-in-time' Labour." *Time and Society* 12 (2–3): 293–314. doi:10.1177/0961463X030122008.

Olivier, S. 2006. "Moral Dilemmas of Participation in Dangerous Leisure Activities." *Leisure Studies* 25 (1): 95–109. doi:10.1080/02614360500284692.

Palmer, C. 2004. "Death, Danger and the Selling of Risk in Adventure Sports." In *Understanding Lifestyle Sports: Consumption, Identity and Difference*, edited by B. Wheaton, 55–69. London: Routledge.

Pedersen, I. K. 2001. "Athletic Career: 'Elite Sports Mothers' as a Social Phenomenon." *International Review for the Sociology of Sport* 36 (3): 259–274. doi:10.1177/101269001036003001.

Pfister, G. 2001. "The Everyday Lives of Sportswomen: Playing Sport and Being a Mother." In *Women's Leisure Experiences: Age, Stages and Roles*, edited by S. Clough and J. White, 75–86. Eastbourne: Leisure Studies Association.

Quarmby, T., and S. Dagkas. 2010. "Children's Engagement in Leisure Time Physical Activity: Exploring Family Structure as a Determinant." *Leisure Studies* 29 (1): 53–66. doi:10.1080/02614360903242560.

Quirke, L. 2006. "'Keeping Young Minds Sharp': Children's Cognitive Stimulation and the Rise of Parenting Magazines, 1959–2003." *Canadian Review of Sociology* 43 (4): 387–406. doi:10.1111/j.1755-618X.2006.tb01140.x.

Ribbens McCarthy, J., R. Edwards, and V. Gillies. 2000. "Moral Tales of the Child and the Adult: Narratives of Contemporary Family Lives under Changing Circumstances." *Sociology* 34 (4): 785–803. doi:10.1017/S003803850000047X.

Richardson, D. 1993. *Women, Motherhood and Childrearing*. Basingstoke: MacMillan.

Richardson, L. 1994. "Writing: A Method of Inquiry." In *Handbook of Qualitative Research*, edited by N. Denzin and Y. Lincoln, 516–529. Thousand Oaks, CA: SAGE.

Rinehart, R. 1998. "Fictional Methods in Ethnography." *Qualitative Inquiry* 4 (2): 200–224. doi:10.1177/107780049800400204.

Rinehart, R., and S. Sydnor, eds. 2003. *To the Extreme: Alternative Sports, Inside and Out*. Albany: State University of New York Press.

Robinson, V. 2008. *Everyday Masculinities and Extreme Sport: Male Identity and Rock Climbing*. Oxford: Berg.

Rowe, D. 2000. "Amour Improper, or Fever Pitch Sans Reflexivity." *Sociology of Sport Journal* 17 (1): 95–97.

Shaw, S. 1994. "Gender, Leisure and Constraint: Towards a Framework for the Analysis of Women's Leisure." *Journal of Leisure Research* 26 (1): 8–22.

Shaw, S. 1997. "Controversies and Contradictions in Family Leisure: An Analysis of Conflicting Paradigms." *Leisure Sciences* 14 (3): 271–286.

Smart, C., and B. Neale. 1998. *Family Fragments*. Cambridge: Polity.

Smith, B., and A. C. Sparkes. 2011. "Exploring Multiple Responses to a Chaos Narrative." *Health: An Interdisciplinary Journal for the Social Study of Health, Illness and Medicine* 15 (1): 38–53. doi:10.1177/1363459309360782.

Sparkes, A. C. 1996. "The Fatal Flaw." *Qualitative Inquiry* 2 (4): 463–494. doi:10.1177/10778 0049600200405.

Sparkes, A. 2002. *Telling Tales in Sport and Physical Activity: A Qualitative Journey*. Leeds: Human Kinetics.

Spowart, L., L. Burrows, and S. Shaw. 2010. "'I Just Eat, Sleep and Dream of Surfing': When Surfing Meets Motherhood." *Sport in Society* 13 (7–8): 1186–1203. doi:10.1080/17430431003 780179.

Spowart, L., J. Hughson, and S. Shaw. 2008. "Snowboarding Mums Carve Out Fresh Tracks: Resisting Traditional Motherhood Discourse?" *Annals of Leisure Research* 11 (1–2): 187–204. doi:10.1080/11745398.2008.9686792.

Stirling, S. 2009. "Mountaineering Mums." UK Climbing. Accessed March 3, 2009. http://www.ukclimbing.com/articles/page.php?id=1739.

Stranger, M. 1999. "The Aesthetics of Risk: A Study of Surfing." *International Review for the Sociology of Sport* 34 (3): 265–276. doi:10.1177/101269099034003003.

Such, E. 2006. "Leisure and Fatherhood in Dual-earner Families." In *Fathering through Leisure*, edited by T. Kay, 185–199. Eastbourne: Leisure Studies Association.

Such, E. 2009. "Fatherhood, the Morality of Personal Time and Leisure-based Parenting." In *Fathering through Sport and Leisure*, edited by T. Kay, 73–87. London: Routledge.

Summers, K. 2007. "Unequal Genders: Mothers and Fathers on Mountains." Sheffield Online Papers in Social Research. Accessed July 10, 2008. http://www.shef.ac.uk/shop/10.html.

Trussell, D. 2009. "Organized Youth Sport, Parenthood Ideologies and Gender Relations: Parents' and Children's Experiences and the Construction of 'Team Family'." PhD diss., University of Waterloo.

Van Maanen, J. 1988. *Tales of the Field*. Chicago, IL: University of Chicago Press.

Wearing, B. 1998. *Leisure and Feminist Theory*. London: SAGE.

Weeks, J. 1995. *Invented Moralities*. Cambridge: Polity.

Wengraf, T. 2001. *Qualitative Research Interviewing: Biographic Narrative and Semi-Structured Methods*. London: SAGE.

Wheaton. B., ed. 2004. *Understanding Lifestyle Sports: Consumption, Identity and Difference*. London: Routledge.

Wheaton, B., and B. Beal. 2003. "'Keeping It Real': Subcultural Media and the Discourses of Authenticity in Alternative Sport." *International Review for the Sociology of Sport* 38 (2): 155–176. doi:10.1177/1012690203038002002.

Wheaton, B., and A. Tomlinson. 1998. "The Changing Gender Order in Sport? The Case of Windsurfing Subcultures." *Journal of Sport and Social Issues* 22 (3): 252–274. doi:10.1177/019372398022003003.

Wimbush, E. 1988. "Mothers' meeting." In *Relative Freedoms: Women and Leisure*, edited by E. Wimbush and M. Talbot, 48–59. Milton Keynes: Open University Press.

Woolger, C., and T. Power. 1993. "Parent and Sport Socialization: Views from the Achievement Literature." *Journal of Sport Behaviour* 16 (3): 171–189.

'We have not seen the kids for hours': the case of family holidays and free-range children

Marie Vestergaard Mikkelsen and Bodil Stilling Blichfeldt

Department of Culture and Global Studies, Aalborg University, Aalborg, Denmark

The purpose of this paper is to explore what 'children having a good time' means in the context of a mundane type of holidaying, namely caravanning. Focusing on families, this paper draws on 210 qualitative in situ interviews with 437 people spending the holidays at 5 different Danish caravan sites.The study points to 'family time' and children's 'own time' as interdependent entities that allow for the balancing of social identities (pursued through family time) and more individual interests (pursued through own time). Compared to extant theory, caravanning seems to allow for more 'own time' and 'spouse time' for adults, because children have extraordinary opportunities to engage in 'own time'. Furthermore, the study suggests that 'real, quality family time' is best achieved insofar one 'has not seen the kids for hours' in between the precious moments of thick sociality and family togetherness that involve all family members.

Introduction

Researchers taking an interest in family holidays have probably come across parents voicing the mantra 'when the kids are having a good time, we have a good time'. Unfortunately, not much research focuses on exactly what parents mean when they refer to children 'having a good time'. Furthermore, research on family holidays rarely addresses enactments of 'children having a good time' as dependent on specific holiday contexts and settings. This is rather surprising as one would expect children's 'having a good time' to differ when, for example, the family goes wildlife trekking for a month; spends a fortnight visiting Disneyworld and other amusement parks in Florida; goes on an all-inclusive holiday to a sun and sea resort abroad; or takes a more mundane type of holiday (e.g. going to a close-by caravan site). Focusing on the latter, mundane type of family holidaying, the aim of this paper is to discuss what 'children having a good time' means in the context of this type of holidaying. The specific holiday addressed is family holidays at either a domestic caravan site or a caravan site in a neighbouring country.

When it comes to family holidays, on the one hand, there is much emphasis on strengthening family bonds by engaging in leisure activities together and 'doing' sociality and family. On the other hand, 'doing' family holidays is also potential for conflicts, compromising and stressful coordination of different family members' wishes, wants, needs and preferences (Schänzel and Smith 2014; Gram 2005). This paper focuses on traditional, nuclear families going caravanning and during these holidays engaging, not only in touristic activities, but also in a welter of more mundane, everyday activities. The paper especially emphasizes the more mundane, everyday activities and practices that families engage in during their holidays as the study of these more mundane aspects of holidaying may open up deeper insights into what families, children and leisure behaviour mean in today's societies.

Literature review

Several researchers (e.g. Schänzel, Yeoman, and Backer 2012; Obrador 2012; Wang 2000) argue that sociality should be focal to studies on family holidays. Furthermore, Gram (2005); Schänzel, Yeoman, and Backer (2012) and Haldrup and Larsen (2004) point to the need for research that addresses how families 'do family' and perform 'thick sociality' during the holidays – thus pointing to the need to study what is often labelled 'family time' and the ideal of family togetherness during the holidays. The fundamental idea that 'the family that plays together stays together' underlies many family leisure activities and practices – including holidaying (Zabriskie and McCormick 2001; Kelly 1990; West and Merriam 1970; Lehto et al. 2012). Simultaneously, though, researchers also underline the need to gain a better understanding of family members' 'own time' and freedom from family constraints during the holidays. In order to further knowledge on both 'family time' and family members' own time, this paper focuses on what family time and own time more precisely mean in the context of more mundane family holidays. The choice to focus on both families and family members' own time during the holidays originates from our empirical data pointing to these issues being more complex than suggested by existing theories. However and as further discussed below, the study predominately gives voice to parents and grandparents. As a result, the voices of children are less prominent, and consequently, understandings of children 'having a good time' are mainly developed through observations and adult family members' enactments hereof.

Families are the main target group for many tourist destinations, however, tourist research has tended to overlook children's and families' holiday experiences (Gram 2005; Schänzel and Smith 2014; Carr 2011; Nanda, Hu, and Bai 2006; Small 2008). To compensate for these deficits, Larsen (2008) calls for a 'de-exoticization' of tourism research and Obrador (2012) for studies of domesticity and thick sociality 'by the pool'. Furthermore, research focusing more specifically on children and their own time away from the family on holidays is sparse. Rarely have children been the key focus of research, and in the few cases they have, the focus is on their influence on decision-making processes (e.g. Blichfeldt et al. 2011; Gram 2007; Nanda, Hu, and Bai 2006; Nickerson and Jurowski 2001; Therkelsen 2010) or their say in adult decision-making (Johns and Gyimóthy 2002). A few studies focus on how children actually experience family holidays (Cullingford 1995; Hilbrecht et al. 2008; Schänzel and Smith 2014). This topic deserves more attention, as family holidays hold a plethora of potentials, both on micro and macro levels. Family holidays are seen as a time where family is created (Shaw 2008) as well as a 'utopian place' for realizing imagined family relations (Haldrup and Larsen 2004). The family holiday is seen as a way to fulfil needs that are not fulfilled in everyday life, as Nickerson and Jurowski argues 'Working parents with more expendable income and less time to spend with their children use the vacation as a time to reconnect as a family' (2001, 19). However, the idea of family holidays as space and time for reconnecting as a family may paint a somewhat rosy picture of the whole family spending harmonious time together. According to Obrador, 'Beneath the image of a united, stable, loving family there are multiple conflicts and tensions' (2012, 416) and he goes on to say that one of them is 'parents that are tired of being with their children all the time'. Miller (1995, 414) also discusses this issue and concludes that ' It can be problematic trying to live up to the ideal of the family doing everything together, possibly even causing "claustrophobia of family togetherness"'.

Daly (2001, 283) argues that 'the hegemonic view of family time reflects the romanticized version of family life', in which ideals of togetherness and positive valence for all family members predominate. However, as is now increasingly recognized, the family is not to be seen as a homogeneous unit but as consisting of individuals, each with their own wishes and needs for experiences that make up an 'ideal' family holiday. As found by Gram (2005), when on holiday, parents face a dilemma between togetherness with their children and making a space for themselves. Other studies show that parents want to relax during the holidays (Blichfeldt 2007; Gram 2005), whereas for children, activities are the main attraction (Therkelsen and Gram 2003; Hilbrecht et al. 2008). Furthermore, children prefer more physical activities than their parents (Schänzel 2010), and play and 'fun' (Hilbrecht et al. 2008) are main elements of what constitutes a nice holiday for children, made possible usually through beaches, swimming pools and theme parks (Swarbrooke and Horner 2007). As Schänzel and Smith (2014, 136) argue, a delicate balancing of family time and own time is achieved through *cooperation*, *compromises* and *conflicts* while families are on holiday. Furthermore, Obrador (2012) demonstrates that family holidays include compromising between parents, who want to go sightseeing and children, who want to stay by the pool.

Caravanning is a rather mundane type of holiday that might offer opportunities for balancing these dynamics. There has not been much recent research on caravanning, only a few studies focusing mainly on long-term travelling in recreational vehicles (RVs) (e.g. Becken and Wilson 2007; Viallon 2012; Counts and Counts 2004) or the social aspect of caravanning (Blichfeldt and Mikkelsen 2013). Furthermore, even though it can be argued that 'families are the backbone of the commercial campground industry' (Janiskee 1990, 396), research on families going caravanning is even sparser. Another aspect that has been ignored is the mundane practices that prevail at caravan sites. Historically, tourism and leisure have been seen as liminal spaces, counter to everyday life and the mundane (Franklin 2003; Rojek 1995). Additionally, according to Larsen (2008), there has been too much research devoted to the extraordinary, exotic tourist places and experiences, while the everyday, ordinary tourist spaces remain under-researched. In line with Larsen (2008), Blichfeldt and Mikkelsen (2014) criticize existing understandings of tourism as extraordinary experiences in sharp contrast to everyday life's more ordinary, mundane and banal endeavours, and argue that the richness and complexities of everyday life practices and routines that people bring with them on holiday are largely ignored. However, the families going caravanning actually spend a large part of their holidays engaging in quite ordinary ordeals. In this particular setting, the boundaries between tourism and leisure are blurred as the practices people engage in 'away' do not differ fundamentally from those at 'home'. When going caravanning, families even bring with them elements from home such as their own linen, pots and pans, the children's favourite toys, board games, etc. In this way, families engaging in caravanning use tactics 'to home oneself' (Winther 2006), perhaps even more nowadays as the concept of 'home' has become more fluid, however still fundamental to most family holidays (Obrador 2012) as it renders 'family members available and present to each other' (Larsen, Urry, and Axhausen 2007, 250). Accordingly, caravanning might be an especially interesting context to study as this type of holidaying enables families with children to go away while bringing with them not only a feeling of home, but also a wide range of material elements of home. Accordingly, the aim of this study is to illuminate these experiences in a de-exotisized manner, in a mundane, closer-to-everyday setting in order to counterbalance dominant discourses within tourism and leisure.

There is a need to focus specifically on children's 'own time' and to take a closer look at children's worlds. As Waksler (1986) argues, there is a tendency to ignore children's own experiences and understandings, both in academic research and in everyday life, however, '(C)hildren are responsible social actors in their own right, adept at managing their own space and time' (Valentine 1997, 67). They are not just 'human becomings', but human beings' (Qvortrup 1987, 5). Today, children are seen as individuals in their own right, capable of making choices on their own and having substantial influence on parents' choices. Hence, although parents may still be the ones taking on the responsibility to ensure a nice vacation for the whole family, perhaps that especially means the child being happy, vacations (especially caravanning) are often planned with the children in mind, both in terms of possible enjoyment, but also possible learning outcomes (Shaw 2008). Additionally, when planning a family holiday, safety is considered important as it gives children an element of independence and parents a space away from their children (Johns and Gyimóthy 2002).

The happiest family may not necessarily be the family that spends the most time together during the holidays or, quantitatively, 'does' most thick sociality as the widespread use of the term 'quality family time' indicates. Therefore, this paper takes a closer look at interdependencies between own time and family time during a mundane type of holidaying that enables families to both do family and to split up, thus potentially dissolving some of the tensions family members enact during holidays. The calls for more focus on families spending time apart are consequently addressed in this paper by focusing on a popular type of family holiday, where opportunities for time together as well as apart can be found in full bloom. Accordingly, the paper contributes to a much needed deconstruction of family time, and questions romanticized and idealized perceptions of family togetherness as always being desirable.

Methodology

Caravanning has a long tradition as a part of Danish tourism. The caravan holiday spread with the increase in the privately owned car and it rapidly became a popular type of holiday in Denmark (Den Jyske Historiker 2012). Caravanning soon became the epitome of freedom (Green 1978; Hardy et al. 2006), as it made it possible to travel over longer distances for longer periods of time while bringing along all amenities necessary. This 'home on wheels' still appeals to many people as it offers both comfort and freedom (Jantzen et al. 2007). Danish caravan sites welcome all ages arriving in tents, RVs, caravans and the like, typically spending from one night to around a fortnight at the site (some longer; Jantzen et al. 2007). However and as also reflected in this study, most guests are families with young children and empty nesters. Caravan sites are bounded areas and can span from primitive sites with electricity and running water, to sites with swimming pools, mini-golf and restaurants. The present study was predominantly carried out at sites with more activities and experience offers for families with children.

This paper draws on 210 qualitative in situ interviews with 437 people spending the holidays at 5 different Danish caravan sites. The interviews are complemented by observations and visual data as visualized in Figure 1.

Data were collected over a period of two summers (see Figure 1). The first round of data collection was more explorative, based on a minimum amount of control and letting

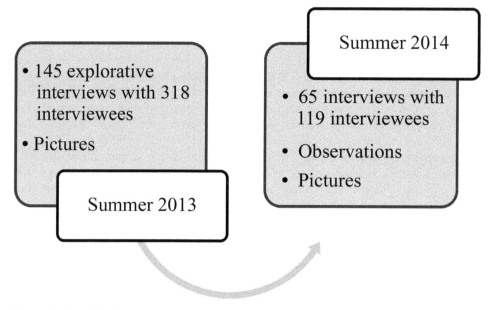

Figure 1. Data collection process.

the terminology rise from the world of caravanning itself (Vannini and Taggart 2012). During the second round, the aim was to get more into depth with the main themes developed through the analysis of the first round of data. After the first round of data collection, analysis therefore focused on identification of main themes, whereas the second round of analysis centres on 'saturation' of these themes. As a result, the interview guide evolved during this process and the second round of interviews became more focused around main themes such as family time, situations qualifying as family togetherness, adult time, quality time, the children's range and details on how family members spend their time, both together and apart. The interviews were digitally recorded and transcribed. Furthermore, the interviews were supported by observations and visual data, to a larger extent during the second round of data collection.

All in all we conducted 210 interviews with 437 interviewees. This might seem a large number given that the guests were disturbed by researchers during their holiday. One explanation of tourists' willingness to partake in the study could be the many quasi- or semi-public places such as playgrounds, common kitchens and barbeque plots at caravan sites, where it is easy and acceptable to approach people. Another could be the element of sociability that characterizes the caravan holiday (Blichfeldt and Mikkelsen 2013), making dominant the discourse of openness towards others. In practice, we mostly approached people when they were sitting in front of their RV, caravan, tent or the like, eating, reading, talking, sunbathing, relaxing, etc. Apart from that, we contacted people in the common areas such as at playgrounds or pools (while they were watching theirs, and others children), or while cooking or dishwashing in the kitchen. However, a choice was made never to contact children unless they were together with adults. Traditional nuclear families with one to three younger children are highly over-represented in the study, and although some blended families participated in the study, we met no single parents or rainbow families at the caravan sites. We have checked this issue with industry experts, and it seems that over-representation of nuclear families and under-representation of other types of families characterizes not only our study, but also families that visit Danish caravan sites in general. Around half of the interviewees (200) are domestic (Danish) tourists whereas the rest of the interviewees are from Germany (155), Norway (44), Holland (19), Sweden (12) and elsewhere (7). Most interviewees stay in caravans (236), tents (31) or RVs (79). Most interviewees are either families with children (177) or empty nesters (163). As we wanted to keep interviews informal, we did not ask explicitly for household income or occupational status and therefore, we only obtained such harder facts when they 'naturally came up' during the interviews.

People seem to 'take a break' from going caravanning around the time the oldest child becomes a teenager, which might be the reason why we mostly encountered families with younger children and empty nesters – with or without grandchildren. This may be due to teenagers' increasing disassociation with this type of holidaying, perhaps because it accommodates many families with young children. Around the teenage years, parents find it difficult to persuade children to engage in family holiday experiences (Hilbrecht et al. 2008). This break usually came up in the interviews with empty nesters as the interviewees talked about their entire travel careers, including other types of holidays and caravanning done previously. The majority of empty nesters sometimes take the grandchildren caravanning, and during the interviews they also reminisced about going caravanning when their children came along. This topic was always brought up before the researchers addressed it, indicating that this is an important and memorable part of their holiday (see Snelgrove and Havitz 2010 on retrospective accounts).

The average length of interviews is around 30 minutes. However, some interviews are very short (often when family members were on their way to 'do something') whereas other interviews were well over an hour in length. Furthermore, the quality of interviews varies considerably – from very short interviews where interviewees mostly offered very factual information, to in-depth conversations covering both this type of holidaying and contrasts to other types of holidays as well as everyday life. Although we intended, and tried, to give children voice during the in situ interviews, children's voices are under-represented and parents' and grandparents' voices dominate our interviews. The reasons for this under-representation of children's voices relate very much to what actually 'goes on' during these holidays. As an example, one hour into an interview with grandparents holidaying with their grandchildren, the adults in the caravan next to the interviewees came by and asked whether the interviewees had seen any of the children and the response was 'maybe they are in our caravan, perhaps they have gone to the playground – but the eldest one, he's on top of everything'. As another example, while doing an interview with parents in their 30s and their two daughters (age 6 and 12) in front of their caravan, the 6 years old asked for, and got, permission to go bicycling. Around 15 minutes later she came back, bringing with her a girl her own age and the following conversation took place:

Daughter: 'Can we go play at her [pointing to the other girl] place?'

Mother: 'Where do you live [at the caravan site]?'

The other girl: 'I live where she [pointing at the interviewer] has just been.'

Interviewer: 'Oh yes, on the second "street" on the left from here, right?'

Mother: 'Yes, that's fine, you can go there.'

As exemplified by the conversation above, during the interviews, most children were actively pursuing 'own time' activities. Furthermore, as we would only talk to children in the presence of one or both parents, we had no chance of contacting all the 'free ranging children' we observed at the caravan sites.

To try to understand the families' holiday experiences better, observations supported by visual data were an important part of the second round of data collection. As mentioned previously, when caravanning, a great deal of time is spent engaging in everyday practices. As Daly (2007, 66) argues: 'Reality as it is lived on a day-to-day basis, is often experienced as mundane and unremarkable'. People seemed to find these everyday activities to be too unremarkable and mundane, and they struggled to give words to them, even in the more detailed, focused interviews. Perhaps this is also because these activities were very embodied and 'habitualized'. In order to move beyond these limits of discourse, we did observations to illuminate some of these mundane, embodied experiences. The focus was mainly on the children's places of concentration, play areas, both formal, such as indoor and outdoor playgrounds (Figure 2) and informal, such as paths and open spaces (Figure 3). Children would play at the formal, structured play areas in the shape of bounded playgrounds with swing sets, jumping pillows, slides and the like. However, older children, or younger children in the company of older siblings, would also play in informal places such as the shrubbery, the streets[1] and the site more in general.

The older children would roam freely around the site on bikes, scooters or by foot, or they would, for example, spend an entire afternoon building a primitive tree hut in the bushes.

Figure 2. Children playing in front of the reception.

Figure 3. Children playing on the jumping pillow.

Out of the 437 interviewees, the forthcoming analysis predominantly draws on those of families with children and grandparents with grandchildren engaging in more performative, mundane and everyday enactments. Conclusively, we are not 'concerned with representation and meaning, but with the performative "presentations", "showings", and "manifestations" of everyday life' (Thrift 1997, 126–27). The analysis is divided into two parts, the first emphasizing first-order interpretations and the second offering a discussion of higher order theoretical interpretations.

Findings

Most interviewees have tried many different types of holidays, and argue that they keep returning to caravanning because this type of holidaying gives families 'something' they cannot get during other holidays. For example, a pregnant mother of two (girl, 4 years old and boy, 6 years old), spending a fortnight in her parents' caravan together with the children and her husband, explained why she resents the kids clubs they have encountered when spending the holidays at resorts and family friendly hotels as follows:

> That is to take a packaged holiday and park your kids in a club. But we go on holiday to be *with* our kids. They should also go on holiday and get to relax. A kids club would be kindergarten all over again. We have a very busy everyday life and the kids have to relate to lots of people. But being here, the kids can choose if it should just be the two of them, all four of us or they can go to the playground to be with other children. They can choose to and from: So if they want to go to the playground, it's cool and if they choose to stay here it is also cool.

93

This mother of two underpins Carr's (2011, 19) statement that 'in addition to adults, children may increasingly be motivated to take a holiday by a desire to escape, in this case the pressures on their free time'. According to this mother of two, to 'park' your children in a kids club is not acceptable, but she does not mind it when her children *choose* to spend time away from her and her husband at the caravan site. In the same vein, a man in his mid-50s tells the following about the first time he and his wife took their son caravanning 25 years ago:

> He was 6 years old and we hardly saw him. In the morning he went off [...]. And later he went to the playground or something. He had a holiday and we had a holiday. So many parents rent a holiday house and for the entire holiday, the kids pester. The parents don't have a vacation and neither do the kids.

What is interesting in this story is not so much that parents have a hard time having a holiday if they have to entertain the children (which is well covered by Blichfeldt 2007 and Gram 2005). What is more interesting, is that the interviewee points to holidays comprised of too much family time, thick sociality and togetherness as something that neither satisfies the needs of the parents nor the children. Another granddad tells of a holiday with his sons when they were tweens as follows:

> Every time, we'd suggest a trip to an amusement park or the likes, our sons would respond: 'Only if we are back before 4 pm, because we [children of different nationalities at the caravan site] are to play football, the 'European championships'. [...] It's really rewarding to be with your kids in that way; the kids learn to be with other kids of other nationalities and the parents can relax because the kids are having a good time and don't need to be entertained. (24–27)

As this interviewee expresses it, there is an element of learning connected to some of the activities that takes place on a caravan site. The children get more opportunities to experience being independent, not only as a playing child but also as a learning child, as also exemplified by one dad saying:

> When you have kids, well, there are so many plusses (when caravanning), when you see these little girls walking with their toilet bags up to the bathrooms and brush their teeth and what not, they get ten feet tall 'cause they can do it themselves, it's wonderful to see.

Other parents and grandparents talk about learning experience in the form of the children helping with everyday practicalities such as dishwashing and cooking, as one dad expresses it, 'When [the child] says "I'm hungry!" yes, well, the food doesn't make itself, we have to go and make it first, and if we haven't washed the dishes then that needs to be done first [...] they get more insight into these things when caravanning'.

Parents often expressed the advantages of their children having the opportunity to help with various mundane, everyday chores. However, although parents emphasize the things they do together with their children, across the quotes, as well as across practically all interviewees, the common denominator is that children, seemingly, need time away from their parents (and grandparents) in order to have 'a good time'. Although the quotes above predominately relate to children's 'own time' as time spent playing with other children (sometimes siblings, but mostly with children they meet at the caravan site), children's 'own time' manifests itself in many different ways: From tweens and teens who have their own tent to sleep in so that they do not need to sleep close to the parents (and younger siblings), over the nine-year-old girl, who goes to the store at the site to buy sweets with her friends (Figure 4), to younger children that go to the toilet themselves. Children around the age of six to seven were often allowed to make small purchases at the on-site stores on their own, such as sweets, icecream or rolls for breakfast. As one mother tells it:

> The children got a small allowance and we told them that they could go and buy a lollipop or an icecream. Then they ask the man in the store how much it costs, so they've done that a couple of times.

Parents feel comfortable in letting their older children make purchases at the on-site store by themselves. Furthermore, there are parents who choose a lot (the small piece of land where people put up their tent, RV or caravan) so close to a playground that toddlers can go there, but still see, and be seen by the parents, using vocal and visual criteria as

Figure 4. Children buying sweets on their own in the on-site store.

'markers of range boundaries' (Matthews 1992, 20). Accordingly, when the parents can see and hear their children, they are within a zone of comfort and the children can go no further.

Across interviewees, reasons why children need their 'own time' relate both to this being necessary to satisfy parents' needs to relax and to satisfying children's needs (not being bored; being freed from family constraints; and having learning experiences). For example, one grandmother argues that one should not take vacations with 'too much' family time, but that one ought to let both children and grandchildren 'run around – let the children have some freedom!' and she proudly tells how their own children played with children of different nationalities long before they understood any foreign languages. Nevertheless, to all interviewees, letting the children have freedom relates to safety, or as a 32-year-old mother of two younger children opines:

> For the kids, this is just a great way to get out and get to know other children. It's just, they run to the playground and find tons of children to play with. So they have freedom and the parents can get to relax – still keeping clued-in. As a parent you feel safe. I just feel it is and if there is anything, they'll come back to the tent. So they go and play and then they return. It's free. But I mean, if you see a kid crying, you take care of it, you don't ignore a child crying. It's just a very nice environment.

As exemplified by this mother of two, children can 'run free' while the parents still feel 'clued-in' and rely on their children being safe as caravan sites are perceived and enacted as safe. The degrees of freedom children have, and how much adults need to feel 'clued-in' differ with the age of the children and the proximity of things. Whereas teenagers have much freedom (and may, for example, stay out late, or go to the swimming pool or beach alone when they are around 15), toddlers are not allowed to go further than to the nearest playground (where the parents can still see them). Teens are mostly allowed to go for walks or bicycle rides around the caravan site, but need to come back and ask for parental permission if they want to go to other children's 'homes'. As a general rule of thumb, it seems that when children 'can find their way back' they are allowed to be without strict supervision. However, deciding when exactly this happens is difficult for the adults to assess. More than one interviewee pointed to the example with toddlers having the lot number written on the diaper (including the comment: 'That's something you can do at a caravan site, not in other places and not abroad, but when caravanning everybody is part of one big family') and kids with lot numbers written on their arms. As an example of the differences in what children are allowed to do, a woman in her 40s (who has taken many of her nephews and nieces caravanning over the years) said:

> Well, Toby was 4 or 5 when he started to go to the playground on his own, […], but we do take the bicycles once in a while and go and check up on the kids. With the pool, I'm much more 'fussy', they don't get to do that alone.

As indicated by this quote, what children are allowed to do depends on assessment of both the individual child's competencies (with Toby being allowed to go to the playground alone at a younger age than the other children) and general rules (e.g. never allowing them to go to the pool alone). Furthermore, most interviewees regularly 'check up' on children younger than around six years. Nonetheless, children do get lost occasionally, but as a woman in her 50s talking about the family holidays when her children were around 6 years old pinpointed:

It did happen that they were gone for a couple of hours, but then they were just playing in somebody else's caravan. They were actually very good at swinging by and telling us 'we are there or there.

What is interesting, is that the interviewees do not voice or exhibit much anxiety, guilt or fear when they tell about 'not having seen the kids for hours' (depending on age), but argue that the children are *safe* at the site – albeit they would not feel so in other holiday settings or contexts.

When the children are spending time away from the family, the parents also get to have some alone time. The time spent apart does not only provide children with own time, but it also gives the adults opportunities to satisfy their own needs, freed from their traditional family roles as mothers, fathers or grandparents. While the children are away engaging in activities and play, the adults pursue individual needs like relaxing, reading books, going for a run or spending time together as a couple. One mother talks about how she uses her alone time: 'I use it as a sanctuary where I can read books and go for a run and those things (…) and we [she and her husband] get to talk more'. To her, the caravan site becomes a 'sanctuary' where she gets to do the things that she might not have time for at home. As another woman explains more in detail:

Woman: 'We [she and her husband] get to talk to one another more here. It can be limited how much you get to talk to one another at home during a very structured day where you are trying to maintain two careers. (…) Here we're just going to be together and have a good time, and do what we feel like doing, together and apart.'

Interviewer: 'What do you mean by that?'

Woman: 'Well, some things we do together, and then sometimes it's nice to be able to say, I just feel like doing this, well, then [her husband] takes the children, or has a lie down and then we go for a walk. There's room for that here too'.

This interview fragment shows how the parents spend time 'alone together', talking more than they would at home. Also, it portrays how families split up into different groupings, so that the adults can have some time together, or one of the spouses can have alone time. This was not only done so one of the parents could have alone time but also in order for a parent to spend time alone with one or all children.

Although our adult interviewees say that children's 'own time' is necessary in order for the entire family to have a good vacation, and although the children actually did spend much time apart from their parents, this does not mean that 'family time' is irrelevant for these families. On the contrary, a key finding is that children, during this mundane type of holiday, constantly shift back and forth between family time (family togetherness) and own time (freedom from family constraints).This is reflected in their daily spatial-temporal choreography of leaving the immediate space of the caravan/tent/RV to go play or engage in other activities and to come back for meal times together with the other family members. Most days are structured around a somewhat repetitive pattern with the caravan/RV/tent as the nub. From this base, the children gradually increase their familiarity with the environment, making the whole site their 'habitual range' (Moore and Young 1978), referring to the range that both children and parents are comfortable with. This would usually include places that become part of everyday patterns, extending into playgrounds, the facilities buildings, the common areas and the site as a whole. Additionally, children's own time seems necessary for families to successfully engage in family time, and interviewees argue that this particular type of holiday is especially good at providing space and time for children's own time. Furthermore, both adults and children point to the situations in which the family 'reunites' as the highlights of their holiday (e.g. when taking their time eating breakfast together; taking a bicycle ride together; doing the dishes together; or, especially, playing cards and board games in the evenings). Accordingly, caravanning allows for families to spend time together, as well as apart, and parents and children constantly separate and connect their paths, fulfilling both collective and individual needs. The safety of the site and proximity of things aid parents to broaden the 'free range' and space for their children.

Discussion

Compared to existing theories on family holidays that emphasize sociality (i.e. family time) more than individuality (i.e. own time), our study points to 'family time' and parent's and children's 'own time' as interdependent entities that allow for the balancing of social identities (pursued through family time) and more individual interests (pursued through own time). Our study also emphasizes that children's own time is necessary in order for the family to successfully engage in family time. Concordant with existing theory (e.g. Blichfeldt 2007; Gram 2005; Larsen 2013), during the holidays, adults need own time and spouse time (i.e. 'the two of us together alone') to be freed from their traditional family roles as mothers, fathers or grandparents. However, compared to extant theory, caravanning seems to allow for more 'own time' and 'spouse time' for adults, because children have extraordinary opportunities to engage in 'own time'. Furthermore, children's own time is time spent actively in the companionship of other children (although a child may occasionally play on its own), but without the parents being present. Children would spend a majority of their own time together with peers more so than adults (also found by Schänzel 2010). Compared to other holidays, during which children's time apart from parents is organized, supervised and structured (exemplified by the kids clubs at resorts), children's own time at caravan sites is non-supervised and non-organized, and adults highlight this as being healthy and offering learning experiences for children, where they get to know how to interact with other children (often of different nationalities) without adult interference. There is little need for structured playtime or 'organized play activity' (Valentine 1997) at a caravan site and due to the site being experienced as a safe place, children are allowed to 'run free'. As an example, a mother of three (aged 12, 9 and 6) told about how the family is caravanning for the very first time and she proudly told how the children took a tour of the site (including getting the youngest to the toilets) while the parents set up the caravan and afterwards came back and took the parents on a tour showing them the site and the facilities. This mother further argued that 'our children are very shy, so a good thing about caravanning is that they meet other children. I think our kids are going to learn a lot from this'. Caravanning seems to provide opportunities for children to be independent; to explore the site on their own; and to get in contact with other children. This is also exemplified by a mother telling of her daughter being nowhere in sight despite knowing that it was 'pizza night', and when the parents arrived at the (on-site) pizza place, there she was, 'her bike parked by the wall, waving at us, 'I'm down here', 'it's fantastic'. The dad continuing:

> Just the fact that she says 'I'll just go for a ride' and then 'prrrt!' (biking away fast), she just goes for a ride, and when you go to check, then you see her, riding her bike down there, you know, how she just rides about, takes a look around, what's going on, it's amazing!

These parents proudly telling of their daughter's bicycle rides indicates that not only does the child get to have own time of play and explore, but also the parents get to experience their children as increasingly independent and maturing individuals, causing them much joy and pride. As Shaw suggested, family leisure is seen by parents as a part of child-rearing, 'through which children will be exposed to a range of positive developmental influences and will learn lessons important for their success in life' (Shaw, 2008, 698). These everyday simplicities may thus be part of wider, developmental processes. This is further supported by Carr (2011, 18) who argues that 'the freedom and exploration available in leisure and unstructured play may result in the development of children into functioning members of adult society'. Within the safe boundaries a caravan site provides, there is room and opportunity for children to do things on their own, where exploration becomes a sort of 'forerunner to adult participation' (Matthews 1992, 37). Accordingly, through the seemingly mundane, everyday practices and activities children engage in at caravan sites (such as playing, taking a bike ride, exploring or simply brushing teeth and helping with dinner) lies immanent potential for wider developmental processes. These holidays thus provide both children and parents with own time, where the adults get to relax and the children to explore and mature, an element that further fuels proud parents. The everyday at home typically does not allow time for children to engage in these processes 'on their own' as most days are scheduled and fast-paced. Furthermore, most parents cannot disclaim either helping or hurrying the child. At the caravan site the 'disintegration' of structure and planning and the loose, slow-paced, safe ecology facilitate 'own time' for children. There are few 'have to do's' and everything seems to happen at a slower pace, giving the much needed and necessary extra time for smaller children. This is further aided through the proximity of things, and the homely atmosphere of one's own 'street' and socializing with 'neighbours'. The habitus of the caravan site thus enables children to run free, however children also play at informal places, creating their own pathways through the vegetation, transforming the site into adventurous experience-scapes.

The caravan site may consequently act as an intermediary space between the everyday and wider cultural contexts, which provide a place for children to mature, play and engage in socializing processes. This constellation is further aided by the site being experienced as safe. Parents explain the safety of the caravan site by everyone watching out for one another, often seen against and contrasted to the neighbourhood at home. As Jobes (1984, 195) argues when referring to retirees in RV's: 'A community of identity, "weeness", and even language emerge with shared activities and the unique leisure lifestyle'. Families going caravanning share a common space for a short period of time, and engage in similar activities in close proximity to one another, or, as one grandmother explains:

> It's a kind of safe environment, I mean you trust people (...) sometimes you think people trust each other so much in this place, I don't know if you can, but it doesn't matter where you go, for example, there's a slab of beer, it's so easy to take it if you wanted, you just trust each other here (...) it's like we belong together at this site, and we also look after each other's children.

As she expresses it people 'belong together' and thereby the caravan site thus provides a sense of temporary community, and this enables parents to let their children run free. Carver, Timperio, and Crawford (2008) argue that lack of neighbourhood safety (and particularly 'stranger danger') is a key reason why children, nowadays, spend less time free-playing outdoors. However, the caravan site is constructed as a welcoming neighbourhood, a safe place. This is a delicate balance that does not seem to be questioned, although when talking about the trusting atmosphere at a caravan site the grandmother adds 'I don't know if you can', exemplifying the fact that it is a constructed safety. As one mother travelling with two young children also shortly ponders:

> The children run in an out of all the caravans. And sometimes you do think 'uh-oh', but you just can't have that thought, 'cause then you're not free when caravanning, so you just have to remember to put that thought away and just be positive'.

This mother is one of the few interviewees fleetingly addressing this construction, concluding that if it is questioned you cannot let your children run and be 'free'. The trust and safety that prevail at a caravan site consequently facilitate parents' and children's own time, a culture that it seems is not as common in interviewees' everyday life contexts as they could wish for.

Family leisure ideologies suggest 'that parents need to be involved in every aspect of their children's lives, including their children's "free time"–a notion that may have been given less attention by previous generations of parents' (Shaw, 2008, 699). Today, a large part of parenting is spent structuring and planning children's 'own' time, where earlier generations told their children to 'go outside and play' (Shaw 2008, 694). One explanation why parents spend more time supervising children may be growing fears concerning public spaces (Wyness 2006). As Valentine and McKendrick (1997) argue, today, children do not have the same outdoor play opportunities as previous generations. As our findings show, caravanning allows for children's own time, freed from the structured, planned and organized everyday life. Furthermore, this allows the adults to be freed from their role as parents and to engage in alone time, together or individually. Perhaps going caravanning fulfils a nostalgic desire to go back to the (imagined) 'good old days' where one could simply tell the children to 'go outside and play'. Furthermore, parents stress the importance of not bringing too many of the children's electronic devices and limiting the time spent using them, as compared to everyday life at home. Also, the children seem to opt out of spending the entire day on their iPads as they prefer spending time with their newfound friends. This nostalgia surrounding caravanning may for some families represent a purer, simpler time where children spent their time playing outside. These findings link to wider historical ideologies within leisure and tourism where people would go on a quest for freedom (Rojek 1995), simplicity and nostalgia in nature (Löfgren 1999; Laing and Crouch 2011). Thus, the cultural context framing these experiences are part of wider ideas of spaces of leisure and tourism providing safety, simplicity, freedom and nostalgia affording a caravan culture of own time and a free-range ecology for children. However, instead of exploring these subjects within liminal and counter-spaces, our findings illuminate these experiences within a more banal, everyday context. Western ideals of family togetherness, positive engagement and child-centeredness (Daly 2001) are widespread and 'a sense of "time famine" is pervasive in late-twentieth-century Europe and America' (Gillis 1996, 5). Notwithstanding, the families we met at the caravan sites take a 'time out' from their everyday life experience of time famine, hereby making room for both family time and own time.

Schänzel, Yeoman, and Backer (2012) argue that family holidays depend on a balance between 'family time' and 'own time' and Schänzel and Smith (2014) propose a model suggesting that families try to balance family time and own time during the holidays through cooperation, compromise and conflict. Furthermore, Larsen (2013, 6) argues that in regard to family holidays the experience of 'being together' is a 'complex and hybrid structure of different, though interrelated, experiences'. Building on Schänzel and Smith's (2014) model and continuing Larsen's (2013) line of reasoning, our data point to 'family time' and children's 'own time' not only being part of a complex structure, but also that children's spending time apart from their (grand)parents is necessary for family time to be successful. As a result, 'family time' and 'own time' should not be investigated separately as they, in an almost cyclic manner, enrich and inform one another. According to the parents and grandparents (and to the extent they actively took voice, the children) in our study, 'real, quality family time' is best achieved insofar one 'has not seen the kids for hours' in between the precious moments of thick sociality and family togetherness, that all interviewees point to as peak holiday experiences. Caravanning is highly poly-dimensional as our study suggests the transformative possibilities of the uneventful, everyday practices families engage in. The habitus of the caravan site enables families to pursue both collective and individual interests in the shape of ostensibly ordinary practices. The caravan holiday gives rise to relaxation, re-charging adults, socializing couples, proud parents and exploring, maturing free-range children.

Although our results are tentative, the study does suggest that studies of more mundane holidays may have much to offer if we wish to better understand children as individuals, who actively shift back and forth between enjoying family time, thick sociality and family togetherness, and individuals, who pursue their own interests and gratifications freed from family constraints and the role as 'their parents' child'. Contemporary ritualization of family time and the moments of time-out-of-time labelled 'quality time' (whether it be the daily family dinner or an annual holiday) did not emerge before the second half of the nineteenth century (Gillis 1996) and are no less and no more than cultural constructions of family ideology. That said, in today's Western societies, family time, togetherness and quality time are ideals that families, more or less intensively and more or less successfully, live with and by. Contrary to dominant romanticized and idealized views on family time (i.e. 'the more, the merrier') and enactments of the family holiday as a time where 'we can be a family 24/7', our study suggests that quality time does not over-shine the full family holiday, but instead twinkles in those precious points in time and space in-between own time and family time, where family members truly (re)connect.

Conclusion

This paper set out to contribute to understandings of parents' and children's own time in the context of caravanning. Sociality and family togetherness are important during these holidays. Nevertheless, children and parents also immensely enjoy being apart during the holidays. Moreover, research focusing specifically on children and their own time away from the family on holidays is sparse and through interviews, observations and visual data, we attempted to flesh out the practices and activities families engage in during a more mundane type of holiday.

It was found that children's own time is essential for families to successfully engage in family time, and caravanning allows for more 'own time' and 'spouse time' for adults, as children have extraordinary opportunities to engage in 'own time'. At a caravan site people share common space for a short period of time, and engage in similar activities. Furthermore, as caravan sites are enacted as safe, they create a temporary community enabling parents to let their children run free. Caravanning is experienced as an antidote to a stressful and highly organized everyday life. The slow-paced, unstructured ecology, paired with the enactments of safety open up for own time for both adults and children. Within the safe boundaries a caravan site provides, there is room and opportunities for children to do things on their own, and engage in free play and independent environmental exploration while the parents relax or spend time as a couple.

The simplicity and safety that prevail at a caravan site may help fulfil a nostalgia for the (imagined) past where one could simply tell the children to go outside and play, providing the outdoor play opportunities the adults reminisce having as children. Thus, the caravan cultures of naturalness, simplicity and freedom extend into wider historical ideologies within tourism and leisure. However, they counterbalance dominant discourses by highlighting these findings within everyday and banal settings. The poly-dimensionality of the caravan holiday lies in the transformative possibilities of the uneventful, everyday practice as 'real, quality family time' is best achieved insofar one 'has not seen the kids for hours' in between the precious moments of thick sociality and family togetherness. This study has touched upon potential different generational perspectives relating to parents' and grandparents' views on the 'good holiday'. Additional contributions are needed to flesh out generational differences further. More research should also further substantiate the complex constructions of mobile communities. Lastly, future research could shed further light on what constitutes the freedom experienced in more mundane contexts.

Note

1. Referring to the on-site paths in between the caravans, tents and RVs.

Notes on contributors

Marie Vestergaard Mikkelsen is a PhD fellow at Aalborg University. She teaches tourism and consumption studies at the Master of Arts level. Her research focuses on consumer studies within the field of tourism with specific emphasis on caravanning.

Bodil Stilling Blichfeldt holds a PhD in marketing and is an Associate Professor at Aalborg University. She teaches tourism, consumption studies and philosophy of science/methodology at the Master of Arts level and has published extensively within tourism and family research in e.g. *Journal of Youth Studies, Journal of Vacation Marketing, Tourist Studies, Current Issues in Tourism, World Leisure Journal, Young Consumers and Higher Education.*

References

Becken, Susanne, and Jude Wilson. 2007. "Trip Planning and Decision Making of Self-Drive Tourists." *Journal of Travel & Tourism Marketing* 20 (3–4): 47–62. doi:10.1300/J073v20n03_04.
Blichfeldt, Bodil S. 2007. "A Nice Vacation: Variations in Experience Aspirations and Travel Careers." *Journal of Vacation Marketing* 13: 149–164. doi:10.1177/1356766707074738.
Blichfeldt, Bodil S., and Marie V. Mikkelsen. 2013. "Vacability and Sociability as Touristic Attraction." *Tourist Studies* 13 (3): 235–250. doi:10.1177/1468797613498160.
Blichfeldt, Bodil S., and Marie Mikkelsen. 2014. "The Extraordinariness of Ordinariness in Tourism Research." *Revista Turismo & Desenvolvimento* 20 (21): 1–22.
Blichfeldt, Bodil S., Bettina M. Pedersen, Anders Johansen, and Line Hansen. 2011. "Tweens on Holidays. In-Situ Decision-making from Children's Perspective." *Scandinavian Journal of Hospitality and Tourism* 11 (2): 135–149. doi:10.1080/15022250.2011.588444.
Carr, Neil. 2011. *Children's and Families' Holiday Experience.* London: Taylor & Francis.
Carver, Alison, Anna Timperio, and David Crawford. 2008. "Playing It Safe: The Influence of Neighbourhood Safety on Children's Physical Activity – A Review." *Health & Place* 14: 217–227. doi:10.1016/j.healthplace.2007.06.004.

Counts, David R., and Dorothy Ayers Counts. 2004. *Over the Next Hill: Ethnography of RVing Seniors in North America*. Peterborough, ON: Broadview Press.

Cullingford, Cedric. 1995. "Children's Attitudes to Holidays Overseas." *Tourism Management* 16 (2): 121–127. doi:10.1016/0261-5177(94)00022-3.

Daly, Kerry J. 2001. " Deconstructing Family Time: From Ideology to Lived Experience." *Journal of Marriage and Family* 63 (2): 283–294. doi:10.1111/j.1741-3737.2001.00283.x.

Daly, Kerry J. 2007. *Qualitative Methods for Family Studies and Human Development*. Thousand Oaks, CA: SAGE.

Den Jyske Historiker [The Jutlandic Historian] 2012. *Fra Frihed til Fritid – Det europæiske fritidsmenneske mellem forbrug og fornøjelse* [From Freedom to Leisure – The European Leisure Individual between Consumption and Pleasure]. Denmark: Aarhus University, 127–128.

Franklin, Adrian. 2003. *Tourism. An Introduction*. London: SAGE.

Gillis, John. 1996. "Making Time for Family: The Invention of Family Time(s) and the Reinvention of Family History." *Journal of Family History* 21 (4): 4–21. doi:10.1177/036319909602100102.

Gram, Malene. 2005. "Family Holidays. A Qualitative Study of Family Holiday Experiences." *Scandinavian Journal of Hospitality and Tourism* 5: 2–22. doi:10.1080/15022250510014255.

Gram, Malene. 2007. "Children as Co-decision Makers in the Family? The Case of Family Holidays." *Young Consumers: Insight and Ideas for Responsible Marketers* 8 (1): 19–28. doi:10.1108/17473610710733749.

Green, F. B. 1978. "Recreation Vehicles. A Perspective." *Annals of Tourism Research* 5 (4): 429–443. doi:10.1016/0160-7383(78)90322-5.

Haldrup, Michael, and Jonas Larsen. 2004. "The Family Gaze." *Tourist Studies* 3: 23–45. doi:10.1177/1468797603040529.

Hardy, Anne, Bill Carter, Bob Beeton, Mark Olsen, and Louise Horneman. 2006. *Users' Motivations, Attitudes and Behaviours in Queensland and Tasmania*. Gold Coast: Sustainable Tourism.

Hilbrecht, Margo, Susan M. Shaw, Fern M. Delamere, and Mark E. Havitz. 2008. "Experiences, Perspectives, and Meanings of Family Vacations for Children." *Leisure/Loisir* 32 (2): 541–571. doi:10.1080/14927713.2008.9651421.

Janiskee, Robert L. 1990. "Resort Camping in America." *Annals of Tourism Research* 17: 385–407. doi:10.1016/0160-7383(90)90005-C.

Jantzen, Christian, Bodil Stilling Blichfeldt, Per Østergaard, and Anna Lund Jepsen. 2007. "I slaraffenland. Oplevelsen af "ingenting" på campingpladsen [In the Land of Milk and Honey. Experiencing "Nothing" at the Caravan Site]." In *Forbrugssituationer. Perspektiver på oplevelsesøkonomi* [Consumption Situations. Perspectives on the Experience Economy], edited by Christian Jantzen and Tove Arendt Rasmussen, 83–120. Aalborg: Aalborg Universitetsforlag.

Jobes, Patrick C. 1984. "Old Timers and New Mobile Lifestyles." *Annals of Tourism Research* 11 (2): 181–198. doi:10.1016/0160-7383(84)90069-0.

Johns, Nick, and Szilvia Gyimóthy. 2002. "Mythologies of a Theme Park: An Icon of Modern Family Life." *Journal of Vacation Marketing* 8 (4): 320–331. doi:10.1177/135676670200800403.

Kelly, John R. 1990. *Leisure*. Englewood Cliffs, NJ: Prentice-Hall.

Laing, Jennifer H., and Geoffrey I. Crouch. 2011. "Frontier Tourism. Retracing Mythic Journeys." *Annals of Tourism Research* 38 (4): 1516–1534. doi:10.1016/j.annals.2011.02.003.

Larsen, Jacob R.Kirkegaard. 2013. "Family Flow: The Pleasures of 'Being Together' in a Holiday Home." *Scandinavian Journal of Hospitality and Tourism*, 13 (3): 153–174. doi:10.1080/15022250.2013.808523.

Larsen, Jonas. 2008. "De-exoticizing Tourist Travel: Everyday Life and Sociality on the Move." *Leisure Studies* 27 (1): 21–34. doi:10.1080/02614360701198030.

Larsen, Jonas, John Urry, and Kay W. Axhausen. 2007. "Networks and Tourism Mobile Social Life." *Annals of Tourism Research* 34 (1): 244–262. doi:10.1016/j.annals.2006.08.002.

Lehto, Xinran Y., Yi-Chin Lin, Yi Chen, and Soojin Choi. 2012. "Family Vacation Activities and Family Cohesion." *Journal of Travel & Tourism Marketing* 29 (8): 835–850. doi:10.1080/10548408.2012.730950.

Löfgren, Orvar. 1999. *On Holiday: A History of Vacationing*. Berkeley: University of California Press.

Matthews, M. H. 1992. *Making Sense of Place. Children's Understanding of Large-Scale Environments*. Hemel Hempstead: Harvester Weatsheaf, Barnes & Noble Books.

Miller, Laura J. 1995. "Family Togetherness and the Suburban Ideal." *Sociological Forum* 10 (3): 393–418. doi:10.1007/BF02095828.

Moore, Robin, and Donald Young. 1978. "Childhood Outdoors: Toward a Social Ecology of the Landscape." In *Children and the Environment. Human Behavior and Environment*, edited by Irwin Altman, Vol. 3. 83–130. New York: Plenum Press.

Nanda, Dipti, Clark Hu, and Billy Bai. 2006. "Exploring Family Roles in Purchasing Decisions during Vacation Planning: Review and Discussions for Future Research." *Journal of Travel and Tourism Marketing* 20 (3/4): 107–125. doi:10.1300/J073v20n03_08.

Nickerson, Norma P., and Claudia Jurowski. 2001. "The Influence of Children on Vacation Travel Patterns." *Journal of Vacation Marketing* 7 (1): 19–30. doi:10.1177/135676670100700102.

Obrador, Pau. 2012. "The Place of the Family in Tourism Research: Domesticity and Thick Sociality by the Pool." *Annals of Tourism Research* 39: 401–420. doi:10.1016/j.annals.2011.07.006.

Qvortrup, Jens. 1987. "Introduction." *International Journal of Sociology* 17 (1): 1–26.

Rojek, Chris. 1995. *Decentring Leisure: Rethinking Leisure Theory*. London: SAGE.

Schänzel, Heike A. 2010. "Whole-family Research: Towards a Methodology in Tourism for Encompassing Generation, Gender, and Group Dynamic Perspectives." *Tourism Analysis* 15 (5): 555–569. doi:10.3727/108354210X12889831783314.

Schänzel, Heike A., and Karen A. Smith. 2014. "The Socialization of Families Away from Home: Group Dynamics and Family Functioning on Holiday." *Leisure Sciences: An Interdisciplinary Journal* 36 (2): 126–143. doi:10.1080/01490400.2013.857624.

Schänzel, Heike A., Ian Yeoman, and Elisa Backer, eds. 2012. *Family Tourism: Multidisciplinary Perspectives*. Bristol: Channel View.

Shaw, Susan M. 2008. "Family Leisure and Changing Ideologies of Parenthood." *Sociology Compass* 2 (2): 688–703. doi:10.1111/j.1751-9020.2007.00076.x.

Small, Jennie. 2008. "The Absence of Childhood in Tourism Studies." *Annals of Tourism Research* 35 (3): 772–789. doi:10.1016/j.annals.2008.06.002.

Snelgrove, Ryan, and Mark E.Havitz. 2010. "Looking Back in Time: The Pitfalls and Potential of Retrospective Methods in Leisure Studies." *Leisure Sciences* 32: 337–351. doi:10.1080/01490400.2010.488199.

Swarbrooke, John, and Susan Horner. 2007. *Consumer Behaviour in Tourism*. 2nd ed. Oxford: Butterworth Heinemann.

Therkelsen, Anette. 2010. "Deciding on Family Holidays—Role Distribution and Strategies in Use." *Journal of Travel & Tourism Marketing* 27 (8): 765–779. doi:10.1080/10548408.2010. 526895.

Therkelsen, Anette, and Malene Gram. 2003. " Børnefamilieferie: en kvalitativ undersøgelse af tyske og danske børnefamiliers idealer for og beslutninger om ferie med særlig fokus på Danmark som ferieland [Families with Children on Holiday: A Qualitative Study of German and Danish Families with Children's Ideals on, and Decisions about Holidays with Special Focus on Denmark as a Holiday Destination]." www.danskturisme.dk/web/alliance. nsf/dok.

Thrift, Nigel. 1997. "The Still Point." In *Geographies of Resistance*, edited by Steve Pile and Michael Keith, 124–151. London: Routledge.

Valentine, Gill. 1997. "'Oh Yes I Can.' 'Oh No You Can't': Children and Parents Understandings of Kids' Competence to Negotiate Public Space Safely." *Antipode* 29 (1): 65–89. doi:10.1111/ 1467-8330.00035.

Valentine, Gill, and John McKendrick. 1997. "Children's Outdoor Play: Exploring Parental Concerns about Children's Safety and the Changing Nature of Childhood." *Geoforum* 28 (2): 219–235. doi:10.1016/S0016-7185(97)00010-9.

Vannini, Phillip, and Jonathan Taggart. 2012. "Doing Islandness: A Non-representational Approach to an Island's Sense of Place." *Cultural Geographies* 20: 225. doi:10.1177/1474474011428098.

Viallon, Philippe. 2012. "Retired Snowbirds." *Annals of Tourism Research* 39 (4): 2073–2091. doi:10.1016/j.annals.2012.06.001.

Waksler, Frances C. 1986. "Studying Children: Phenomenological Insights." *Human Studies* 8: 171–182. doi:10.1007/BF00142910.

Wang,Ning. 2000. *Tourism and Modernity: A Sociological Analysis*. Oxford: Pergamon Press.

West, P. C., and L. C. Merriam. 1970. "Outdoor Recreation and Family Cohesiveness: A Research Approach." *Journal of Leisure Research* 2: 251–257.

Winther, Ida W. 2006. "Kids' Rooms as Plus Territory." *Interaccoes* 2: 9–26. http://www.eses.pt/interaccoes.

Wyness, Michael. 2006. *Childhood and Society: An Introduction to the Sociology of Childhood.* Basingstoke: Palgrave Macmillian.

Zabriskie, R., and B. McCormick. 2001. "The Influences of Family Leisure Patterns on Perceptions of Family Functioning." *Family Relations* 50 (3): 281–289. doi:10.1111/j.1741-3729.2001.00281.x.

A review of gay and lesbian parented families' travel motivations and destination choices: gaps in research and future directions

Rodrigo Lucena, Nigel Jarvis and Clare Weeden

School of Sport and Service Management, University of Brighton, Eastbourne, UK

Academic tourism research is traditionally concerned with individual decisions and fails to address the viewpoint of the family unit. Indeed, while family tourism remains unexplored, lesbian and gay parented family tourism is further overlooked, with little attention in tourism research given to families whose configurations do not fit the heteronormative model, namely the 'mother-father-children' trinomial. This paper critically reviews the literature on the topics that offer insight into same-sex parented family tourism and identifies gaps in knowledge in four different areas: travel motivations, destination choice, family decision-making, and strategies used by lesbians and gay men to manage sexuality in public spaces. The paper ends with recommendations designed to progress theoretical and empirical research.

Introduction

This paper provides a critical review of literature that illuminates holiday motivations and destination choices of same-sex parented families whilst identifying knowledge gaps and potential for future research in the area. For the scope of this paper, same-sex parented families are units formed of at least one child and one gay father or one lesbian mother. A family holiday is construed as encompassing travel made by a family with the purpose of leisure, recreation and/or to visit relatives and friends, as well as the activities performed during the trips and the decisions that precede them.

Although same-sex parented families are not a new phenomenon, increased legal protection has resulted in greater recognition, especially in Western nations. For example, 14 countries worldwide have legalized same-sex marriage and 15 countries globally now accept joint adoption, which allows children of lesbian and gay couples to be registered under both parents' names (ILGA 2014). Like all families, gay and lesbian parented families are leisure consumers and tourists. Lesbian and gay travel is an increasingly important market segment to the tourism and hospitality industries (Hughes and Southall 2012; Blichfeldt, Chor, and Milan 2013). If, as reported by a 40,000 people survey conducted by Out Now (2011), a marketing agency catering for the lesbian, gay, bisexual and transgender (LGBT) market, 40% of lesbians and gays are keen to become parents in the future, then these families may become a significant consumer group for the tourism industry. More importantly, while these groups have gained increased social acceptance in some countries, their voices and experiences need to be listened to not only in the tourism context but also as expressions of a fair and just society.

Nonetheless, academic tourism research on families parented by gay men and lesbians is scarce. Indeed, all types of family tourism remain largely unexplored in research with theory mostly centred on individual decision-making (Carr 2011). An overrepresentation of the individual tourist (Schänzel 2012) fails to address the complexity of family holiday decisions (Decrop 2006), and thus creates a gap in tourism knowledge. In addition, the voices of children are often neglected in family tourism. This is due to numerous factors, such as a lack of researchers' expertise, the ethical issues involving research with children, and a lack of theories and conceptual models that contemplate the children's viewpoints (Poria and Timothy 2014). This indicates more studies are needed that address the complexity of family tourism.

The underrepresentation of the family in tourism research is even more apparent in the case of families who do not fit the 'conventional' heteronormative model, namely the 'mother-father-children' trinomial. Yet, the notion of the 'family' as a social institution constantly evolves, with historic configurations of families no longer considered the norm (Yeoman et al. 2012). While the single parent family has undergone recent recognition as a focus for tourism research (Quinn 2013), 'traditional' nuclear layouts of families remain the benchmark for 'the family' (Hughes and Southall 2012).

Thus, research about families that differ from the heteronormative paradigm is needed, especially with regard to their holiday motivations and decisions, which are central to tourism marketing and management. Against this background, this paper builds on Hughes and Southall's (2012) call for further research on lesbian and gay family tourism and offers several areas of contributions. First, it provides insight into the holiday motivations and decisions of lesbians and gay men, and, thus, calls into question the heteronormativity that prevails in tourism research. Second, it sheds light upon family travel choice, adding to a greater understanding of group decisions in tourism scholarship. Third, it highlights the gaps in knowledge of non-heteronormative families' travel motivations and choices. Finally, this paper illuminates the mechanisms through which lesbians and gay men may navigate their sexuality in public spaces and offers insight into how heteronormativity impacts their leisure choices when part of a family unit.

The paper is structured in three sections. The first part reviews current research into travel motivations while the second investigates holiday destination choice. In both sections, there is a particular focus on the travel decisions of lesbians and gay men, and those of families as a way of investigating potential intersections and gaps. The third section examines the literature on same-sex parented families focusing on how gay men and lesbians manage their sexual identities in heteronormative tourist spaces. The paper ends with recommendations designed to progress theoretical and empirical research.

Travel motivations

Understanding tourist motivations has long been the focus of research (see Crompton 1979; Iso-Ahola 1980; Dann 1981; Gnoth 1997; Gountas and Carey 2000; Li and Cai 2012). Motivation, from the Latin word movere (to move), is what generates action (Dann 1981), or, as Li and Cai (2012) suggest, the underlying force that propels behaviour. Motivations encompass a state of mind and a meaningful action (Dann 1981). However, this does not imply motivations are synonymic with reasons. Reasons are cognitive justifications of motivations (Dann 1981). On the other hand, motivations, although possibly target-oriented, are not always rational. They may be driven by additional factors such as emotions, yet, rationalized through logical articulations of thought. As Decrop (2006) clarifies, holiday decisions are not always based on rational choices; they may also be the product of hedonistic pleasure. Therefore, travel motivations, and not reasons, should ground a study on holiday choices. Furthermore, travel motivations are important for the tourism industry as they can be helpful to differentiate tourism sub-groups (Biran, Poria, and Oren 2011). Weber (1978, 11) described motivations as the 'complex of subjective meaning which seems to the actor himself and to the observer an adequate ground for conduct'. Thus, motivations are inseparable to the meanings people attribute to them, which underpins their subjectivity and fluidity.

Motivations have been the focus of academic inquiry in diverse fields and disciplines. Most theories of motivations explain them as responses to something that is missing (Maddi 1996) or as action-generating forces that are propelled by the projection of a result (Vroom 1964). Tourism research is no different, and travel motivations are traditionally explained through two different perspectives: need- and expectation-based theories.

For need-based theories, motivation is a result of a need, namely a lack that creates an internal conflict which in turn causes an individual to act towards the fulfilment of that absence (Crompton 1979). The intersecting point among need-based theories is the understanding and elaboration of motivations as binary constructs. Crompton's (1979) seminal work, for instance, built upon Dann's (1977) notion of push and pull factors, which relate to the desire to go on holiday and the attraction exerted by destination attributes, respectively (Gountas and Carey 2000). Dann (1981) further expanded the idea of push factors via another binary construct: anomie, namely the lack of meaning in daily life that drives people to escape chaos, and ego-enhancement, the need for prestige and status. From a socio-psychological standpoint, Iso-Ahola (1980) stated motivation involves two forces acting in parallel: escaping, the need to shun the pressures of the world, and seeking, the need to search for rewards, such as knowledge, relaxation or social interaction.

Need-based theories are not without their critics. These theories assume needs are the source of motivations and are, thus, considered insufficient to explain how motivations are converted into action (Gountas and Carey 2000). The main weakness of these theories is their simplistic approach, grounded on dichotomies that ignore the multi-layered, pluralistic and fluid nature of travel motivations. They also lack depth and oversimplify the diversity of human behaviour. For example, they do not offer specific insight into the impact of sexuality on motivations, which, alongside other factors, may be relevant for the understanding of gay and lesbian parented families' travel motivations.

Rather than explaining motivations as the result of a need, expectation-based theories associate them with the production of a desired outcome. For Witt and Wright (1992), motivations are formed as functions of three factors: expectancy, which relates to the anticipation of the outcome, instrumentality, linked with the evaluation of the viability of the outcome, and valence, connected with the value and appeal of an outcome. Gnoth (1997) explained that motivations are created around mental projections of the outcome. On the one hand, expectation-based theories clearly elaborate and reinforce the link between motivations and personality, while, on the other hand, they emphasize the rational aspect of motivations. Because they assume human behaviour as utilitarian, they are deployments of economic theories that adopt a positivistic approach and reduce human action to target-driven processes.

Both need- and expectation-based theories suffer from a similar limitation. They are constructed around individual actions and fail to address group motivations, and families in particular (Obrador 2012). A holistic understanding of gay parented families' travel motivations should, as stated, address the impact of sexuality on travel motivations and the holiday motivations of the family unit. Therefore, the next sections explore the literature on both lesbian and gay, and family travel motivations.

Travel motivations of gay men and lesbians

An important yet scant body of academic literature on lesbian and gay tourism was produced in the late 1990s and 2000s. This mainly addressed the holiday motivations of gay men and lesbians, and compared them to those of heterosexuals. Whilst some academic work suggests gay men's desire to engage in sexual activities may be a motivating factor to go on holiday (Ryan and Hall 2001; López López and Van Broeck 2010), the majority of outcomes pointed to gay men and lesbians being driven by the same aspects as 'straight' people with regard to their travel motivations (see for instance, Clift and Forrest 1999; Pritchard et al. 2000; Hughes 2005).

However, while travel motivations of lesbians and gay men do not largely differ from those of heterosexuals, there is consensus in the doctrine that tourism helps construct and/or reinforce gay and lesbian identity. For example, many gay men and lesbians travel to have their first sexual experience away from their hometown (Hughes 2006). While this may also apply to heterosexuals, Hughes (2006) suggests gays and lesbians are particularly driven to have a first sexual experience in an environment where they are not known, or where they can feel at ease. He implies this is often not the case in their own hometown. If discovering and exploring their sexuality happens when they travel, then travelling and 'coming out of the closet' (accepting and revealing one's own homosexuality) are inextricably linked (Hughes 2006). This is line with Poria and Taylor's (2002) claim that gay and lesbian motivations to be involved in tourism activities are often linked to their coming out process. Therefore, tourism helps construct and reinforce sexual identities. Lesbian and gay identity is also achieved through a search for belonging to a group. In this sense, lesbians and gay men travel to seek spaces where they can feel comfortable among equals, where they can 'learn to be gay' (Cox 2002; Blichfeldt, Chor, and Milan 2013). Consequently, gay and lesbian 'meccas', such as San Francisco and Lesvos, become places of pilgrimage where lesbian and gay identities are learned, constructed and strengthened (Howe 2001), and, thus, remain popular destinations (Gorman-Murray, Waitt, and Gibson 2012).

In addition to a search for homosexual identity, lesbians and gay men are motivated by a need to escape and be themselves (Pritchard et al. 1998; Hughes 2000; Pritchard et al. 2000). This need is not bound with Iso-Ahola's (1980) construct of escaping. Rather, in the context of gay tourism, it refers to a need to avoid the pressures of living in a heteronormative society in which heterosexuality is assumed as the norm (Perlesz et al. 2006). As Waitt and Markwell (2006, 5) remark, travel is a 'mechanism to escape the literal straitjacket of the everyday "closet"'. For Cox (2002), holidays are journeys to the gay self, during which tourists are less interested in gazing at the 'other' than themselves. Hughes (2006, 56) posits that the need to escape heteronormativity depends on the level of 'gayness', namely the extent to which gays and lesbians accept and deal with their own sexuality. Thus, closeted gays are more commonly driven by a need to escape the pressures of the heteronormative world than those who do not conceal, and/or effectively manage their sexuality.

Whether same-sex parented families are, along with other factors, also motivated by a search for gay identity and to escape heteronormativity, and whether sexuality plays a part in their travel motivations are issues worth investigating. It could be, for instance, that for these families, the parents' sexuality (and the meaning and significance they may assign to it) may impact not only on family travel motivations but also the importance ascribed to family holidays themselves. In addition to the motivations that relate to parents' sexuality, these families might be influenced by family dynamics, bonds and structure. To gain greater understanding of why same-sex parented families to go on holidays, it is therefore important to explore family tourism research.

Family travel motivations

As previously indicated, literature on family travel motivation emphasizes more 'conventional' family configurations. As for individuals, a desire to escape the pressures of everyday life and a search for relaxation are common motivations for family holidays (Blichfeldt 2007; Shaw, Havitz, and Delemere 2008). The literature on family travel motivations traditionally revolves around three main themes: togetherness, family bonds and social interaction.

Togetherness is consistently associated with family holidays (Carr 2011; Kluin and Lehto 2012; Schänzel 2012). However, it is important to clarify togetherness is not simply a desire to spend time together but a response to an anxiety which Daly (2004, 9) terms 'time famine'. This refers to a lack of family time in densely structured and busy lifestyles (Southall 2012), which family members are keen to recover when together (Epp, Schau, and Price 2011). It is conjectured that what families perceive and/or define as a need to spend time together could in reality refer to the above-cited desire to escape routine. In other words, what is verbalized as a need for family time could actually be related to a wish to shun the pressures of daily life, both as individuals and as a family unit. Similarly, Carr (2011, 26) argues togetherness can be an expression of guilt by parents who believe they should spend more time with their children, a notion he calls 'good parent'.

Constructing and reinforcing family bonds are also significant drivers for family holidays. In this way, family connections are strengthened by the physical and emotional closeness that families enjoy when away (Shaw, Havitz, and Delemere 2008). This closeness not only reinforces family cohesion but also enhances, and in turn is enhanced by, family adaptability and intra-communication (Olson 2000) thereby strengthening the group structure. Bonding supports family roots and provides a sense of identity (Carr 2011). Memories play a very important part in assuring the maintenance of family bonds (Shaw, Havitz, and Delemere 2008) as they ground a family in its past and preserve its future, thereby perpetuating family history (Epp and Price 2008). The memories holidays create are thus central to bond formation, and protection and maintenance of the family unit.

Whilst families travel to spend time together, they also look for social interaction (Crompton 1979; Kluin and Lehto 2012). This paradox is explained by Bowen and Clarke's (2009, 169) theory of opposing forces, according to which families are preserved by three pairs of forces: 'stability and change, structure and variety, and familiarity and novelty'. If, on the one hand, being together relates to stability, structure and familiarity, on the other hand, interacting with others allows for change, variety and novelty. In this sense, children play a decisive role in facilitating social interactions on holiday (Carr 2006, 2011) and are often the ones who initiate it (Crompton 1979). Likewise, parents encourage children to play with others as a fundamental part of socialization (Rugh 2008).

Family travel motivations are not a homogeneous construct, but composed of many layers, which often eclipse individual needs and desires (Decrop 2006; Kluin and Lehto 2012). For example, parents often perceive holidays as a way of introducing children to physical activities (Carr 2011), education (Rugh 2008; Yeoman et al. 2012) and heritage (Poria, Reichel, and Biran 2006), which might not necessarily be a child's stated need. In this sense, children themselves might be motivations for parents to go on holiday (Carr 2011). Parents may also be more interested in relaxing and enhancing family relationships, while children may be more concerned with having fun and socializing with other children (Schänzel 2012). Children's motivations and needs may also be impacted upon by their age. For instance, younger children look for excitement and demand more energy and time from their parents (Milkie et al. 2004). As they grow, children become more prone to be influenced by advertisements and word of mouth recommendations, which may significantly impact on their motivations (Carr 2011). Adolescents are more vocal about their needs (Carr 2006) and are often more likely to be dissatisfied with family trips as they may find their age-related needs are not adequately met (Schänzel 2012).

Mothers and fathers may also perceive holiday experiences differently and, thus, be motivated by diverse factors. Such (2006) argues that fathers are motivated by the excitement of leisure and recreation with their children. Conversely, mothers may be more interested in less energetic activities (Schänzel 2012) as, due to an ethic of care, they are expected to perform caregiving duties even on holiday (Decrop 2006; Bowen and Clarke 2009; Berdychevsky, Gibson, and Poria 2013). Such (2006, 193–194) posits that fathers' motivations relate to 'being there with' their children whereas mothers' motivations are concerned with 'being there for' them.

As noted previously, research tends to give prominence to the traditional 'mother-father-children' structure. The above-mentioned differences between fathers and mothers' travel motivations are no exception to this rule, with tourism academia focusing on families parented by heterosexuals. To gain a greater understanding of what motivates same-sex parented families to go on holiday, it might be worthwhile to investigate whether there are any significant differences between gay fathers and lesbian mothers in terms of parenthood and the relationship with their children. In this sense, there is an overwhelming gap in research comparing lesbian and gay parenting. Most of the comparative research involving same-sex parented families contrasts them to heterosexual ones (see for instance, Golombok and Tasker 1996; Patterson 2002; Biblarz and Savci 2010). The very scarce scholarship on the theme indicates more similarities than differences between the ways lesbians and gays have and raise their children (Biblarz and Stacey 2010). Yet, lesbian mothers were found to be more prone to have children due to social pressures than gay fathers (Baetens and Brewaeys 2001). Gay fathers are more commonly committed to full-time employment (Biblarz and Stacey 2010), and, thus, spend less time with their children than lesbian mothers. Gay men also challenge gender stereotypes more often than lesbian mothers as they refute preconceived ideas of masculinity more commonly than lesbians dispute femininity (Stacey 2006). Biblarz and Stacey (2010, 17) conclude women are better parents and, thus, families parented by lesbians are more likely to have a 'double dose of caretaking, communication, and intimacy'. How, if at all, these differences inform the choices gay and lesbian parents make when deciding on their holidays should be further scrutinized.

It is therefore not clear how travel motivations are conceptualized within lesbian and gay parented families. For instance, does sexuality impact on their motivations? Are these families, along with other variables, motivated by parents' need to escape heteronorma-tivity and/or desire to seek gay identity? If so, how do these needs intersect with the family's travel motivations? Do the travel motivations of gay fathers differ from those of lesbian mothers? These questions prompt further investigation into same-sex parented families' holiday motivations, and how they link to destination choice. The following section examines the latter in more detail.

Destination choice

Literature on destination choice mostly assumes human behaviour is logical and rational (see Decrop 2006; Moutinho 1987) and is divided between choice-set models and the decision-making process. Choice-set models are grounded in an assumption that people evaluate and eliminate options as they go through the linear stages of decision-making (Um and Crompton 1990). As such they ignore the potential for spontaneity that characterizes decisions, particularly when holiday choices are involved (Smallman and Moore 2010). Holiday decision-making does not necessarily follow a linear approach (Tversky and Kahneman 1986), it may not always be about problem-solving (Blichfeldt 2007) and the process may sometimes involve adding options rather than discarding them (Decrop 2010).

Process-based models focus on the steps of the decision-making process. They either emphasize the chronology of decisions (see Moutinho 1987), the variables that intercede and interfere in the process (see Mayo and Jarvis 1981) or sub-decisions, namely those that follow destination choice, such as the ones that take place during the trip (see Fesenmaier and Jeng 2000). Because these models have been considered too generic, thereby lacking applicability, recent models tend to amalgamate aspects of both choice set and process models. For instance, Lye et al.'s (2005) model acknowledges the interplay between a tourist's values and objectives, and refers to decision waves, thereby highlighting the fluidity of decision-making.

As with motivation studies, decision-making research tends to focus on individual rather than family choice. This ought to be redressed because, Obrador (2012) argues, families are at the core of tourism decision-making. Family choices also involve negotiation and concession (Decrop 2006), which, apart from a few notable exceptions (see for example, Nichols and Snepenger 1988; Bronner and de Hoog 2008) tourism academia has so far failed to grasp. Therefore, to understand same-sex parented families' holiday decisions, a review of the literature on family destination choice is crucial. Moreover, because these families may also have their choices shaped or impacted upon by the parents' sexuality, an overview of gay and lesbian destination choice is equally important.

Destination choice of lesbians and gay men

Destination choice stems first and foremost from travel motivations (Moscardo et al. 1996). As is the case of travel motivations, the holiday destination choices of gay men and lesbians may thus be influenced by a need to escape heteronormativity and be themselves (Scholey 2002). Consequently, they may choose destinations perceived as gay-friendly or gay-centred (Hughes 2006). However, destination avoidance also plays a fundamental part in the holiday decision of gay men and lesbians (Hughes 2002). Destination avoidance is traditionally associated with travel constraints and perceived risk. The former refers to factors that restrict destination choice or cause holidays to be cancelled (McGuiggan 2001). Hughes (2002) and Want (2002) report gay men's travel choices are constrained by the presence of other tourists, with single gay men avoiding destinations and accommodation perceived as child-friendly. Clift and Forrest (1999) suggest these people feel uncomfortable interacting with straight-parented families. If gay men avoid child-friendly destinations when single, then it is important to explore whether their destination choices, as well as those of lesbians, are affected when they go on holiday as part of a family unit.

Destination avoidance also relates to perceived risk, or tourists' perception of the likelihood of loss or peril (Bowen and Clarke 2009). Risks may limit holiday choice if they are considered to threaten personal safety (Sönmez and Graefe 1998). As Brunt, Mawby, and Hambly (2000) put it, a destination is not chosen for being safe but avoided for being unsafe. In his work on LGBT tourism, Hughes (2002, 2006) concluded gay men and lesbians choose the least risky destination. During the decision-making process, places perceived as homophobic (hostile or unfriendly to gay men and lesbians) may be systematically ruled out (Rapp 2010). These risks may affect not only the destination choices of gay men and lesbians but also their behaviour while on holiday, impacting on their feeling of safety and impairing social interaction with locals and other tourists (Poria 2006a). They can also cause anxiety if forced to come out to strangers. In tourism, this may include 'check in phobia', namely the lesbian or gay couple's anxiety for having to ask for a double bed in a hotel when registering on arrival (Hughes 2006, 81).

Travel-related risks need not be real. Rather, it is the perception of risk that actually impacts on destination avoidance (Roehl and Fesenmaier 1992; Sönmez and Graefe 1998; Hughes 2002; Kozak, Crotts, and Law 2007). As subjective constructs, perceived risks may be influenced by gender. Scholarly findings indicate women perceive themselves as more prone to risk than men (Lepp and Gibson 2003; Kozak, Crotts, and Law 2007). Therefore, safety is a more important concern for women than it is for men when choosing their holiday destinations (Brownell and Walsh 2008). This can impact not only on their holiday decisions but also on their planning and organization of tourist activities (Wilson and Little 2008). Such findings are echoed in literature about lesbian and gay leisure choices, with Skeggs (1999) affirming lesbians feel more vulnerable than gay men even when going to gay-friendly destinations since the gay space is predominantly masculine. Conversely, gay men were specifically found to feel unsafe in the presence of other people's children (Poria 2006a). Thus, investigating whether men and women (and gays and lesbians) have diverse risk perceptions and how, if at all, this impacts on their travel choices is an important question that might yield valuable information about same-sex parented families' holiday decisions.

Family decision-making and destination choice

Tourism research into family decision-making has tended to focus on marketing to a single decision-maker (see for instance, Kang and Hsu 2004; Kozak 2010). However, holiday decisions are jointly made by partners in a couple (Jenkins 1980; Kang and Hsu 2004; Kozak 2010). The term 'joint decision', nevertheless, is vague as it can refer to partners participating in decision-making together, or feeling they have an equal, hence, balanced, say in the final decision. Further, joint decisions may be perceived differently by each partner; for instance, one may believe the couple have similar decision powers, while acquiescing to the other's will (Pahl 1990).

Moreover, tourism marketing is mostly targeted at adults (Carr 2006). Nevertheless, understanding whether and how children influence family decisions with respect to travel destination choices could be of value to tourism scholars but also, and especially, to marketers and practitioners. Scholarly findings concerning children's influence in family decision-making in tourism have varied considerably. Earlier studies concluded children have little impact on the process (see for instance, Jenkins 1979; Fodness 1992). More current research, on the other hand, perceives children as more influential in the choice of not only the family's travel destination but also other decisions such as the choice of accommodation and holiday activities (Kang and Hsu 2004; Decrop 2006; Thomson, Laing, and McKee 2007). In this sense, Decrop (2006) clarifies children may not have decision-making powers but they clearly affect parental choice. The mechanisms through which children's influence takes place may range from information search to formation of coalitions with other family members (Thomson, Laing, and McKee 2007). For Carr (2011), rather than discussing whether the children's influence exists or not, theorists would better understand how it changes as they grow. Following this line of reasoning, Schänzel, Yeoman, and Backer (2012) call for a methodological approach that is not limited to the parents' stance and also encompasses the viewpoint of children.

Studies of family decision-making suffer from another significant flaw; they discuss the family from a heteronormative standpoint. Many use terms such as 'husbands', 'wives' or 'spouses' (Bohlmann and Qualls 2001; Kang and Hsu 2005; Kozak 2010), which, in view of the changes the family as an institution has undergone, may be inadequate, especially when same-sex parented families are concerned. Further, this approach, which often equates husbands with key income earners and wives with caregivers, is premised on stereotypical and increasingly obsolete gender roles, which may not be applicable or may manifest differently in lesbian and gay parented families (Clarke and Peel 2007).

Part of the literature on family holiday choices views decision-making using family life stages, a construct found in Wells and Gubar's (1966) oft-cited work. These are defined as key junctures in a family's history, such as the birth of children, the empty nest, or the death of a partner. Family lifecycle theory assumes families at the same stage in their history adopt similar lifestyles and consumption practices. While Wells and Gubar's (1966) taxonomy may have been relevant when first devised, it does not capture the diversity of modern day family structures (Bojanic 2011). For instance, a family with a child raised by two same-sex couples (in other words, four parents) may not have been contemplated by Wells and Gubar (1966), and thus family lifecycles as a framework to understand gay parented families should be viewed with much caution.

Power relations are also significant in research on family decision-making. Decrop (2006) argues that families whose power is centralized with the parents are less likely to involve all members in holiday decisions. Bowen and Clarke (2009) classify families as socio- and concept-oriented. In the former, children learn to respect (and not challenge) parental authority; in the latter, children are encouraged to participate actively in holiday decision-making. Scholarship on same-sex parented families claims they exhibit a more balanced distribution of power and are egalitarian in terms of task division than those parented by heterosexuals (Patterson 2002; Biblarz and Savci 2010). To what extent this is accurate and whether this alleged power balance within same-sex parented families affects their holiday decisions merits scrutiny.

Family destination choices have also been examined through the lens of destination avoidance, which, as previously stated, is bound up with travel constraints and perceived risk. McGuiggan (2001) claims children can be a travel constraint since their presence may cause holiday plans to be modified or cancelled, a view endorsed by Decrop (2006). In addition, families with children have fewer destination choice options and have holiday times restricted or altered to reflect the school calendar (Page and Connell 2009). The holiday choices of a family are also affected by their perception of risk. In this sense, if a child's safety becomes the main concern for a family on holiday, it thus limits destination choice (Roehl and Fesenmaier 1992; Simpson and Siguaw 2008). This may be particularly relevant for same-sex parented families since their destination choices might be restricted by a potential fear of discrimination and/or an anxiety to protect their children. Therefore, the destination choice of lesbian and gay parented families is likely influenced both by the parents' sexuality and the presence of children. However, it is still not clear whether, or how, these factors intersect. For instance, are these aspects conflated and, as a consequence, family choices narrowed? These questions are important not only because they may shape holiday decisions but also because they influence the travel patterns of families, in particular how parents negotiate their sexuality and/or the presence of children on holiday.

Gay parented families' mechanisms to manage sexuality in public spaces

If, as Gabb (2005, 426) states, 'individuals' conformity is established through the marginalization of all "other-ness"', then, in order to feel like they are part of a group, individuals may discriminate against those perceived as different. If heterosexuality is considered the norm, then 'abnormal' sexualities are marginalized (Nathanson 2007). Indeed, homophobia, 'the fear and loathing of those identifying as lesbian, gay, or bisexual accompanied by feelings of anxiety, disgust, aversion, anger and hostility' (Perlesz et al. 2006, 183) is a type of discrimination that affects the lives of many gay men and lesbians. Some may develop feelings of internalized homonegativity, namely the perception and acceptance that being gay is negative (Reilly and Rudd 2006), or shame, which encapsulates a range of emotions such as humiliation, inferiority (Greene and Britton 2013) or even self-hatred (Irvine 2009).

In addition to challenges encountered by all families, lesbian and gay parents may be affected by discrimination and/or the fear of discrimination, which may also have an impact on their children. Research shows children raised by lesbian mothers or gay fathers bear more similarities than differences to those brought up by heterosexuals (Golombok and Tasker 1996; Golombok and Badger 2010). However, children of same-sex couples were found to be more prone to bullying in school (Ray and Gregory 2001; Stacey and Biblarz 2001), emotional stress due to discrimination (Lambert 2005) and homophobia in general (Ryan and Berkowitz 2009).

The public arena may magnify feelings of marginalization. However, it is true that gays and lesbians may find support in particular environments. Poria (2006b), for instance, found in his research with Israeli lesbians that the tourist space may be reassuring for them since it is often equated with anonymity. Nonetheless, gay spaces, whether at home, or in bars away from the heterosexual gaze, are more commonly private (Gabb 2005). Everyday public spaces, such as workplaces or supermarkets, are predominantly heteronormative (Valentine 1996; Skeggs 1999; Waitt, Markwell, and Gorman-Murray 2008). Many lesbians and gay men experience insecurity in the public sphere (Skeggs 1999; Pritchard et al. 2000), which can inhibit their consumption practices, such as hotel experiences, for instance (Poria 2006a). It can also limit public displays of affection with partners (Valentine 1996), with some attempting to 'pass as straight' to lessen their alternative sexuality (Woodruffe-Burton and Bairstow 2013). Negotiating sexuality in the public arena may be even more complex for gay and lesbian parents. While parents may find it easier to 'blend' in the social arena as their offspring facilitates the 'straight look', the presence of children may increase parental anxiety because it 'affects how parents manage their sexual-parental identity and the ways that families are (re)presented in public/private space' (Gabb 2005, 420). For instance, children may unwittingly disclose their parents' sexuality or simply enhance their visibility thus adding to feelings of insecurity (Gianino 2008). Lesbian and gay couples' public anxiety may be further complicated as parents may have to navigate their sexuality differently depending on the ages of the children. For example, the elder children may be aware of the parents' sexual orientation whereas younger ones may not (Demo and Allen 1996).

If most everyday public spaces are dominated by heteronormative presumptions, tourism and leisure spaces are no different. Rather than simply being physical locales, tourism spaces are social constructions where identities are negotiated (Pritchard et al. 2000), and most holiday sites are characterized by a fluidity of the separation between the public and private arenas (Perlesz et al. 2006). Tourists share common areas, like swimming pools and beaches, for considerable amounts of time, causing spatial and social boundaries to blur. This, it is conjectured, may enhance same-sex parented families' visibility. As a result, interacting with straight parented families may be daunting, but could also present empowerment opportunities. As previously reported, social interaction is a key travel motivation for families (Crompton 1979; Kluin and Lehto 2012), but fear of discrimination can generate insecurity and/or shame for lesbians and gay men in social situations.

Given this apparent tension between the need for social interaction and the anxiety it may generate, further questions emerge: how do lesbian and gay parented families navigate their sexuality while on holiday? Is social interaction impaired by the insecurities caused by heteronormative holiday spaces? Or do holidays enable same-sex parented families to openly express pride in their sexuality? Is this pride affected by or does it conflate with other types of pride, such as that of the family as a unit?

Conclusions for future research on same-sex parented family holiday choices

As indicated, tourism studies have predominantly focused on individual decision-making, which has failed to address the group perspective, in particular that of the family unit. Moreover, the scant literature on family tourism has emphasized a heteronormative model, mostly composed of mother, father and children, with stereotypical gender roles. As a consequence, families parented by gay men and lesbians have been largely neglected by tourism research, particularly with regard to their travel motivations and destination choices. Through a critical review of the literature, this paper has identified several knowledge gaps, which open avenues for further research. Such gaps are now discussed under the following four areas: travel motivations, destination choices, family decision-making, and strategies for managing sexuality in public spaces.

Travel motivations are fluid concepts that cannot be entirely encapsulated by rational paradigms; they may be impacted by subjective factors, which include sexuality. Thus, it is worth researching whether, and how, parents' sexuality affects the travel motivations of same-sex parented families. Some gay and lesbian parents might for instance prioritize their own travel needs to the detriment of the family, whereas others consider their own desires less important. Understanding how individual travel motivations impact upon the family unit should also be scrutinized further, because (lesbian) mothers and (gay) fathers may be motivated by diverse aspects. Furthermore, children of lesbian or gay parents may, in addition to other factors, be motivated by a need to escape the heteronormative world as they may themselves be victims of homophobia. Finally, family holidays may add to the children's life quality as they may enhance both family and child identity as well as reinforce and preserve parent-child relationship, thereby helping forge a defence mechanism against discrimination. Whether and how all of this comes into play on the motivations of the family to go on holiday is worth being investigated.

Likewise, destination choices of lesbian and gay parented families might be swayed by parents' sexuality. The literature notes that childless gay men avoid family-friendly destinations, and that many lesbians and gay men visit gay-centric places such as Lesvos and Gran Canaria. However, when later travelling as part of a family unit, to what extent does their previous travel experience impact their current and future holiday choices? Research also indicates lesbians and gays avoid homophobic destinations. Likewise, holiday choice may be restricted because parents seek to protect children from less gay-friendly destinations. How the risks associated with the parents' sexuality impact on the children, and whether these affect holiday choices is therefore worthy of scrutiny. Finally, scholars have suggested children can act as travel constraints. Research should be conducted to explore the veracity of this claim, because children can also act as the driving force for holidays rather than a restriction.

Additionally, destination choice models have so far failed to grasp the complexities of family decisions. Similarly, the traditional framework of the family lifecycle model is unable to effectively address same-sex parented families. As such, new conceptualisations of gay parented families' holiday decision-making are required. Holiday-related decisions often demand negotiation. In this sense, the literature reports lesbian and gay parented families are characterized by equality in power distribution, which might suggest children are vocal about their needs and wants. Investigating whether this holds true and how this impacts on family holiday choices is another topic that deserves further academic attention. Moreover, children's participation in decision-making processes would be better understood if their perspectives were taken into consideration, especially in view of the fact that their influence may vary with age. Thus, research into the children's viewpoint is warranted.

Heteronormativity is prevalent in most public spaces, which may generate tension for gay men and lesbians. Children may heighten gay parents' visibility and inadvertently disclose their sexuality on holiday. More scholarly attention should thus be given to whether and how the presence of children affects the ways parents navigate their sexuality in everyday public spaces. For example, for some parents, their children can reinforce insecurity and apprehensiveness, and even amplify feelings of shame. On the other hand, lesbian and gay parents may be reassured by a belief they mirror heteronormative paradigms of family and therefore 'blend in' more easily at a travel destination. Further complexities stem from the fluid disjuncture between public and private holiday spheres, and so an investigation into the mechanisms they adopt to navigate their sexuality on holiday should be explored in more depth. Furthermore, social interaction is an important tourism driver for families. Whether heteronormative holiday spaces affect their interaction with others also merits investigation as these may influence decisions on destination and accommodation choices as well as travel companions.

Finally, tourism research in general, and theory on travel motivations and destination choices in particular, have been traditionally driven by quantitative approaches, which emphasized the importance of generalizability. However, due to the ethical sensitivity of researching families and their children, quantitative research methods are inadequate in seeking insightful understanding of how parents and children negotiate their holiday decisions. Therefore qualitative methods such as in-depth interviews or travel diaries of families are recommended. Such approaches will not only yield rich data on how sexuality intersects with destination choice and motivations, but also enable deep exploration of the power dynamics operating within and among same-sex parented families. Moreover, qualitative research approaches are better at uncovering the nuances associated with managing sexuality in heteronormative holiday spaces.

In conclusion, this paper reveals the need for further empirical research on same-sex parented family tourism. Such proposed research will fill the gaps in academic knowledge about family travel and gay and lesbian tourism. For instance, it offers contributions about family and children's travel motivations, their holiday experiences, and the role of sexuality in holiday decisions and the host-guest encounter. As it addresses themes such as public spaces and family decision-making, it also has implications for other spheres of academia, such as geography and psychology. Further research will also provide invaluable opportunities for the tourism and hospitality industries to develop new products and refine services and operations to better cater for same-sex parented families. Finally, this research could have very relevant social implications. In adding to an understanding of and giving a voice to lesbian and gay parented families, such research would stretch the limited parameters that currently define the family. It is argued here that amplifying the definition of the family may widen societal perceptions of and attitudes towards lesbian and gay parented families. This may in turn lead to a reduction in their marginalization thereby contributing to wider social justice and equality.

Disclosure statement

No potential conflict of interest was reported by the authors.

Notes on contributors

Rodrigo Lucena is a Ph.D. candidate and part time lecturer at the University of Brighton. He has an M.Sc. in International Hospitality Management from the Manchester Metropolitan University. His research interests include family tourism, gender and sexuality, lesbian and gay parented families and also qualitative research methods, phenomenology, hospitality operations, revenue management and service quality.

Dr Nigel Jarvis is a Senior Lecturer at the University of Brighton, where he completed his Ph.D. on the meaning of sport in the lives of Canadian and British men. Nigel has a keen interest in gender and sexuality issues in leisure and tourism. Further research and teaching interests relate to sport tourism, sport and event sponsorship, the economic, sociocultural and environmental impacts of tourism, attractions management, the politics associated with tourism planning, leisure management and research methods.

Dr Clare Weeden is a Senior Lecturer in tourism and marketing at the University of Brighton, where she has been working since 1992. Clare was awarded her Ph.D. in 2008 from the University of Glasgow, where she explored the influence of personal values on the holiday choice decisions of ethical consumers. This research built on her earlier work and publications, which focused on the emergence of ethical tourism, the motivations of responsible tourists and the competitive opportunities of ethical tourism for UK specialist tour operators.

References

Baetens, Patricia, and Anne Brewaeys. 2001. "Lesbian Couples Requesting Donor Insemination: An Update of the Knowledge with Regard to Lesbian Mother Families." *Human Reproduction Update* 7 (5): 512–519. doi:10.1093/humupd/7.5.512.

Berdychevsky, Liza, Heather Gibson, and Yaniv Poria. 2013. "Women's Sexual Behaviour in Tourism: Loosening the Bridle." *Annals of Tourism Research* 42: 65–85. doi:10.1016/j.annals.2013.01.006.

Biblarz, Tymothy J., and Evren Savci. 2010. "Lesbian, Gay, Bisexual and Transgender Families." *Journal of Marriage and Family* 72 (3): 480–497. doi:10.1111/j.1741-3737.2010.00714.x.

Biblarz, Tymothy J., and Judith Stacey. 2010. "How Does the Gender of Parents Matter?" *Journal of Marriage and Family* 72 (1): 3–22. doi:10.1111/j.1741-3737.2009.00678.x.

Biran, Avital, Yaniv Poria, and Gila Oren. 2011. "Sought Experiences at (Dark) Heritage Sites." *Annals of Tourism Research* 38 (3): 820–841. doi:10.1016/j.annals.2010.12.001.

Blichfeldt, Bodil Stilling. 2007. "The Habit of Holidays." *Tourist Studies* 7 (3): 249–269. doi:10.1177/1468797608092512.

Blichfeldt, Bodil Stilling, Jane Chor, and Nina Ballegaard Milan. 2013. "Zoos, Sanctuaries and Turfs: Enactments and Uses of Gay Spaces during the Holidays." *International Journal of Tourism Research* 15 (5): 473–483. doi:10.1002/jtr.1890.

Bohlmann, Jonathan, and William J. Qualls. 2001. "Household Preference Revisions in Decision-making: The Role of Disconfirmation." *International Journal of Research in Marketing* 18 (4): 319–339. doi:10.1016/S0167-8116(01)00043-X.

Bojanic, David C. 2011. "The Impact of Age and Family Life Experiences on Mexican Visitor Shopping Expenditures." *Tourism Management* 32 (2): 406–414. doi:10.1016/j.tourman.2010.03.012.

Bowen, David, and Jackie Clarke. 2009. *Contemporary Tourist Behaviour: Yourself and Others as Tourists*. Wallingford, CT: CABI.

Bronner, Fred, and Robert de Hoog. 2008. "Agreement and Disagreement in Family Decision-Making." *Tourism Management* 29 (5): 967–979. doi:10.1016/j.tourman.2007.12.001.

Brownell, Judi, and Kate Walsh. 2008. "Women in Hospitality." In *The SAGE Handbook of Hospitality Management*, edited by Bob Brotherton and Roy C. Wood, 107–128. London: Sage.

Brunt, Paul, Rob Mawby, and Zoe Hambly. 2000. "Tourist Victimisation and the Fear of Crime on Holiday." *Tourism Management* 21 (4): 417–424. doi:10.1016/S0261-5177(99)00084-9.

Carr, Neil. 2006. "A Comparison of Parents and Adolescents' Holiday Motivations and Desires." *Tourism and Hospitality Research* 6 (2): 129–142. doi:10.1057/palgrave.thr.6040051.

Carr, Neil. 2011. *Children and Families' Holiday Experiences*. Oxon: Routledge.

Clarke, Victoria, and Elizabeth Peel. 2007. "From Lesbian and Gay Psychology to LGBTQ Psychologies: A Journey into the Unknown (or Unknowable?)." In *Out in Psychology: Lesbian, Gay, Bisexual, Trans and Queer Perspectives*, edited by Victoria Clarke and Elizabeth Peel, 11–27. Chichester: John Willey.

Clift, Stephen, and Simon Forrest. 1999. "Gay Men and Tourism: Destinations and Holiday Motivations." *Tourism Management* 20 (5): 615–625. doi:10.1016/S0261-5177(99)00032-1.

Cox, Martin. 2002. "The Long-haul of the Closet: The Journey from Smalltown to Boystown." In *Gay Tourism: Culture, Identity and Sex*, edited by Stephen Clift, Michael Luongo, and Carrie Callister, 151–173. New York: Continuum.

Crompton, John. 1979. "Motivations for Pleasure Vacation." *Annals of Tourism Research* 6 (4): 408–424. doi:10.1016/0160-7383(79)90004-5.

Daly, Kerry. 2004. *The Changing Culture of Parenting*. Ottawa, ON: Vanier Institute of the Family.

Dann, Graham. 1977. "Anomie, Ego-enhancement and Tourism." *Annals of Tourism Research* 4 (4): 184–194. doi:10.1016/0160-7383(77)90037-8.

Dann, Graham. 1981. "Tourism Motivation: An Appraisal." *Annals of Tourism Research* 8 (2): 187–219. doi:10.1016/0160-7383(81)90082-7.

Decrop, Alain. 2006. *Vacation Decision Making*. Wallingford: CABI.

Decrop, Alain. 2010. "Destination Choice Sets: An Inductive Longitudinal Approach." *Annals of Tourism Research* 37 (1): 93–115. doi:10.1016/j.annals.2009.08.002.

Demo, David H., and Katherine R Allen. 1996. "Diversity within Lesbian and Gay Families: Challenges and Implications for Family Theory and Research." *Journal of Social and Personal Relationships* 13 (3): 415–434. doi:10.1177/0265407596133007.

Epp, Amber, and Linda Price. 2008. "Family Identity: A Framework of Identity Interplay in Consumption Practices." *Journal of Consumer Research* 35 (1): 50–70. doi:10.1086/529535.

Epp, Amber, Hope Jensen Schau, and Linda Price. 2011. "Connected Families: How Consumption Practices Survive Distance." *Marketing Science Institute Paper Series*. Report No. 11–119.

119

Fesenmaier, Daniel, and Jiann Min Jeng. 2000. "Assessing Structure in the Pleasure Trip Planning Process." *Tourism Analysis* 5 (1): 13–27.

Fodness, Dale. 1992. "The Impact of Family Life Cycle on the Vacation Decision-making Process." *Journal of Travel Research* 31 (2): 8–13. doi:10.1177/004728759203100202.

Gabb, Jacqui. 2005. "Locating Lesbian Parent Families: Everyday Negotiations of Lesbian Motherhood in Britain." *Gender, Place and Culture* 12 (4): 419–432. doi:10.1080/09663690 500356768.

Gianino, Mark S. 2008. "Adaptation and Transformation: The Transition to Adoptive Parenthood for Gay Male Couples." *Journal of GLBT Family Studies* 4 (2): 205–243. doi:10.1080/15504 280802096872.

Gnoth, Juergen. 1997. "Tourism Motivation and Expectation Formation." *Annals of Tourism Research* 24 (2): 283–304. doi:10.1016/S0160-7383(97)80002-3.

Golombok, Susan, and Sharlene Badger. 2010. "Children Raised in Mother-parented Families from Infancy: A follow-up of Children of Lesbian and Single Heterosexual Mothers, at Early Adulthood." *Human Reproduction* 25 (1): 150–157. doi:10.1093/humrep/dep345.

Golombok, Susan, and Fiona Tasker. 1996. "Do Parents Influence the Sexual Orientation of their Children? Findings from a Longitudinal Study of Lesbian Families." *Developmental Psychology* 32 (1): 3–11. doi:10.1037/0012-1649.32.1.3.

Gorman-Murray, Andrew, Gordon Waitt, and Chris Gibson. 2012. "Chilling Out in 'Cosmopolitan Country': Urban/Rural Hybridity and the Construction of Daylesford as a 'Lesbian and Gay Rural Idyll'." *Journal of Rural Studies* 28 (1): 69–79. doi:10.1016/j.jrurstud.2011.07.001.

Gountas, John, and Sandra Carey. 2000. "Tourism Satisfaction and Service Evaluation." In *Motivations, Behaviour and Tourist Types: Reflections on International Tourism*, edited by Mike Robinson, Philip Long, Nigel Evans, Richard Sharpley, and John Swarbrooke, 55–70. Sunderland: Centre for Travel and Tourism and Business Education.

Greene, Darrell C., and Paula J. Britton. 2013. "The Influence of Forgiveness on Lesbian, Gay, Bisexual, Transgender, and Questioning Individuals' Shame and Self-esteem." *Journal of Counselling and Development* 91 (2): 195–205. doi:10.1002/j.1556-6676.2013.00086.x.

Howe, Alyssa Cymene. 2001. "Queer Pilgrimage: The San Francisco Homeland and Identity Tourism." *Cultural Anthropology* 16 (1): 35–61. doi:10.1525/can.2001.16.1.35.

Hughes, Howard. 2000. "Holidays and Homosexuals: A Constrained Choice?" In *Motivations, Behaviour and Tourist Types: Reflections on International Tourism*, edited by Mike Robinson, Philip Long, Nigel Evans, Richard Sharpley, and John Swarbrooke, 221–230. Sunderland: Centre for Travel and Tourism and Business Education.

Hughes, Howard. 2002. "Gay Men's Holiday Destination Choice: A Case of Risk and Avoidance." *International Journal of Tourism Research* 4 (4): 299–312. doi:10.1002/jtr.382.

Hughes, Howard. 2005. "A Gay Tourism Market: Reality or Illusion, Benefit or Burden?" *Journal of Quality Assurance in Hospitality & Tourism* 5 (24): 57–74. doi:10.1300/J162v05n02_04.

Hughes, Howard. 2006. *Pink Tourism: Holidays of Gay Men and Lesbians*. Wallingford: CABI.

Hughes, Howard, and Carol Southall. 2012. "Gay and Lesbian Families and Tourism." In *Family Tourism: Multidisciplinary Perspectives*, edited by Heike Schänzel, Ian Yeoman, and Elisa Backer, 125–142. Bristol: Channel View.

International Lesbian Gay Bisexual Trans and Intersex Association (ILGA). 2014. "*State-sponsored Homophobia: A World Survey of Laws, Criminalisation, Protection and Recognition of Same-sex Love*." http://ilga.org/ilga/en/article/1161.

Irvine, Janice M. 2009. "Shame Comes Out of the Closet." *Sexuality Research and Social Policy* 6 (1): 70–79. doi:10.1525/srsp.2009.6.1.70.

Iso-Ahola, Seppo. 1980. *The Social Psychology of Leisure and Recreation*. Dubuque, IA: W C Brown.

Jenkins, Roger L. 1979. "The Influence of Children in Family Decision-making." *Advances in Consumer Research* 6: 413–118.

Jenkins, Roger L. 1980. "Contributions of Theory to the Study of Family Decision-making." *Advances in Consumer Research* 7: 207–211.

Kang, Soo K., and Cathy H. C. Hsu. 2004. "Spousal Conflict Level and Resolution in Family Vacation Destination Selection." *Journal of Hospitality and Tourism Research* 28 (4): 408–424. doi:10.1177/1096348004265281.

Kang, Soo K., and Cathy H. C. Hsu. 2005. "Dyadic Consensus on Family Destination Selection." *Tourism Management* 26 (4): 571–582. doi:10.1016/j.tourman.2004.01.002.

Kluin, Juyeon, and Xinran Lehto. 2012. "Measuring Family Reunion Travel Motivations." *Annals of Tourism Research* 39 (2): 820–841. doi:10.1016/j.annals.2011.09.008.

Kozak, Metin. 2010. "Holiday Taking Decisions: The Role of Spouse." *Tourism Management* 31 (4): 489–494. doi:10.1016/j.tourman.2010.01.014.

Kozak, Metin, John C. Crotts, and Rob Law, R. 2007. "The Impact of the Perception of Risk on International Travellers." *International Journal of Tourism Research* 9 (4): 233–242. doi:10.1002/jtr.607.

Lambert, Serena. 2005. "Gay and Lesbian Families: What We Know and Where to Go from Here." *Family Journal* 13 (1): 43–51. doi:10.1177/1066480704270150.

Lepp, Andrew, and Heather Gibson. 2003. "Tourist Roles, Perceived Risk and International Tourism." *Annals of Tourism Research* 30 (3): 606–624. doi:10.1016/S0160-7383(03)00024-0.

Li, Mimi, and Lipping Cai. 2012. "The Effects of Personal Values on Travel Motivation and Behavioral Intention." *Journal of Travel Research* 51 (4): 473–487. doi:10.1177/0047287511418366.

López López, Álvaro, and Anne Marie Van Broeck. 2010. "Sexual Encounters between Men in a Tourist Environment: A Comparative Study in Seven Mexican Localities." In *Sex and the Sexual during People's Leisure and Tourism Experiences*, edited by Neil Carr and Yaniv Poria, 119–142. Newcastle: Cambridge Scholars.

Lye, Ashley, Wei Shao, Sharyn Rundle-Thiele, and Carolyn Fausnaugh. 2005. "Decision Waves: Consumers' Decisions in Today's Complex World." *European Journal of Marketing* 39 (1/2): 216–230. doi:10.1108/03090560510572098.

Maddi, Salvatore R. 1996. *Personality Theories: A Comparative Analysis.* Pacific Groves, CA: Brooks Cole.

Mayo, Edward, and Lance Jarvis. 1981. *The Psychology of Leisure Travel.* Boston, MA: CABI.

McGuiggan, Robyn. 2001. "Which Determines our Leisure Preferences: Demographics or Personality?" In *Consumer Psychology of Tourism, Hospitality and Leisure.* Vol. 2, edited by Josef Mazanec, Geoffrey Crouch, Brent Ritchie, and Arch Woodside, 195–214. Oxon: CABI.

Milkie, Melissa A., Marybeth J. Mattingly, Kei N. Nomaguchi, Suzanne M. Bianchi, and John P. Robinson. 2004. "The Time Squeeze: Parental Statuses and Feelings about Time with Children." *Journal of Marriage and Family* 66 (3): 739–761. doi:10.1111/j.0022-2445.2004.00050.x.

Moscardo, Gianna, Alastair M. Morrison, Philip L. Pearce, Cheng-Te Lang, and Joseph T. O'Leary. 1996. "Understanding Vacation Destination Choice through Travel Motivation and Activity." *Journal of Vacation Marketing* 2 (2): 109–122. doi:10.1177/135676679600200202.

Moutinho, Luiz. 1987. "Consumer Behaviour in Tourism." *European Journal of Marketing* 21 (10): 5–44. doi:10.1108/EUM0000000004718.

Nathanson, Donald L. 2007. "Foreword." In *Queer Attachments: The Cultural Politics of Shame*, edited by Sally R. Munt, xiii–xiv. Aldershot: Ashgate.

Nichols, Catherine M., and David J. Snepenger. 1988. "Family Decision Making and Tourism Behaviour and Attitudes." *Journal of Travel Research* 26 (4): 2–6. doi:10.1177/004728758802600401.

Obrador, Pau. 2012. "The Place of the Family in Tourism Research: Domesticity and Thick Sociality by the Pool." *Annals of Tourism Research* 39 (1): 401–420. doi:10.1016/j.annals.2011.07.006

Olson, David. 2000. "Circumplex Model of Marital and Family Systems." *Journal of Family Therapy* 22 (2): 144–167. doi:10.1111/1467-6427.00144.

Out Now. 2011. *"The Out Now Global LGBT 2020 Study."* http://www.outnowconsulting.com/latest-updates/lgbt2020-study.aspx.

Page, Stephen J., and Joanne Connell. 2009. *Tourism: A Modern Synthesis.* 3rd ed. Andover, MA: Cengage Learning EMEA.

Pahl, Jan. 1990. "Household Personal Spending, Personal Spending and the Control of Money in Marriage." *Sociology* 24 (1): 119–138. doi:10.1177/0038038590024001009.

Patterson, Catherine J. 2002. "Lesbian and Gay Parenthood." In *Handbook of Parenting.* Vol. 3: *Being and Becoming a Parent*, edited by Marc H. Bornstein, 317–338. New Jersey, NJ: Lawrence Erlbaum Associates.

Perlesz, Amaryll, Rhonda Brown, J. O. Lindsay, Ruth McNair, David deVaus, and Marian Pitts. 2006. "Family in Transition: Parents, Children and Grandparents in Lesbian Families Give

Meaning to 'Doing Family'." *Journal of Family Therapy* 28 (2): 175–199. doi:10.1111/j.1467-6427.2006.00345.x.

Poria, Yaniv. 2006a. "Assessing Gay Men and Lesbian Women's Hotel Experiences: An Exploratory Study of Sexual Orientation in the Hotel Industry." *Journal of Travel Research* 44 (3): 327–334. doi:10.1177/0047287505279110.

Poria, Yaniv. 2006b. "Tourism and Spaces of Anonymity: An Israeli Lesbian Woman's Travel Experience." *Tourism* 54 (1): 33–42.

Poria, Yaniv, Arie Reichel, and Avital Biran. 2006. "Heritage Site Perceptions and Motivations to Visit." *Journal of Travel Research* 44 (3): 318–326. doi:10.1177/0047287505279004.

Poria, Yaniv, and Alex Taylor. 2002. "'I'm Not Afraid to be Gay When I Am on the Net'. Minimising Social Risk for Lesbian and Gay Consumers Searching for Hotel Related Information." *Journal of Travel & Tourism Marketing* 11 (2/3): 127–142. doi:10.1300/J073v11n02_07.

Poria, Yaniv, and Dallen J. Timothy. 2014. "Where are the Children in Tourism Research?" *Annals of Tourism Research* 47: 93–95. doi:10.1016/j.annals.2014.03.002.

Pritchard, Annette, Nigel Morgan, Diane Sedgely, and Andrew Jenkins. 1998. "Reaching Out to the Gay Tourist: Opportunities and Threats in an Emerging Market Segment." *Tourism Management* 19 (3): 273–282. doi:10.1016/S0261-5177(98)80016-2.

Pritchard, Annette, Nigel Morgan, Diane Sedgley, Elizabeth Khan, and Andrew Jenkins. 2000. "Sexuality and Holiday Choices: Conversations with Gay and Lesbian Tourists." *Leisure Studies* 19 (4): 267–282. doi:10.1080/02614360050118832.

Quinn, Bernadette. 2013. "Finding Oneself on Holidays: Some Insights into the Holiday Practices of Lone Parents." Paper presented at the annual international conference for the Royal Geographical Society, London, August 27–30.

Rapp, Linda. 2010. "Puerto Rico and the Caribbean." In *The Politics of Sexuality in Latin America: A Reader on Lesbian, Gay, Bisexual and Transgender Rights*, edited by Javier Corrales and Mario Pecheny, 135–143. Pittsburgh: University of Pittsburgh.

Ray, Vivien, and Robin Gregory. 2001. "School Experiences of the Children of Lesbian and Gay Parents." *Family Matters* 59 (Winter): 28–34.

Reilly, Andrew, and Nancy A. Rudd. 2006. "Is Internalized Homonegativity Related to Body Image?" *Family and Consumer Sciences Research Journal* 35 (1): 58–73. doi:10.1177/1077727X06289430.

Roehl, Wesley, and Daniel Fesenmaier. 1992. "Risk Perceptions and Pleasure Travel: An Exploratory Analysis." *Journal of Travel Research* 30 (4): 17–26. doi:10.1177/004728759203000403.

Rugh, Susan. 2008. *Are We There Yet? The Golden Age of American Family Vacations*. Lawrence: University Press of Kansas.

Ryan, Maura, and Dana Berkowitz. 2009. "Constructing Gay and Lesbian Families 'beyond the Closet'." *Qualitative Sociology* 32 (2): 153–172. doi:10.1007/s11133-009-9124-6.

Ryan, Chris, and Colin Michael Hall. 2001. *Sex Tourism: Marginal People and Liminalities*. London: Routledge.

Schänzel, Heike. 2012. "The Inclusion of Fathers, Children and the Whole Family Group in the Tourism Research on Families." In *Family Tourism: Multidisciplinary Perspectives*, edited by Heike Schänzel, Ian Yeoman, and Elisa Backer, 67–80. Bristol: Channel View.

Schänzel, Heike, Ian Yeoman, and Elisa Backer. 2012. "Introduction: Families in Tourism Research." In *Family Tourism: Multidisciplinary Perspectives*, edited by Heike Schänzel, Ian Yeoman, and Elisa Backer, 1–16. Bristol: Channel View.

Scholey, Richard. 2002. "Going Far This Holiday? A UK HIV-prevention Intervention with Gay Male Travellers." In *Gay Tourism: Culture, Identity and Sex*, edited by Stephen Clift, Michael Luongo, and Carrie Callister, 250–266. New York: Continuum.

Shaw, Susan, Mark Havitz, and Fern Delemere. 2008. "'I Decided to Invest in my Kids' Memories': Family Vacation, Memories and the Social Construction of the Family." *Tourism, Culture and Communication* 8 (1): 13–26. doi:10.3727/109830408783900361.

Simpson, Penny M., and Jenny Siguaw. 2008. "Perceived Travel Risks: The Traveller Perspective and Manageability." *International Journal of Tourism Research* 10 (4): 315–327. doi:10.1002/jtr.664.

Skeggs, Beverley. 1999. "Matter out of Place: Visibility and Sexualities in Leisure Spaces." *Leisure Studies* 18 (3): 213–232. doi:10.1080/026143699374934.

Smallman, Clive, and Kevin Moore. 2010. "Process Studies of Tourists' Decision-making." *Annals of Tourism Research* 37 (2): 397–422. doi:10.1016/j.annals.2009.10.014.

Sönmez, Sevil, and Alan Graefe. 1998. "Determining Future Travel Behavior from Past Travel Experience and Perceptions of Risk and Safety." *Journal of Travel Research* 37 (2): 171–177. doi:10.1177/004728759803700209.

Southall, Carol. 2012. "UK Family Tourism: Past, Present and Future Challenges." In *Family Tourism: Multidisciplinary Perspectives*, edited by Heike Schänzel, Ian Yeoman, and Elisa Backer, 50–66. Bristol: Channel View.

Stacey, Judith. 2006. "Gay Parenthood and the Decline of Paternity as We Knew It." *Sexualities* 9 (1): 27–55. doi:10.1177/1363460706060687.

Stacey, Judith, and Timothy J. Biblarz. 2001. "(How) Does the Sexual Orientation of Parents Matter?" *American Sociological Review* 66 (2): 159–183. doi:10.2307/2657413.

Such, Elizabeth. 2006. "Leisure and Fatherhood in Dual-earner Families." *Leisure Studies* 25 (2): 185–199. doi:10.1080/02614360500504610.

Thomson, Elizabeth S., Angus W. Laing, and Lorna McKee. 2007. "Family Purchase Decision Making: Exploring Child Influence Behaviour." *Journal of Consumer Behaviour* 6 (4): 182–202. doi:10.1002/cb.220.

Tversky, Amos, and Daniel Kahneman. 1986. "Rational Choice and the Framing of Decisions." *Journal of Business* 59 (4): S251–S278. doi:10.1086/296365.

Um, Seoho, and John Crompton. 1990. "Attitude Determinants in Tourism Destination Choice." *Annals of Tourism Research* 17 (3): 432–448. doi:10.1016/0160-7383(90)90008-F.

Valentine, Gill. 1996. "(Re)negotiating the 'Heterosexual Street': Lesbian Productions of Space." In *BodySpace: Destabilizing Geographies of Gender and Sexuality*, edited by Nancy Duncan, 146–155. New York: Routledge.

Vroom, Victor H. 1964. *Work and Motivation*. New York: Wiley.

Waitt, Gordon, and Kevin Markwell. 2006. *Gay Tourism: Culture and Context*. Binghamton, NY: Haworth Hospitality.

Waitt, Gordon, Kevin Markwell, and Andrew Gorman-Murray. 2008. "Challenging Heteronormativity in Tourism Studies: Locating Progress." *Progress in Human Geography* 32 (6): 781–800. doi:10.1177/0309132508089827.

Want, Philip. 2002. "Trouble in Paradise: Homophobia and Resistance to Gay Tourism." In *Gay Tourism: Culture, Identity and Sex*, edited by Stephen Clift, Michael Luongo, and Carrie Callister, 191–213. New York: Continuum.

Weber, Max. 1978. *Economy and Society*. Berkeley: University of California Press.

Wells, William D., and George Gubar. 1966. "Life Cycle Concept in Marketing Research." *Journal of Marketing Research* 3 (4): 355–363. doi:10.2307/3149851.

Wilson, Erica, and Donna Little. 2008. "The Solo Female Experience: Exploring the Geography of Women's Fear." *Current Issues in Tourism* 11 (2): 167–186. doi:10.2167/cit342.0.

Witt, Christine A., and Peter L. Wright. 1992. "Tourist Motivation: Life after Maslow." In *Choice and Demand in Tourism*, edited by Peter Stewart Johnson and Barry Thomas, 33–55. London: Mansell.

Woodruffe-Burton, Helen, and Sam Bairstow. 2013. "Countering Heteronormativity." *Gender in Management: An International Journal* 28 (6): 359–374. doi:10.1108/GM-01-2013-0015.

Yeoman, Ian, Una McMahon-Beattie, Damian Lord, and Luke Parker-Hodds. 2012. "Demography and Societal Change." In *Family Tourism: Multidisciplinary Perspectives*, edited by Heike Schänzel, Ian Yeoman, and Elisa Backer, 30–49. Bristol: Channel View.

Intersection of family, work and leisure during academic training

Stephanie Chesser

Department of Recreation and Leisure Studies, University of Waterloo, Canada

For advanced academic trainees (i.e. doctoral students and postdoctoral trainees), success in the academy often involves stepping away from an ordinary '9 to 5' working environment and into a space where workaholic tendencies are largely encouraged. While the daily care and nurturing of a family can be demanding (and itself represents a form of unpaid, often gendered, labour), evidence suggests that children can offer positive emotional benefits for parents, help curb workaholic tendencies, and offer a reason to step away from work and have fun with the family through leisure. This conceptual paper examines the realities of managing family and work lives for academic trainees, a group that has been largely under-recognized in published literature. Issues such as the current work-related expectations for academics (and the ways these expectations can influence leisure), the gendered experience of the academy and family life among academic trainees and the potential benefits of family to academic pursuits will be discussed. Specific strategies that could be implemented to assist academic trainee families, including enrolment and work schedule flexibility, increased institutional support policies and more family-friendly trainee leisure opportunities will also be explored. This conceptual work suggests that academic trainees may face unique challenges with regard to work/family management and, thus, require specific consideration by the research community and academic administrators.

Introduction

It can be said that the pursuit of advanced academic training is not an undertaking for the weak-willed. Signing on the dotted line with a college or university typically involves a serious restructuring of one's entire lifestyle in order to meet the very demanding commitments of the scholarly community. The hectic pace of this schedule no doubt has the potential to dramatically impact the quality of one's life. Sleep, the ability to 'shut off' from work, leisure time and even time spent nurturing personal relationships are often sacrifices deemed essential by many universities, and numerous academic disciplines, for a chance at success (Austin 2002; American Association of University Professors 2001; Demers 2014). I contend that such a culture can make the decision to become a parent, an equally time-consuming and energy depleting endeavour, seem unimaginable (Evans and Grant 2009).

While research has steadily been produced over the past several decades on the topic of motherhood within the academy from the perspective of female faculty (Cuddy, Fiske, and Glick 2004; Evans and Grant 2009; Huang 2009; Krais 2002; Kemkes-Grottenthaler 2003), I would argue that less attention has been paid to the experiences of graduate student and postdoctoral trainee parents and the role that leisure and family may play in both their personal and professional lives. Additionally, while established academics and academic trainees share some similarities with regard to combining parenthood and teaching/research, there are some important (and perhaps under-recognized) distinctions that create additional challenges for graduate student and postdoctoral parents. Consequently, through this feminist-informed conceptual paper, I aim to make academic trainees more visible by highlighting the specific ways that family (and its associated work and leisure activities) may factor into their lives, work and leisure.

My feminist guiding framework

My conceptions of feminism, and, certainly the feminist scholars whose work I draw from, are the ones who challenge the negative views of the movement that still permeate society today (i.e. that feminism is radical, angry, man-hating and uncompromising). To me, feminism remains a distinctly individualized concept that will be experienced and lived differently by all of the women (and men) who choose to fly its banner. Indeed, Hesse-Biber (2011) has emphasized that feminist praxis leaves room for a multitude of approaches to feminist inquiry.

I see feminism as involving the recognition that women's lives function differently and are shaped by different societal pressures than those of men. However, I also believe that both women *and* men remain trapped by societal power structures that seek to privilege some by subordinating others (Henderson and Shaw 2006). Consequently, I assert that the social and political change necessary to create equal opportunities and treatment for women in our society will only be achievable if men are recruited as allies in the fight. For me, a better world for women must leave an equivalent place for men. While I agree that feminist objectives will not be achievable if men speak *for* women, I believe that men speaking *with* women is a necessary step to help create social change (Lyons 2006).

Gender within family life

It has been argued that parenthood has the potential to both differentiate individuals based on gender (Belsky and Kelly 1994; Katz-Wise, Priess, and Hyde 2010; Sanchez and Thomson 1997) and reinforce gender identities (McMahon 1995; Vissing 2002; Walzer 2010) by slotting parents into the socially defined roles of 'mother' and 'father'. This gendering process is perhaps most evident when one looks at the traditional roles of mothers and fathers and the debated inequalities that these roles can create (Belsky and Kelly 1994; Doucet 2001; Katz-Wise, Priess, and Hyde 2010; Sanchez and Thomson 1997). For example, men as fathers have historically been cast in the role of 'breadwinner', shouldering the bulk of the economic responsibility for their household as well as for the physical safety and security of their families (Beaujot 2000; Cowan and Cowan 1992; Glauber and Gozjolko 2011). Women, conversely, have been primarily tasked socially with the role of 'caretaker' in relation to their homes, children and significant others (Beaujot, 2000; O'Reilly 2010).

Although larger institutions (i.e. political, religious and economic) may help to shape gender expectations at a societal level, gender remains something that is demonstrated and reinforced daily by individuals in the ways that they interact with one another, particularly within the family (Belsky and Kelly 1994; Courtenay 2009; O'Reilly 2012; Sanchez and Thomson 1997). Indeed, I would contend that the concepts of 'mother' and 'father' are largely shaped by the economic and social conditions of a given time, and by the historically dominant ideologies that have come before. For example, following the Industrial Revolution's separation of 'home' (i.e. female responsibility) and 'work' (i.e. male responsibility), each gender found itself socially, and arguably morally, accountable for its respective realm of 'labour'.

In the several hundred year wake of this huge societal shift, many women have found themselves bombarded by messages from the media, family, friends, peers and clergy to prioritize the care of their families and homes above many others aspects of their lives (including paid employment, education and leisure) (Henderson et al. 1996; O'Reilly 2010, 2012). This pressure in many ways implied that it was, in fact, a woman's moral duty to ensure a safe and nurturing upbringing for her children (Risman 2004). It could be suggested that these nurture-related notions are tied to the 'ethic of care' that has been described in the feminist literature and implies that a 'good' woman should put the needs of others before her own (O'Reilly 2010, 2012; Rich 1977). Given the importance society places on this care role, it is unsurprising to see women's competency as mothers under scrutiny within society. Indeed, we see women measured against socially idealized mothering traits (i.e. patient, nurturing, self-sacrificing and devoted) every time they visit a playground, a paediatrician's office, or even a friend or family member's home (Blackford 2004; Mulcahy, Parry, and Glover 2010). Men, on the other hand, have historically been made solely accountable for the financial care of their families and, thus, are expected to put in long hours of paid work in order to accomplish this task (Glauber and Gozjolko 2011; Townsend 2002). In many ways, it could be argued that a man's perceived ability to live up to this societal masculine ideal (i.e. being a 'real man') is intimately associated with his ability and willingness to be a good worker and earner for his family.

While the gendered nature of the parenting role has been well documented in the literature (Doucet 2001; Fox 2009; Katz-Wise, Priess, and Hyde 2010; McMahon 1995; Shaw 2008; Walzer 2010), I propose that this gendering process takes place long before a child is even born. Indeed, decisions concerning whether to conceive (in addition to the choices and actions that expectant parents make preceding the births of their children) can often slot mothers and fathers into traditional gender roles, each heavily influenced by societal expectations and norms, as well as by the attributes of the other role. For example, White and Burke (1987) suggest that 'the role of mother takes on meaning in connection with the role of father' (312), in that each gendered role can be seen to occupy a complementary or counter-role status for the other (e.g. men as financial providers and disciplinarians in families versus women as caretakers and nurturers) (Beaujot 2000). Regardless of gender, evidence indicates that both men and women who opt to become parents report being largely motivated by their desire to form close and special relationships with their children (Asselin 2008; Cowan and Cowan 1992; Lahman 2008). Others have reported feeling as though the decision to become a parent signals a willingness to progress into the role of 'adult' by taking on the responsibility for a life (Cowan and Cowan 1992; Lynch 2002).

Academic training

Seemingly far from this world of parenthood lies the realm of academia. Indeed, the academic domain, whether it be at the level of student or professor, involves stepping away from the stereotypical '9 to 5' workday and into an environment where 'work' never seems to end (American Association of University Professors 2001; Anaya et al. 2009). From the perspective of many departments, graduate students are 'trained to be monkish in their devotion and slavish in their pursuit of knowledge' in order to properly prepare for a future in the academy (Springer, Parker, and Leviten-Reid 2009, 438). Unfortunately, the 'greedy' nature of this academic role can leave those students who are not working 60-hour weeks (a trait that could very well constitute a label of 'workaholism' in many other professions) deemed 'uncompetitive' by their institutions (Anaya et al. 2009; Gappa and MacDermid 1997; Grant, Kennelly, and Ward 2000; Ward and Wolf-Wendel 2004). Indeed, the risks posed to the health and well-being of those individuals who do choose to equate a workaholic lifestyle with graduate school can be immense, and may include poor work–life balance, physical and mental 'burnout' and, in extreme cases, increased rates of attrition (Golde 2000; Wall 2008).

While certain elements of academic training (at the graduate or postdoctoral level) remain relatively universal (e.g. coursework, committee and supervisor meetings, publication writing, teaching and grading responsibilities), other components remain significantly dependent upon the stage of one's academic training. Indeed, the levels of autonomy one is able to maintain, in addition to productivity expectations, will differ for doctoral students versus postdoctoral trainees. For instance, postdoctoral trainees would typically not be expected to complete coursework or committee meetings, but might have a higher teaching or publication writing commitment than a doctoral student. However, for the purposes of this theoretical work, I have chosen to group these two trainee categories together, as each requires a significant academic commitment (i.e. years of training above the undergraduate level) that could potentially lead to greater challenges for the management of work and life.

In addition to the stage of training, the discipline in which a trainee works can impact the expectations they will need to fulfil academically. For instance, within the areas of science, technology, engineering and mathematics (STEM), doctoral students are often viewed as 'apprentices' in the eyes of their academic supervisors (often termed principle investigators), as they typically work on projects that are directly related to their supervisor's research interests (Peters 1997). Potential research grant funding for a principle investigator's laboratory often depends largely on a doctoral student's productivity; consequently, students in scientific disciplines may experience less flexibility with regard to their working schedules (i.e. laboratory work cannot be conducted from home) and may feel a degree of pressure to put in long work hours in order to achieve publishable results. Additionally, doctoral students in the STEM disciplines often hold research assistantships (which increases their opportunity to publish academically) and are generally expected to work collaboratively as a laboratory in order to achieve publishable material (Austin 2002).

Conversely, doctoral and postdoctoral trainees in the humanities and social sciences often conduct research projects that are only loosely related to the work conducted by their supervisors (Peters 1997). As a consequence, these individuals may not experience the same degree of pressure as STEM students, as a supervisor's future funding may not be directly tied to the research published by their students. Unlike their science counterparts, trainees in the social sciences and humanities also more commonly hold teaching assistantships, thus they are afforded slightly more autonomy with regard to their day-to-day duties (Austin 2002). Several published narratives written by humanities and social science doctoral students have also discussed the flexibility that their discipline affords them with regard when and where they work (Asselin 2008; Evans and Grant 2009; Lynch 2002). For example, Gabriel Asselin (2008), a parent and doctoral student in anthropology, has expressed the ways that his student status allowed him greater freedom to structure his day around his partner's working schedule. Specifically, he reported being able to independently structure when he takes his classes, works on his academic writing and completes his data collection depending on when his wife has free time to care for their children.

Complexities of academic trainee leisure

Although demonstrating academic proficiency through research, teaching, publications and coursework[1] remains the dominant component of the graduate student and postdoctoral life, the process of integrating into a larger university and/or departmental culture also requires that trainees be willing and able to interact with students and faculty. While some of these interactions could take place in hallways or over semi-working breakfast or lunch meetings, many will take place in more informal, leisure settings outside of normal working hours (i.e. departmental holiday parties, gatherings at pubs, restaurants or homes). Although these social opportunities may possess several characteristics of leisure (i.e. they are optional and are intended to be fun and relaxing), they could also be perceived by some as 'work', in that they are often important for honing one's social skills and building networking contacts (Ali and Kohun 2007; Golde 2000). Undoubtedly, developed social traits are promoted as essential elements for success in academia, as the ability to form connections with one's peers and superiors can often prove pivotal to the acquisition of scholarships and funding, as well as future research and academic positions (Henkel 2005). As a result, 'voluntary' academic activities might seem mandatory (and, thus, not leisurely) for students or postdoctoral trainees looking to get ahead in their careers, and may contribute to feelings of work/life imbalance (Bair, Haworth, and Sandfort 2004; Myers-Walls et al. 2011).

Unfortunately, making the time to connect socially with one's colleagues can prove extremely problematic for graduate student parents. The often impromptu social outings that are common among students (and can carry over into future postdoctoral or faculty positions) can be challenging for parents with extremely scheduled lives (e.g. day care, children's activities and children's sleep schedules) and can leave mothers and fathers feeling isolated from aspects of their academic roles (Anaya et al. 2009; Gardner 2008; Lind 2008). Additionally, student parents who choose to partake in these work-related leisure opportunities may do so at the cost of some of their family leisure time (i.e. time spent with one's partner and/or children).

Family and advanced academic training

It would appear that the decision to even consider starting a family is one that involves accepting that life will need to alter in some way. Indeed, major life transitions in all of our lives generally require not only that we be open to adapting to change, but also that we be willing to re-evaluate the roles we occupy for others (e.g. wife, husband, daughter, son and student), as well as our boundaries, priorities and motivations (Mattessich and Hill 1987; Sevón 2012). For many couples, however, the decision-making process surrounding the possibility of parenthood can be a stressful one, as it is not always assured that intimate partners will agree on when or even whether to have children (Rosina and Testa 2009). I assert that the stress associated with such decisions can certainly be amplified if one, or both, parents are students. For some couples, entry into parenthood may not be planned and, thus, will likely require life changes that individuals may not willing to make (i.e. taking leave from school/work; obtaining a second job and changes in living arrangements).

For those individuals who decide to have children during their academic training, the reality of juggling the demands of both parent and student roles can be sobering. Indeed, student parents have reported increased levels of stress, likely attributable to the conflicting priorities associated with each role (Cohen 2011; Demers 2014; Desrochers, Hilton, and Larwood 2002; Duxbury, Higgins, and Lee 1994; Fowlkes 1987; Sorcinelli and Near 1989). The reality remains that a baby is not going to cease needing to be fed, changed and cuddled because one has a paper due in the morning and, conversely, academic institutions are likely going to continue to have the expectation that students will attend meetings and meet deadlines, despite having a child at home. This conflict associated with managing dual roles for student parents does appear, however, to have a noticeable gender bias (Elliott 2008).

Both male and female academics report work–family role conflict, in that each has described feeling that a parental role is often incongruent or incompatible with an academic role, primarily due to the time that each requires (Elliott 2008; Myers-Walls et al. 2011; O'Laughlin and Bischoff 2005). Specifically, Elliott's work found that female academics report increased conflict related specifically to their parental/caregiver role, while men report feeling greater strain associated with their work-related identities. This conflict appears to manifest either as feelings of inadequacy (e.g. 'I am a poor parent who is not spending enough time playing with my child because I work too much' or 'I am a lagging behind as a graduate student because I am not working hard enough') or as guilt (e.g. women expressing feeling guilty about taking time away from their families to work, while men feel guilty that they are not living up to their work expectations due to their responsibilities at home).

It has been proposed that commitment for student parents may also play a major role in the management of both their 'student' and 'parent' identities (Burke and Stets 2009; Hogg, Terry, and White 1995; Stryker and Burke 2000). Within the context of identity, commitment is seen to involve how invested a person is in maintaining an identity because it holds meaning for them; thus, the greater the commitment to an identity, the more ingrained an identity is likely to become in an individual's conception of themselves (Hogg, Terry, and White 1995; Stryker and Burke 2000). When applied to the potential dual management of parental and graduate student identities, the concept of commitment can become exceedingly complicated. It has been suggested that if an individual is not committed to multiple identities equally, the potential for conflict and stress increases, seemingly because an individual is not inherently motivated to find ways to effectively manage both roles concurrently (Cinamon and Rich 2005). Consequently, if a graduate student is exceedingly committed to their parental role and only somewhat committed to their student role, I would suggest that there is a likelihood that they will experience stress and may make changes to remedy this tension (e.g. they may choose to leave their graduate programme). However, if an individual is seen to have equivalent commitment to two or more identities, research has demonstrated that a decreased level of stress will be experienced (O'Neill and Greenberger 1994). Thus, I would propose that graduate student parents who are equally committed to (and satisfied with) their roles as parent and academic are more likely to experience less role-related stress.

Unfortunately, the roles of parent and academic are not necessarily afforded equal status in the eyes of society and the academy (Solomon 2011). From a societal perspective, parenthood, conceivably, is a role that should supersede all others, as it is widely accepted that those individuals who have taken on the responsibility for a child have an obligation to make the needs of that child a priority in their lives (Baker 2010). The views of the academy sit in direct opposition to this belief system, in that one's work is often required to take precedence over many aspects of one's life for an opportunity at long-term success (Ward and Wolf-Wendel 2004).

Historically, feminist leisure scholars such as Shaw (2001) and Henderson et al. (1996) have asserted that societal pressure concerning familism may be one contributor to these sentiments. The notion of familism has been described in the literature as an 'idealized' approach to family life that can directly or indirectly influence how men and women 'do' everyday family life (e.g. decisions about who takes care of children; who participates in paid employment; who has more time to engage with leisure either alone or with the family) (Edgell 2006; Hull 2006). In many ways, this idealized concept of family has traditionally suggested that the principle roles of mothers and fathers are heavily tied to traditional gendered expectations for women and men within society (Bem 1993; Hochschild 1989; Hochschild and Machung 2012).

It has also, in part, been feminist leisure scholars who have drawn research attention to the disproportionate amount of time that women appear to devote to unpaid household labour (when compared to men), which arguably may contribute to a decreased amount of time women have reported having available for leisure (Henderson et al. 1996; Hilbrecht 2012; Samdahl 2013). Indeed, leisure, for many mothers, is a 'luxury' that they may feel that they do not have time for or entitled to, possibly because they may believe (and society may reinforce) that their family's needs and happiness should be prioritized above their own (Fullagar 2009; Henderson and Bialeschki 1991; Shaw and Henderson 2005; Sullivan 2013). Therefore, it can be debated that such sentiments suggest that women's choices may be restricted by a society that believes that a woman's free time is owed to her family. Mothers who do try to prioritize leisure in their lives may do so by finding ways to incorporate children into their own leisure time (e.g. running pushing a stroller, mom and child swim days at community centres), or may structure specific family leisure time (i.e. family picnics, family game nights or family vacations) (Craig and Mullan 2010; Shaw 2008; Wearing 1990). Unfortunately, such strategies can limit the sense of escape from the 'job' of motherhood that leisure provides and, specifically with regard to family leisure, may cause women to feel as though their 'free time' is yet another household chore to perform (Shaw 2008; Shaw and Dawson 2001).

Academic/parent gender roles

Feminist scholars (myself included) contend that the academy has historically been built on a traditionally male-oriented work model involving a highly demanding and sometimes inflexible work schedule. In the past, those academics who also wanted to have a family needed to either have paid help or a spouse at home to take care of any household or childcare responsibilities (Coltrane 2004; Knights and Richards 2003). In this male-centred model, I would suggest that it would likely be possible for established academics/academic trainees (historically, predominately male) to 'have it all' with regard to school and family because there would frequently be a partner at home (historically, predominately female) to ensure that one's focus remained primarily on work (Acker and Armenti 2004). Indeed, several male graduate students have reported that this arrangement works well for their careers and families (Lynn 2008; Marotte, Reynolds, and Savarese 2011). However, such an approach to family structure could be argued to be gender biased in that it assumes that men will occupy and prioritize their academic role over parenthood, while women will be assumed to prioritize the role of mother over that of trainee (Anderson and Miezitis 1999; Huang 2009; Wall 2008). Indeed, this type of androcentric approach to paid/unpaid divisions of labour may not be overly conducive to modern graduate and post-doctoral trainees (who are now composed of increasingly large numbers of women), as well as partnerships in which both individuals are academic trainees or where the male partner wishes to stay at home to care for their children (Bane 2011).

Due to the decades-old contention that the bulk of the day-to-day responsibilities for children often fall on the shoulders of mothers (Hochschild 1989; Hochschild and Machung 2012; Maume and Sebastian 2012), women may find themselves faced with increased questioning from both the academy and society regarding exactly where their priorities lie. From the perspective of some institutions, academic mothers may not be considered 'ideal workers' in that they may be assumed to be more committed to their families than their studies or careers (Correll, Benard, Paik 2007; Cuddy, Fiske, and Glick 2004; Ward and Wolf-Wendel 2004). Such expectations may also be contributing factors to the increased stress female academics have reported with regard to the balancing of their professional and personal lives (O'Laughlin and Brischoff 2005).

Perhaps in an attempt to counteract this perceived lack of commitment to an academic role, some women have chosen to put off having children until they have a 'break' in their schedules (e.g. try to time their pregnancies so they will give birth in the summer months when one's academic commitments are often lessened) or wait until after they have completed a research project or their degree to conceive, largely to minimize the impact a baby could have on their work (Huang 2009). Such practices can potentially result in couples having smaller families than they had initially planned for or no children at all (Kemkes-Grottenthaler 2003; Krais 2002, Krakauer and Chen 2003). Men also appear susceptible to this perceived lack of commitment to work after becoming fathers, with studies suggesting that academic fathers are less likely to take parental leave than their female counterparts, largely due to fear of career-related repercussions (Haas, Allard, and Hwang 2002; Mason, Goulden, and Frasch 2009).

Benefits of juggling parenthood and academia

It is important to highlight that there is evidence to suggest that 'parent' and 'academic trainee' are roles that can successfully coexist in peoples' lives and that the time spent with one's children can actually contribute to academic success. Within the literature, opinions about the potential impact of young children on research and academic productivity (most often measured in numbers of publications), particularly among mothers, have been varied and hotly debated. While a negative relationship between children and research productivity has historically been reported (Hargens,

McCann, and Reskin 1978; Hunter and Leahey 2010; Kyvik and Teigen 1996; Long 1990; Sonnert and Holton 1995), likely due to the potential for children to be both distracting and time-consuming for academic parents, other studies have found no correlation to exist between children and the time one devotes to research activities (Cole and Zuckerman 1987; Fox 2005; Sax et al. 2002; Stack 2004; Zuckerman 1987). It should be noted, however, that intersecting factors, such as one's stage of career (i.e. pre- or post-tenure), the number of children one has and the age of one's children can complicate the measurable impact family might have on research productivity (Fox 2005; Hunter and Leahey 2010; Kyvik 1990; Stack 2004). Still other studies have found that, in particular, academic mothers report developing increased focus and time management skills within their research after having children, due simply to their need to more closely structure their scholarly activities around their children's schedules (Lynch 2002; Ward and Wolf-Wendel 2004). Indeed, it is this flexibility in one's working schedule that can make graduate school a more ideal place for young parents than many employment venues (Asselin 2008; Eyre-White 2009; Lynch 2002).

Children have also been reported to provide emotional benefits for parents, which can be applied in positive ways to an academic career, particularly for those in social science disciplines. One study suggests that graduate student parents are better able to curb workaholic tendencies in their studies after having children (i.e. children provide a reason to step away from work on a regular basis), allowing them to feel more recharged with regard to the execution of their work-related duties (Ward and Wolf-Wendel 2004). Asselin (2008) has articulated that his and his partner's choice to become parents during their master's degrees provided both with the opportunity to grow as individuals. Each described becoming more patient and better able to connect with other people (including research participants) following their entry into parenthood. Lynn (2008) has also reported that one's status as a parent can provide an opening for communication and trust with research participants. Such studies suggest that the learned personal attributes attached to parental roles can be seen to strengthen parents' abilities to succeed as academics (Thomas 2005).

Strategies to assist academic trainee parents

In this conceptual work, I have asserted that the social roles of 'parent' and 'academic trainee' are both heavily influenced by societal values and expectations; however, men and women appear to experience these pressures differently. While I recognize that the process of combining academic training and parenthood will likely never become stress free, I believe that there are some strategies that academic institutions could implement to help ease the process for their trainees.

First, institutional flexibility in the ways trainees go about completing their work may be one of the most powerful ways colleges and universities could assist academic trainee parents. For example, allowing both male and female graduate student parents to assume part-time statuses within their academic programmes could allow for greater time to complete their training activities, while also allowing for increased time for both mothers and fathers to bond with their children. Despite there being evidence to suggest that part-time enrolment in North American graduate studies programmes is increasing (Gardner 2008), this status has been shown to be unpopular within some institutions, as it can impact the ability for students to receive and/or retain scholarships and graduate in a standard time frame (Williams, Manvell, and Bornstein 2006).

Second, flexibility with regard to when and where academic parents work could provide some assistance with the juggling of work and family, and could be particularly useful to trainees in the STEM fields who have traditionally had less flexible working arrangements. While individual support from supervisors related to 'telecommuting' (i.e. using the internet to work from home) or flexible hours has been a possibility for individual students in many faculties for some time, I would assert that greater institutional and departmental support could help to make this type of arrangement more common among greater numbers of academic trainees. It should be noted, however, that this type of work-related flexibility also has the potential to 'blur' the boundaries between work and home for workers and could contribute to even greater levels of work/life imbalance if individuals are not cognizant of their schedules (Heijstra and Rafnsdottir 2010).

Third, institutional policies and programmes designed to directly benefit academic trainee parents (i.e. subsidized on-site day care, paid parental leave and bursaries for student parents) could provide support to trainees and their families. Such resources, I would argue, could also provide students increased flexibility with regard to their finances and their ability to fit their working schedules around the care needs of their children.

Lastly, I feel that academic trainee leisure could be an effective site for making changes that could benefit parents. Indeed, strategies such as creating more child-friendly academic social events (e.g. providing advanced notice of events to allow time for child care arrangements to be made; refraining from holding events in non-child-friendly environments such as pubs or bars) or holding events during more regular working hours or on weekends (when childcare is often easier for parents to arrange) could help to ease some of the social isolation that may be experienced by trainee parents (Wall 2008). Additionally, the creation of on-campus support groups for trainee parents could allow individuals to find solidarity among their peers and perhaps share strategies for addressing the challenges associated with the juggling of multiple life roles (Demers 2014).

Where we go from here ...

What is, unfortunately, currently missing from much of the published academic literature is research that brings together the topics of parenthood and doctoral/postdoctoral training. While we do have the benefit of the knowledge shared in individual accounts of the experience of juggling these two roles (e.g. anthologies and short narrative works) (Anaya et al. 2009; Asselin 2008; Evans and Grant 2009; Lynch 2002; Marotte, Reynolds, and Savarese 2011), more in-depth explorations have been much more sparsely published. Those accounts that do exist come almost exclusively from the perspective of female academic trainees at the doctoral level; consequently, men's and postdoctoral experiences have been largely under-represented. As a result, it seems prudent for those of us in the academy to turn our gaze to the personal experiences and needs of our trainees. Indeed, the information that such inquiry could provide would help not only to make the lives of academic trainee parents more visible, but could help to further devise strategies to address the challenges this group faces. Even though discussions about trainee parenthood may be uncommon or relatively new for many institutions (and may cause a certain degree of trepidation for some, given the personal nature of the topic), I would contend that they are essential to the process of building productive and thriving academic environments for all.

Acknowledgements

I would like to thank my supervisor Dr Diana Parry (Department of Recreation and Leisure Studies, University of Waterloo) and my dissertation committee members Dr Troy Glover (Department of Recreation and Leisure Studies, University of Waterloo) and Dr Toni Serafini (Sexuality, Marriage and Family Studies Program, St. Jerome's University) for their assistance with this work. This work has been supported by the Social Science and Humanities Research Council of Canada.

Note

1. I would like to recognize that while coursework is a common component of doctoral degrees in North American countries, many doctorates completed globally (in countries such as the UK, New Zealand and Australia) provide research-only programmes of study. As a result of these alternate degree expectations, trainees may experience differing workload stresses and, thus, may need to utilize diverse coping strategies to manage academically and in their personal lives.

Notes on contributor

Stephanie Chesser is a doctoral candidate in the Aging, Health and Well-being programme at the University of Waterloo. She holds a Master of Public Health degree and diploma in Health Services and Policy Research from Lakehead University. Her research interests focus largely on gender and well-being and often involve the intersection of these issues with the concepts of family and leisure. Her dissertation work looks specifically at the factors that influence family planning among couples where one or both partners are enrolled in doctoral or postdoctoral training.

References

Acker, S., and C. Armenti. 2004. "Sleepless in Academia." *Gender and Education* 16 (1): 3–24.
Ali, A., and F. Kohun. 2007. "Dealing with Social Isolation to Minimize Doctoral Attrition – A Four Stage Framework." *International Journal of Doctoral Studies* 2 (1): 33–49.
American Association of University Professors. 2001. *Statement of Principles on Family Responsibilities and Academic Work.* http://www.aaup.org/ statements/re01fam.htm.
Anaya, L., A. Glaros, I. Scarborough, and N. Tami. 2009. "Single Parenthood and the PhD Journey." *Anthropology News*, September.
Anderson, B. J., and S. Miezitis. 1999. "Stress and Life Satisfaction in Mature Female Graduate Students." *Initiatives* 59 (1): 33–43.
Asselin, G. 2008. "Balancing Personal and Educational Priorities." *Anthropology News*, September.
Austin, A. E. 2002. "Preparing the Next Generation of Faculty: Graduate School as Socialization to the Academic Career." *The Journal of Higher Education*, 73 (1): 94–122.
Bair, C. R., J. G. Haworth, and M. Sandfort. 2004. "Doctoral Student Learning and Development: A Shared Responsibility." *Naspa Journal* 41 (3): 709–727.
Baker, M. 2010. "Motherhood, Employment and the "Child Penalty." *Women's Studies International Forum* 33 (3): 215–224.
Bane, C. 2011. "Balancing Diapers and a Doctorate: The Adventures of a Single Dad in Grad School." In *Papa PhD*, edited by M. Marotte, P. Reynolds, and R. Savarese, 196–200. New Brunswick, NJ: Rutgers University Press.
Beaujot, R. P. 2000. *Earning and Caring in Canadian Families.* Toronto, ON: University of Toronto Press.
Belsky, J., and J. Kelly. 1994. *The Transition to Parenthood – How a First Child Changes a Marriage: Why Some Couples Grow Closer and Others Apart.* New York: Delacorte Press.
Bem, S. L. 1993. *"The" Lenses of Gender: Transforming the Debate on Sexual Inequality.* New Haven, CT: Yale University Press.

Blackford, H. 2004. "Playground Panopticism: Ring-Around-the-Children, a Pocketful of Women." *Childhood* 11 (2): 227–249.

Burke, P., and J. Stets. 2009. *Identity Theory.* New York: Oxford University Press.

Cinamon, R. G., and Y. Rich. 2005. "Work–Family Conflict among Female Teachers." *Teaching and Teacher Education* 21 (4): 365–378.

Cohen, S. M. 2011. "Doctoral Persistence and Doctoral Program Completion among Nurses." *Nursing Forum* 46 (2): 64–70.

Cole, J. R., and H. Zuckerman. 1987. "Marriage, Motherhood and Research Performance in Science." *Scientific American* 256 (2): 119–125.

Coltrane, S. 2004. "Elite Careers and Family Commitment: It's (Still) About Gender." *The ANNALS of the American Academy of Political and Social Science* 596: 214–220.

Correll, S. J., S. Benard, and I. Paik. 2007. "Getting a Job: Is There a Motherhood Penalty?" *American Journal of Sociology* 112 (5): 1297–1339.

Courtenay, W. 2009. "Theorizing Masculinity and Men's Health." In *Men's Health: Body, Identity and Social Context*, edited by A. Broom and P. Tovey, 9–30. West Sussex: Wiley-Blackwell.

Cowan, C., and P. Cowan. 1992. *When Partners Become Parents: The Big Life Change for Couples.* Mahwah, NJ: Lawrence Erlbaum Associates.

Craig, L., and K. Mullan. 2010. "Parenthood, Gender and Work-Family Time in the United States, Australia, Italy, France, and Denmark." *Journal of Marriage and Family* 72 (5): 1344–1361.

Cuddy, A. J. C., S. T. Fiske, and P. Glick. 2004. "When Professionals Become Mothers, Warmth Doesn't Cut the Ice." *Journal of Social Issues* 60 (4): 701–718.

Demers, D. 2014. "Back to School: The Balancing Act Graduate Student Mothers Play Between Home and School". Unpublished doctoral dissertation, Southern Illinois University, Carbondale.

Desrochers, S., J. M. Hilton, and L. Larwood. 2002. *Predicting Work-Family Role Strain among Business Professors from Their Identity-Based and Time-based Commitments to Professional and Parenting Roles.* BLCC Working Paper #02-05. Ithaca, NY: Cornell University, Cornell Careers Institute.

Doucet, A. 2001. "You See the Need Perhaps More Clearly than I Have: Exploring Gendered Processes of Domestic Responsibility." *Journal of Family Issues* 22 (3): 328–357.

Duxbury, L., C. Higgins, and C. Lee. 1994. "Work-Family Conflict: A Comparison by Gender, Family Type, and Perceived Control." *Journal of Family Issues* 15 (3): 449–466.

Edgell, P. 2006. *Religion and Family in a Changing Society.* Princeton, NJ: Princeton University Press.

Elliott, M. 2008. "Gender Differences in the Causes of Work and Family Strain among Academic Faculty." *Journal of Human Behavior in the Social Environment* 17 (1–2): 157–173.

Evans, E., and C. Grant. 2009. *Mama PhD.* New Brunswick, NJ: Rutgers University Press.

Eyre-White, J. 2009. "Engineering Motherhood." In *Mama PhD*, edited by E. Evans and C. Grant, 31–38. New Brunswick, NJ: Rutgers University Press.

Fowlkes, M. R. 1987. "Role Combinations and Role Conflict: Introductory Perspective." In *Spouse, Parent, Worker: On Gender and Multiple Roles*, edited by F. J. Crosby, 347–360. New Haven, CT: Yale University.

Fox, M. F. 2005. "Gender, Family Characteristics, and Publication Productivity among Scientists." *Social Studies of Science* 35 (1): 131–150.

Fox, B. 2009. *When Couples Become Parents: The Creation of Gender in the Transition to Parenthood.* Toronto, ON: University of Toronto Press.

Fullagar, S. 2009. "Governing Healthy Family Lifestyles Through Discourse of Risk and Responsibility." In *Biopolitics and the Obesity Epidemic: Governing Bodies*, edited by J. Wright and V. Harbood, 108–126. London: Routledge.

Gappa, J. M., and S. M. MacDermid. 1997. *Work, Family, and the Faculty Career. New Pathways: Faculty Career and Employment for the 21st Century.* Working Paper Series, Inquiry #8. Washington, DC: Association of American Higher Education.

Gardner, S. K. 2008. "Fitting the Mold of Graduate School: A Qualitative Study of Socialization in Doctoral Education." *Innovative Higher Education* 33 (2): 125–138.

Glauber, R., and K. L. Gozjolko. 2011. "Do Traditional Fathers Always Work More? Gender Ideology, Race, and Parenthood." *Journal of Marriage and Family* 73 (5): 1133–1148.

Golde, C. 2000. "Should I Stay or Should I Go? Student Descriptions of the Doctoral Attrition Process." *The Review of Higher Education* 23 (2): 199–227.

Grant, L., O. Kennelly, and K. Ward. 2000. "Revisiting the Gender, Marriage, and Parenthood Puzzle in Scientific Careers." *Women's Studies Quarterly* 28 (1/2): 62–83.

Haas, L., K. Allard, and P. Hwang. 2002. "The Impact of Organizational Culture on Men's Use of Parental Leave in Sweden." *Community, Work, and Family* 5 (3): 319–342.

Hargens, L., J. McCann, and B. Reskin. 1978. "Productivity and Reproductivity: Fertility and Professional Achievement among Research Scientists." *Social Forces* 57 (1): 154–163.

Heijstra, T. M., and G. L. Rafnsdottir. 2010. "The Internet and Academics' Workload and Work–family Balance." *The Internet and Higher Education* 13 (3): 158–163.

Henderson, K. A., and D. Bialeschki. 1991. *"A Sense of Entitlement to Leisure as Constraint and Empowerment for Women." Leisure Sciences* 13 (1): 51–65.

Henderson, K. A., M. D. Bialeschki, S. Shaw, and V. Freysinger. 1996. *Both Gains and Gaps.* State College, PA: Venture.

Henderson, K. A., and S. M. Shaw. 2006. "Leisure and Gender: Challenges and Opportunities for Feminist Research." In *A Handbook of Leisure Studies*, edited by C. Rojek, S. M. Shaw, and A. J. Veal, 216–230. New York: Palgrave Macmillan.

Henkel, M. 2005. "Academic Identity and Autonomy in a Changing Policy Environment." *Higher Education* 49 (1–2): 155–176.

Hesse-Biber, S. N. 2011. *Handbook of Feminist Research: Theory and Praxis.* Thousand Oaks, CA: Sage.

Hilbrecht, M. 2012. "Time Use in Daily Life: Women, Families, and Leisure." In *Leisure, Women and Gender*, edited by V. J. Freysinger, S. M. Shaw, K. A. Henderson, and M. D. Bialeschki, 177–192. State College, PA: Venture.

Hochschild, A. R. 1989. *The Second Shift: Working Parents and the Revolution at Home.* New York: Viking Penguin.

Hochschild, A., and A. Machung. 2012. *The Second Shift: Working Families and the Revolution at Home.* London: Penguin Books.

Hogg, M. A., D. J. Terry, and K. M. White. 1995. "A Tale of Two Theories: A Critical Comparison of Identity Theory with Social Identity Theory." *Social Psychology Quarterly* 58 (4): 255–269.

Huang, P. 2009. *Gender Bias in Academia: Findings from Focus Groups.* http://www.worklifelaw. org/GenderBias_index.html.

Hull, K. 2006. *Same-Sex Marriage: The Cultural Politics of Love and Law.* New York: Cambridge University Press.

Hunter, L., and E. Leahey. 2010. "Parenting and Research Productivity: New Evidence and Methods." *Social Studies of Science* 40 (3): 433–451.

Katz-Wise, S. L., H. A. Priess, and J. S. Hyde. 2010. "Gender-Role Attitudes and Behavior Across the Transition to Parenthood." *Developmental Psychology* 46 (1): 18–28.

Kemkes-Grottenthaler, A. 2003. "Postponing or Rejecting Parenthood? Results of a Survey among Female Academic Professionals." *Journal of Biosocial Sciences* 35 (2): 213–226.

Knights, D., and W. Richards. 2003. "Sex Discrimination in UK Academia." *Gender, Work & Organization* 10 (2): 213–238.

Krais, B. 2002. "Academia as a Profession and the Hierarchy of the Sexes: Paths Out of Research in German Universities." *Higher Education Quarterly* 56 (4): 407–418.

Krakauer, L., and C. P. Chen. 2003. "Gender Barriers in the Legal Profession: Implications for Career Development of Female Law Students." *Journal of Employment Counseling* 40 (2): 65–79.

Kyvik, S. 1990. "Motherhood and Scientific Productivity." *Social Studies of Science* 20 (1): 149–160.

Kyvik, S., and M. Teigen. 1996. "Child Care, Research Collaboration, and Gender Differences in Scientific Productivity." *Science Technology Human Values* 21 (1): 54–71.

Lahman, M. 2008. "Dreams of My Daughter: An Ectopic Pregnancy." *Qualitative Health Research* 19 (2): 272–278.

Lind, I. 2008. "Balancing Career and Family in Higher Education – New Trends and Results." In *Gender Equality Programmes in Higher Education*, edited by S Grenz, B Kortendiek, M Kriszio, and A Löther, 193–208. Wiesbaden: VS Verlag für Sozialwissenschaften.

Long, J. S. 1990. "The Origins of Sex Differences in Science." *Social Forces* 68 (4): 1297–1316.

Lyons, K. 2006. "Wolves Among Sheep? The Role of Men in a Feminist Leisure Studies." *Leisure Sciences* 28 (3): 305–309.

Lynch, K. 2002. "An Immodest Proposal: Have Children in Graduate School." *The Chronicle of Higher Education.* http://grad-affairs.uchicago.edu/academic-resources/An%20Immodest%20Proposal%20Have%20Children%20in%20Grad%20School.pdf.

Lynn, C. D. 2008. "Parent seeking PhD." *Anthropology News*, September.

Marotte, M., P. Reynolds, and R. Savarese. 2011. *Papa PhD*. New Brunswick, NJ: Rutgers University Press.

Mason, M. A., M. Goulden, and K. Frasch. 2009. "Why Graduate Students Reject the Fast Track." *Academe.* http://www.aaup.org/aauP/pubsres/academe/2009/JF/Feat/maso.htm.

Mattessich, P., and R. Hill. 1987. "Life Cycle and Family Development." In *Handbook of Marriage and the Family*, edited by M. B. Sussman and S. K. Steinmetz, 437–469. New York: Plenum Press.

Maume, D. J., and R. A. Sebastian. 2012. "Gender, Nonstandard Work Schedules, and Marital Quality." *Journal of Family and Economic Issues* 33 (4): 477–490.

McMahon, M. 1995. *Engendering Motherhood: Identity and Self-transformation in Women's Lives.* New York: Guilford.

Mulcahy, C. M., D. C. Parry, and T. D. Glover. 2010. "Play-Group Politics: A Critical Social Capital Exploration of Exclusion and Conformity in Mothers Groups." *Leisure Studies* 29 (1): 3–27.

Myers-Walls, J. A., L. V. Frias, K. A. Kwon, M. J. M. Ko, and T. Lu. 2011. "Living Life in Two Worlds: Acculturative Stress among Asian International Graduate Student Parents and Spouses." *Journal of Comparative Family Studies* 42 (4): 455–478.

O'Laughlin, E., and L. Bischoff. 2005. "Balancing Parenthood and Academia: Work/Family Stress as Influenced by Gender and Tenure Status." *Journal of Family Issues* 26 (1): 79–106.

O'Neil, R., and E. Greenberger. 1994. "Patterns of Commitment to Work and Parenting: Implications for Role Strain." *Journal of Marriage and Family* 56 (1): 101–118.

O'Reilly, A. 2010. "Outlaw(ing) Motherhood: A Theory and Politic of Maternal Empowerment for the Twenty-First Century." *Hecate* 36 (1/2): 17–29.

O'Reilly, A. 2012. *From Motherhood to Mothering: The Legacy of Adrienne Rich's of Woman Born.* Albany, NY: SUNY Press.

Peters, R. L. 1997. *Getting What You Came for: The Smart Student's Guide to Earning a Master's or Ph.D.* New York: Farrar, Straus and Giroux.

Rich, A. C. 1977. *Of Woman Born: Motherhood as Experience and Institution.* New York: Bantam Books.

Risman, B. J. 2004. "Gender as a Social Structure Theory Wrestling with Activism." *Gender & Society* 18 (4): 429–450.

Rosina, A., and M. R. Testa. 2009. "Couples' First Child Intentions and Disagreement: An Analysis of an Italian Case." *European Journal of Population* 25 (4): 487–502.

Samdahl, D. 2013. "Women, Gender, and Leisure Constraints." In *Leisure, Women and Gender*, edited by V. J. Freysinger, S. M. Shaw, K. A. Henderson, and M. D. Bialeschki, 109–126. State College, PA: Venture.

Sanchez, L., and E. Thomson. 1997. "Becoming Mothers and Fathers: Parenthood, Gender, and the Division of Labor." *Gender & Society* 11 (6): 747–772.

Sax, L., L. S. Hagedorn, M. Arredondo, and F. Dicrisi. 2002. "Faculty Research Productivity: Exploring the Role of Gender and Family-Related Factors." *Research in Higher Education* 43 (4): 423–446.

Sevón, E. 2012. "'My Life Has Changed, But His Life Hasn't': Making Sense of the Gendering of Parenthood During the Transition to Motherhood." *Feminism & Psychology* 22 (1): 60–80.

Shaw, S. M. 2001. "The Family Leisure Dilemma: Insights from Research with Canadian Families." *World Leisure Journal* 43 (4): 53–62.

Shaw, S. 2008. "Family Leisure and Changing Ideologies of Parenthood." *Sociology Compass* 2 (2): 688–703.

Shaw, S., and D. Dawson. 2001. "Purposive Leisure: Examining Parental Discourses on Family Activities." *Journal of Leisure Research* 23 (4): 217–231.

Shaw, S., and K. Henderson. 2005. "Gender Analysis and Leisure Constraints: An Uneasy Alliance." In *Constraints to Leisure*, edited by E. Jackson, 23–34. State College, PA: Venture.

Solomon, C. R. 2011. "'Sacrificing at the Altar of Tenure': Assistant Professors' Work/Life Management." *The Social Science Journal* 48 (2): 335–344.

Sonnert, G., and G. Holton. 1995. *Who Succeeds in Science: The Gender Dimension*. New Brunswick, NJ: Rutgers University Press.

Sorcinelli, M. D., and J. Near. 1989. "Relations Between Work and Life Away from Work among University Faculty." *Journal of Higher Education* 60 (1): 59–66.

Springer, K., B. Parker, and C. Leviten-Reid. 2009. "Making Space for Graduate Student Parents Practice and Politics." *Journal of Family Issues* 30 (4): 435–457.

Stack, S. 2004. "Gender, Children and Research Productivity." *Research in Higher Education* 45 (8): 891–920.

Stryker, S., and P. J. Burke. 2000. "The Past, Present, and Future of an Identity Theory." *Social Psychology Quarterly* 63 (4): 284–297.

Sullivan, A. M. 2013. "Becoming a Mother: Where Does Leisure Fit?" In *Leisure, Women and Gender*, edited by V. J. Freysinger, S. M. Shaw, K. A. Henderson, and M. D. Bialeschki, 297–310. State College, PA: Venture.

Thomas, A. 2005. "Terms of Inclusion? Rejecting the Role of 'Honorary Man' in the Ivory Tower." In *Parenting and Professing: Balancing Family Work with an Academic Career*, edited by R. H. Bassett, 182–191. Nashville, TN: Vanderbilt University Press.

Townsend, N. 2002. *Package Deal: Marriage, Work and Fatherhood in Men's Lives*. Philadelphia, PA: Temple University Press.

Vissing, Y. 2002. *Women Without Children: Nurturing Lives*. New Brunswick, NJ: Rutgers University Press.

Wall, S. 2008. "Of Heads and Hearts: Women in Doctoral Education at a Canadian University." *Women's Studies International Forum* 31 (3): 219–228.

Walzer, S. 2010. *Thinking About the Baby: Gender Transitions into Parenthood*. Philadelphia, PA: Temple University Press.

Ward, K., and L. Wolf-Wendel. 2004. "Academic Motherhood: Managing Complex Roles in Research Universities." *The Review of Higher Education* 27 (2): 233–257.

Wearing, B. 1990. "Beyond the Ideology of Motherhood: Leisure and Resistance." *Journal of Sociology* 26 (1): 36–58.

White, C. L., and P. J. Burke. 1987. "Ethnic Role Identity among Black and White College Students: An Interactionist Approach." *Sociological Perspectives* 30 (3): 310–331.

Williams, J. C., J. Manvell, and S. Bornstein. 2006. *Opt Out or Pushed Out? How the Press Covers Work/Family Conflict: The Untold Story of Why Women Leave the Workforce*. University of California, Hastings College of the Law. http://www.uchastings.edu/site_files/WLL/OptOutPushedOut.pdf.

Zuckerman, H. 1987. "The Careers of Men and Women Scientists: A Review of Current Research." In *Women: Their Underrepresentation and Career Differentials in Science and Engineering*, edited by L. S. Dix, 127–156. Washington, DC: National Academy Press.

Family leisure and the coming out process for LGB young people and their parents

Dawn E. Trussell, Trisha M.K. Xing and Austin G. Oswald

Department of Recreation and Leisure Studies, Brock University, Canada

This article examines how the coming out process for young people who identify as lesbian, gay, and bisexual (LGB) shaped the meanings and experiences of their family leisure engagement. The data draws on a purposive sample of 20 participants (7 young people and their parents). The findings emphasize that shared family activities (media in the family home, family outings and vacations, visiting extended family members) could be altered in relation to the coming out process and cultural norms related to heterosexism and homophobia. It highlights the significant role of mothers as well as extended family members who identified as LGB (i.e. aunts, uncles) in mediating familial relationships. Issues of identity formation (i.e. LGB young person, the parent of a LGB child) and the ongoing process of acceptance are emphasized.

Early research on family leisure focused primarily on the benefits of family activities, and although this research provided an important beginning, it did not reflect the reality of lived-experiences that includes positive and negative attributes (Shaw 2008). As Kelly (1997) argued: "In family there is both community and alienation. In relationships there is both bonding and violence. In nurture there is love and exploitation" (134). In recent years, a more critical lens has highlighted the purposive and contradictory aspects of family leisure practices (e.g. Hebblethwaite and Norris 2010; Shannon and Shaw 2008; Trussell and Shaw 2012) and the multiplicity of meanings that may be experienced by individual family members as well as among diverse family forms (e.g. Harrington 2013; Hilbrecht et al., 2008; Schänzel 2012). Moreover, family scholarship has emphasized the important role that leisure experiences may have for families confronting different forms of adversity. For instance, the demise of the family farm (Trussell and Shaw 2009), the deployment of a partner in the military during a time of war (Werner and Shannon 2013), and the reconstruction of the family unit following a divorce (Hutchinson, Afifi, and Krause 2007).

One type of family that may be facing adversity is that which has a child who has a developing lesbian, gay, and bisexual (LGB) identity during their adolescent years. Despite the proliferation of research that has emerged over the last three decades, it remains largely centred on the risks and challenges that young people may encounter

(Horn, Kosciw, and Russell 2009). For example, attention has been given to under-standing the impact of coming out on rates of family rejection and poor health out-comes such as suicide, depression and illegal drug use (Horn et al., 2009). Further, most of the research on parents' initial reactions and the subsequent outcomes for the child emphasizes a negative, traumatic and even violent context (Bertone and Pal-lotta-Chiarolli 2014). Yet, research has also pointed to accepting parents that may counter the heterosexist nature of the family home, and by "queering" this space, provide a supportive environment for developing LGB identities (Gorman-Murray 2008).

Despite the potential for change to family life and leisure practices during this time period, there has been a lack of understanding given to the collective familial unit. This is problematic given "events that occur in the life of one family member also affect others in the family" (Bertone and Pallotta-Chiarolli 2014, 1). The paucity of research in understanding parental perspectives is evident not only in leisure studies, but across the broader social sciences. That is, existing research relies heavily on young people's recollections of parental responses (Grafsky 2014). In part, this may be because, "families of origin of GLBT people have been a hard-to-reach-popu-lation" (Bertone and Pallotta-Chiarolli 2014, 10).

These realities speak to the significance of the study on which this paper is based. Not only is the study and paper situated at a time when gay rights are at the forefront of media and scholarly attention in North America and beyond, it also seeks to address a noted gap in the literature. We intend to expand the current understanding of the coming out process by integrating the shared experiences of parents and young people who identify as LGB. With this in mind, the purpose of this paper was to examine how the coming out process for young people who identified as LGB, shaped the meanings and experiences of family leisure engagement. Specifically, an interpretive interview study was conducted with young people and their parents to explore the extent to which it affected their family leisure activities, values, and relationships. It also sought to understand how broader cultural attitudes related to heterosexism and homophobia influenced family experiences and access to leisure. As Kivel and Johnson (2013) wrote, young people who identify as LGB(T)

> are more likely to find support for their sexual identity today than in the distant and recent past, but prejudice, discrimination, heterosexism (the unquestioned assumption that everyone is heterosexual) and homophobia (an irrational fear and hatred of LGBT people) are pervasive. (440)

Families of origin and the coming out process

As Bertone and Pallotta-Chiarolli (2014) point out, there is limited research that has examined the lives of LGB people and relations with their families of origin (i.e. parents, siblings, grandparents, and other members of the extended family). The limited research exists mainly in the field of psychology and has "mostly been con-cerned with their [the parents] reactions to disclosure and with the conditions fostering a development of their attitudes towards full acceptance" (5). Young people who identify as LGB are more likely to experience conflict at home, and consequently, are over-represented in foster care, juvenile detention, and among homeless youth (Ryan et al. 2009). Indeed parent–child relationships may be challenged and the "fear of negative parental reactions to the disclosure of sexual orientation has been found to be the major reason that LGB youth do not tell their families" (D'Augelli, Grossman, and Starks 2005, 474). As D'Augelli (2005) et al. assert, the initial reaction may be negative, however, through time more positive parental responses and support may become evident.

Research that has considered the possible developmental benefits of family acceptance and supportive behaviours for LGB youth has emphasized the protective factors it may foster. For example, family acceptance has been found to be associated with positive health outcomes such as enhanced self-esteem, social support and general health status (Ryan et al. 2010). It may also protect against negative health outcomes such as depression, substance abuse, and suicidal ideation and behaviours (Ryan et al. 2010).

Although some parents may exhibit family acceptance and support, they too may go through a coming out process that parallels their child's. For instance, parents may feel the need to conceal their child's LGB identity from others, there may be enhanced conflict between siblings as well as parents, and there may be a plethora of negative emotions ranging from self-blame to despair by the parent (Pallotta-Chiarolli 2005 as cited in Bertone and Pallotta-Chiarolli 2014). Thus, understanding parental perspectives, in addition to the young person's recalling of parental reactions, may be essential to a holistic understanding of how the coming out processes shape the collective family unit.

It is clear, too, that popular family leisure practices such as watching television (Shaw 2001) may influence the coming out process and mediate familial attitudes and relationships. For example, Malici (2014), in his Italian based study, argued that queer television programming facilitated a broader sense of family acceptance during the coming out process. He asserts, "television is an important source of support in that it provides an initial opportunity for discussion and reciprocal understanding within the family of origin, while also easing conflicts and helping with the coming-out process" (194). Moreover, he refers to *Queer Television Moments* as "unpredictable instances of confrontation with sexual dissidence, LGBT visibility, and political issues coming from the public sphere" (189). Yet, Malici noted that media censorship often restricts queer television moments to late at night when viewing is minimal and portrays stereotypical roles of the overly effeminate gay and hyper-masculine lesbian. Consequently, his research alludes to the interplay between the private sphere of the family home and the public sphere's social and cultural norms.

Historical moments, cultural contexts and shifting societal attitudes

Weststrate and McLean (2010) argued that the coming out experience is constructed within a "dynamic cultural context" (226) in that cultural norms, political views, and legal standpoints shape how sexuality is conceptualized. They posit, "to understand the development of sexual identity it is critical to understand both the *cultural* and *personal* developments relevant to the person" (emphasis in original, 227). As such, the unique socio-cultural, geographical, and temporal context may shape how young people with developing LGB identities and their families negotiate their coming out stories.

There is a burgeoning body of literature that explores the coming out process at the interface of different cultural systems. For example, Furnham and Saito (2009) conducted a cross-cultural investigation of attitudes toward gay men in Japan and

Britain. They found that both cultures held disparate ideologies about sexuality that shaped participants' attitudes toward men who openly identified as gay (i.e. Japanese participants were less tolerant and less accepting of gay men when compared to the British participants). Similarly, other research has pointed to the dominant cultural script of a particular region that plays a discerning role in moderating how sexuality is communicated in public and private spaces (e.g. Khanna 2013; Klein et al. 2015). Cuddy et al. (2009) argue: "Culture shapes the ideologies that legitimate prejudice. Cultural ideologies govern what people see as good and bad, thereby stipulating which groups will become the targets of prejudice" (8). Therefore, broader cultural norms and political ideologies will inevitably impact the coming out process for individuals who identify as LGB and their families of origin.

Dominant norms about sexuality are not fixed; rather, they are dynamic forces that evolve through historical and political moments. In some countries, historical events such as the gay rights movement may have re-defined the coming out experience for individuals who identify as LGB and their families. For instance, a young person coming out today in a Westernized country may make sense of their sexuality in vastly different ways than a young person coming out during the 1970s liberation movement and the 1980s AIDS epidemic (Weststrate and McLean 2010). Moreover, a young person coming out (and their family of origin) in a culture that supports gay rights may experience different challenges than those coming out in cultures with strong homophobic biases and legislature that criminalizes homosexuality (see, for example, Thoreson 2008).

Another important consideration is that even with recent legislation that supports the gay rights movement, heterosexism and homophobia persist. For example, schools and other youth programmes in the USA continue to be unsafe for LGB youth as they navigate hostile environments (Johnson, Singh, and Gonzalez 2014). In Canada, homophobia and the lack of support available in school systems continues to exist (Klein et al. 2015). As Mishna et al. (2009) point out, "bullying of lesbian and gay youth continues despite an overall increased level of acceptance of lesbian and gay individuals by society" (1602).

In sum, the overarching historical moment and dominant cultural discourses play a seminal role in shaping coming out stories. Moreover, the family of origin is important to consider as "accepting and rejecting behaviors can co-occur as families adjust to learning about their child's LGBT identity" (Ryan et al. 2010, 206). In turn, this may influence familial attitudes and collective family leisure experiences within the public gaze.

Project design

Theoretical perspective

General principles of constructivism provided the guiding framework for the study on which this paper is based. In constructivism, "the aim is to understand aspects of human activity from the perspectives of those who experience it" (Jones, Torres, and Arminio 2006, 18). This approach views reality as subjective, disparate and multiple, as people construct different meanings from their lived experiences (Crotty 2006). Grounded within the interpretive paradigm, a constructivist perspective sees knowledge as contextually based and seeks to shed light on the subjective complexities of reality through interpretation and translation (Jones et al. 2006). As Guba (1990) explained: "constructivism thus intends neither to predict and control the 'real' world nor to transform it but to *reconstruct* the 'world' at the only point at which it exists: in the minds of constructors" (emphasis in original, 27).

Aligned with a constructivist perspective, an inductive qualitative methodology was appropriate. Specifically, principles from Charmaz's (2005, 2006) constructivist grounded theory approach provided the guiding framework. In this approach, the researcher-participant co-construct the emergent data. That is, "researchers view themselves as embedded in the research process" (Charmaz 2008, 160) and assume an influential role alongside the participants in the co-creation of knowledge. Consequentially, the research process is emergent and not linear, consisting of "simultaneous data collection and analysis, with each informing and focusing the other throughout the research process" (Charmaz 2005, 508).

Methods

Our research team consisted of one faculty member and two graduate students at a publicly funded university in Canada. We are diverse in our own sexual identities with two members identifying as heterosexual and one member identifying as LGB. The first author lived in Canada and the USA during the data collection and analysis phase of the project. Two of the team members identify as White, while one identifies as West Indian. All three-research team members are married and embrace political ideals related to human rights and liberties through our scholarship and personal lives.

The participants for this study were (i) young people between the ages of 18 and 25 who openly self-identified as LGB in high school and (ii) their parent(s). Purposeful sampling strategies were used to find participants best suited to illuminate understanding of the research questions. Initial recruitment of the young people involved contacting LGBTQ centres at publicly funded universities in Canada and the USA, resulting in nine young people being interviewed.

After completion of the young people's interviews, we asked if they would be interested in their parents' participation in the project. Seven young people agreed to have their parents participate, thus, included in this study are the insights of seven young people (four from Canada and three from the USA), seven mothers (one single mother) and six fathers. Of these seven young people, three self-identified as male and gay; four self-identified as female and lesbian; with several of the participants identifying as bisexual in their initial coming out stories.

Although we were open to including parents with diverse sexual identities, all of the parents in this study identified as heterosexual. All of the participants were White (as well as their families of origin), and six of the seven families were from a relatively privileged socio-economic background. All of the young people came out to their parents in the mid-2000s to early 2010s and, their experiences are grounded in a particular historical and social context. At the time of data collection, same-sex marriages were legal in Canada and became legal shortly thereafter where the young people resided in the USA.

The design of the study was a qualitative, retrospective one that facilitated an opportunity for the participants to be reflective of their experiences, rather than during the initial difficult moment of transition. The primary method of data collection was two semi-structured interview guides, one for the young people and one for the parents. Due to the potential for sensitive conversations, separate interviews were conducted with each family member. All of the interviews occurred in a location deemed appropriate and "safe" by the individual family member (e.g. coffee shop, family home, park, telephone) and our conversations were somewhat unstructured, ranging from 34 minutes to more than two hours in duration. Although the young people and parental interview guides were tailored to their perspectives, the questions were grounded in broader related themes: (i) how did the coming out process shape family life and dynamics, (ii) the role of leisure activities and immediate family member interactions, (iii) the role of leisure activities and extended family members, and (iv) advice giving and words of wisdom. All interviews were audio-recorded and transcribed verbatim for data analysis.

As outlined by Charmaz (2006), the strategies of memoing, coding, comparative method, and theoretical sampling procedures provided the guiding principles for analysis. First, we immersed ourselves in the data by reviewing and assessing the transcripts individually. We each developed a general sense of the information and engaged in preliminary analysis of the data through initial, line-by-line coding. Reflective notes were made on each transcript to develop an overall meaning as well as begin the early stages of the coding process. We then met to discuss the initial analysis and combine our insights. Effort was made to identify salient themes shared among the group as initial codes were accepted, altered, or eliminated to determine key themes. In turn, these key themes guided us as we engaged in focused coding procedures. The final phase involved what Charmaz describes as theoretical coding. Here, we continued to focus our analysis in effort to reach larger theoretical representations of the data. Theoretical coding continued until we achieved theoretical saturation; a process of continued analysis until "gathering more data sheds no further light on the properties of their theoretical category" (Charmaz 2008, 167).

Findings

The analysis of the family member discourse discovered that the meanings of shared family activities could be altered in relation to the coming out process and cultural norms related to heterosexism and homophobia. Three main themes that best reflected the parents' and young peoples' experiences emerged: (a) coming out in the family home and the significance of media consumption; (b) coming out of the family closet in the public gaze; and (c) coming out to grandma and extended family members. What emerged as a major, overarching theme was the significant role of mothers as well as extended family members who identified as LGB in mediating familial relationships. These three main themes and the major, overarching theme are discussed in the following sections.

Coming out in the family home and the significance of media consumption

The first theme revealed the significance of everyday leisure experiences within the home as a vehicle that provided opportunities to open and enhance communication. Specifically, the significance of media consumption played an instrumental role in helping with the coming out process for the young people, their parents, and the parent–child relationship.

It was within the context of media consumption and artefacts found within the family home that conversations were initiated. For example, some parents started to question their child's sexual orientation when they stumbled upon print or electronic media that suggested an LGB identity:

> My husband and I kind of wondered for a long time if [our son] was gay. When he was in eighth grade we found on the Internet some pictures of young men in their underwear. They weren't like porn but they were in their underwear. (Mother, family #1)

Indeed for this family, finding their son's magazines was how the conversation was initiated:

> So my husband was cleaning my son's car. There were these newspapers called Prairie Flame, which is the local gay lesbian magazine. And he came in and he just showed those to me. I said: "Okay, I'll go ask him." So I went upstairs to his room and I said: "What are these, why do you have these?" And he was still in bed and just said, "Mom, you know I'm gay." And I said: "Well I gotta go get your dad" and he said: "I know." (Mother, family #1)

For other families, the young person initiated the coming out conversation with their parents through electronic media. Several participants cited the use of emails or MSN, and in particular, it was their mothers who received the initial form of correspondence. A mother and son best exemplified this:

> I wrote her a pretty lengthy email for being only 14 and told her everything. I think even in the subject line it said: "Do not tell dad" because I figured he would take it a bit rougher than she would. (Son, family #2)

> My son emailed me ... so he revealed it in that. I still have it. As well as some follow up emails that he wrote. (Mother, family #2)

Parents also used electronic media during their child's coming out process. As one father explained, the Internet was used as a support resource to help him better understand his son's gay identity as well as his new identity as a parent of a child who identified as LGB: "I think even the day of [our son] coming out, we found PFLAG[1] and did a lot of research on the Web, trying to identify with other parents ... on what we are supposed to do now" (Father, family #1).

It was clear, too, that television programming played a central role in the coming out process, in that, the young people used it to explore and understand their sexual identity. Consequently, some parents started to question their child's sexual orientation when LGB programming was viewed and this created the opportunity for communication – whether or not the young person was ready. As one daughter explained:

> When I first came out to my mom it was because she had started figuring it out. She found out that someone in the family had been watching *The L Word*, which is a show that was very predominantly about lesbians. At first she thought it was my brothers but then I was like: "No, I'm watching it!" She was like: "Why would you want to watch that?" I was like: "Maybe I want to figure out what it's like ... I just want to learn about different cultures, like different experiences" and she would not let it drop. (Daughter, family #6)

Media consumption was also seen as a way to help educate and shape parental perspectives. For example, some of the young people believed that media (i.e. television sitcoms and movies) sensitized their parents to diverse sexual identities and experiences. Other comments by parents emphasized how media was used as a forum in which they could learn how to relate to their child and their sexual orientation. As this son and father explained:

> I remember my mom watched the movie *The Family Stone* … it's got like this very functional gay couple. And I remember she told me she was like bawling at the end of that because my mom was really focused on learning to make it work. (Son, family #1)

> My wife and I watched the movie *The Family Stone*. It's a great movie. I was so impressed by how they accepted him [a gay partner] into the family … At the end of the movie, I remember looking over at my wife and saying: "I want to be a dad like that. I want that for our family." (Father, family #1)

While yet others pointed to the increased conflict that television sitcoms and movies could create. For some young people they felt it marginalized their sexual identity and further privileged heterosexuality within the family unit. The daughter from family #6 best exemplified this:

> Even watching movies with her became hard. My mom likes romantic comedies so every time we watched a romance movie it was always heterosexual couples. With each movie I was reminded that she would never watch a gay movie with me. So she would never experience what would be my life and I always had to experience what was her life. Now it doesn't matter at all. I would just make comments throughout the entire movie about how it is so heterosexist and this movie is so stereotypical and she'd be like: "Just shut up and watch the movie with me!" (Daughter, family #6).

Thus, media consumption played a particularly significant role in the family home facilitating opportunities to open and enhance communication within the family unit. For the young people, it provided an opportunity to explore and understand their emerging sexual identity. It also provided a forum in which they could educate and alter their parent(s)' heterosexist perspectives and attitudes. Media consumption was important to the parents as they sought to process their child's LGB identity, and what it meant for their own parenting beliefs and support systems. It also provided the parents with role models that they could aspire to be.

At the same time, parent–child relational conflict could occur during moments of media consumption. This was particularly evident during the early stages of the coming out process within the family home as parents and children appeared to struggle with the exploration of their LGB identities (i.e. the young person as LGB; the parent of a child who identified as LGB). Parent–child relational conflict was also heightened when the parental choice of media content was seen to privilege and reinforce heterosexism.

Coming out of the family closet in the public gaze

Underlying much of the parental and young adult discourse was the purposive, yet at times, contradictory nature of family outings. For example, it was evident that parent–child conflict could be heightened depending upon the recency of the coming out process. This was exacerbated when a parent had difficulty accepting their child's LGB identity. While on a family vacation after shortly coming out, one daughter explained the initial emotional conflict and strained parent–child relationship:

> I know my mom didn't enjoy that vacation as well because she was constantly upset about me coming out. We were arguing a little bit and there was also that whole gay issue because she would make a comment and I would make one back sort of thing. Like: "Oh man that guy's so hot!" And I'm like: "Meh, he's okay looking but look at that

girl!" Just because I knew she was doing it on purpose, I would do it on purpose too. So there was definitely clashing a lot – so that was the initial coming out. That's how things were. (Daughter, family #5)

However, after the initial adjustment, for some families, day trips and vacations were intentionally organized by parents to help facilitate the coming out process. For example, some parents decided to purposively visit gay and lesbian friendly communities as the destination for family excursions. Although this was something that the parents might not have been interested in before their child's coming out, they wanted to demonstrate support and acceptance for their son's or daughter's LGB identity. This was evident in families who appeared to accept their child's identity more readily (i.e. family #3) as well as those that took several years to find acceptance (i.e. family #1). As the father from family #3 and the mother from family #1 recalled:

> A zeal to be accepting. And I think things like the trips to the Castro Theater [in San Francisco] for example – going into the heart of the gay community. There was a certain part of me that was like I'm going to go into this environment and there was a certain degree of pride – to say that I'm willing to take my family into this environment and feel really good about the fact that we're just going to go there and just do it and embrace it. It's not we're just going to the Wizard of Oz; we're going to the Wizard of Oz in the Castro. (Father, family #3)

> There's an area north of Chicago called Wicker Park – and Wicker Park is a very almost Bohemian part of Chicago. On the edge of that is what's called Boys Town and that's a large gay community. We would walk around Wicker Park and everything. It became a comfort level. (Mother, family #1)

The notion of normalizing their child's developing LGB identity was embedded in some of the parents' comments, particularly with parents who were readily accepting of the identity. The father from family #3 best exemplified this: "Cause we can go to this cool neighborhood [Castro Theatre] and our daughter can look around and see lots of other gay people and see how normal it is and how cool it is."

Moreover, as the children entered their late teens, some of them expressed the desire to bring their partners on family vacations. The parent–child negotiations of bringing along a partner could create conflict. At the same time, this important step seemed to symbolize a level of understanding and acceptance for both the children and their parents. For example: "Our relationship has really evolved to a point now where we accept his partner. We accept our son. We took our son and his partner when he graduated [from high school]. We took them to Disney World" (Father, family #1).

Even with acceptance, it was clear too, there were moments when the parents would have to (re)confront their heterosexist ideals and conflicting emotional responses. As the mother from family #1 revealed, taking her child's partner on a family vacation was not without its difficulties:

> They both slept in the same bed and my husband was just like "Ugh, do they have to sleep in the same bed?" … And whenever they would show affection. I thought I was so proud of myself and I even said that to my son. But when they would hold hands or anything … on the inside … I was like "don't do that" but at the same time I was like "dammit!" (Mother, family #1)

As father #1 continued to explain, the public gaze on their family outings/vacations altered the meanings and experiences of the activity. Rather than enjoying the moment with his family he became aware of other people's reactions to his son's public displays of affection.

> I saw a lot of nobody cared. But I did notice in some – they would do double takes or they would stare or especially if we were taking a picture of the kids. I felt my parental instinct of immediately protecting. (Father, family #1)

Thus, underlying much of the parental and young people's discourse was the purposive, yet, contradictory nature of family outings. As the above participant comments revealed, some of the parents were purposive in their family outing/vacation destinations, as they wanted to be perceived as forward thinking and find moments to help normalize a developing LGB identity. The parents felt a sense of pride when showing acceptance for their child's LGB identity – and family outings were one way in which this was achieved. Yet, at times, family leisure experiences were negotiated with parent–child conflict, the negotiation of parents' conflicting feelings about their child's sexual identity, and their child's public displays of affection with their partner. In part, the presence of the public gaze and living in a culture of heterosexism and homophobia appeared to alter the families' leisure meanings and experiences; and this was particularly expressed by the parents.

Coming out to grandma and extended family members

The third theme revealed the significance of the coming out process and how it impacted the parents and young people's experiences of family functions and holiday gatherings. Specifically, the centrality of grandma and other extended family members and their familial attitudes shaped and influenced the leisure experiences of young people who identified as LGB and their parents. Consequently, the participant discourse focused on when it was appropriate (if ever) to disclose the young person's LGB identity to extended family members. Although both parents and young people expressed these concerns, comparative analysis showed a tendency for the young people to express how it was kept hidden in the early years of the coming out process.

> Extended family – that was pretty much just … that stays at home. We don't bring it there. I have some pretty conservative family members. (Son, family #1)

> I think my dad took it harder socially. He didn't want anyone to find out. He didn't want his friends or any of the rest of the family to find out. I think they [my parents] had their own motives behind who we shared it with, why we did not share it with certain people. (Son, family #2)

Some of the parents explained that they would need time to "process it all in their mind" (Mother, family #2) or it was initially thought that their child might be going through "an experimental phase in life" (Mother, family #2). Some parents explained that they needed time before they could come out to extended family members. For example: "it was probably more us than anything because he would say: 'I would like to bring [my boyfriend] to gatherings' and we probably just weren't ready for that" (Father, family #1).

As the young people grew older the perceived heterosexist values of extended family members and the potential for homophobia would alter the nature of the family gathering experiences for the parents and their children. For example, the young adults would bring their respective partner under the guise of being *just a friend* or they felt that they could not bring them at all. As these comments illustrated:

> Several years [my son] would have a guy friend come for a holiday. We just did our best to lead my mom to believe that they were just friends. (Mother, family #2)

> My grandparents didn't know yet and it kind of sucked. Especially when I started growing to care about her [girlfriend] more and more. I wanted her to meet them. I wanted them to know each other. (Daughter, family #4)

As time passed, many young people explained that it became more difficult to hide their LGB identity, in that, their experiences at extended family functions/ holiday gatherings were altered by feelings of emotional exhaustion, fatigue and disappointment.

> I remember at family functions I just wouldn't talk at all, because if I can't talk about who I am, then what's the point of talking at all? (Daughter, family #6)

> I did have a conversation with my cousin. I said: "I don't want it to be this huge process. … I just want people to know. I'm tired of saying pronouns and being careful and being very gender neutral. I'm tired of that." (Son, family #7)

Despite the fear of heterosexist values from extended family members, embedded throughout the parental and young people's discourse was a sense that the majority of extended family members were eventually accepting of the young person's LGB identity. Indeed, the word *accepting* was consistently used throughout the interviews. If there was conflict with extended family members, it seemed to centre on religious values firmly entrenched in a heterosexist system. This comment was reflected in a statement by one of the mothers that illustrated the emotional tension/conflict that could be created and how it could potentially alter the family gathering experience.

> My sister who is a very strong Catholic faithed person – she had a little bit of issues with it … [My son] was clearly upset by it and the situation was unfortunate. It was my niece's wedding. My sister in her drunken state – she was out dancing with [my son] and said: "You know, you being gay, you're going to end up going to hell because in the Bible it says … " (Mother, family #2)

It was clear, too, that grandma held a particularly significant role in the coming out process. Surprisingly, a great deal of discussion with the participants focused on the coming out stories to their grandmothers. Consequently, the emotional turmoil and stress of grandmothers knowing meant that they were often the last to find out. As one mother recalled: "My son was like: 'I don't want grandma to know, I don't want to tell her. I don't want her to know'" (Mother, family #2).

A major source of concern for some of the young adults was the heterosexist and homophobic comments that had been shared at earlier family gatherings. For example: "My grandma's the most conservative out of everyone in my family. A year before, she had said at dinner one time: 'God I can't even imagine if I had a child who's gay! It would just be so terrible'" (Daughter, family #4). One of the most emotional memories of homophobia was recalled during a sleepover:

> When I go visit grandma's house I would stay in her room that has just shelves of books, religious books, and I would go through them and look. There'd be books lined up: *Why Homosexuality is Wrong*. I'd just pick them up and I'd cry and I'd cry and I'd cry. Not because I thought they were true, but because that's what my grandma thought. (Daughter, family #3)

Through time most of the grandmothers were told about their grandchild's LGB identity and many of them became accepting and supportive to varying degrees. For some, this was a process that took many years, for others a supportive hug was given to the young person almost immediately. Further, the complexity of their relationships was also evident, in that, some grandmothers supported their grandchild's sexual identity within the public gaze. For example, one young person explained: "I danced at a gay event last weekend and she came to it and it was hosted by a drag queen. So my grandma met her first drag queen" (Son, family #1). Other grandmothers' seemed to respond with a sense of evangelism. As one mother explained: "My mom is a real evangelist and I think there is part of her that is hoping that if she can get a close relationship with [our daughter] that she can fix her ... so there's that agenda going on" (Mother, family #3).

Generational differences were often cited as one of the reasons that the young people's LGB identity should be kept hidden and why grandmothers were perceived as potentially less accepting. As the father from family #3 explained:

> You can see it in grandma's eyes. You can kinda see a level of awareness and a level of understanding and acceptance that we can't talk about this publicly ... and a lot of people grandparents age – they're from a generation where people just didn't talk about this stuff, but everybody knew about it ... people didn't deal with it, they just pretended it didn't exist.

Finally, the risk of rejection or homophobic attitudes towards the young people and their parents was so strong, that some grandmothers were never told. As these comments illustrated: "It was agreed upon that nobody told grandma – that grandma didn't know" (Mother, family #6) and "Grandma died before I was comfortable ... grandma died not knowing" (Son, family #7).

The role of mothers and LGB extended family members

As the analysis progressed, it became evident that embedded within each of the three main themes was the significant role of mothers as well as extended family members who identified as LGB in mediating familial attitudes and beliefs related to heterosexism and homophobia. Throughout the interviews, there was an overall sense from participants (parents and young people) that these groups of individuals were instrumental in mediating relationships, not only within the immediate family unit, but also with extended family.

It was clear that mothers were an important source of support and they seemed to manage the family relationships during the coming out process. Six of the seven mothers in this study were the first parent that the young people confided in and also whom they maintained ongoing conversations with. As one young person explained: "Mom, like we always chatted about things so I felt that I could chat with her more openly about more things that were important to me after coming out" (Son, family #7). Mothers also played a significant role in trying to reconstruct family relationships and reduce father–child and sibling–sibling conflict. For some young people, this appeared to facilitate a sense of understanding: "My mom was really interested in coping with it and how she can make everything comfortable" (Son, family #1). The emotional work that mothers undertook was also evident in the grandchild-grandmother relationship:

> It was really hard for my mother-in-law. And she grieved and would cry easily for quite some period of time. I just kept saying to my daughter: "If anybody in the world … you're the one who has the power to help her see things in a different way." (Mother, family #4)

However, the role that mothers played in mediating family relationships was not without judgment by their children as well as the grandmothers. Indeed, they were often in an intermediary role that had emotional consequences. For example, one daughter explained: "And she asked me not to tell my grandmother … I felt like I was constantly getting mixed messages. Like, "it's okay to be who you are, just don't tell anyone!" (Daughter, family #6) As best exemplified by one mother, reactions embedded with heterosexism, accusation, and blame could also be directed towards them:

> She [her mother-in-law] told us more than once, and me alone more than once, that maybe if we just got him a prostitute – for him to have a social experience with a woman that is professional and has experience in pleasing a man, that maybe that would set him straight … It was almost like she was blaming us, like we did something wrong, and that we could fix him. (Mother, family #2)

Underlying the parental and young peoples' discourse was also the significance of having an extended family member who identified as LGB. More than half of the young people in this study had an aunt or uncle who identified as gay or lesbian and this seemed to bring a quicker sense of acceptance within the immediate as well as extended family units. These extended family members were conceptualized as trailblazers and their experiences appeared to normalize diverse sexual identities. Further, family members who identified as LGB were seen as a source of support for both the parents and young people. As two participants said:

> She [her mom upon learning the news] seemed very frazzled and confused and she didn't know how to react … and then she talked to my uncle – her brother who was gay. (Daughter, family #7)

> I think for [our daughter] having her aunt and her current partner in her life, they've taken her under their wing. I mean they are so there for her and they just love her so much and [our daughter] knows that and I think she loves going to see them 'because they're just there for her and they understand. (Mother, family #3)

Moreover, there was a sense of aunts and uncles who identified as LGB helping to normalize diverse sexual identities within the extended family context. For example, one of the mothers shared this story:

> My husband's sister was very helpful and supportive of our daughter because she's in a lesbian relationship for the past 15 years with the same person. We were there last summer and they had a family gathering and we were like twenty plus people. We walked into the dining room area and they were sitting, my sister-in-law and her

partner and our daughter, and they were talking about it and it was open. And then people just sat down and continued listening to the conversation. (Mother, family #5)

Discussion and conclusion

Although research has demonstrated the social significance of the coming out process on young people's leisure (Johnson 1999; Kivel and Kleiber 2000; Kivel and Johnson 2013; Theriault 2014) this paper revealed that it also has a significant impact on the collective family unit's leisure experiences. Similar to earlier research, the analysis of the data revealed the significance of shared family leisure engagement in fostering a sense of togetherness, intra-familial communication, and overall relationship building (e.g. Shaw 2008; Werner and Shannon 2013). In particular, the importance of shared media experiences in the family home, family outings and vacations, and visiting extended family members was highlighted. The analysis of the family member discourse discovered that the meanings of these shared family activities could be altered in relation to the coming out process and cultural norms related to heterosexism and homophobia. It also identified the significant role of mothers as well as extended family members (i.e. aunt or uncle) who self-identified as LGB in mediating familial relationships.

The power of the consumption of media during leisure moments within the home environment was emphasized in this study. Media representations can "inform, confirm, trouble and launch our understandings of gender and sexualities" (Johnson and Dunlap 2011, 210). Similar to Johnson and Dunlap (2011) and Kivel and Kleiber (2000) the young people in the study on which this paper is based used media (e.g. television sitcoms, movies, Internet, magazines) as a vehicle to access information about being gay and to seek out positive gay role models. The findings in this paper also revealed how the young people used the Internet as a way to open communication channels with their parents (e.g. coming out through written emails, MSN chats). The significance of the media was also noted for parents processing their child's developing LGB identity. This was evident in parental accounts of the importance of on-line forums used to seek support as well as movies and television sitcoms that had positive role models that they could aspire to be. However, shared media experiences could also become problematic (e.g. movies), particularly when the young people felt that it privileged normative forms of heterosexuality.

The ways in which family members that identify as heterosexual influence experiences of and access to leisure for the young people within the family home, community, and extended family gatherings was evident. For example, coming out to their grandmother(s) was an important marker in the coming out process for both the young people and parents. Although the narratives of the young people and their parents illustrated diverse and complex reactions from grandmothers (as well as extended family members), the fear and apprehension of telling their grandmother(s) underscored all participant interviews. In part, this may be because of intergenerational differences whereby family members believed that grandmothers' possessed heterosexist beliefs that could not be altered. The very possibility of rejection and the fear of their relationship changing weighed heavily on their minds. Thus, for some young people and/or their parents, they were unwilling to challenge intergenerational differences that they did not feel could be reconciled (Hebblethwaite and Norris 2010), while others eventually invited grandmothers into their queer leisure spaces and were able to resolve the perceived differences.

It was clear, too, that mothers played a significant role in the coming out process within the immediate family unit as well as with extended family members. This builds on the existing family leisure literature that emphasizes the gendered work of mothers and the emotional labour they undertake to facilitate family activities and holiday gatherings to ensure their success (Shaw 2001, 2010). The emotional work that the mothers endure in relation to the young people's coming out process may exacerbate a sense of conflict and exhaustion between immediate family relations (parent–child; sibling–sibling; parent–parent). Moreover, the potential for mothers to be negatively judged and blamed through homophobic remarks by extended family members (e.g. grandmothers), speaks to perceived and real external pressures to reinforce heterosexist values within the family unit (Tyler 2015).

As Johnson and Dunlap (2011) point out, most youth do not have access to positive gay role models. However, as this study revealed, the significance of older extended family members who identified as LGB was important to the young people and their parents. These family members became important role models as the young people tried to re-imagine what their life could be like outside of their parents' heterosexist model. Extended family members who were openly LGB were also able to help the parents navigate the coming out process by acting as a source of support and easing conflicts between the parent–child relationships.

The findings in our paper may also have important insights to contribute to how the family unit may enact broader social change through resistant acts or attempts to enhance personal power. Resistance is viewed as individual or collective acts that seek to challenge power relations that oppress individuals or groups based on categorical definitions like race, class, sexual identity, and gender. Drawing on the work of Wearing (1998), Shaw (2006) explained that while resistance can occur in all settings and circumstances, leisure provides enhanced opportunities for resistant acts because of greater opportunities for self-expression and self-determination. Indeed, the potential for young people and their aunts and uncles who were LGB trailblazers to shift and destabilize family members' heterosexist beliefs and values may be one form of resistance.

Moreover, essential to the idea of resistance is the public and social interactional nature. Some of the parents desire to purposively visit gay-friendly communities; have political discussions at the (extended) family dinner table; and take the young people's partners on family vacations may be some ways that a heterosexist cultural system is challenged within public spaces. As Shaw (2006) points out: "the political significance of resistance lies in the process of communication and the impact such acts may have on other people and on the potential for influencing political beliefs and ideologies" (535). Through engaging in these leisure practices within the public gaze, LGB young people and their families may challenge how parenting ideologies are constructed and their connection to the (re)production of dominant cultural ideals such as heterosexism.

By revealing these aspects of family leisure and the coming out process for LGB young people, this paper also served to emphasize issues of social identity for the young people and their families of origin. That is, both parent and child go through a process of identity (re)formation (i.e. LGB young person, the parent of a LGB child) that requires a family adjustment process (LaSala 2010). Through this process various nonlinear stages may be evident such as the initial disclosure to parent(s), relational tension, and relational adjustment (Tyler 2015). Moreover, as a collective unit, the parent–child relationship becomes an evolving relational identity that constructs a shared narrative in response to family life events (Tyler 2015). As this study shows, this shared narrative may in part be constructed through the parent and young people's access to and experiences of family leisure in the home, community, and with extended family members.

Further, the ongoing process of acceptance was significant in this paper. Similar to Wakeley and Tuason (2011) the acceptance process included, "behaviors and perceptions that changed, emotional struggles, seeking and utilizing resources, and undertaking actions that helped [the parents] to accept" (21) their LGB child. Shared family leisure activities became an important vehicle through which the process of acceptance was facilitated (e.g. watching movies with LGB characters, dinner conversations with extended family members) as well as demonstrated (e.g. family outings in gay and lesbian friendly communities; taking LGB partners on family vacations).

Finally, our paper calls attention to the conceptualization of family leisure as "inherently contradictory". The notion of family leisure as contradictory is defined by previous theorizing about the inevitable co-existence of divergent experiences, expectations, meanings and realities that are associated with family time (e.g. Shaw 2010; Trussell and Shaw 2009). However, as this retrospective study revealed, although the family leisure activities may be seen to create parent–child support and conflict through divergent perspectives related to heterosexism and diverse sexual identities, it was through the process of conflict and family adjustment that a reciprocal understanding was cultivated. Thus, what might initially be seen as inherently contradictory during the early stages of family leisure engagement (positive and negative attributes of the shared experience) has the potential to facilitate a more supportive and empathetic familial relationship through time.

Our study was limited to the experiences of parents and grandparents who were heterosexual-identifying family members. As family leisure meanings and experiences may be shaped by family members with diverse beliefs and value systems, clearly it will be important for future research to consider diverse family forms (e.g. LGBTQ parents and grandparents). In addition, as siblings have an important role in the coming out process (Gorman-Murray 2008; Jenkins 2008), future research may want to capture their experiences and meanings. Research that explores the potential for leisure to help LGB young people navigate the coming out process may help better understand their lives and their families' lives. Moreover, it may help inform our understanding of the (re)construction of new dimensions to familial relationships within the private and public spheres of family life.

Note

1. PFLAG is one of the largest family and ally organizations found in the United States and Canada. It has a vast grassroots network with local chapters and a national governing body. It was founded by parents who wanted to help themselves and others understand and accept children with diverse sexual and gender identities. Its aim is to advance equality and a more accepting society for LGBTQ people.

Notes on contributors

Dawn E. Trussell is an Assistant Professor in the Department of Recreation and Leisure Studies at Brock University in Ontario, Canada. Her research programme seeks to understand leisure meanings and experiences in relation to diverse social contexts and issues of power and social inclusion, particularly related to the constructs of family, children and youth, gender and sexuality. She has written in the areas of family leisure; organized youth sport; the transition to motherhood; homelessness; methodological and ethical issues in the research process. Dawn has served as an Associate Editor for the *Journal of Leisure Research* since 2011 and is currently serving as the Vice-President/Treasurer for the Canadian Association for Leisure Studies.

Trisha M.K. Xing is a doctoral candidate in the Applied Health Sciences programme (Social and Cultural Health Studies) at Brock University in Ontario, Canada. Her research is rooted in a desire to better understand the leisure needs and issues of diverse profiles of youth, particularly those who are vulnerable or marginalized. She is interested in critically exploring the nature of leisure experiences, focusing on factors that shape leisure engagement, and examining the issues and implications of power in leisure settings.

Austin G. Oswald has a Master of Arts in Applied Health Sciences (Leisure Studies) from Brock University in Ontario, Canada. Upon graduation he was employed as a Psychosocial Rehabilitation Specialist at the New York-Presbyterian Hospital. He currently works in geriatric psychiatry and has specialized training in psychiatric care. He has a keen interest in research ethics and methodology. His research agenda explores constructs of mental health, gender and sexuality, childhood and adolescence, ageing, and families.

References

Bertone, C., and M. Pallotta-Chiarolli. 2014. "Putting Families of Origin into the Queer Picture: Introducing This Special Issue." *Journal of GLBT Family Studies* 10: 1–14. doi:10.1080/1550428x.2013.857494.

Charmaz, K. 2005. "Grounded Theory in the 21st Century: Applications for Advancing Social Justice Studies." In *Handbook of Qualitative Research*, edited by N. Denzin and Y. Linclon, 3rd ed., 507–536. Thousand Oaks, CA: Sage.

Charmaz, K. 2006. *Constructing Grounded Theory: A Practical Guide Through Qualitative Analysis.* Thousand Oaks, CA: Sage.

Charmaz, K. 2008. "Grounded Theory as an Emergent Method." In *Handbook of Emergent Methods*, edited by S. N. Hesse-Biber and P. Leavy, 155–172. New York: Guilford Press.

Crotty, M. 2006. *The Foundations of Social Research. Meaning and Representation in the Research Process.* Thousand Oaks, CA: Sage.

Cuddy, A. J. C., S. T. Fiske, V. S. Y. Kwan, P. Glick, S. Demoulin, P. Leyens, M. H. Bond, et al. 2009. "Stereotype Content Model Across Cultures: Towards Universal Similarities and Some Differences." *British Journal of Social Psychology* 48: 1–33. doi:10.1348/014466608X314935.

D'Augelli, A. R., A. H. Grossman, and M. T. Starks. 2005. "Parents' Awareness of Lesbian, Gay, and Bisexual Youths' Sexual Orientation." *Journal of Marriage and Family* 67: 474–482.

Furnham, A., and K. Saito. 2009. "A Cross-cultural Study of Attitudes Toward and Beliefs About, Male Homosexuality." *Journal of Homosexuality* 56: 299–318. doi:10.1080/00918360902728525.

Gorman-Murray, A. 2008. "Queering the Family Home: Narratives From Gay, Lesbian and Bisexual Youth Coming out in Supportive Family Homes in Australia." *Gender, Place and Culture* 15 (1): 31–44.

Grafsky, E. L. 2014. "Becoming the Parent of a GLB Son or Daughter." *Journal of GLBT Family Studies* 10: 36–57. doi:10.1080/1550428x.2014.857240.

Guba, E. C. 1990. "The Alternative Paradigm Dialog." In *The Paradigm Dialog*, edited by E. C. Guba, 17–27. London: Sage.

Harrington, M. 2013. "Families, Gender, Social Class, and Leisure." In *Leisure, Women, and Gender*, edited by V. J. Freysinger, Susan M. Shaw, Karla A. Henderson, and M. Deborah Bialeschki, 325–341. State College, PA: Venture.

Hebblethwaite, S., and J. Norris. 2010. "You Don't Want to Hurt his Feelings … ": Family Leisure as a Context for Intergenerational Ambivalence." *Journal of Leisure Research* 42 (3): 489–508.

Hilbrecht, M., S. Shaw, F. Delamere, and M. Havitz. 2008. "Experiences, Perspectives, and Meanings of Family Vacations for Children." *Leisure/Loisir* 32 (2): 541–571. doi:10.1080/14927713.2008.9651421.

Horn, S. S., J. G. Kosciw, and S. T. Russell. 2009. "Special Issue Introduction: New Research on Lesbian, Gay, Bisexual, and Transgender Youth: Studying Lives in Context." *Journal Youth Adolescence* 38: 863–866. doi:10.1007/s10964-009-9420-1.

Hutchinson, S., T. Afifi, and S. Krause. 2007. "The Family that Plays Together Fares Better: Examining the Contribution of Shared Family Time to Family Resilience Following Divorce." *Journal of Divorce & Remarriage* 46 (3/4): 21–48. doi:10.1300/J087v46n03_03.

Jenkins, D. A. 2008. "Changing Family Dynamics: A Sibling Comes Out." *Journal of GLBT Family Studies* 4 (1): 1–16. doi:10.1080/15504280802084365.

Johnson, C. 1999. "Living the Game of Hide and Seek: Leisure in the Lives of Gay and Lesbian Young Adults." *Leisure/Loisir* 24 (3–4): 255–278.

Johnson, C. W., and R. J. Dunlap. 2011. "'They Were Not Drag Queens, They Were Playboy Models and Bodybuilders': Media, Masculinities and Gay Sexual Identity." *Annals of Leisure Research* 14 (2–3): 209–223.

Johnson, C. W., A. A. Singh, and M. Gonzalez. 2014. "It's Complicated": Collective Memories of Transgender, Queer, and Questioning Youth in High School." *Journal of Homosexuality* 61: 419–434. doi:10.1080/00918369.2013.842436.

Jones, S. R., V. Torres, and J. Arminio. 2006. *Negotiating the Complexities of Qualitative Research in Higher Education. Fundamental Elements and Issues.* New York: Routledge.

Kelly, J. 1997. "Changing Issues in Leisure-Family Research – Again." *Journal of Leisure Research* 29: 132–134.

Khanna, A. 2013. "Three Hundred and Seventy Seven Ways of Being – Sexualness of the Citizen in India." *Journal of Historical Sociology* 26 (1): 120–142. doi:10.1111/johs.12007.

Kivel, B. D., and C. W. Johnson. 2013. "Activist Scholarship: Fighting Homophobia and Heterosexism." In *Leisure, Women, and Gender*, edited by V. J. Freysinger, S. M. Shaw, Karla A. Henderson, and M. D. Bialeschki, 439–450. State College, PA: Venture.

Kivel, B. D., and D. Kleiber. 2000. "Leisure in the Identity Formation of Lesbian/Gay Youth: Personal, But Not Social." *Leisure Sciences* 22: 215–232.

Klein, K., A. Holtby, K. Cook, R. Travers. 2015. "Complicating the Coming Out Narrative: Becoming Oneself in a Heterosexist and Cissexist World." *Journal of Homosexuality* 62: 297–326. doi:10.1080/00918369.2014.970829.

LaSala, M. 2010. *Coming Out, Coming Home: Helping Families Adjust to a Gay or Lesbian Child.* New York: Columbia University Press.

Malici, L. 2014. "Queer TV Moments and Family Viewing in Italy." *Journal of GLBT Family Studies* 10: 188–210. doi:10.1080/1550428X.2014.857234.

Mishna, F., P. A. Newman, A. Daley, and S. Solomon. 2009. "Bullying of Lesbian and Gay Youth: A Qualitative Investigation." *The British Journal of Social Work* 39: 1598–1614. doi:10.1093/bjsw/bcm148.

Pallotta-Chiarolli, M. 2005. *When Our Children Come Out: How To Support Gay, Lesbian, Bisexual and Transgendered Young People.* Sydney: Finch Publishing.

Ryan, C., D. Huebner, R. Diaz, and J. Sanchez. 2009. "Family Rejection as a Predictor of Negative Health Outcomes in White and Latino Lesbian, Gay, and Bisexual Young Adults." *Pediatrics* 123: 346–352. doi:10.1542/peds.2007-3524.

Ryan, C., S. T. Russell, D. Huebner, R. Diaz, and J. Sanchez. 2010. "Family Acceptance in Adolescence and the Health of LGBT Young Adults." *Journal of Child and Adolescent Psychiatric Nursing* 23 (4): 205–213.

Schänzel, H. A. 2012. "The Inclusion of Fathers, Children and the Whole Family Group in Tourism Research on Families." In *Family Tourism: Multidisciplinary Perspectives*, edited by H. Schänzel, I. Yeoman, and E. Backer, 67–80. Toronto, ON: Channel View.

Shannon, C., and S. M. Shaw. 2008. "Mothers and Daughters: Teaching and Learning About Leisure." *Leisure Sciences* 30: 1–16. doi:10.1080/01490400701544659.

Shaw, S. 2001. "The Family Leisure Dilemma: Insights from Research with Canadian Families." *World Leisure* 43: 53–62.

Shaw, S. M. 2006. "Resistance." In *A Handbook of Leisure Studies*, edited by C. Rojek, S. Shaw, and A.J. Veal, 533–545. New York, NY: Palgrave Macmillan Ltd.

Shaw, S. M. 2008. "Family Leisure and Changing Ideologies of Parenthood." *Sociology Compass* 2 (2): 688–703.

Shaw, S. M. 2010. "Diversity and Ideology: Changes in Canadian Family Life and Implications for Leisure." *World Leisure* 52 (1): 4–13.

Theriault, D. 2014. "Organized Leisure Experiences of LBGTQ Youth: Resistance and Oppression." *Journal of Leisure Research* 46 (4): 448–461.

Thoreson, R. R. 2008. "Somewhere over the Rainbow Nation: Gay, Lesbian and Bisexual Activism in South Africa." *Journal of Southern African Studies* 34 (3): 679–697. doi:10.1080/03057070802259969.

Trussell, D. E., and S. M. Shaw. 2009. "Changing Family Life in the Rural Context: Women's Perspectives of Family Leisure on the Farm." *Leisure Sciences* 31 (5): 434–449. doi:10.1080/01490400903199468.

Trussell, D. E., and S. M. Shaw. 2012. "Organized Youth Sport and Parenting in Public and Private Spaces." *Leisure Sciences* 34 (5): 377–394. doi:10.1080/01490400.2012.714699.

Tyler, T. R. 2015. "Our Story: The Parent and LGBTQ Child Relational Process." *Journal of Gay & Lesbian Social Services* 27: 17–45. doi:10.1080/10538720.2015.988313.

Wakeley, M. D., and M. T. Tuason. 2011. "Tasks in Acceptance: Mothers of Lesbian Daughters." *Journal of Gay & Lesbian Social Services* 23: 1–29. doi:10.1080/10538720.2010.541027.

Wearing, B. M. 1998. *Leisure and Feminist Theory.* London: Sage.

Werner, T., and S. Shannon. 2013. "Doing More with Less: Women's Leisure During Their Partners' Military Deployment." *Leisure Sciences* 35: 63–80. doi:10.1080/014900400.2013.739897.

Weststrate, N. M., and K. C. McLean. 2010. "The Rise and Fall of Gay: A Cultural-historical Approach to Gay Identity Development." *Memory* 18 (2): 225–240. doi:10.1080/09658210903153923.

Family experiences of visitor attractions in New Zealand: differing opportunities for 'family time' and 'own time'

Joanna Fountain[a], Heike Schänzel[b], Emma Stewart[a] and Nora Körner[c]

[a]Department of Tourism, Sport & Society, Lincoln University, Lincoln, New Zealand; [b]School of Hospitality & Tourism, AUT University, Auckland, New Zealand; [c]Formerly at Department of Tourism, Sport & Society, Lincoln University, Lincoln, New Zealand

Studies of family leisure and holidays reveal that an important goal of these experiences is the fostering of family togetherness and social connectedness away from usual work/life pressures. As outlined by [Schänzel, H. A., and K. A. Smith. 2014. "The Socialization of Families Away from Home: Group Dynamics and Family Functioning on Holiday." *Leisure Sciences* 36 (2): 126–143], however, family experiences of leisure include opportunities for both 'family time' and 'own time'. Family time incorporates opportunities for strengthening family bonds by creating family memories and allowing learning to occur. By contrast, own time encapsulates freedom from those family commitments to pursue one's own interests and to seek respite from the obligatory commitments of family life. Using data collected in face-to-face questionnaires completed with 221 New Zealand family groups, this paper seeks to explore the extent to which family time and own time experiences are differently perceived by parents accompanying their children to three family-friendly visitor attractions in Christchurch, New Zealand. In particular, the paper explores the motivations and experiences sought by fathers visiting with their child/ren at these attractions and compares these with mothers' motivations and experiences. Findings show that fathers have differing motivations and seek different experiences than mothers at these attractions, and that these motivations vary based on whether they are attending visitor attractions as sole parents or accompanied by a co-parent.

Introduction

Family leisure has been defined as 'time that parents and children spend together in free time or recreational activities' (Shaw 1997, 98). A multitude of theories indicate that well-functioning families spend leisure time together and this demonstrates meaningful interaction (Lehto et al. 2009). On the basis of these various conceptualizations of family leisure, societal norms related to family leisure have espoused a variety of benefits, one of the most common being the old adage, 'The family that plays together stays together'. The emphasis then lies on togetherness rather than using family leisure as an escape from the obligatory commitments of family life. Schänzel and Smith (2014) outlined that family experiences of leisure include opportunities for both 'family time' and 'own time' and are experienced differently by different family members. Family time incorporates opportunities for strengthening family bonds by creating family memories and allowing learning to occur. By contrast, own time encapsulates freedom from those family commitments to pursue one's own interests and to seek respite from the obligatory commitments of family life. However, there has been little research on fathers' engagement with their children in leisure and tourism research (Schänzel and Smith 2011), and virtually nothing is known about fathers' experiences at family-friendly visitor attractions. There is, therefore, little known about how family leisure is experienced differently for mothers and fathers with regard to visitor attractions.

Using data collected in face-to-face questionnaires completed with 221 New Zealand family groups, the main objective of the research on which this paper is based was to explore the extent to which 'family time' and 'own time' experiences are differently perceived by parents accompanying their children to three family-friendly visitor attractions in Christchurch, New Zealand. In particular, the paper explores the motivations and experiences sought by fathers visiting with their child/ren at these attractions and compares these with mothers' experiences and motivations of spending time with their children and creating time for themselves. Furthermore, the paper examines how contextual differences (such as whether the mother or father are sole parents or have another adult with them) might impact experiences at the attraction. For this study, families are defined as multigenerational social groups that include at least one child under the age of 18 years and one adult affiliated by blood-relationship or affinity (Schänzel, Yeoman, and Backer 2012).

Family leisure, children, mothers and fathers in the literature

Parents value the opportunity to spend quality time (indicating meaningful inter-action) with their children and this has become ever more desired in modern society (Lehto et al., 2009). Increasing importance is placed by society on families spending time together because of the perception that parents are too busy and have less time to relax, play, communicate and share meals with their children (Mintel 2009). This is despite most studies of family time use suggesting that parents are now more involved in their children's lives than previous generations (Bianchi, Robinson, and Milkie 2006; Gauthier, Smeeding, and Furstenberg 2004). Research indicates that for a family to function well, time spent together is key (e.g. Lehto et al. 2009; Shaw and Dawson 2001; Zabriskie and McCormick 2001), and visitor attractions become increasingly important for families as enablers of this desired quality family time. Family holidays, family leisure and family outings are identified in the literature to have positive contributions to families (e.g. Lee, Graefe, and Burns 2008; McCabe, Joldersma, and Li 2010; Petrick and Durko 2013), such as strengthening of relation-ships, enhanced communication and an increased sense of well-being. However, motivations for family leisure are multifarious constructs and often eclipse individual needs and desires (Decrop 2006). For example, parents take their children to leisure activities to entertain and educate them (Carr 2011) rather than going of their own volition. Much centres on the adage: 'when children are happy, parents are happy' (Gram 2005, 5) as reasons for commercial activities. Children themselves then become the motivation to visit a family attraction.

Many visitor attractions are designed for families (DeVault 2000), for example, zoos (Hallman and Benbow 2007; Mowen and Graefe 2006; Turley 2001), theme parks (Johns and Gyimothy 2002) and museums (Blud 1990; Sterry and Beaumont

2006; Wu, Holmes, and Tribe 2010). However, relatively little is known about the social experiences and benefits gained by visitors at these attractions. A study into managers' perspectives of leisure facilities in Christchurch found that they needed to be more accessible, welcoming and safe for families (Lamb 2010). It also highlighted how mothers used the facilities as meeting places and to relax while their children are entertained. Wu, Holmes, and Tribe (2010) found that for children the primary goal of family outings was having fun and that museums need to ensure they offer enjoyable and interactive activities. It appears that social interaction, rather than learning, has the most memorable effects on families in art museums (Sterry and Beaumont 2006). Johns and Gyimothy's (2002) study found that there is a dichotomy between the 'fun' experienced at theme parks and the perceived penance and self-sacrifice of the parents. By contrast, Hallman and Benbow (2007) report that visits to the zoo are regarded as providing emotional connection between family members and enjoyable educational experiences for children and are redolent with purpose and meaning. This highlights the need for children to have active fun while parents might seek rest and relaxation, a common dilemma on holidays (Gram 2005). Overall, existing research emphasizes that parents and children seek different outcomes on holiday; parents are more deliberate about educational outcomes and social identity formations while children seek social fun (Schänzel and Smith 2014).

Contradictory perspectives seem to exist in the literature on the social experiences of family leisure and family holidays. The main motivation is for families to spend time together. However, a central distinction appears between parents' emphasis on togetherness and relaxation in contrast to children's preferences for fun and social activities (Carr 2011; Gram 2005; Hilbrecht et al 2008; Schänzel 2010; Shaw, Havitz, and Delamere 2008). With regard to on-site experiences a study by Schänzel and Smith (2014) introduces a theoretical model of the sociality of family holiday experiences that centre on 'family time' and 'own time', maintaining that successful family holidays contain a balance of togetherness and separateness (see Figure 1). While there is the ideal of family togetherness in family time, every family member also seeks freedom from family commitments in their own time. Larsen (2013) argues that achieving an intra-group dynamic of creating a harmonic balanced set of different individual pleasures or 'family flow' provides optimal holiday experiences for both parents and children. Although these theories concentrate on the family holiday, the experiences outlined could be equally applied to experiences at family-oriented leisure sites. There are, however, gender role differences in how leisure experiences can be perceived by mothers and fathers.

Tourism and leisure studies informed by a feminist research perspective found that the genderized roles of mothers are mostly maintained on family holidays (Mottiar and Quinn 2012; Small 2005) and in family leisure (Clough 2001; Hall, Swain, and Kinnard 2003). This highlights the never-ending domestic and emotional work of motherhood both at home and when away. Women already experience the everyday tasks of family life as more stressful than men (Helms and Demo 2005). Instead of a break from home, leisure travel for women can contain obligation, work, social disapproval and responsibility (McCormack 1998). Increasingly, women resist the social expectations created by the 'ideology of motherhood' by redefining what it means to be a good mother through creating spaces and time for themselves to achieve their own happiness (Spowart, Hughson, and Shaw 2008; Wearing and Fullagar 1996). This includes seeking freedom from the care of children on family holidays (Small 2005) through more restful relaxation in

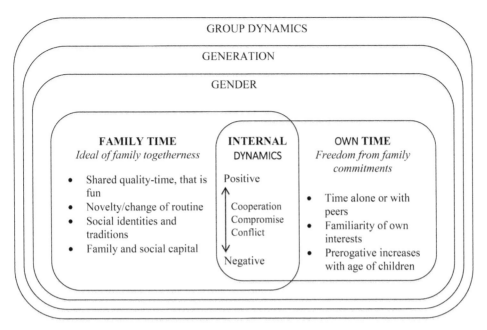

Figure 1. Model of the sociality of family holiday experiences.
Source: Schänzel and Smith (2014, 133)

their own time, for example reading or shopping (Schänzel and Smith 2014). It high-lights that fathers become the entertainers of the children partly to enable the mothers to pursue their own interests, a role that has not been acknowledged suffi-ciently in the literature (Schänzel and Smith 2011).

Fatherhood within the family leisure literature is a relatively new theme (Jeanes and Magee 2011; Such 2006). Kay (2006b) considers fathers and fatherhood as an 'absent presence' in leisure studies but also argues leisure-based activities (such as sport) are potentially more prominent in fathering than in mothering. It allows fathers to show emotional connection to their children (Harrington 2006), including for non-resident fathers (Jenkins and Lyons 2006). There is also a sense of fostering the next generation through children's leisure activities or for 'generativity' to occur (Erikson 1950), which is central to the generative notion of fathering (Harrington 2006). Fathers' involvement in family leisure can be the strongest predictor of all aspects of family functioning (Buswell et al. 2012). Kay (2006a) showed that mothers perceived family leisure as more work-like or 'being there' for the children. By contrast, fathers described leisure to mean 'being with' their children, resulting in a kind of 'leisure-based' parenting (Such 2006, 194). This points to the difficulties experienced by mothers in finding respite from caring for their children while fathers seem to be embracing more the opportunities of spending time with their chil-dren through being engaged in leisure activities. There are then qualitative differences in how family leisure time is experienced by mothers and fathers, and also quantitative differences in that mothers spend more time with their children than fathers, regardless of their work status (Sayer, Bianchi, and Robinson 2004). The reality of role divisions in most households is that a substantial amount of time mothers spend with their chil-dren involves childcare and maintenance, whereas fathers get to spend more time with their children playing (Craig 2006; Roxburgh 2006).

Facilitating family leisure through visiting attractions, which is the focus of this paper, then can provide differing opportunities for different family members. This is despite the emphasis of family activities being on spending time together or having family time for improved family cohesion (Lehto et al. 2012). Children primarily seek fun at family attractions which reflects their self-interest and this fun is fundamentally experienced as socially interactive (Schänzel and Smith 2014). Mothers seek more of a respite from their child-care duties and an opportunity to meet up with other mothers (Lamb 2010). Less is known about how fathers use visitor attractions, on which this paper sheds light. Traditionally mothers are considered the gatekeepers with regard to research in the family but with true gender scholarship there is recognition that more studies are needed on the role of fathers in leisure and tourism research (Schänzel and Smith 2011). The aim of this paper is to explore the extent to which 'family time' and 'own time' experiences are differently perceived by mothers and fathers accompanying their children to three family-friendly visitor attractions in Christchurch, New Zealand.

The family, including children, represents one of the largest markets for the leisure and tourism industry (Carr 2006; Obrador 2012). For example, in 2013 there were 469,290 two-parent with children families and 201,804 one parent with children families comprising 43% of households in New Zealand (Statistics New Zealand 2013). Over 1 million New Zealanders, or about 26% of the population, are under 18 years old and most of them live within the context of the family (Statistics New Zealand 2013). Families with children, thus, represent a significant proportion of the population and an important current and future market for leisure and tourism service providers in New Zealand. Although the concept of the family has changed, New Zealand and international studies reveal that family life continues to be important and increasingly includes family leisure activities to facilitate bonding experiences (Schänzel, Yeoman, and Backer 2012; Shaw, Havitz, and Delamere 2008). There is, however, a need to better understand how these leisure experiences are perceived differently by mothers and fathers at visitor attractions primarily catering for the family market.

Study sites

Willowbank Wildlife Reserve was established in 1975 and can be best described as a 'Kiwi Wildlife Experience' offering a tour through a wildlife reserve, an interactive Maori cultural experience, and a restaurant/cafe which offers traditional New Zealand meals. The wildlife park, which is separated from the Maori cultural experience, provides a collection of exhibits which allow visitors to interact with farm animals and to experience a selection of New Zealand native and introduced wildlife in natural bush surroundings first hand by watching, touching and feeding animals. 'Wild New Zealand' acquaints visitors with introduced species such as deer and wallabies, 'Heritage New Zealand' is a farmyard setting which includes pigs, rabbits, goats and cattle, and 'Natural New Zealand' showcases native birds like the kiwi and kea, flora, and the role of this wildlife in New Zealand cultural expressions. The relatively intimate nature of this attraction and its small scale makes it particularly appealing for pre-school and primary school-aged children.

Orana Park, set on 80 hectares of park-like grounds, is located on the outskirts of Christchurch, and is New Zealand's only open range zoo. The park opened to the public in 1976 and currently the collection has over 400 animals from 70 different species. Animal encounters are a park speciality and this enables visitors to get close to endangered animals (e.g. tigers, rhinoceros, cheetahs and keas). Where possible, only streams, moats and banks are used as barriers to allow visitors the opportunity to see the animals in a natural setting. During daily animal feeds visitors can experience and learn about the individual abilities of the animals. Visitors can also hand feed giraffes and a range of animals in the farmyard and they can travel through the lion habitat on board of a specially modified vehicle. For those visitors who do not want to walk through the park, a complimentary shuttle bus (with expert commentary) is provided. The park also includes a restaurant with both inside and outside seating and a gift shop located at the exit of the attraction. This attraction is appealing to all age groups, from pre-schoolers to adults.

Established in 1992, the Antarctic Attraction is the visitor centre at the International Antarctic Centre (IAC) located in the heart of a working Antarctic campus which include the headquarters of a number of National Antarctic Programmes. The Antarctic Attraction is designed to bring a powerful and memorable experience of Antarctica to visitors in a fun, exciting, informative and commercially successful way. The opportunity to experience thrilling fun is provided to visitors via the Hägglund ride, an amphibious all-terrain tracked vehicle driving over an adventure course. Visitors are also able to experience a virtual sea voyage to Antarctica via a four dimensional extreme movie presentation. Other exhibits include New Zealand's first combined indoor/outdoor penguin viewing area serving as a penguin life support space, which provides the opportunity to learn about how to protect New Zealand's and Antarctica's natural wildlife. The Antarctic Storm blows at −18°C in an all-weather indoor polar room chilled to −5°C where visitors can slide down an icy slope and shelter in an ice cave. These experiences aim to be fun and educational, and are aimed to appeal to those of primary school age and older.

Methodology

The data presented in this paper were collected by means of an interviewer-completed survey administered at the three visitor attractions in Christchurch, New Zealand identified above. Face-to-face questionnaires, containing closed- and open-ended questions, were completed with 300 New Zealand family groups at these attractions ($n = 00$ at each attraction) in 2010. The response rate during the whole research process was 79%. The findings reported here relate only to situations where it was a mother or father of the children completing the survey. Amongst the 300 respondent family groups, not surprisingly mothers and fathers made up the majority of respondents, with 149 mothers completing surveys, and 72 fathers ($n = 221$). Approximately one-third of the surveys with mothers and fathers were completed at each of the three attractions (Willowbank 35.7%; Orana 32.6%; Antarctic, 31.7%). The remainder of the surveys were completed by other relatives, such as grandparents or aunts and are excluded from the analysis.

Based on the literature and conceptual frameworks outlined above, the questionnaire was developed to explore the characteristics of domestic family visitors and their experiences prior to and during the attraction visit. Although the questionnaire was designed to survey only one family member, on certain questions family members answered the questions jointly which resulted in responses that contained the views and opinions of the whole family group including adults and children alike. This was the case particularly on questions regarding the activities the children had enjoyed.

The overall questionnaire included sections on family travel and attraction visitation information, motivation, experiences at the attraction, satisfaction with the visit, and changes in holiday and attraction visitation patterns. Closed questions were included in the questionnaire in order to easily group answers concerning family characteristics, motivation and demographics, while open-ended questions were included to gather in-depth spontaneous answers based on ideas and issues raised by the participants themselves concerning family motivations, experiences and satisfaction (McIntosh 1998). The sections reported in this paper focus in particular on two areas; the motivations of parents visiting the attraction, and the parent's most enjoyable experience at the attraction. The motives for attendance were measured using a Likert-scale question, with items generated by reviewing previous research (e.g. Burns and Burns 2008; Chuo and Heywood 2006; Pearce and Lee 2005). To explore the most enjoyable experience for the individual parent at the attraction, an open-ended question was asked ('What did you most enjoy today? Why did you enjoy that?') which enabled participants to define and describe their experiences in their own words, and it is from these latter questions that the researchers were able to identify elements that reflected expressions of family time and own time experiences. The questions reported on in this paper were answered by one respondent only, for example, the mother or the father.

A convenience sampling technique was chosen to select potential respondents on each day within the two week research period coinciding with New Zealand school holidays. Potential respondents needed to be current New Zealand residents visiting the attraction with a family group. Surveys were completed at different times of the day and different days of the week in order to obtain a cross section of visitors. As a result of human ethics considerations, respondents completing the survey had to be 18 years or older, and were selected on the basis of being the person most closely related to the child or children in the group. If two or more respondents were equally as closely related (e.g. a mother and a father), the person who had had the most recent birthday was selected as the respondent. Families were surveyed on a 'next to pass' basis as they left the attraction in order to ensure information about their whole visitor attraction experience could be gathered. After introducing the research, the visitor was given plenty of time to read the research information sheet, decide whether to participate, and make an informed oral consent.

After completing data collection, the quantitative survey responses were analysed with SPSS (Statistical Package for Social Science), using t-tests and chi-square tests and the findings were significant at the .05 level of confidence. Qualitative responses from the open-ended questions were entered into an Excel spreadsheet, from where data were analysed in the search for themes and patterns using open, axial and selective coding (Strauss and Corbin 1994). A starting point for this coding came from knowledge of previous literature, and was informed also by the quantitative analysis, however additional themes were identified through a close reading of the responses.

Findings

Characteristics of the sample

When comparing the mothers and fathers, there was no significant differences in education level or household income between them; both groups were more highly

Table 1. Travel party.

	n	%
Father alone	16	22.2
Father with others	3	4.1
Father as part of a couple	53	73.6
Mother alone	63	42.3
Mother with others	37	24.8
Mother as part of a couple	49	32.9

educated and from higher earning households than the average New Zealander. The majority of mothers (58.3%) and fathers (54.0%) held a university degree qualification or higher, and half of the fathers (56.9%) and mothers (50.0%) lived in households earning $NZ 80,000 or more per annum which is at or above the average annual household income in New Zealand (Statistics New Zealand 2013).

There were highly significant differences ($\chi^2 = 34.362$, $p < .001$) in the composition of travel parties of mothers and fathers visiting the attractions (see Table 1). Of the fathers, 16 visited alone with children (22.2%), while 53 (73.6%) were visiting with their spouse. The remaining three fathers were accompanied by another adult. The mothers were most likely to be visiting as a sole adult with children (42.3%), while 32.9% were visiting with a spouse. Another noticeable difference is that a quarter (24.8%) of all mothers were visiting with at least one other adult in their group. In addition, comments from mothers visiting as sole adults suggest a number of them were meeting up with other family groups at the attraction itself for socializing (so not considered part of their travel party, but important to their experience on the day).

There were significant differences also in the attractions visited ($\chi^2 = 34.659$, $p < .001$). Fathers were most likely to be interviewed at the Antarctic Attraction (41.7%) with an equal proportion interviewed at Willowbank and Orana Park (29.2% each), while mothers were most likely to be found at Willowbank (38.9%), followed by Orana Park (34.2%) and the Antarctic Attraction (26.8%) (Table 2). The differences are even more significant when parents visiting as sole adults with children was analysed. More than half (56.3%) of sole fathers were visiting the Antarctic Attraction, while a similar proportion of sole mothers (50.8%) were surveyed at Willowbank, with the smallest proportion at the Antarctic Attraction (17.5%). Mothers visiting with other adults were most likely to be at Willowbank also (51.4%). Of groups including couples, 43.1% were visiting the Antarctic Attraction, compared with 36.3% at Orana and 20.6% at Willowbank.

Table 2. Attractions visited.

	% Fathers	% Mothers
Willowbank	29.2	38.9
Orana Park	29.2	34.2
Antarctic Centre	41.7	26.8

Table 3. Age of children.

Age of children	n	%
All pre-school children (under 5 years of age)	54	25.5
Mix of pre-school and primary school	58	27.3
All primary school children (aged 5–12 years)	68	32.1
Mix of primary and secondary school	19	9.0
All secondary school children (aged 13–18 years)	6	2.8
Total	212	

In terms of the age of children accompanying their parents to these visitor attractions, the majority were primary school aged or younger (Table 3). Over half of the families interviewed included pre-school children (52.8%), while two-thirds (68.4%) included primary school-aged children. By comparison, families with high school children represent only 11.8% of those interviewed.

There were no significant differences between fathers and mothers regarding the age of children accompanying them, although fathers were somewhat more likely to be attending an attraction with groups containing no pre-schoolers than mothers. However, when the travel party of the fathers and mothers are compared there are more significant differences in the age of accompanying children ($\chi^2 = 29.996$, $p < .001$). For example, while only one father visiting as a sole adult was accompanied by a pre-school child, almost half (48.3%) of the mothers visiting as sole adults were in travel parties including pre-school children and 83.3% of mothers who were visiting with other adults had pre-schoolers in their party. What this indicates is that virtually all the pre-schoolers (96.4%) in families interviewed for this study were experiencing the attraction with their mother. This brief summary suggests that the experiences of mothers and fathers at visitor attractions might be expected to be different in some noticeable ways.

'Why we are here': the motivations of mothers and fathers at visitor attractions

Fathers and mothers reported very similar motivations for attending these visitor attractions (Table 4). When comparing the means for the ratings of the various motivations on a 5-point Likert scale, where 1 is 'strongly agree' and 5 'strongly disagree', the most highly rated values for each group are 'to spend time with the family' (fathers 1.46; mothers 1.30) and 'to have fun' (fathers 1.58; mothers 1.42), with mothers scoring each of these slightly higher than fathers. This finding confirms the absolute importance of togetherness and fun in family leisure as identified by parents (Schänzel, Yeoman, and Backer 2012). Perhaps somewhat surprisingly, given previous literature and the 'child-friendly' nature of these attractions, the third most important motivation for the parents was 'to learn new things' (fathers 1.93; mothers 1.98). These top three motivations are substantially ahead of all other motivations for visiting these attractions. The least important motivation for both mothers and fathers was 'to have others know I have been there' (fathers 3.49; mothers 3.64). A further key finding arising from this research is that t-tests revealed no statistically significant differences between the mean scores of the motivations of mothers and fathers, however chi-square analysis reveals a statistical difference in the importance of the motive: 'to develop personal interests', with fathers rating this

Table 4. Motivations for visiting attraction.

	Fathers *mean* (rank)	Mothers *mean* (rank)
To spend time with family	1.46 (1)	1.30 (1)
To have fun	1.58 (2)	1.42 (2)
To learn new things	1.93 (3)	1.98 (3)
To rest and relax	2.46 (4)	2.62 (5)
To experience thrills/excitement	2.67 (5)	2.61 (4)
To develop my personal interests	2.76 (6)	2.83 (6)
To escape from daily life	3.03 (7)	2.86 (8)
To maintain friendship	3.11 (8)	2.85 (7)
To gain a new perspective on life	3.17 (9)	3.21 (9)
To have others know I have been there	3.49 (10)	3.64 (10)

motivation more highly (χ^2 = 10.485, p < .05). This difference may be influenced by the older age of the children accompanying the fathers, and in particular, the much lower proportion of fathers visiting with pre-school children. A t-test analysis shows that the only motivational statement which was significantly affected by age of children, and in particular the presence of pre-schoolers in the travel party, is 'to develop personal interests'. For example, in travel parties where the youngest child was primary school aged the mean on this statement is 2.56, compared with 3.01 in travel parties with pre-schoolers (t = 3.062, p < . 01).

It is interesting to note that there is a distinct split in the sample of both fathers and mothers on the importance of the motivation 'to escape from daily life' in their decision to visit the attraction, with a substantial proportion of respondents agreeing with the statement, but a similar proportion disagreeing or strongly disagreeing. While there was no statistical difference, fathers were somewhat less likely to agree, and more likely to disagree, with the statement than mothers; 45.6% of mothers and 38.9% of fathers agreed or strongly agreed that an important motivation for visiting the attraction was to escape from daily life, while 31.9% of fathers and 28.8% of mothers disagreed or strongly disagreed with the statement. Fathers rate the motive 'to rest and relax' more highly than mothers, perhaps again reflecting the older age of the children accompanying them, who require less intense supervision, and the tendency of men to parent their children through play (Craig 2006; Roxburgh 2006). Overall, the most important motive to visit was to spend time together, confirming findings in the literature (e.g. Carr 2011; Gram 2005).

When comparisons are made between fathers visiting as sole adults (albeit a small sample) and mothers as sole adults the latter rate one motivation significantly more highly; this is the motivation 'to maintain friendship' (2.84 vs. 3.75; t = 2.466, p < .05), reflecting the fact that even when visiting as a sole parent, many of these mums were catching up with friends and other family groups at the attraction, a point reinforced in the comments about their experiences. This confirms Lamb's (2010) findings that mothers used these types of attractions to meet with other mothers and relax while their children were entertained in a safe environment. Many mothers visited the attractions with other adults too, suggesting a social motive to the visit, which may not be fully reflected in the motivational statement 'to maintain friendship' presented to them.

Enjoyable experiences for fathers and mothers

Respondents were asked to explain what they personally had enjoyed most about their visit to the attraction, and no one reported that they enjoyed nothing. Interestingly, despite the top ranking for motivation being the opportunity to spend time as a family, unprompted responses reveal the largest proportion of all responses mentioned some feature of the attraction as being the most enjoyable element of the day, with mothers (43%) more likely to mention an attraction feature than fathers (36%). These revolved around close interactions with animals and sensory and embodied experiences which are particularly relevant for children (Small 2008). Typical examples of this category of responses are as follows:

> Feeding [and] stroking eels, being able to get close and interact with animals, enjoyed because able to do these things with little/few barriers. (Mother visiting with other adults, Willowbank, children 11–15 yrs)
>
> Feeding the farm animals. Most interactive activity and no waiting in huge queues. Everyone could get involved and a variety of farm animals to interact with. (Father sole adult, Orana Park, children 2–10 yrs)
>
> Seeing penguins up close. One had its feet redressed and lady showed us him close up. Seeing penguins in their nest because don't usually see things that close up. (Mother with father, Antarctic Attraction, children 9–12 yrs)

The second highest set of responses, mentioned by one-quarter of all respondents (25%), referred to watching their children have fun, or watching them learn as the most enjoyable aspect of the experience. There are purposeful aspects of family leisure at play here, such as providing enjoyable educational experiences for children (Hallman and Benbow 2007; Shaw and Dawson 2001). Again, the percentage of mothers (26%) and fathers (22%) mentioning this as their favourite aspect was quite similar:

> Watching the kids enjoying themselves. Also loved kids seeing and pointing out things you wouldn't normally see. (Mother with other adults, Willowbank, children 6–9 yrs)
>
> Watching my youngest one feed the giraffe. Interested to see her match her understanding of giraffes with being close to one in real life – could see her adjusting her concepts of giraffes. (Father with mother, Orana Park, children 3–9 yrs)

Fathers (12.5%) were more likely than mothers (8%) to mention that they had explicitly learnt something at the attraction, supporting the higher ranking by fathers on the motivation 'to develop my personal interests'. This emphasis on learning may be due to their greater likelihood of being interviewed at the Antarctic Attraction, which is more focused around education and aimed at older families. Interestingly, however, fathers were more likely to mention 'being with the family' as the most enjoyable part of the day than mothers (15.3% compared to 6.6%) – 'getting out of the house and having family time' – being a typical response, perhaps reflecting the more leisure-based parenting of fathers reported elsewhere (Such 2006).

By comparison, mothers were more likely to state that what they most enjoyed was the change of scene, or the chance to relax than fathers (8.6% vs. 5.6%). Only mothers mentioned enjoying spending time with their friends in these open response answers. The attractions then provided important spaces for socializing, reinforcing the point made above about the existence of a social motive for these mothers, and some much needed respite from active care as the children could entertain themselves.

The following quotations are indicative of the opportunities provided at the attractions for 'own time' (Schänzel and Smith 2014) or to take a break from the endless tasks of motherhood (Small 2005):

> Spending time with friends in a relaxed, outdoor environment. Sitting down to have lunch – doesn't often happen as a mother. (Mother sole adult, Willowbank, children 1–3yrs)
>
> It was relaxing and the kids had fun. It was a good way to spend a Friday. (Mother with other adults, Willowbank, children 1–12yrs)

It should be noted that many responses included a number of elements, which combined to create an enjoyable day:

> Interaction with family (cousins), coffee and sunshine, watching children have a lovely time. (Mother sole adult, Orana Park, children 3–5yrs)
>
> The sunshine, the animals and great friends and time with my son. (Father with other adults, Willowbank, child 3yrs)

The family leisure provided at these family-friendly attractions then revolve around multiple opportunities for social interaction, interaction with animals, outdoor experiences, educational experiences, playfulness, relaxation and bonding time with children. While the focus of family leisure is on spending time together, these attractions also allowed for own time, especially for the mothers, that was perceived as more restful relaxation (Schänzel and Smith 2014). The social family experience of 'being together' then may not require 'doing everything' together, but can also refer to a psychological and emotional closeness fostered by individual pleasures (Larsen 2013). Watching children having fun while creating spaces and time for themselves is an important part of what attracts parents to these attractions.

Conclusion

The findings presented in this paper suggest that on the whole, while fathers and mothers are likely to be visiting different family attractions with children of different ages and abilities, their motivations for visiting and the experiences they find enjoyable are generally similar. Mothers and fathers alike are motivated to enjoy family time, have fun and to learn new things. This is reflected in their reported experiences at the attractions, whereby they find pleasure and enjoyment in the attractions themselves and in the enjoyment these attractions give to their children, largely confirming the literature on family leisure (e.g. Carr 2011; Gram 2005; Lehto et al. 2012; Schänzel, Yeoman, and Backer 2012). It is interesting to note that there is no evidence in these responses of any perception by parents of penance or self-sacrifice (cf. Johns and Gyimothy 2002), with all respondents being able to identify something that they personally enjoyed, with many mothers and fathers naming multiple enjoyable experiences. Active fun, however, was central to the children while the fun experienced by the parents was more connected with ensuring children had fun, rather than themselves. These family-friendly attractions in Christchurch then succeed in fulfilling the motivations of parents by providing opportunities for meaningful interactions and social connection for parents and children which is increasingly desirable in modern society (Lehto et al. 2012). The research also highlights that providing leisure experiences filled with relaxation, interaction, learning and fun for the entire family requires complex planning and management.

This paper has identified some differences, however, in the motivations of fathers and mothers and the experiences they seek out and enjoy at family attractions which could be explored further. It would sensible to assess the specific needs of parents and design appropriate products and services that facilitate family time as well as adult time alongside time for the children. Mothers (single or partnered) seem to relish the opportunities provided for adult time on their own or in socializing with other adults while the children are happily engaged in their own time or child(ren) time. The emphasis for the fathers (single or partnered) in their experiences appears to be more on family time with the children rather than socializing with other adults or adult time alone. Products and services provided at visitor attractions catering to the family market then need to facilitate family time experiences that are fun for the whole family; adult time experiences that are relaxing and allow for socializing as well as children time experiences that are safe and provide entertainment. The focus of family leisure experiences at visitor attractions has been on family time but more emphasis is needed on own time experiences in the form of adult time and child(ren) time or peer time for adults and children through socializing. This supports the theoretical model of the sociality of family holiday experiences (Schänzel and Smith 2014) in that own time encompasses time alone or with peers and this prerogative increases with the age of children. However, it is clear that more research is needed to understand how children perceive leisure experiences at visitor attractions.

Mothers are more likely than fathers to be motivated on these visits to family attractions by an opportunity to take a break from everyday life, if not from the everyday tasks of mothering. In that, mothers increasingly resist the motherhood discourse and exert their rights to create their own spaces of happiness for themselves (Spowart, Hughson, and Shaw 2008), by having a coffee while the children are playing or meeting up with other mothers or relatives. Mothers then use the facilities to create adult time for themselves and other adults. This allows mothers time to provide social and emotional support for others, to allow for the relief of shared childcare and to engage in social connections; a motive which could be explored further in future research. While these experiences are not always seen as particularly relaxing by the mothers, this might be partly a reflection on the high likelihood that they are accompanied by pre-school children, who generally require much closer supervision than older children. Despite this, the novelty of the exhibits and the presence of friends and other relations, including grandparents, for their children mean these mothers still have an opportunity to personally enjoy the exhibits on display and enjoy the pleasure these exhibits bring to their children. Most significantly, perhaps, it is clear that these attractions are places for mothers to socialize with friends; watching their children having fun, but also able to take 'time out' from their busy lives at home. Another explanation for the differences between the experiences of fathers and mothers is that mothers still spend more time with their children involving childcare and maintenance (Craig 2006), and perceive more of a need for respite from these duties. Facilities at family-friendly attractions then need to accommodate mothers' need for restful relaxation and social interaction, such as through a café area offered as a refuge to rest over a coffee alone or with other mothers while the children are entertained and safe.

This 'time out' or own time component (Schänzel and Smith 2014) seems to be missing from the accounts of fathers. Fathers, more than mothers, report enjoying the opportunity to be with their families, but there is not the sense that this marks a break from everyday life to the same extent. It may be that 'being with' their children in a leisure environment is their normal pattern of engagement with their children through more leisure-based fathering (Such 2006). There is little evidence either that socializing with members outside the family group is a priority in fathers' experiences. Compared to mothers, fathers seem somewhat more motivated by the attraction's learning opportunities which support their personal interests, as well as watching their children learn which is part of the generative notion of fathering (Harrington 2006). An explanation for this may be that fathers were significantly more likely to have been interviewed at the Antarctic Attraction, which provides information and exhibits aimed at children aged 8–16 years. What is not known is if their presence at this attraction is a choice by these men, based on the fact that it will enable them and their children to learn more, or the fact that there is a greater emphasis on learning *because* they are at this attraction. The fact that fathers are much less likely than mothers to be accompanied by pre-schoolers on their visits mean that learning is more likely to be an outcome for both themselves and their offspring. Further research is needed to explore why this is the case: is it that fathers are more willing to take children to visitor attractions (on their own, in particular) when their children are at least of school age so that their own motive of fulfilling personal interests can be fulfilled? Or could it be that the differing parental role of fathers – being the 'fun' parent or entertainer (Schänzel and Smith 2011), rather than the one more responsible for domestic and emotional care – means that visits to family attractions such as these seem more onerous for fathers of pre-schoolers without adult backup. It indicates that more research is needed into how family leisure is experienced differently for mothers and fathers which will add to the scarce research on fatherhood within the family leisure and tourism literature.

Notes on contributors

1. Joanna Fountain is a senior lecturer in Tourism Management at Lincoln University, New Zealand. Key research interests include tourist behaviour and experiences, particularly involving wine and other agrifoods, cultural heritage tourism, and regional and destination branding.
2. Heike Schänzel is a senior lecturer in International Tourism Management at Auckland University of Technology, New Zealand. Research interests include tourist behaviour and experiences, sociality in tourism, theory development in tourism and hospitality and qualitative research methods.
3. Emma J. Stewart is a senior lecturer in Parks and Tourism at Lincoln University, New Zealand. Research interests include human dimensions of climate change; resident responses to tourism; polar tourism; community-based research approaches and qualitative research methods.
4. Nora Körner completed a Master of Parks, Recreation and Tourism Management at Lincoln University, New Zealand. Since completing her studies she has returned home to Germany to work.

References

Bianchi, S. M., J. P. Robinson, and M. A. Milkie. 2006. *Hanging Rhythms of American Family Life.* New York: Russell Sage Foundation.
Blud, L. M. 1990. "Social Interaction and Learning Among Family Groups Visiting a Museum." *Museum Management and Curatorship* 9 (1): 43–51.
Burns, R. B., and R. A. Burns. 2008. *Business Research Methods and Statistics using SPSS.* London: Sage.

Buswell, L., R. B. Zabriskie, N. Lundberg, and A. J. Hawkins. 2012. "The Relationship between Father Involvement in Family Leisure and Family Functioning: The Importance of Daily Family Leisure." *Leisure Sciences* 34 (2): 172–190. doi:10.1080/01490400.2012.652510.

Carr, N. 2006. "A Comparison of Adolescents' and Parents' Holiday Motivations and Desires." *Tourism and Hospitality Research* 6 (2): 129–142.

Carr, N. 2011. *Children's and Families' Holiday Experiences.* London: Routledge.

Chuo, H.-Y., and J. L. Heywood. 2006. "Theme Park Visitors' Dynamic Motivations." In *Advances in Hospitality and Leisure*, edited by J. S. Chon, 73–90. Oxford: Elsevier.

Clough, S. 2001. "A Juggling Act: Women Balancing Work, Family and Leisure." In *Women's Leisure Experiences: Ages, Stages and Roles*, edited by S. Clough & J. White, 129–138. Eastbourne: Leisure Studies Association.

Craig, L. 2006. "Does Father Care Mean Father Share? A Comparison of How Mothers and Fathers in Intact Families Spend Time with Children." *Gender & Society* 20 (2): 259–281.

Decrop, A. 2006. *Vacation Decision Making.* Wallingford: CABI.

DeVault, M. L. 2000. "Producing Family Time: Practices of Leisure Activity Beyond the Home." *Qualitative Sociology* 23: 485–503.

Erikson, E. H. 1950. *Childhood and Society.* New York: Norton.

Gauthier, A. H., T. M. Smeeding, and F. F. Furstenberg. 2004. "Are Parents Investing Less Time in Children? Trends in Selected Industrialized Countries." *Population and Development Review* 30 (4): 647–672. doi:10.1111/j.1728-4457.2004.00036.x.

Gram, M. 2005. "Family Holidays. A Qualitative Analysis of Family Holiday Experiences." *Scandinavian Journal of Hospitality & Tourism* 5 (1): 2–22.

Hall, D., M. B. Swain, and V. Kinnard. 2003. "Tourism and Gender: An Evolving Agenda." *Tourism Recreation Research* 28 (2): 7–11.

Hallman, B. C., and S. M. P. Benbow. 2007. "Family Leisure, Family Photography and Zoos: Exploring the Emotional Geographies of Families." *Social & Cultural Geography* 8 (6): 871–888.

Harrington, M. 2006. "Sport and Leisure as Contexts for Fathering in Australian Families." *Leisure Studies* 25 (2): 165–183.

Helms, H. M., and D. H. Demo. 2005. "Everyday Hassles and Family Stress." In *Families and Change*, edited by P. C. McKenry & S. J. Price, 355–378. Thousand Oaks, CA: Sage.

Hilbrecht, M., S. M. Shaw, F. M. Delamere, and M. E. Havitz. 2008. "Experiences, Perspectives, and Meanings of Family Vacations for Children." *Leisure/Loisir* 32 (2): 541–571.

Jeanes, R., and J. Magee. 2011. "Come on My Son! Examining Fathers, Masculinity and 'Fathering through Football'." *Annals of Leisure Research* 14 (2–3): 273–288.

Jenkins, J., and K. Lyons. 2006. "Nonresident Fathers' Leisure with their Children." *Leisure Studies* 25 (2): 219–232.

Johns, N., and S. Gyimothy. 2002. "Mythologies of a Theme Park: An Icon of Modern Family Life." *Journal of Vacation Marketing* 8 (4): 320–331.

Kay, T. 2006a. "Editorial: Fathering through Leisure." *Leisure Studies* 25 (2): 125–131.

Kay, T. 2006b. "Where's Dad? Fatherhood in Leisure Studies." *Leisure Studies* 25 (2): 133–152.

Lamb, D. 2010. "A View from the Top: Managers perspectives on family leisure in New Zealand." *Annals of Leisure Research* 13 (3): 439–458. doi:10.1080/11745398.2010.9686857.

Larsen, J. R. K. 2013. "Family flow: The pleasures of 'being together' in a Holiday Home." *Scandinavian Journal of Hospitality and Tourism* 13 (3): 1–22. doi:10.1080/15022250.2013.808523.

Lee, B., A. Graefe, and R. Burns. 2008. "Family Recreation: A Study of Visitors Who Travel with Children." *World Leisure Journal* 50 (4): 259–267. doi:10.1080/04419057.2008.9674565.

Lehto, X. Y., S. Choi, Y. C. Lin, and S. M. MacDermid. 2009. "Vacation and Family Functioning." *Annals of Tourism Research* 36 (3): 459–479.

Lehto, X. Y., Y. C. Lin, Y. Chen, and S. Choi. 2012. "Family Vacation Activities and Family Cohesion." *Journal of Travel & Tourism Marketing* 29 (8): 835–850. doi:10.1080/10548408.2012.730950.

McCabe, S., T. Joldersma, and C. Li. 2010. "Understanding the Benefits of Social Tourism: Linking Participation to Subjective Well-being and Quality of Life." *International Journal of Tourism Research* 12 (6): 761–773. doi:10.1002/jtr.791.

McIntosh, A. 1998. "Mixing Methods: Putting the Tourist at the Forefront of Tourism Research." *Tourism Analysis* 3 (2): 121–127.

McCormack, C. 1998. "Memories Bridge the Gap between Theory and Practice in Women's Leisure Research." *Annals of Leisure Research* 1 (1): 37–50.

Mintel. 2009. *Family Leisure, Leisure Intelligence, December 2009*. London: Mintel International Group.

Mottiar, Z., and D. Quinn. 2012. "Is a Self-catering Holiday with the Family Really a Holiday for Mothers? Examining the Balance of Household Responsibilities While on Holiday from a Female Perspective." *Hospitality & Society* 2 (2): 197–214. doi:10.1386/hosp.2.2.197_1.

Mowen, A. J., and A. R. Graefe. 2006. "An Examination of Family/Group Roles in the Decision to Visit a Public Zoological Park." *Journal of Park & Recreation Administration* 24 (1): 104–123.

Obrador, P. 2012. "The Place of the Family in Tourism Research: Domesticity and Thick Sociality by the Pool." *Annals of Tourism Research* 39 (1): 401–420.

Pearce, P. L. and U.-I. Lee. 2005. "Developing the Travel Career Approach to Tourist Motivation." *Journal of Travel Research* 43: 226–237.

Petrick, J. F., and A. M. Durko. 2013. "Family and Relationship Benefits of Travel Experiences: A Literature Review." *Journal of Travel Research* 52 (6): 720–730. doi:10.1177/0047287513496478.

Roxburgh, S. 2006. "I Wish we had more Time to Spend Together … The Distribution and Predictors of Perceived Family time Pressures Among Married Men and Women in the Paid Labor Force." *Journal of Family Issues* 27 (4): 529–553.

Sayer, L. C., S. M. Bianchi, and J. P. Robinson. 2004. "Are Parents Investing Less in Children? Trends in Mothers' and Fathers' Time with Children." *The American Journal of Sociology* 110 (1): 1–43.

Schänzel, H. A. 2010. "Whole-Family Research: Towards a Methodology in Tourism for Encompassing Generation, Gender, and Group Dynamic Perspectives." *Tourism Analysis* 15 (5): 555–569.

Schänzel, H. A., and K. A. Smith. 2011. "The Absence of Fatherhood: Achieving True Gender Scholarship in Family Tourism Research." *Annals of Leisure Research* 14 (2–3): 129–140.

Schänzel, H. A., and K. A. Smith. 2014. "The Socialization of Families Away from Home: Group Dynamics and Family Functioning on Holiday." *Leisure Sciences* 36 (2): 126–143. doi:10.1080/01490400.2013.857624.

Schänzel, H., I. Yeoman, and E. Backer, eds. 2012. *Family Tourism: Multidisciplinary Perspectives*. Bristol: Channel View.

Shaw, S. M. 1997. "Controversies and Contradictions in Family Leisure: An Analysis of Conflicting Paradigms." *Journal of Leisure Research* 29 (1): 98–112.

Shaw, S. M., and D. Dawson. 2001. "Purposive Leisure: Examining Parental Discourses on Family Activities." *Leisure Sciences* 23 (4): 217–231.

Shaw, S. M., M. E. Havitz, and F. M. Delamere. 2008. "I Decided to Invest in My Kids' Memories: Family Vacations, Memories, and the Social Construction of the Family." *Tourism Culture & Communication* 8 (1): 13–26.

Small, J. 2005. "Women's Holidays: Disruption of the Motherhood Myth." *Tourism Review International* 9 (2): 139–154.

Small, J. 2008. "The Absence of Childhood in Tourism Studies." *Annals of Tourism Research* 35 (3): 772–789.

Spowart, L., J. Hughson, and S. Shaw. 2008. "Snowboarding Mums Carve out Fresh Tracks: Resisting Traditional Motherhood Discourse?" *Annals of Leisure Research* 11 (1/2): 187–204.

Statistics New Zealand. 2013. "Families and Households in New Zealand." Accessed November 26, 2014. http://www.stats.govt.nz/.

Sterry, P., and E. Beaumont. 2006. "Methods for Studying Family Visitors in Art Museums: A Cross-Disciplinary Review of Current Research." *Museum Management and Curatorship* 21 (3): 222–239.

Strauss, A., and J. Corbin. 1994. "Grounded Theory Methodology: An Overview." In *Handbook of Qualitative Research*, edited by N. K. Denzin and Y. S. Lincoln, 1–8. London: Sage.

Such, E. 2006. "Leisure and Fatherhood in Dual-earner Families." *Leisure Studies* 25 (2): 185–199.

Turley, S. K. 2001. "Children and the Demand for Recreational Experiences: The Case of Zoos." *Leisure Studies* 20 (1): 1–18.

Wearing, B., and S. Fullagar. 1996. "The Ambiguity of Australian Women's Family Leisure: Some Figures and refiguring." In *Women, Leisure and the Family in Contemporary Society: A Multinational Perspective*, edited by N. Samuel, 15–34. Wallingford: CABI.

Wu, K. L., K. Holmes, and J. Tribe. 2010. "Where Do You Want to Go Today? An Analysis of Family Group Decisions to Visit Museums." *Journal of Marketing Management* 26 (7–8): 706–726. doi:10.1080/02672571003780007.

Zabriskie, R. B., and B. P. McCormick. 2001. "The Influences of Family Leisure Patterns on Perceptions of Family Functioning." *Family Relations* 50 (3): 281–289.

Understanding ambivalence in family leisure among three-generation families: 'It's all part of the package'[†]

Shannon Hebblethwaite

Department of Applied Human Sciences, Concordia University, Montreal, QC, Canada

Although family leisure plays a central role in the development of close family bonds, it is not without its challenges and has been found to be both consensual and conflictual. Furthermore, family leisure researchers have neglected the voices of older adults. Building on Shaw's [1997. "Controversies and Contradictions in Family Leisure: An Analysis of Conflicting Paradigms." *Journal of Leisure Research* 29 (1): 98–112] call for a contradictory theory of family leisure and framed by the model of intergenerational ambivalence [Luscher, K., and Pillemer, K. 1998. "Intergenerational Ambivalence: A New Approach to the Study of Parent-child Relations in Later Life." *Journal of Marriage and Family* 60 (2): 413–425], the purpose of this interpretive study is to address these two significant gaps in the literature and explore how intergenerational ambivalence is experienced in family leisure in three-generation families (grandparents, parents, and adult grandchildren). Sixteen family triads were interviewed and reflected on both the benefits and challenges of family leisure. The findings provide valuable insights into the ambivalence that is experienced in family leisure across generations. The purposive nature and the generative effect of family leisure, along with the norm of non-interference help families to cope with the feelings of ambivalence that are commonly experienced in their relationships.

Family leisure has important implications for family relations. The bulk of the family leisure literature, however, privileges the nuclear family (heterosexual couples with young children) and fails to attend to extended family relationships, including grandparents and grandchildren (Hebblethwaite and Norris 2010, 2011; Holland 2013; Scraton and Holland 2006). Similarly, family research has been criticized for an implicit acceptance of the status quo, with continued emphasis on families with young children (Walker 2009), including research on grandparenting that mainly focuses on younger grandchildren (Hayslip and Page 2012). Given that much of the life course is spent in adult intergenerational relationships, that nearly 70% of older adults are grandparents, and that 75% of children born in 2000 will have at least one grandparent still living when they reach age 30 (Kemp 2003; Uhlenberg and Kirby 1998), 'the significance of these ties for everyday living and personal well-being cannot be over-stated' (Cooney and Dykstra 2013, 356). Increased longevity and decreased fertility rates have changed families significantly over the past two decades (Olshansky et al. 2009) and grandparent–grandchild relationships are lasting longer than ever before. Grandparents today are more likely to live longer, be in better health, be more highly educated, be more likely to have retired, and have fewer grandchildren. This results in more time for each grandchild and allows grandparents to make more meaningful investments in their grandchildren's lives (Uhlenberg 2009). This stage of the grandparent–grandchild relationship, when grandchildren are emerging adults, has been largely ignored (Hayslip and Page 2012).

Recent literature has begun to explore the implications for family leisure in intergenerational relationships between grandparents and grandchildren (Havitz 2011; Hebblethwaite and Norris 2010, 2011; Holland 2013; Scraton and Holland 2006). This work highlights both benefits and challenges in these family leisure experiences. Hebblethwaite (2014) expands upon this literature to include three generations (grandparents, parents, and adult grandchildren) and finds that family leisure is a key contributor to strong family ties. To deepen our understanding of family leisure in extended families and to understand both consensus and conflict in these experiences, the purpose of this paper is to explore how intergenerational ambivalence is experienced in family leisure among grandparents, parents, and adult grandchildren.

Literature

Family leisure and family relations in three-generation families have received scarce attention from both leisure and family scholars. Literature that does address these relationships highlights both benefits and challenges and notes experiences of both consensus and conflict. To understand these relationships in more depth, I draw on theoretical and empirical literature on purposive leisure, generativity, and intergenerational ambivalence. Additional work focusing on grandparenting has sensitized me to the contributions of socioemotional selectivity and the norm of non-interference. Each of these will be discussed in relation to family leisure.

Purposive leisure

Leisure has been defined in terms of the form, time, and place of the activity, but also some sense of its meaning to the individuals engaged in leisure (Kelly and Godbey 1992). The emphasis, however, is on relaxation, diversion, knowledge, social participation, and creativity (Gordon, Gaitz, and Scott 1976). Neulinger (1974) proposed an attitudinal approach to defining leisure that included perceptions of freedom, intrinsic motivation, and the non-instrumentality of the pursuit. Leisure researchers have been criticized for relying too strongly on individual, social–psychological understandings of leisure experiences and failing to account for the influence of the social context or interactional aspects of leisure (Edwards and Matarrita-Cascante 2011; Rojek 2005; Shaw and Dawson 2001).

Family leisure researchers have responded to this critique, investigating social structures and exploring how family activities may not typically be freely chosen, intrinsically motivated, or even necessarily enjoyable (Freysinger et al. 2013; Schwab and Dustin 2015; Shaw and Dawson 2001; Watson 2000). Shaw and Dawson (2001) propose purposive leisure as a term that best describes the meaning and experience of family leisure. They suggest that purposive leisure is 'planned, facilitated, and executed by parents in order to achieve particular short- and long-term goals' (228), including enhanced family cohesion and moral value teaching. Recent literature supports the concept of purposive leisure in the context of family vacations (Shaw, Havitz, and Delamere 2008), social class (Harrington 2014), women's experience of breast cancer (Shannon and Shaw 2005), rural farm women (Trussell and Shaw 2009), fathers' involvement in family leisure (Harrington 2006), and three-generation family leisure (Hebblethwaite 2014). More recently, Harrington (2013) interrogates gendered approaches to purposive leisure, suggesting that mothers and fathers may emphasize different aspects of purposive leisure. One key goal often implicated in purposive leisure is the imparting of family values through leisure experiences. Holland (2013) found that sharing similar activities across generations and 'learning leisure' from female relatives were common in three-generation families of women. This is a central feature of generativity, but little scholarly work has implicated generativity due to the narrow focus in family research on the nuclear family and lack of interdisciplinary work in this area (Hebblethwaite and Norris 2011). Generativity may be one of the central purposes of engaging in family leisure.

Generativity and family leisure

Generativity refers to the midlife concern for, and care of, future generations as a legacy of the self (Erikson 1963). This commitment to the next generation may be expressed through parenting, teaching, mentoring, leadership, religious involvement, and civic or political engagement (de St. Aubin, McAdams, and Kim 2004). Although generativity is frequently treated as a midlife construct, recent research shows that generativity exists across the lifespan, including in adolescence (Frensch, Pratt, and Norris 2007; Lawford et al. 2005) as well as older adulthood (Hebblethwaite and Norris 2011; Kleiber and Nimrod 2008). Generativity is positively associated with successful ageing (Peterson and Duncan 2007), as well as psychological well-being (Rothrauff and Cooney 2008) and life satisfaction (Ackerman, Zuroff, and Moscowitz 2000).

Family leisure is associated with similar benefits. Family leisure is defined as 'time that parents and children spend together in free time or recreational activities' (Shaw 1997, 98). Societal norms related to family leisure espouse a variety of benefits, one of the most common being the old adage, 'The family that plays together, stays together'. Most family-related leisure research, in fact, focuses on these benefits, including improved communication among family members, higher quality of family relationships, and enhanced family cohesiveness and strength (Freeman and Zabriskie 2002; Orthner and Mancini 1990; Palmer, Freeman, and Zabriskie 2007). Family leisure positively impacts family communication and overall family functioning (Poff, Zabriskie, and Townsend 2010). It is an important context for teaching, mentoring and creating a family legacy (Hebblethwaite and Norris 2011). Harrington (2001, 2006) notes that a key feature of family leisure is the purposeful sharing of values, interests, and a sense of family. This research highlights important generative features of family leisure.

According to Erikson (1963), the dialectical conflict of generativity vs. stagnation reflects an internal resolution of the conflict between self-preoccupation or self-indulgence (stagnation) and the nurturing concern for those individuals, ideas, traditions, and cultural productions that will inevitably outlive oneself (generativity) (Manheimer

2004). Generativity is exhibited beyond midlife in grandparents' stories of teaching their grandchildren (Norris, Kuiack, and Pratt 2004) and in older adolescents who tell stories of how their own grandparents teach them important values (Pratt et al., "Intergenerational Transmission of Values," 2008). Generativity has also been studied in three-generation families. Generative parents are more optimistic and forgiving of grandparent behaviours that they perceive to be problematic in interacting with their young grandchildren (Pratt et al., "Parents' Stories of Grandparenting Concerns," 2008). Family leisure facilitates the development and expression of generativity across the lifespan through the processes of building a legacy, sharing wisdom, and reciprocal experiences of teaching and learning (Hebblethwaite and Norris 2011). Manheimer (2004) suggests that the emphasis should be on interacting life stages, rather than the isolated ones proposed in Erikson's (1950) original conceptualization. He expands on Erikson's (1986) process of grand-generativity, and suggests that generativity is evident in multiple life stages, rather than just midlife. Generativity, therefore, may play a more significant role for grandchildren and grandparents than previously illustrated. Given the role that family leisure can play in enhancing family relationships, and the recognition that the family can be an important context for the development and expression of generativity, further exploration of the relationship between generativity and family leisure in intergenerational relationships is warranted.

Ambivalence and family leisure

Imparting family values and leaving a legacy may be one of the key motivators of family leisure. Yet not all family leisure is consensual in nature. In recent years, family researchers have critically deconstructed the normative assumptions associated with family research. Leisure scholars, for example, suggest that family leisure is not always a categorically positive experience and highlight challenges associated with family leisure experiences (Freysinger 1997; Hebblethwaite and Norris 2010; Kay 1998, 2000; Scraton and Holland 2006; Shaw 1992, 1997; Shaw and Dawson 2003; Trussell and Shaw 2007, 2009; Watson 2000). Although family leisure can help families to develop personal histories, common interests, and strong intergenerational bonds, contradictory thoughts and emotions are regularly experienced in these family leisure experiences (Hebblethwaite and Norris 2010).

Shaw (1997) suggests that a contradictory theory of family leisure would be useful in understanding both the positive and negative aspects of the experience. The intergenerational ambivalence model (Luscher and Pillemer 1998) addresses these concerns and has recently been applied to the study of family leisure (Hebblethwaite and Norris 2010). Relationships within families inherently involve *both* consensus and conflict (Bates and Taylor 2013; Birditt, Fingerman, and Zarit 2010). Intergenerational ambivalence relates to the experience of contradictions in relationships between parents and offspring (Luscher and Pillemer 1998). This includes contradictions at both the level of social structure, including institutional resources and requirements, such as statuses, roles, and norms, and at the subjective level, in terms of cognitions, emotions, and motivations (Luscher and Pillemer 1998). More specifically, Luscher (2000, 16) states that ambivalence exists when 'dilemmas and polarizations of feelings, thoughts, actions, and, furthermore, contradictions in social relations and social structures, which are relevant for personal and societal development, are interpreted as being basically irreconcilable'.

The intergenerational ambivalence framework, therefore, moves away from theorizing about the typical 'love-hate relationship' (Luscher 2000) and towards an understanding of the complexity of intergenerational relations. The emphasis in this model is not solely on conflict, but reflects the simultaneous existence of both positive and negative thoughts and emotions that cannot be reconciled, thus avoiding the dualistic view of family relationships as either running smoothly or being fraught with conflict (Pillemer and Luscher 2004). Connidis (2012) suggests that ambivalence is useful in exploring the 'negotiation (action) of family ties in the context of current institutional arrangements (family, work, health, education) and structured social relations (gender, age, class, race ethnicity, sexual orientation)' (37). Intergenerational ambivalence, therefore, accounts for both the individual sentiments (psychological ambivalence) and the negotiation of family ties as influenced by social structures and relations (sociological ambivalence) (Connidis 2012). Thus, ambivalence can be applied at the levels of individuals, relationships, social institutions, and societies (Lettke and Klein 2004).

The norm of non-interference is one key normative social construct that grandparents negotiate in their relationship with their grandchildren. Grandparent input and authority into family relationships is contingent on the request and/or sanctioning by the parent (Cherlin and Furstenberg 1986). This norm has been found to be one of the strongest associated with grandparenting behaviours (Douglas and Ferguson 2003; Kemp 2004).

Carstensen's (1992) theory of socioemotional selectivity may also be implicated in how older adults cope with ambivalence (Hebblethwaite and Norris 2010). Older adults are strongly motivated by emotional regulation and, therefore, minimize conflict in their lives, often choosing to participate in relationships that are closer and more rewarding. This may lessen the ambivalence they perceive in their family leisure.

Family leisure research demonstrates that intergenerational ambivalence exists in family leisure experiences. Havitz (2011) presents his authoethnographic struggle with ambivalence in family vacations. Scraton and Holland (2006) outline grandfathers' ambivalence in their relationships with their grandchildren. Hebblethwaite and Norris (2010) highlight the evolving nature of ambivalence in family leisure over time among grandparents and adult grandchildren. How families negotiate this ambivalence, however, is less clear. Since higher levels of ambivalence are associated with decreased well-being (Lowenstein 2007; Fingerman et al. 2008), it is necessary to understand how families cope with their experiences of ambivalence. The generative nature of family leisure, along with socioemotional selectivity and the norm of non-interference may give purpose and temper the ambivalence experienced in family leisure.

Methodology

A social constructionist approach to grounded theory (Charmaz 2006) guides the study on which this paper is based. This approach accounts for the social context of experiences and acknowledges the active process of generating meaning that occurs between the researcher and the participant. Theory may be generated initially from the data or elaborated upon, if pre-existing theories seem appropriate to the area of investigation (Strauss 1987).

Data collection

Triads of adult grandchildren, one parent, and one grandparent were recruited using snowball sampling across Canada from 2011 to 2012. Grandchildren were eligible to

Table 1. Participant characteristics.

$N = 48$	Grandparents	Parents	Grandchildren
Sex (female:male)	8:8	9:7	9:7
Mean age (age range)	77.6 (62–91)	50.8 (37–60)	21.8 (18–27)
Education	5 college/university 6 high school 5 did not complete high school	16 college or university	16 college or university
Marital status	Married (1 widowed)	Married or common-law	Single
Employment	Retired	11 full-time 5 part-time	4 full-time 12 students (6 employed part-time)

participate in the study if they were between the ages of 18–27 and had a parent and a grandparent who were also willing to participate in the study. No age requirements were placed on the parents or grandparents.

The study included 16 grandparent–parent–grandchild triads ($N = 48$) (see Table 1). Participants were dispersed across Canada, living in the provinces of Ontario, Quebec, Newfoundland, and British Columbia. Most families had three generations living in the same province, but two families had members who lived in different provinces. There was an equal distribution of families living in rural and urban areas (for further examination of this context, see Hebblethwaite 2014). Grandparents, parents, and grandchildren were interviewed separately. Interviews were conducted by the first author or by a research assistant. The grandchildren chose which parent and grandparent (if they had more than one) that they invited to participate in the study.

Participants were asked to speak specifically about their family members who were participating in the study, but they were also encouraged to speak about other family members in order to develop a broad understanding of their families. The following research questions guided the interviews: How do grandparents, parents, and adult grandchildren participate in family leisure? What is the meaning of family leisure for grandparents, parents, and adult grandchildren? How is the experience of family leisure related to the intergenerational relationship? How do families experience ambivalence in their family leisure? Participants were asked to describe the time they spent together in free time or recreational activities and were asked to reflect upon both the positive and negative aspects of these experiences. They were also asked to consider the role that these experiences played in their relationships with their family members. The interviews were conducted separately, rather than together, in order to encourage participants to be open and honest in their discussion of their experiences. Since family leisure has the potential to be conflictual, we were concerned that participants would feel uncomfortable presenting this aspect of their experience if they were not guaranteed this confidentiality.

A total of 48 interviews were conducted, audio-recorded with participant consent, and then transcribed verbatim. Detailed fieldnotes, analytical memos, and a reflective journal were maintained throughout this process, the data from which further informed the emergent understanding of participants' experiences. Participation in the study was strictly confidential and pseudonyms have been used in the data presented here to ensure that confidentiality was maintained.

Data analysis

Each interview was analysed individually using a social constructivist grounded theory approach (Charmaz 2006). Data were gathered from family triads, but analysis occurred across generations, not by family triad. All data were coded separately by the author and the research assistant. This method consisted of initial, line-by-line coding, focused coding, raising codes to categories, and theorizing based on these categories and grounded in the experiences of the participants (Charmaz 2004). The research assistant participated in the initial line-by-line coding and the author conducted the remaining focused coding and raising codes to categories. Data were systematically compared to the current literature on family leisure and intergenerational relations. Analytic memos were essential throughout the analysis to move beyond descriptions and concepts and to theorize about the experience. Data were stored and organized using the QSR NVivo software package to facilitate the development of categories and comparison of codes applicable to each category. The final stage of the data analysis involved the theoretical integration of the categories that emerged from the data.

Findings

Experiencing ambivalence as a normal part of family life

All three generations experienced ambivalence to some degree in their family leisure. There was always some level of enjoyment of the experiences, but it was often discussed in a comparative sense. For example, one grandson alluded to family leisure as important but not the most exciting leisure experience, stating,

> Well they are always enjoyable moments. We take advantage of the time to see each other, talk, and exchange on subjects, get news from each other. It's nice to see each other. Obviously we don't jump excitedly each time but it's definitely enjoyable.

Another father acknowledged ambivalence in family relationships, but noted differences between the relationship with his parents compared to his children, saying 'Well its not an obligation but families are made that way. Obviously I'm going to have more of an emotional connection with the activities that I do with my children than the ones I share with my parents'. Relationships with grandparents were valued, but were consistently seen as less important than relationships within the nuclear family.

The grandparents were sometimes hesitant to talk about negative aspects of their relationships as evident in one grandmother's statement, 'I don't know if I really want to talk about the challenges'. Despite this initial hesitation, most grandparents did reveal ambivalence in their relationships, but often minimized this ambivalence, framing it as a normal part of their relationships. One grandfather stated, 'He has his own activities and, I mean he doesn't inform us of his activities, I mean he is 22! We don't meddle in his schedule'.

Ambivalence was accepted as a normative aspect of all family relations. This was clearly stated by one grandson who said, 'I think you're crazy to think any relationship can be one side or the other. If it is, it's probably not really a true relationship'. One mother reflected on the co-existing positive and negative emotions involved in the same activity. There was a sense of obligation, but a co-existing gratefulness about their involvement in family leisure. She stated,

> Right now, any leisure – any sports or school stuff, or any hobbies that the kids have – my going with them and watching them is sort of like a motherly duty, kind of still. But I get such sense of gratefulness that I can be part of that.

Another mother spoke about how family relations and family leisure changed over time and how ambivalence ebbed and flowed over the course of their relationship. She accepted this as a normative experience, saying, 'And you can have great years and then, you know, you can have years full of issues. But it's all part of the package'.

Coping with ambivalence

Using family leisure to share family values

Ambivalence was accepted as normative in these intergenerational relationships. It was not something that would go away, but the families did find ways of adjusting to the irreconcilable experience of ambivalence. The most salient way was by emphasizing the importance of family leisure to engender and impart family values between the generations. This was very clear in the grandparents' interviews, evident in this grandfather's statement,

> It gives a sense to our life. Personally I have my own activities, my wife as well, and we often go to the movies or to the opera and we have our own activities. But it wouldn't be enough to say that we have an interesting life. On the family level it's important. But on the personal level even more because it's what we leave behind and our values that matter.

Similarly, one grandmother reflected on her obligation to share family values. When speaking about the importance of family leisure, she reflected,

> I think children and the next generation are really crucial. It's where you can be happy very easily, and much of what goes on in a family reflects what will happen later in their lives. So, of course, in terms of an obligation, I guess, it would be to set a good example and morally and ethically kind of lead them the way you think you should see them go.

Sharing family values and engendering a strong sense of commitment to the family were highly regarded by all three generations. In some cases, there were explicit values shared through stories, but there was also a more subtle learning that came through role-modelling from previous generations, as one mother reflected,

> Well, I think my mom and her mom and that generation, they did stuff together all the time. So then that's been passed down to me and my mom and my family. So it's just kind of something that we've grown up with and come to appreciate. It's been built in.

Another mother was more explicit about the specific values that her family shared. These values were generated through shared family leisure experiences.

> I think it's [leisure] an expression of what we all value in terms of valuing our family relationships, in terms of valuing our health, in terms of valuing even commitment. And so that sense of values I think has been reinforced by the number of things that

we've always done together. It was our commitment to family, it's our commitment to each other, it was maybe even loyalty to each other to a certain extent.

As the grandchildren passed through the stage of emerging adulthood, they too became acutely aware of the importance of family connections. They recognized the importance, for their grandparents in particular, of being able to share their knowledge and experiences with their grandchildren. One granddaughter, who characterized her grandmother as a strong feminist, stated, 'I think she's always had this feeling that it's important for her to impart, you know, some, like feminist wisdom onto her granddaughters'. She encouraged her granddaughter to participate in any sports she wanted and to not be constrained by gender stereotypes.

Although some of the grandchildren recognized the importance for their grandparents of being able to share their experiences and impart wisdom to the younger generations, others were explicit about the benefit that they gained from their grandparents' knowledge and wisdom. They were extremely grateful for the opportunities they had to learn from their grandparents. One grandson stated,

> I'm older, I'm more mature and my interests have changed as well. You kind of see you've got such a valuable resource there and hopefully keep that because everybody in the family has got something Grandpa built them. That's important to me too, like that connection to family.

Across all three generations, the purposeful use of family leisure experiences to create strong family values tempered the ambivalence in their relationships. By engendering a generative commitment, they became more accepting of any ambivalence that they had experienced.

Turning points

Grandchildren, specifically, began to value their family leisure experiences with their parents and grandparents as they navigated emerging adulthood. Beyond this developmental stage, however, were key turning points in their lives that engendered a greater appreciation for their families and their family leisure. For some grandchildren, when they moved away from home to attend college or university, they suddenly realized that they had taken that family time for granted. One grandson reflected, 'But maybe I'm just more cognizant of spending that time because I didn't get to do it for a while'. Another granddaughter contemplated the change in her perspective over time. This change was influenced by her observation of other families that did not have the same emotional closeness.

> It means a lot. Yeah. It's definitely something that, you know, when you were young you were like, 'Oh, I don't really want to go with my parents to go play tennis.' We always had the tennis membership. And you know, I would rather go with my friends. But now that I'm older, I've come to really appreciate it, actually. And I've seen other families that aren't as close. And, maybe even if it's just having dinner together every night. We always have dinner together. And I've really come to enjoy that. And, you know, depend on it, like, 'Okay. That's my family time and I know we're going to be together.' So definitely means a lot to me.

For others, it was more unexpected events that caused them to reflect on their relationships and re-evaluate their thoughts about family leisure and the ambivalence they experienced. Heath issues were common turning points, as illustrated by one granddaughter who said,

> I remember when my grandmother had her heart surgery and we thought she was going to die. It really made me aware of how often we'd put off seeing somebody. I guess it really made me aware of how important it is to spend the time that we have with people because you only have so much time to get to know someone, and then after that they're gone and all that there is left is what you remember and what other people remember and you can never ask them these questions that you always wanted to know.

These turning points reinforced the importance of family and helped to moderate the ambivalence that the grandchildren had experienced when they were younger.

Not meddling

While grandchildren's ambivalence was tempered by these turning points, grandparents engaged in other strategies to help them cope with the ambivalence that was inherent in their intergenerational relationships. They repeatedly emphasized the importance of not meddling in their children's and grandchildren's lives. They used family leisure to subtly impart their wisdom and values, but were very careful not to give unsolicited advice. One grandfather explained how this helped he and his wife to avoid conflict in their relationships, stating,

> Each person educates their children like they want to educate them. We have no business meddling in that and I never will. Unless they ask us for advice. This is very important. Because if we start meddling in their situations, that is when the problems start.

This strategy was common among grandparents. It was also apparent to the parents and grandchildren, who were aware of the grandparents' use of this strategy. By not meddling, the grandchildren were more appreciative of the grandparents' advice when it was given, as evidenced by one grandson who reflected,

> Grandpa, he'll step in if he thinks it's needed. But at the same time I think he just garners that respect from the family that if Grandpa's telling you something, it's probably the right thing. So he'll step in if he needs to. And when I was a teenager he would tell me if I wasn't acting up to his standards, which I appreciated. Probably at the time a few times I probably didn't like it so much, but now when you think about it he was right, so I appreciate that now.

Discussion

The experience of family leisure among grandparents, parents, and adult grandchildren is multifaceted and evolves over the life course. It is complex and simultaneously challenging and rewarding. Theoretically integrating these findings, I suggest that purposive and generative family leisure, turning points, and the norm of non-interference all play key roles in facilitating coping with intergenerational ambivalence. Family leisure is a meaningful and purposive context for the development and expression of generativity in all three generations.

Coping with ambivalence

Using intergenerational ambivalence to guide the investigation of family leisure in three-generation families, I build upon previous family leisure research that has highlighted the consensual (Orthner and Mancini 1990) and contradictory nature of family leisure (Shaw and Dawson 2003). Psychological ambivalence was evident in the individual sentiments expressed by the participants. Family leisure was not always the preferred, or most exciting way to engage in leisure. Sociological ambivalence was reflected in the active negotiation of family ties as influenced by normative social structures and relations, such as feelings of obligation or the norm of non-interference. Ambivalence was a normative part of the relationships between grandparents, parents, and adult grandchildren. The thoughts and emotions were irreconcilable with the social structures and resulted in constant negotiation between individual needs and family expectations. As Connidis (2012) suggests, individuals do not mindlessly follow prescribed norms, nor do they create family life just as they would like it to be. Rather, in the face of pressures exerted by social structure, they make choices to negotiate relationships that they believe contribute to a meaningful family life. Negotiation involves agency as individuals navigate the management of new situations. 'Exercising agency applies both to paths taken or not taken – the decisions and choices that we make – and how we handle a specific chosen or imposed transition' (Connidis 2012, 42). Purposive leisure was crucial to this negotiation.

Purposive leisure and generativity

Engaging in purposive leisure that met the generative needs of all three generations was central to this negotiation of ambivalence. This allowed families to attain their goal of developing a strong family history and sharing family values across generations, thereby achieving the family legacy that is an essential component of generativity. This supports previous work that emphasizes the important role that teaching and mentoring play in the lives of grandparents (Hebblethwaite and Norris 2011; Kemp 2004; Waldrop et al. 1999). These findings also contribute to the expansion of our understanding in recent years of generativity beyond midlife. All three generations in this study focused on the generative aspects of their family leisure. This supports recent research by family scholars who have found evidence of generativity in both adolescents and young adults (Hebblethwaite and Norris 2011; Lawford et al. 2005; Pratt et al., "Intergenerational Transmission of Values," 2008) as well as in older adults (Hebblethwaite and Norris 2011; Manheimer 2004). The range of generative concern and behaviours were expanded in the current study to encompass the expression of generativity that younger generations exhibit towards older generations. Adult grandchildren strongly valued opportunities to develop their family legacies by actively engaging in family leisure with their parents and grandparents. This extends Peterson's (2002) suggestion that generativity can be exhibited as care for older generations and provides evidence that grandchildren begin to think about their own and their families' legacy at an early stage of emerging adulthood.

Socioemotional selectivity and norms of non-interference

Parents and grandchildren reported substantially more ambivalence than the grandparents did. This exposes a similar relationship between age and ambivalence that has been demonstrated in parent-child relationships whereby ambivalence appears to peak in adolescence and early adulthood and begins to decrease in midlife and continue the downward trend through older adulthood (Fingerman and Hay 2004). This effect can be linked to Carstensen's (1992) theory of socioemotional selectivity. This theory posits that older adults are strongly motivated by emotional regulation and, therefore, minimize conflict in their lives, often choosing to participate in relationships that are closer, more rewarding (Charles and Carstensen 2010) and which cause less ambivalence. This thinking can be extended to Pratt et al. (1999) work, for example, which analysed older adults' narratives about moral values and found that older adults tend to describe more positive events and speak about more positive social content in their narratives than younger adults do. It is thought that, by selecting and presenting positive events and/or relationships in the context of their interviews, older adults seek to maximize the positive nature of their experiences and, therefore, optimize their sense of self.

Grandparents did, however, acknowledge some ambivalence in their family leisure experiences with their children and grandchildren. They were quick to point out their concerted efforts to avoid the perception of interfering or 'meddling' in the lives of their offspring. This is reflective of the norm of non-interference (Cherlin and Furstenberg 1986) whereby grandparent input and authority into family relationships is contingent on the request and/or sanctioning by the parent. This norm has been found to be one of the strongest norms associated with grandparenting behaviours (Douglas and Ferguson 2003; Kemp 2004). Grandparents were eager to be supportive and involved, but were extremely cautious about giving unsolicited advice. This norm was reinforced by parents and adult grandchildren who identified this non-interference as a strategy employed by grandparents. Interestingly, however, as the grandchildren emerged into adulthood, they expressed gratitude for the advice that was shared when they were younger, even if this advice was unsolicited. This norm, therefore, appears to hold significant importance when families are presently engaged in family relationships, but they seem to be more accepting of some level of 'interference' when they reflect on the past and can connect the experience to generative commitments. If the advice was seen as a means of transmitting family values and developing a family legacy, it was appreciated retrospectively despite being unsolicited and interfering at the time.

Turning points

As the grandchildren emerged into adulthood, their experience of ambivalence often decreased from the level they had retrospectively reported experiencing during adolescence. They became more generative in their thinking and began to highly value their relationships with their parents and grandparents. Contrary to Kemp's (2004) suggestion that adult grandchildren are mainly focused on independence and individualism, the grandchildren in this study developed a strong investment in their relationships, particularly with their grandparents. This shift often followed a key turning point in their life stories. McAdams (1985, 2001) argues that it is in this stage of emerging adulthood that people begin to construct self-defining life stories. The stage of emerging adulthood (Arnett 2000) is increasingly self-reflective and strongly focused on identity formation (Erikson 1959). Turning points are characterized as nuclear episodes (along with high points and low points) that help emerging adults construct their life stories (McAdams 1985).

In the study on which this paper is based, grandchildren spoke of life events of significant import that strongly influenced a shift in their commitment to their families. Death of a grandparent or a serious health issue were more obvious examples, but even moving away from the family to attend university shaped grandchildren's relationships with their families. These turning points lead to the expression of more generative commitments among the adult grandchildren which, in turn, tempered the ambivalence that they experienced in their family leisure. This is consistent with McLean and Pratt's (2006) work that emphasized the important role of turning points in facilitating generativity and meaning-making for emerging adults.

Conclusion

Purposive family leisure facilitates generativity across three generations. This, along with socioemotional selectivity and the norm of non-interference in grandparents, as well as key turning points for grandchildren facilitate successful coping with intergenerational ambivalence as grandchildren emerge into adulthood. Researchers find that closer relationships and enhanced communication results from grandparent participation in recreation activities with grandchildren (Fingerman 2004; Goodsell, Bates, and Behnke 2011; Silverstein and Marenco 2001). Bates and Taylor (2013) hypothesize that ambivalence negatively moderates the impact of grandparent–grandchild activity involvement. On the contrary, I suggest that leisure experiences pursued with a purposeful and generative intent mediate the experience of ambivalence in a positive way and help families to cope with their feelings of ambivalence. Similarly, socioemotional selectivity and the norm of non-interference help grandparents to cope with ambivalence in their family relations. Turning points facilitate a shift in grandchildren's perspective on the importance of family relationships.

These findings are important to both research and practice. Facilitating purposeful and meaningful leisure engagement in three-generation families and helping families to understand how to cope with the ambivalence that they experience will have long-term effects. Whether grandparents feel they are important influences in their families will influence how they define their roles and how they will be involved in the development of their grandchildren (Hayslip and Page 2012). Grandparents who find their roles satisfying and are in generative relationships report more personal benefits when they get older and report feeling younger and less depressed (Kaufman and Elder 2003; Thiele and Whelan 2006). Grandchildren who have closer relationships when they are younger with their grandparents have more positive perceptions of growing older (McGuinn and Mosher-Ashley 2002). Hayslip and Page (2012, 192) suggest that,

> Through the transmission of values (Pratt, Norris, Hebblethwaite, and Arnold 2008) and in serving as a support system in times of crisis, grandparents can positively influence grandchildren (Ruiz 2004). In this respect, having meaningful contact with a grandparent can buffer the effect of a parent's divorce, mental illness or death (Henderson, Hayslip, Sanders, and Louden 2009).

It is important to note that the meaning of being a family member is actively constructed (Hayslip and Page 2012) and multidimensional (Connidis 2010). Connidis (2012, 36) suggests that it is necessary,

> to view family relationships as the outcome of negotiations among individuals in the context of socially constructed arrangements and structures that can change; to take an interpretive rather than normative approach to family life and to aging; to consider the interconnections of multiple levels of analysis and multiple facets of social life; and to consider ways of improving the lives of older persons, in part through improving family life and the social process of aging.

Schwab and Dustin (2015) attend to these issues and develop family leisure models for three individual nuclear families. Future research could include analysis by family triad to further explore this active and multidimensional experience of intergenerational family leisure. Attention to structural and cultural changes across generations can also expand our understanding (Wheeler and Green 2014).

This interdisciplinary examination of ambivalence in family leisure strengthens the body of family leisure literature by integrating theoretical insights from psychology, sociology, gerontology, leisure studies, and family relations. Taking an inclusive view of family relationships and including grandparent perspectives broadens the scope of understanding of family leisure. Attending to the experiences of adult grandchildren also helps us to understand family leisure across the life course. Longitudinal studies would be crucial in facilitating an even more in-depth understanding of how three-generation families engage in purposive leisure and develop generativity across generations in relation to time and space.

The study on which this paper is based is limited in its scope, having only been able to recruit a White, middle-class sample. Families are not homogeneous and future research should endeavour to address intersectionality, attending to social structure and context. Gender, race, class, and ability all influence families and family leisure. Culture reflects internalized, shared norms as well as intergenerationally transmitted values (Hayslip and Page 2012). Cultural values of familism and individualism, views of grandparents as mentors for younger parents, as transmitters of cultural values and heritage, or as agents of socialization for grandchildren are all implicated in the meaning-making around family leisure. For example, African-American grandparents have almost twice the degree of involvement with grandchildren than non-Hispanic Whites (Szinovacz 1998). This may result in a different experience around the norm of non-interference. Likewise, the experience of this middle-class sample may reflect both time and monetary resources not available to families of lower socioeconomic status. An explicit investigation of the intersections of age, culture, race, gender, and ability would strengthen our understanding of family leisure experiences.

The participants discussed in this paper were self-selected and, therefore, may represent more positive family relationships than those who chose not to participate. Although ambivalence exists in both consensual and more conflictual family relationships, the study of family leisure would benefit from a closer study of families who experience more challenging relationships. This sample was also involved in normative family relationships. Future research into non-normative experiences (e.g. blended families, custodial grandparenting, great-grandparenting, and step-grandparenting) could make important contributions to our understanding of family leisure. Additionally, families are increasingly geographically dispersed. Understanding the role of digital media in facilitating purposive leisure and generative commitments is essential in our increasingly networked society. Attending to the evolving nature of family relations will contribute to a more in-depth understanding of the experience of family leisure.

Acknowledgements

I gratefully acknowledge all of the families who shared their stories, as well as the reviewers for their constructive review of this article. Special thanks to Lori Gallagher, Lynn Curley, Judy Hebblethwaite, and Leah Lewis for their assistance with recruitment and interviewing.

Funding

This research was supported by a grant from the Fonds Québécois de la Recherche sur la Société et la Culture (FQRSC) under grant # RAS210.

Notes on contributor

Shannon Hebblethwaite is Associate Professor in the Department of Applied Human Sciences, Concordia University, 1455 DeMaisonneuve Blvd W, Montreal, Quebec, Canada, H3G 1M8.

References

Ackerman, S., D. Zuroff, and D. S. Moscowitz. 2000. "Generativity in Midlife and Young Adults: Links to Agency, Communion, and Well-being." *International Journal of Aging and Human Development* 50: 17–41.

Arnett, J. 2000. "Emerging Adulthood: A Theory of Development from the Late Teens Through the Twenties." *American Psychologist* 55: 469–480.

Bates, J. S., and A. C. Taylor. 2013. "Taking Stock of Theory in Grandparent Studies." In *Handbook of Family Theories: A Content-Based Approach*, edited by M. A. Fine and F. D. Fincham, 51–70. New York: Routledge.

Birditt, K. S., K. L. Fingerman, and S. H. Zarit. 2010. "Adult Children's Problems and Successes: Implications for Intergenerational Ambivalence." *The Journals of Gerontology Series B: Psychological Sciences and Social Sciences* 65B (2): 145–153.

Carstensen, L. L. 1992. "Social and Emotional Patterns in Adulthood: Support for Socioemotional Selectivity Theory." *Psychology & Aging* 7: 331–338.

Charles, S. T., and L. L. Carstensen. 2010. "Social and Emotional Aging." *Annual Review of Psychology* 61: 383–409.

Charmaz, K. 2004. "Grounded Theory." In *Approaches to Qualitative Research*, edited by S. N. Hesse-Biber and P. Leavy, 496–521. New York: Oxford University Press.

Charmaz, K. 2006. *Constructing Grounded Theory.* Thousand Oaks, CA: Sage.

Cherlin, A. J., and F. F. Furstenberg. 1986. *The New American Grandparent: A Place in the Family, A Life Apart.* New York: Basic Books.

Connidis, I. A. 2010. *Family Ties and Aging.* 2nd ed. Los Angeles: Pine Forge Press.

Connidis, I. A. 2012. "Theoretical Directions for Studying Family Ties and Aging." In *Handbook of Families and Aging*, 2nd ed., edited by R. Bliezner and V. Hilkevitch Bedford, 35–60. Santa Barbara, CA: Praeger.

Cooney, T. M., and P. A. Dykstra. 2013. "Theories and Their Empirical Support in the Study of Intergenerational Family Relationships in Adulthood." In *Handbook of Family Theories: A Content-Based Approach*, edited by M. A. Fine and F. D. Fincham, 356–378. New York: Routledge.

Douglas, G., and N. Ferguson. 2003. "The Role of Grandparents in Divorced Families." *International Journal of Law, Policy and the Family* 17 (1): 41–67.

Edwards, M. B., and Matarrita-Cascante, D. 2011. "Rurality in Leisure Research: A Review of Four Major Journals." *Journal of Leisure Research* 43 (4): 447–474.

Erikson, E. 1950. *Childhood and Society.* New York: Norton.

Erikson, E. 1959. "Identity and the Life Cycle: Selected Papers." *Psychological Issues* 1: 5–165.

Erikson, E. 1963. *Childhood and Society.* 2nd ed. New York: Norton.

Erikson, E. 1986. *The Life Cycle Completed.* New York: Norton.

Fingerman, K. L. 2004. "The Role of Offspring and In-laws in Grandparents' Ties to Their Grandchildren." *Journal of Family Issues* 25: 1026–1049.

Fingerman, K. L., and E. L. Hay. 2004. "Intergenerational Ambivalence in the Context of the Larger Social Network." In *Intergenerational Ambivalences: New Perspectives on Parent-Child Relations in Later Life*, edited by K. Pillemer and K. Luscher, 133–152. New York: Elsevier.

Fingerman, K. L., L. Pitzer, E. S. Lefkowitz, K. S. Birditt, and D. Mroczek. 2008. "Ambivalent Relationship Qualities Between Adults and Their Parents: Implications for the Well-being of Both Parties." *The Journals of Gerontology Series B: Psychological Sciences and Social Sciences* 63 (6): 362–371.

Freeman, P. A., and R. B. Zabriskie. 2002. "The Role of Outdoor Recreation in Family Enrichment." *Journal of Adventure Education and Outdoor Learning* 2 (2): 131–145.

Frensch, K. M., M. W. Pratt, and J. E. Norris. 2007. "Foundations of Generativity: Personal and Family Correlates of Emerging Adults' Generative Life-story Themes." *Journal of Research in Personality* 41 (1): 45–62.

Freysinger, V. J. 1997. "Redefining Family, Redefining Leisure: Progress Made and Challenges Ahead in Research on Leisure and Families." *Journal of Leisure Research* 29 (1): 1–4.

Freysinger, V. F., S. M. Shaw, K. A. Henderson, and M. D. Bialeschki. 2013. *Leisure, Women and Gender*. State College, PA: Venture.

Goodsell, T. L., J. S. Bates, and A. O. Behnke. 2011. "Fatherhood Stories: Grandparents, Grandchildren and Gender." *Journal of Social and Personal Relationships* 28: 134–154.

Gordon, C., C. M. Gaitz, and J. Scott. 1976. "Leisure and Lives: Personal Expressivity Across the Life Span." In *Handbook of Aging and the Social Sciences*, edited by R. Binstock and E. Shanas, 310–341. New York: Van Nostrand Reinhold.

Harrington, M. 2001. "Gendered Time: Leisure in Family Life." In *Minding the Time in Family Experience: Emerging Perspectives and Issues*, edited by K. J. Daly, 343–382. Oxford: Elsevier Science.

Harrington, M. 2006. "Sport and Leisure as Contexts for Fathering in Australian families." *Leisure Studies* 25 (2): 165–183.

Harrington, M. 2013. "Families, Gender, Social Class, and Leisure." In *Leisure, Women, and Gender*, edited by V. J. Freysinger, S. M. Shaw, K. A. Henderson, and M. D. Bialeschki, 325–341. State College, PA: Venture.

Harrington, M. 2014. "Practices and Meaning of Purposive Family Leisure Among Working- and Middle-Class Families." *Leisure Studies* 34 (4), 471–486. doi:10.1080/02614367.2014.938767.

Havitz, M. E. 2011. "Trip of a Lifetime: An Autoethnographic Retrospective on a Life-Altering Family Vacation." Paper presented at the 13th Canadian congress on leisure research. St. Catharines, ON: Canadian Association for Leisure Studies, May 18–21.

Hayslip, Jr., B., and K. S. Page. 2012. "Grandparenthood: Grandchild and Great-Grandchild Relationships." In *Handbook of Families and Aging*, 2nd ed., edited by R. Bliezner and V. Hilkevitch Bedford, 183–212. Santa Barbara, CA: Praeger.

Hebblethwaite, S. 2014. "'Grannie's Got to Go Fishing': Meanings and Experiences of Family Leisure for Three-Generation Families in Rural and Urban Settings." *World Leisure Journal* 56 (1): 42–61.

Hebblethwaite, S., and J. E. Norris. 2010. "'You Don't Want to Hurt His Feelings': Family Leisure as a Context for Intergenerational Ambivalence." *Journal of Leisure Research* 42 (3): 489–508.

Hebblethwaite, S., and J. E. Norris. 2011. "Expressions of Generativity Through Family Leisure: Experiences of Grandparents and Adult Grandchildren." *Family Relations* 60 (1): 121–133.

Henderson, C., Hayslip, B., Sanders, L., and Louden, L. 2009. "Grandmother-Grandchild Relationship Quality Predicts Psychological Adjustment Among Youth from Divorced Families." *Journal of Family Issues* 30: 1245–1264.

Holland, S. 2013. "Three Generations of Women's Leisure: Changes, Challenges and Continuities." *Journal of Gender Studies* 22: 309–319.

Kaufman, G., and G. H. Elder. 2003. "Grandparenting and Age Identity." *Journal of Aging Studies* 17 (3): 269–282.

Kay, T. A. 1998. "Having It All or Doing It All? The Construction of Women's Lifestyles in Time-crunched Households." *Leisure and Society* 21 (2): 435–454.

Kay, T. A. 2000. "Leisure, Gender and Family: The Influence of Social Policy." *Leisure Studies* 19 (3): 247–265.

Kelly, J. R., and G. Godbey. 1992. *The Sociology of Leisure*. State College, PA: Venture.

Kemp, C. L. 2003. "The Social and Demographic Contours of Contemporary Grandparenthood: Mapping Patterns in Canada and the United States." *Journal of Comparative Family Studies* 34 (2): 187–212.

Kemp, C. L. 2004. "'Grand' Expectations: The Experiences of Grandparents and Adult Grandchildren." *Canadian Journal of Sociology* 29 (4): 499–525.

Kleiber, D., and G. Nimrod. 2008. "Expressions of Generativity and Civic Engagement in a 'Learning in Retirement' Group." *Journal of Adult Development* 15 (2): 76–86.

Lawford, H., M. Pratt, B. Hunsberger, and M. Pancer. 2005. "Adolescent Generativity: A Longitudinal Study of Two Possible Contexts for Learning Concern for Future Generations." *Journal of Research on Adolescence* 15 (3): 261–273.

Lettke, F., and D. M. Klein. 2004. "Methodological Issues in Assessing Ambivalences in Intergenerational Relations." In *Intergenerational Ambivalences: New Perspectives on Parent-child Relations in Later Life*, edited by K. Pillemer and K. Luscher, 85–113. New York: Elsevier.

Lowenstein, A. 2007. "Solidarity-conflict and Ambivalence: Testing Two Conceptual Frameworks and Their Impact on Quality of Life for Older Family Members." *The Journals of Gerontology Series B: Psychological Sciences and Social Sciences* 62 (2): S100–S107.

Luscher, K. 2000. "Ambivalence: A Key Concept for the Study of Intergenerational Relations." In *Family Issues Between Gender and Generations*, edited by S. Trnka, 11–25. Vienna: European Communities.

Luscher, K., and Pillemer, K. 1998. "Intergenerational Ambivalence: A New Approach to the Study of Parent-Child Relations in Later Life." *Journal of Marriage and Family* 60 (2): 413–425.

Manheimer, R. J. 2004. "Rope of Ashes: Global Aging, Generativity, and Education." In *The Generative Society: Caring for Future Generations*, edited by E. de St. Aubin, D. P. McAdams, and T. C. Kim, 115–130. Washington, DC: APA Press.

McAdams, D. P. 1985. *Power, Intimacy, and the Life Story: Personological Inquiries into Identity*. New York: Guilford Press.

McAdams, D. P. 2001. "The Psychology of Life Stories." *Review of General Psychology* 5 (2): 100–122.

McGuinn, K., and P. Mosher-Ashley. 2002. "Children's Fears About Personal Aging." *Educational Gerontology* 28: 561–575.

McLean, K. C., and M. W. Pratt. 2006. "Life's Little (and Big) Lessons: Identity Statuses and Meaning-Making in the Turning Point Narratives of Emerging Adults." *Developmental Psychology* 42 (4): 714–722.

Neulinger, J. 1974. *The Psychology of Leisure*. Springfield, IL: Charles C. Thomas.

Norris, J. E., S. L. Kuiack, and M. W. Pratt. 2004. "'As Long as They Go Back Down the End of the Day': Stories of the Satisfactions and Challenges of Grandparenthood." In *Family Stories and the Life Course*, edited by M. W. Pratt and B. H. Fiese, 353–374. Mahwah, NJ: Lawrence Erlbaum Associates.

Olshansky, S., Goldman, D., Zheng, Y., and Rowe, J. 2009. "Aging in America in the 21st Century: Demographic Forecasts from the MacArthur Foundation Network on an Aging Society." *The Milbank Quarterly* 87: 842–862.

Orthner, D. K., and J. A. Mancini. 1990. "Leisure Impacts on Family Interaction and Cohesion." *Journal of Leisure Research* 22 (1): 125–137.

Palmer, A. A., P. A. Freeman, and R. B. Zabriskie. 2007. "Family Deepening: A Qualitative Inquiry into the Experience of Families Who Participate in Service Expeditions." *Journal of Leisure Research* 39 (3): 438–458.

Peterson, B. E. 2002. "Longitudinal Analysis of Midlife Generativity, Intergenerational Roles and Caregiving." *Psychology and Aging* 17: 161–168.

Peterson, B. E., and L. E. Duncan. 2007. "Midlife Women's Generativity and Authoritarianism: Marriage, Motherhood, and 10 years of Aging." *Psychology and Aging* 22 (3): 411–419.

Pillemer, K., and K. Luscher (Eds.). 2004. *Intergenerational Ambivalences: New Perspectives on Parent-child Relations in Later Life*. New York: Elsevier.

Poff, R. A., R. B. Zabriskie, and J. A. Townsend. 2010. "Australian Family Leisure: Modelling Parent and Youth Data." *Annals of Leisure Research* 13 (3): 420–438.

Pratt, M. W., J. E. Norris, M. L. Arnold, and R. Filiyer. 1999. "Generativity and Moral Development as Predictors of Value-socialization Narratives for Young Persons Across the Adult Life Span: From Lessons Learned to Shared." *Psychology and Aging* 14 (3): 414–426.

Pratt, M. W., J. E. Norris, K. Cressman, H. Lawford, and S. Hebblethwaite. 2008. "Parents' Stories of Grandparenting Concerns in the Three-generational Family: Generativity, Optimism and Forgiveness." *Journal of Personality* 76 (3): 581–604.

Pratt, M. W., J. E. Norris, S. Hebblethwaite, and M. L. Arnold. 2008. "Intergenerational Transmission of Values: Family Generativity and Adolescents' Narratives of Parent and Grandparent Value Teaching." *Journal of Personality* 76 (2): 171–198.

Rojek, C. 2005. *Leisure Theory: Principles and Practices.* New York: Palgrave Macmillan.

Rothrauff, T., and T. M. Cooney. 2008. "The Role of Generativity in Psychological Well-being: Does it Differ for Childless Adults and Parents?" *Journal of Adult Development* 15 (3/4): 148–159.

Ruiz, D. S. 2004. *Amazing Grace: African American Grandmothers as Caregivers and Conveyors of Traditional Values.* Westport, CT: Praeger.

Schwab, K. A., and D. L. Dustin. 2015. "Towards a Model of Optimal Family Leisure." *Annals of Leisure Research* 18 (2): 1–25.

Scraton, S., and S. Holland. 2006. "Grandfatherhood and Leisure." *Leisure Studies* 25 (2): 233–250.

Shannon, C. S., and S. M. Shaw. 2005. "'If the Dishes Don't Get Done Today, They'll Get Done Tomorrow': A Breast Cancer Experience as a Catalyst for Changes in Women's Leisure." *Journal of Leisure Research* 37 (2): 195–215.

Shaw, S. M. 1992. "Derifying Family Leisure: An Examination of Women's and Men's Everyday Experiences and Perceptions of Family Time." *Leisure Sciences* 14: 271–286.

Shaw, S. M. 1997. "Controversies and Contradictions in Family Leisure: An Analysis of Conflicting Paradigms." *Journal of Leisure Research* 29 (1): 98–112.

Shaw, S. M., and D. Dawson. 2001. "Purposive Leisure: Examining Parental Discourses on Family Activities." *Leisure Science* 23: 217–231.

Shaw, S. M., and D. Dawson. 2003. "Contradictory Aspects of Family Leisure: Idealization Versus Experience." *Leisure/Loisir* 28 (3–4): 179–201.

Shaw, S. M., M. E. Havitz, and F. M. Delamere. 2008. "'I Decided to Invest in My Kids Memories': Family Vacations, Memories, and the Social Construction of the Family." *Tourism Culture and Communication* 8 (1): 13–26.

Silverstein, M., and A. Marenco. 2001. "How Americans Enact the Grandparent Role Across the Family Life Course." *Journal of Family Issues* 22 (4): 493–522.

de St. Aubin, E., D. P. McAdams, and T. C. Kim. 2004. *The Generative Society: Caring for Future Generations.* Washington, DC: American Psychological Association.

Strauss, A. 1987. "Introduction." In *Qualitative Analysis for Social Scientists*, edited by A. Strauss, 22–39. Cambridge, MA: Cambridge University Press.

Szinovacz, M. E. 1998. *Handbook on Grandparenthood.* Westport, CT: Greenwood.

Thiele, D. M., and T. Whelan. 2006. "The Nature and Dimensions of the Grandparent Role." *Marriage and Family Review* 40: 93–108.

Trussell, D. E., and S. M. Shaw. 2007. "'Daddy's Gone and He'll Be Back in October': Farm Women's Experiences of Family Leisure." *Journal of Leisure Research* 39 (2): 366–387.

Trussell, D. E., and S. M. Shaw. 2009. "Changing Family Life in the Rural Context: Women's Perspectives of Family Leisure on the Farm." *Leisure Sciences* 31 (5): 434–449.

Uhlenberg, P. 2009. "Children in an Aging Society." *The Journals of Gerontology Series B: Psychological Sciences and Social Sciences* 64B: S489–S496.

Uhlenberg, P., and Kirby, J. 1998. "Grandparenthood Over Time: Historical and Demographic Trends." In *Handbook on Grandparenthood*, edited by M. Szinovacz, 23–39. Westport, CT: Greenwood Press.

Waldrop, D. P., J. A. Weber, S. L. Herald, J. Pruett, K. Cooper, and K. Juozapavicius. 1999. "Wisdom and Life Experience: How Grandfathers Mentor Their Grandchildren." *Journal of Aging and Identity* 4 (1): 33–46.

Walker, A. J. 2009. "A Feminist Critique of Family Studies." In *Handbook of Feminist Family Studies*, edited by S. A. Lloyd, A. L. Few, and K. R. Allen, 18–27. Thousand Oaks, CA: Sage.

Watson, B. 2000. "Motherwork – Motherleisure: Analysing Young Mother's Leisure Lifestyles in the Context of Difference." Unpublished PhD thesis, Leeds Metropolitan University.

Wheeler, S., and K. Green. 2014. "Parenting in Relation to Children's Sports Participation: Generational Changes and Potential Implications." *Leisure Studies* 33 (3): 267–284.

Families in the forest: guilt trips, bonding moments and potential springboards

Alice Goodenough[a], Sue Waite[b] and Jade Bartlett[c]

[a]The Silvanus Trust, Cremyll, Cornwall, UK; [b]Plymouth Institute of Education, Plymouth, UK; [c]Freelance Researcher for The National Trust, Southwest Region, Exeter, UK

The article is based upon practitioner research supported by the BIG Lottery funded *Good from Woods* programme that aimed to develop research capacity in the third sector and explore social cohesion and well-being outcomes derived from woodland activities. The location of the research was the Family Places project run by the UK National Trust, which organized family friendly activities in woodland. Using interviews and fieldnotes, our research found that popular discourse around children's disconnection from nature was experienced as a pressure by some parents who sought opportunities to reduce 'guilt'. An English cultural tendency to romanticize 'natural childhood' may underpin parental references to their own outdoor childhoods and explain some parents' expressed desires to offer nature opportunities for their children through shared experience. The intervention seemed to alleviate pressure to provide positive outdoor experiences, engendering both self-confidence as 'competent parents' in guided events and possibly stimulating independent family engagement with nature.

Introduction

In this paper, we examine and problematize the character of 'shared experience' in nature for supporting families' sense of well-being. We draw on theory about the importance of parent–child play and shared leisure time for family cohesion and well-being (Zabriskie and McCormick 2003; Shaw, Havitz, and Delemere 2008; Coyl-Shepherd and Hanlon 2013), and the role of early experience and memories of nature in encouraging future engagement and well-being (Chawla 2006; Waite 2007; Humberstone and Stan 2009).

The article is based upon research conducted by an intern at the UK National Trust,[1] who focused on the Trust's 'Family Places Project' in their 'Good from Woods' practitioner research. The Family Places Project sought to inspire confidence in families using National Trust sites, including woodlands; while Good from Woods is a BIG Lottery funded project, where woodland activity providers explore well-being benefits of the activities they provide. Family Places worked through children's centres[2] to recruit participants, with National Trust and children's centre staff anticipating that parents would be drawn from lower socio-economic groups as the centres were set up to improve outcomes for those families in greatest need.

193

In the article, we consider theory about the value and purposes that family leisure in nature may bring and then discuss the findings of a case study in the light of relevant literature around emergent themes of guilt trips, bonding moments and springboards. In particular, we examine the phraseology used by parents' discussing their families' enjoyment of outdoor leisure to understand their investment in this activity on behalf of their children. The semantic content of what was being said helped us discern the aims and significance of families' excursions to the forest, and their contribution to well-being and cohesion.

Family leisure, cohesion and resilience

Positive outcomes for family functioning and parent and child well-being are consistently identified in the literature exploring family leisure activity. Multiple studies highlight how shared leisure by parent and child can beneficially impact upon family closeness, interaction and collective resilience (Zabriskie and McCormick 2001; Swinton et al. 2008; Coyl-Shepherd and Hanlon 2013). Furthermore, research demonstrates that satisfaction with family leisure time correlates highly with increased satisfaction with family life (Zabriskie and McCormick 2001; Swinton et al. 2008).

Family leisure patterns and their relation to family functioning can be divided into two categories. 'Core family leisure' has been used to describe the relatively unplanned, day to day, inexpensive, frequently home-centred recreational activities that bring families together, such as TV watching, cooking, gardening, and game playing (Zabriskie and McCormick 2001; Ward and Zabriskie 2011). Such leisure tends to be familiar, recurrent and well established and may impact primarily on families' feelings of cohesion and group identification. 'Balance family leisure' refers to recreation that is typically more structured, less frequent and located away from home, requiring greater investment of time, energy and expenditure and includes activities such as holidays, special occasions, and trips out (Zabriskie and McCormick 2001; Minnaert 2012). The more novel, challenging and less familiar character of balance type activities are argued to stimulate learning, growth and flexibility amongst family groups, contributing to their collective ability to function positively. Together core and balance leisure can meet families' needs for security and novelty and affect both kinship and resilience. Access to both appears to have the most positive impact on parental perceptions of family well-being (Zabriskie and McCormick 2001; Ward and Zabriskie 2011). However, while core leisure activity seems most significant in shaping perceptions of family cohesion and happiness for young people; parental views appear more influenced by participation in balance activities (Ward and Zabriskie 2011). The structured activity provided by the National Trust's Family Places Project involved parents' signing up for and travelling to specially designed activity days with their children and would be classified as a balance leisure activity.

Purposive employment of leisure for increased family cohesion and development

Some studies reveal parents' active use of balance type shared leisure as a tool for increasing positive family functioning and enhancing their children's development (Shaw et al. 2008). Such 'purposive' family leisure is deliberately employed by parents to support family integration and advancement. Engagement of the family in this may be driven by a sense of obligation and responsibility on the part of the parent and may be understood by them as an integral task of parenting (Trussell and Shaw 2007; Shaw et al. 2008).

It may also be regarded as a way of reinforcing collective identification as 'family'. For example, Shaw et al. (2008) present the family holiday as a context in which parents seek to generate positive, shared memories of family life. Memories are actively constructed and subsequently reinforced to nurture a sense of mutuality through shared experience. Parents organize memorable activities and supervise family dynamics as part of managing this process and perceive a lack of competing distractions (such as work and school) as helping to support it (Ibid). Parents' (positive and negative) recollections of their childhood holidays may drive this construction of family history; personal recall influencing their awareness that memories of success-fully shared leisure can help nurture kinship (Shaw et al. 2008).

Purposive recreation is also utilized by parents to encourage children's adherence to family norms and values (Trussell and Shaw 2007; Shaw et al. 2008). When building holiday memories, for example, parents suggest they may help guide their offspring's future decision-making about the way they live their lives (Shaw et al. 2008). Likewise, parents may champion and support involvement in particular family leisure activities if they understand them to be fostering attitudes and behaviours which they regard as advantageous to their children's development (Harrington 2002; Coakley 2006). Par-ental coaching of children's sports, for example, provides an adult supervised context, where skills and attributes perceived as useful to future positive functioning, such as co-operation, or competitiveness, are nurtured (Coakley 2006, 161).

Socio-economic background may be a determinant in parents' motivations for pursuing purposive family leisure (Harrington 2002). Harrington's research (2002) suggests that many parents value family leisure time for its role in pulling together family members and connecting them. However, the author suggests that middle-class parents are more likely to use purposive leisure as a tool for promoting their chil-dren's personal growth and skills gain. According to Harrington, middle-class parents are more likely to value the anticipated long-term benefits of family activity to their children. In contrast, families on lower incomes were less likely to structure their chil-dren's activities towards long term or specific goals and their children were corre-spondingly more likely to engage in 'free play'. Lower income parents were more frequently focused on family leisure's more immediate impacts on interpersonal relationships and bonding. Harrington (2002, 2003) suggests that regardless of socio-economic background however, parents within her study were united by their deriving of 'considerable pleasure and satisfaction from their children's enjoyment of leisure and sport activities' (Harrington, 2002, 2).

Whilst purposive recreation may be aimed at nurturing very specific family cul-tures, its pursuit is set within and informed by wider cultural patterns and norms, as the evidence above suggests. The influence of cultural ideas and ideals concerning child development, and contemporary notions of how 'good' parenting can support it, are also explored within the literature (Coakley 2006; Shaw et al. 2008). Coakley (2006), for example, identifies a shift in western child-rearing cultures towards increased parental responsibility for children's happiness and success, as well as their failures. Within this cultural paradigm, 'good' parents are expected to devote considerable time, energy and money to supporting their children's development. Coakley (2006) suggests that achievement on the part of the child has become, by extension, achievement on the part of the parent; a return on their investment and visible proof of their 'good' parenting. Enabling and supporting particular types of leisure activity may be part of this asset building. Coakley (2006) refers to fathers' coaching and management of their children's sports interests in the USA and suggests that parents, who fail to support their children's engagement in such contexts, are judged to be less 'good' parents, less morally worthy (Coakley 2006). Such studies confirm that family leisure time can be understood as a space of both active and more passive management of family cohesion, development, and well-being.

Family leisure, memory and the outdoors

There are several strands of literature with relevance to exploring the importance of the outdoors and natural settings in relation to family leisure time. Within the UK there is a longstanding cultural and historical habit of understanding childhood as a period spent somehow closer to 'nature'. The historical character of this perception has altered in relation to contemporary norms and concerns, but is recognizable through its connection of youth with 'natural' attributes and environments. In terms of discipline, for example, society sometimes appears to fear children running 'wild' or 'feral' and perhaps behaving in an untamed way without the civilizing influence of parental socialization (Sibley 1995a, 1995b; Gittins 1998). Closeness of childhood to nature is also interpreted more positively, however. Within western literature, a childhood spent in the countryside is often characterized as innocent, healthy and sheltered from sophisticated, often urban influences. In association of the natural world and youth, being instinctive tends to be considered a virtue and nature is often seen as an educator in its own right (Hendrick 1997; Gittins 1998). This romanticized interpretation of childhood's relationship with nature is a powerful idea which appears to often correspond with unease in adult society with aspects of modern life (Jones 1997; Matthews et al. 2000). The recalled or imagined country childhood can be seen as an influential representation of simplicity and continuity in times of rapid change.

Valentine's research (1997) offers a rare and significant exploration of how concepts of idealized nature may impact within a family context. The author's interviews with rural parents of 8–11–year-olds found that they actively contrasted idealized notions of their children's childhoods with ideas of urban, 'streetwise' upbringings to suggest that the countryside was a protective space (Valentine 1997, 140). The parents suggested that their rural children would be less exposed to stresses they associated with modern, urban life, such as awareness of fashion and sex or involvement in substance abuse or violence (Valentine 1997). However, work exploring young rural residents' perspectives suggests that country childhood is actually a diverse experience, responsive to many more factors than its location (Matthews et al. 2000).

The pursuit of outdoor family leisure is likely to be affected both by cultural constructions of 'natural' childhoods and their desirability and ideas of 'good' parenting. UK-based campaigns which seek to stimulate parents to take the family into outdoor natural environments, such as the National Trust's 'Natural Childhood' venture or 'Project Wild Thing', in which it collaborated, reflect such popular influences (National Trust 2014; Project Wild Thing 2014). These schemes are part of a growing movement across the western world that both look to evidence the impact of children spending less time outside in the natural world and to promote families and children increasing their engagement with the outdoors (Louv 2005). Discourse associated with this cause regularly emphasizes the process and importance of memory making in nature (Kellert and Kahn 2002; Chawla 2006; Waite 2007).

'There's nothing quite like fresh air, exercise and family time. You can't beat the fun you have in the Great Outdoors and creating memories that will last a lifetime'. (National Trust '50 things to do before your 11¾' campaign, 2015)

'Time spent outdoors can give children a lifetime of memories ... The vast majority of people point to similar memories when asked when they felt happiest and safest as children. I've asked hundreds of children the same question during the making of my documentary **PROJECT WILD THING**. Thankfully the majority of them still recall an outside memory. But by no means all of them do'. (David Bond, Memories of a natural childhood, 2013)

Memory access to a 'golden age' of outdoor childhoods may not be universal, but some commentators contend that a markedly steeper drop in engagement with natural environments since the 1980s does now influence our ability to recall 'natural' childhood experiences (Louv 2005; Chalquist 2009). Arguably, more parents today may not have personal early experience of the outdoors to provide an impetus for and knowledge about engaging with natural environments. If this pattern is repeated generationally, then previously established ways of knowing and understanding the natural world may be diminished, and enjoyment of the outdoors could be impacted.

Kellert and Kahn (2002) argue that there is a critical period in early childhood to develop a love of nature and that early experience creates a lasting positive attitude towards nature and a wish to participate in outdoor activity in later life. Such participation has also been demonstrated by research (Lovell and Roe 2009; Chalquist 2009) to have clear personal, social and health benefits. Recent findings in Natural England's longitudinal study 'Monitoring Engagement in the Natural Environment (MENE)' have included the motivational and facilitating role of children in encouraging parents to go to natural places (Hunt, Burt, and Stewart 2014), which suggests that outdoor family leisure may also influence intergenerational interaction and well-being. Indeed, there is a large literature that points to the value of nature for happiness and health. A thorough and wide ranging review by Bowler et al. (2010) concluded that outdoor contexts promoted physical exercise and physical health but also contributed to mental, social and psychological well-being through opportunities for social interactions.

Our study thus focused on an intervention into an area of family life, engagement with nature, frequently regarded as attenuated through general societal disconnection from nature (Louv 2005). National Trust and children's centre staff anticipated that participants within The Family Places Project would indeed demonstrate just such a lack of connection with the natural world, potentially exacerbated by parents' relative youth and low socio-economic status (Chalquist 2009). This expectation reflects children's centres' focus on families in challenging circumstances, and that attending parents are frequently, although controversially, perceived as lacking certain parenting skills (Coakley 2006; Lavelle 2014). Our interest lay in whether the balance leisure activities provided as part of the Family Places project could impact on core leisure pastimes and upon families' ongoing perception of their cohesion and well-being (Ward and Zabriskie 2011). This article examines a case study evidencing the outcomes for families of spending time in woodland-based activities. Through determining the relationship of its findings with the various theoretical perspectives and cultural assumptions discussed above, it aims to contribute to our understanding of the value of forest-focused family leisure time.

Our methods

The case study was part of the Lottery funded *Good from Woods* project. Lcd in partnership between Plymouth University and The Silvanus Trust, this research explored the well-being benefits associated with spending time in woodland. Good from Woods supported 12 woodland-based activity providers to examine the outcomes of the activities they provided to identify the people, places and practices associated with tangible impacts for participants. These providers became practitioner–researchers. Practitioner–researchers employed a qualitative, action research methodology. This seemed to offer the most satisfactory approach both pragmatically (suiting a wide range of research contexts and types of respondent) and also as a means of gaining an understanding of research processes as well as outcomes (McNiff and Whitehead 2002; Kemmis 2009).

The focus of this particular case study was woodland-based activities delivered through The National Trust's 'Family Places Project', another Lottery funded partnership between the National Trust and Family Learning in the southwest of England, running between 2008 and 2011. 'Family Places' identified National Trust owned properties and landscapes that could inspire learning and grow confidence in family learners visiting them. The Good from Woods case study examined the outcomes achieved by family learners visiting National Trust woodlands and participating in Trust organized forest school and bushcraft styles of recreation that encouraged engagement with the outdoor, natural environment. For instance, such activities might emphasize examining nature in close up, such as hunting for bugs, or using the natural world as both inspiration and material for creativity, such as building stick men sculptures.

The research took place between 2010 and 2011 during these activities at various woods open for public use and focused on the adults, who were visiting with their children as part of the Family Places Project. Parents were recruited to the scheme through children's centres. Staff at the centres specifically steered some families towards attendance if they were felt to be a good match with the project's stated aims and those who chose to participate in its woodland-based activities then formed the sample for this research.

The term 'parent' is used in this article to indicate the adult accompanying the child on the activity. The majority took part with their mothers and fathers, but children were sometimes taken by grandparents or a childminder. Thirty-two adult respondents participated within the activities and the study. Just under a third of adult attendees were estimated by children's centre staff to have learning differences of some type and a sixth perceived to have social or emotional differences. Ten families were identified as coming from areas of known social deprivation and there were a range of rural and urban backgrounds amongst them. Twenty three adults were female, 9 male, attending with a total of 38 children under 4 (21 female, 17 male) and 6 children aged 5–11 (2 female, 4 male). All participants were white British. Demographic details of participants were given in anonymous format by children's centres, precluding any detailed analysis of how these interact with expressed perspectives. Although quotes from respondents have been anonymized, they include the gender of the parent and children attending.

Five minute, walking or activity-centred, snapshot interviews with adult respondents were the main research method. The use of mobile methods to hold conversations has been advocated for reducing tension associated with formal interviews and to support research about place and activity, where the prompts for thinking are present during the interview (Moles 2008). Interviews were semi-structured with questions informed by Good from Woods' overarching focus on well-being derived from woodland activity and feedback on earlier drafts from stakeholders in the research (see below for further discussion). Parents were asked why they had chosen to attend, whether they undertook any similar activities with their child on other occasions and what they had done during the event. The researcher was alert to who, what and where were identified by respondents as significant during their experience and asked respondents to expand on these themes. This brief, concentrated approach suited parents whose attention was centred on their children and the activities and who might need to shift their focus quickly. Their immediacy also helped prompt reflection about ongoing experiences. Interviews were recorded with a Dictaphone, which supported them being conducted flexibly. However, for some respondents, audio-recording introduced some anxiety, with one respondent comparing audio recording to her experience of being filmed for local TV; 'I was like "oh my god, I don't want to get out of the car" [laughs] [Angela, Mum with partner, three sons and daughter]'.

The researcher used semi-participatory observation. She engaged in conversation during activities and helped as needed, but did not fully engage in the activities as she made contemporaneous fieldnotes as a secondary research method. Notes made during data collection sessions reflected both on the observed experiences of families and the experience of capturing this evidence. The observations provided a means of interrogating the interview evidence; to consider the observed experiences that respondents' did not appear to verbalize, or perhaps deem relevant to the researcher, compared with those they mentioned often and felt were significant to the enquiry.

Longer semi-structured interviews (around 30 minutes long) were conducted with 7 stakeholders regarding anticipated outcomes of the woodland-based activity before the events. These took place with National Trust staff leading the project and its activities and children's centre staff referring families to the project. They aimed to establish the ideas underlying the design and implementation of the Family Places project and motivations for promoting it to families. Exploration of this data was undertaken in relation to the parents' views to highlight where expectations were being met or where outcomes were unexpected.

Data was examined using a guiding analytical framework, an understanding of types of subjective well-being and indicators developed for Good from Woods in collaboration with practitioner–researchers. This shared conception of well-being (emotional, social, psychological, physical and biophilic) and feelings and behaviours likely to be indicative of its achievement was formulated in the early stages of the wider *Good from Woods* project. The model built on the literature, empirical evidence gathered in pilot projects (Good from Woods 2015), and measures and approaches employed within UK governmental and non-governmental organizations' (DCLG 2007; Abdallah et al. 2008; Nevill 2009; DEFRA 2010; Mguni and Bacon 2010; ONS 2011; Bragg, Wood, and Barton 2013). Space precludes full inclusion of this aspect of the research, but it should be noted that the suggested components of subjective well-being provided a frame of reference (helping to shape research questions, methods, thematic analysis and cross study comparison) rather than a definitive model. Each practitioner–researcher was encouraged to engage with it critically, exploring how well it worked for their context and dataset and where it could be modified or expanded (Goodenough and Waite 2011).

Findings and discussion

Guilt trips

In this section we consider some cultural expectations for what constitutes 'good' parenting and how these can underpin stated motivations for taking part in balance type leisure activities in the woods. We explore the possible association of this guilt with idyllic concepts of nature and the location of these within some parents' memories of their own 'natural' childhoods.

'Good' parenting and feeling good

In line with Ward and Zabriskie's findings (2011), most parents who took their children to the woods to participate in the National Trust's activities appeared to feel good about the experience. The majority of respondents described the activities, the people leading the activities and their location in positive terms. In particular, parents appeared to feel good about themselves as parents. Attending and participating in the woodland activities allowed adult attendees to experience themselves as competent, confident, in control and progressing; feelings that can be associated with psychological well-being (Keyes, Shmotkin, and Ryff 2002; Deci and Ryan 2004; Abdallah et al. 2008; Bauer, Mcadams, and Pals 2008; Ryan 2009). These feelings appeared to be associated with how attendance and involvement in the events allowed them to meet parenting goals that they perceived as important, but may not always manage to achieve. These parenting goals were multiple, but appeared to overlap and be linked in character. As Coakley (2006) observes parents in western cultures appear to feel themselves responsible for children's success or otherwise, therefore in order to be a 'good parent', they must provide opportunities for increasing their child's happiness and success.

Making a 'good' choice on behalf of a child

A number of parents participating in the activities with their children appeared influenced in their decision to attend by a sense that they would be meeting their children's needs through doing so.

> So why did you come?
> Only because I thought he would really enjoy it. [Kathy, Mum with son]

Some parents in particular anticipated that activities children took part in would increase their access to and engagement with the outdoors and the natural world. Further, they understood that this enhanced contact with nature would help meet their child's developmental needs.

> I think it's great for the children; it's wonderful for them to be in nature in the outdoors, I think it feeds their soul; it feeds their imagination. [Robin, Mum with daughter]
> For the exercise, so they can do something tangible ... I think a lot of life these days is not something you can touch is it ... so the more they, they can affect change in their environment then the happier they'll be, I fancy. Good preparation for life really. [Mark, Dad with two daughters]

Evidence of purposive parenting and perceptions that, in the western world, 'good' parents make choices about family leisure that will help meet the developmental and future needs of their child (Coakley 2006; Shaw et al. 2008), can be detected within these responses. Some adult attendees appeared grateful to the National Trust for helping them to be a 'good' parent, supporting them to provide a valued stimulus for their children's growth.

> When I'm on my own with him or something … I'm always thinking 'right, got to do more things with him' all the time, but when you're with a group, it's somehow a bit more relaxing, as long you can just go with the pace and they're telling you where to go next and what to do next, which I think is better. [Dave, Dad with son]
>
> More outdoor orientated and more nature [than routine activity] – you know to do with nature and things which is good for him – something new. [Ruth, Mum with son]
>
> I mean to be honest with you I'd have never thought of coming here with a picnic so that's something, that's nice so I'll do again. Yeah and the mudslinging – I'd never do that – too messy, lazy mummy. [Lucy, Mum with son]

Some of this feedback hints at parents experiencing guilt associated with the moral parameters associated with 'good' parenting (Coakley 2006). A mother who finds it hard to accommodate her child playing with mud, even whilst perceiving it to be a worthwhile activity, fears she will be perceived to be lazy, for example. Some parents engaging their children in woodland-based activity appeared to experience time in the woods as a relief from pressures to provide 'good' parenting without support.

The disconnection of children from nature (Louv 2005) is a powerful popular discourse and may account for some parents' apologetic tone in relation to mud and the outdoors. The guilt it may engender is a troubling aspect of parents' motivations for joining in this balance leisure (Zabriskie and McCormick 2001). Their comments suggest a deficit view of the core leisure they share day-to-day with their children as insufficient for 'good' parenting. Evidence from the MENE study in the UK (Hunt et al. 2014) shows lower socio-economic families are less likely to access natural places and as Harrington (2002) notes, research also suggests that lower socio-economic groups are less likely to purposively pursue balance leisure. An emergent identity of the 'good parent' as one who provides novelty and nature to stimulate learning and growth may therefore be class-based and, as Lavelle (2014) argues, a widely held deficit view of parents attending children's centres may compound this. Yet, whilst the whole family unit can potentially benefit from improvements to interpersonal relationships achieved via shared balance leisure activity, some parents' comments suggest that their primary focus in visiting the woods are benefits to their children's development (Minnaert 2012). This conforms to further findings in the MENE study which suggest that children are a powerful influence on whether adults access natural places themselves (Hunt, et al. 2014).

Bonding moments

Not all parents seemed to experience the chosen purposive leisure activities as purely altruistic. Some parents saw the woodland experience as a learning opportunity not only for their children, but also for themselves. A shared learning context appeared to offer opportunities to bond; however, close semantic analysis suggests that this sharing may be complex and conflicted.

Providing a learning experience

Parents repeatedly perceived time spent in woods as providing learning opportunities through the diverse, novel and distinctive, nature-focused experiences they were understood to support, possibly leading them to feel that attendance was a positive decision made on behalf of their children (Hunt et al. 2014).

> I think it's very important as well, you know you're talking about bringing children into woodlands ... well being outdoors in general but, yeah they just learn so much – and they're not scared of you know a twig or ... it's good for them. [Erin, Mum with son]
>
> [Elaborating on why they would visit the woods again] *It's the most natural learning environment.* [Judith, Mum with son]

For some parents, attendance was felt to have enhanced their own learning about the environment or ways of engaging with it. This was sometimes equated with personal growth for the adult, but was also understood by some as providing skills that would both help them meet their children's needs in the future, and potentially repeat the experience.

> We haven't really gone a lot of places like this and it's something ... little games that we can play with him and 'there's the trees' or 'there's the sticks or stones' and he can pick each thing up and play little games with them ... seeing him what he's been like today; he loves it. [Lisa, Mum with son]

For some, however, feeling like a competent, confident parent was derived more from their learning to care for their child in a novel environment.

> It gives me a chance to kind of get out, and practice like looking after her on my own and things like that you know. Dealing with feeding and all those situations. [Will, Dad with daughter]

Several stakeholders had also anticipated that learning to be outside together would help families to bond and adults to increase their parenting skills.

> What I've seen is that they get to enjoy outdoor play as a family, so parents and children interacting and all the positive outcomes within that, bonding, attachment, parents and children increasing their confidence with skills ... collecting firewood for a fire together is not usually what families get a chance to do, so doing something a little bit different but as a family ... being outside will be very beneficial to their [parents] wellbeing and therefore the knock on effect for the family if the parents are feeling happier in themselves ... Some parents don't know how to or feel anxious about playing with them, with their children, so doing something like this activity where it is presented in a way where there is an informal structure – it is less threatening. [Sarah, children's centre staff member]

In this way, nature appears not only valued for its own qualities by stakeholders, but also because it perhaps offers a looser cultural context (Waite 2013), in which to model enjoyment and playing within families than children's centres' parenting courses. Stakeholders appeared to support the contention that parents may feel less likely to be perceived by others as deficient in parenting skills through shared activity in a novel environment that is associated with fewer preconceived expectations. (Swinton et al. 2008; Coyl-Shepherd and Hanlon 2013)

Potential springboards

Perhaps forest-focused family activities form a foundation for repeating similar experiences by addressing areas which parents may not feel competent to provide for their child alone and by offering a shared learning environment. This might be through re-affirmation of an existing relationship with nature, but also through providing a new arena for families to be together purposively. The research suggests however that there may be a flaw in expectations that balance family leisure time will translate into core pursuits. Shaw et al. (2008) suggest that for parents some of the value of family balance leisure is because it is recollected more than regular shared activities; its novelty and the lack of competing distractions contributing to its memorability (Waite 2007; Shaw et al. 2008). Whilst children more frequently appreciate repeated, familiar activities compared to one-off experiences in shaping family well-being and cohesiveness (Ward and Zabriskie 2011), conversely, parents accord greater significance to specially arranged events, away from the everyday. However, there were some indications in our data that, aside from their intrinsic value, such experiences might act as a springboard for future core family leisure activity.

> You get different ideas – something like the natural painting … we haven't done that so that's an idea we would take away and go and do. [Robin, Mum with daughter]

Feeling supported in meeting children's needs

For some families who reported already engaging in outdoor-based recreation, attending the National Trust organized woodland activities was part of an ongoing purposive pursuit of this type of leisure.

> *I just like any opportunity to get outside with* [child's name] [Karen, Mum with two daughters].

> We actually love being outdoors. [Robin, Mum with daughter]

Despite feeling their children benefit from deliberate attempts to spend time in natural settings, a few adults appeared to find aspects of outdoor recreation daunting. These families seem to have felt particularly supported by The National Trust's offer of a clearly led, knowledgeable engagement with nature.

> It was tough with a little two year old, I wouldn't have thought they could have done it, but with the groups doing it, they've done it … They [children] take the discipline better from the leader especially when they've started to go to school and it's good for them. [Joan, Grandma with grandson, granddaughter and child-minding one girl]

Within parents' responses there is a recurring sense that whether or not families are already spending time in outdoor recreation, attending *led* activities may provide children with a more expansive, deeper or memorable engagement with the woods. As discussed, the latter of these opportunities, the chance to establish familial reference points which can be recalled by children, can motivate adults' promotion of balance family leisure activity (Shaw et al. 2008).

> … he really loved the fire and when we were late because of the car he was just desperate that he was going to not get the jacket potato – and the whole idea – he's been thinking about it for days – cooking them on the fire – and I think it's things like this because you don't tend to do this yourselves – well I don't. [Kathy, Mum with son]
> We would just walk through them [woods], you know, have a circular walk rather than stop and take it all in, whereas if you do something like this and spend some actual

time here you get much more out of it ... we wouldn't have done stuff like this. [Kirstin, Mum, with daughter]

Sometimes I suppose you might be a little bit reticent yourself about what you can manage to do – like light a fire or bake something, or cook – so I just wanted the chance to come and see how other people do it really and ... because I suppose when we use outdoor spaces we wouldn't normally stop to just savour it the way we, I suppose we are doing here and do things in it – we just keep moving really, so it's a bit different isn't it? [Elle, Mother with daughter]

A number of stakeholders also described how parents introduced to the woods would be supported through the activities with the encouragement of staff to manage their family successfully in an unfamiliar and challenging setting. In addition, some stakeholders hoped that adults feeling good about their increased competency and confidence in this situation might consequently feel more positive about becoming involved in other adult learning opportunities.

The lady, the wellies lady as we call her, she actually went on to do the 'early start' ... an accredited course for doing literacy and they work alongside their children as well and she's going on to do a 'first steps' skills for life course ... my perception is that she would not have done that had we not gone out on the sessions outside. [Kate, Children's Centre staff member]

Whilst some of these predicted outcomes appeared to match the impacts that participants reported during the research, what could not be judged from this study was the extent to which this experience acted as a catalyst for future, similar experiences or sustained changes in parenting practices.

'Natural' childhoods and purposive parenting

It is possible that for some parents a sense of having made a 'good' parenting decision on behalf of a child through choosing woodland activity as family recreation, was reinforced by cultural associations between 'good' childhoods and natural, outdoor environments (Louv 2005). The influence of such ideas can be detected by a tendency by some parents to contrast that day's experience with less esteemed leisure pastimes.

I mean when I was a child I roamed the woods for hours, I feel the children don't get that opportunity as much now, really don't and that really bothers me. To get out as much as possible in non-shopping environments as well, we do so much shopping with our children, we don't do enough nature with them, outdoor stuff, you know. [Lucy, Mum with son]

Several statements, concerning motivation for attending the activity as a family, were characterized by similar temporal references. In one instance a parent suggested that what she particularly liked about the woods was that it was 'Like going back to childhood' [Karen, Mum with two daughters]. Other examples contrast memories of a parent's more 'natural' childhood with contemporary childhoods characterized by more interior or urban pursuits. There are references to a recent change in the nature and texture of childhood.

When I grew up in the summer holidays we used to spend all our time outside, now kids seem to spend all their time indoors playing, playing computers or TV's or stuff, so I just want them to spend as much time as they can outdoors, being happy really. [Richard, Dad with two daughters]

[The children] have an outdoor play area [at home]where they have slides and swings but I think they need to come to places like this because it's sort of healing and they can learn such a lot about flowers ... there's no television, there's no video games and all that stuff that's .... you are away from all that stuff, all that technology that seems to be so prevalent, I just hate it – hate all the technology. [Liz, Grandma with granddaughter]

The theme of recalled childhood appears multi-layered in its significance. There is no doubt that the experience of childhood has altered in parents' lifetimes due to effects associated with modern lifestyles (Matthews et al. 2000). Parents, comparing their childhood with that of their children's, may well find memories provide an impetus to using leisure time for re/creating experiences they remember as beneficial to their own development, as the literature suggests (Shaw et al. 2008). The obverse was noted in one instance, a parent felt their lack of memorized or heritable experience of the natural world was a stimulus to creating a different legacy for his children.

It is a bit different to normal cos my, I'm totally suburban; my knowledge is so limited I can barely tell one tree from another. I think I'm better than I used to be and I'm trying to get better, I'm trying to bring the kids up so they got the complete opposite to that because I just don't have it. [Alan, Dad with two daughters]

As discussed earlier, the recollected home of 'childhood' within the western world is most frequently a natural setting, and this idealization of a youth spent in natural places may express a counterpoint to adults' anxieties about modern life (Holland 1992; Valentine 1997; Matthews et al. 2000). Foy-Phillips and Lloyd-Evans (2011, 381) discuss the effects of white middle-class constructions of risk on parenting and how 'social and cultural dimensions of everyday rural life, such as parenting, are embedded within imaginary and metaphorical spaces of community and the gendered rural idyll, as well as grounded in material worlds'.

Within this study it sometimes seems that modern childhood is seen by parents as a less 'real' foundation for creating lasting memories, with associated implications for the task of creating wholesome narratives of childhood and family cohesion that can act as a resource for resilience in the future (Valentine 1997). One parent described modern childhood as being somehow less 'tangible' than in the past, less material in some way (Mark, Dad with two daughters). It is perhaps the case that parents experience the lack of embodiment implied by increasingly virtual lenses on the world as negatively affecting their ability to create experiences that can build family cohesion and resilience. However, it could also be the case that recalled childhood is reconstructed as more real and more substantial, when it is acting as an antidote to fears and anxieties about the present (Valentine 1997; Waite 2007).

Possibly, adults taking part in woodland-based activities with their children experienced themselves as 'good' parents both for providing experiences they recalled as significant in their own growth and development and for meeting a more ambiguous, cultural requirement that childhood take place in natural environments (Jones 1997; Shaw et al. 2008). Several adults, acknowledging that they infrequently spent family leisure time outside, spoke of 'nature' itself as a desirable destination and contrasted it with where they and their children spend more everyday leisure time.

It's just nice to come along and see other things you might do in nature. [Elle, Mum with daughter]

I think it is nice for the children to be on the whole nature side of things, we do lots indoors – especially this time of year, so it's nice to get out. [Helen, Mum with daughter]

Whilst speaking of 'nature' in this way may be common, a shorthand for various aspects of the natural world; it may also suggest referral to nature as an abstract idea. In this case, 'nature' may offer a refreshing ideal in comparison with other, more familiar modern contexts and possibly offer relief from them; a literal and perhaps more emblematic, breath of fresh air. Yet, its abstraction seems somewhat at odds with the embodied experience of being in nature and the lukewarm adjective 'nice' might suggest that an 'abstract ideal' may not always fully engage the adult.

A number of stakeholders also referred to situations where they perceived the whole family to be disconnected from nature.

[The parent] wrote it down, saying that living, you know they live on an estate – just getting outside into a different environment was refreshing and gave them a feeling of peace and a sense of there's a bigger world out there. [Carl, National Trust staff member]

It's taking them [the participating families] out of their comfort zone ... And especially living in an area like this, I think, it's getting them to actually open their eyes to what's around them. We get families who haven't really experienced the countryside ... I think a lot of parents have had experiences of living in a very, even in this area, living in a very urban controlled environment, so to actually be in a natural environment and especially in woodland, it can be completely new to them. [Kate, children's centre staff member]

Perhaps for parents with limited personal experience of the natural environment who may find taking their children out a big step, structured balance leisure provision may help provide a bridge. However, the practitioner–researcher found that many of the actual participants did have previous exposure to outdoor activities. Whether this reflected an increased likelihood of parents signing up to the woodland-based activities because of this or whether the demographic of the participants was not that anticipated by the activity providers is not known. Lavelle (2014) suggests that staff in children's centres may tend to envisage parental deficits, and expectation here also appeared to anticipate participants more significantly disconnected from the possible value and content of natural experiences than many of those participating in the Family Places project appeared to be.

Engaging with or witnessing moments in nature: critiquing shared experience

An abstraction or sense of being at a remove from direct benefit from the woodland experience is further illustrated in an interesting sub-theme within the data concerning the way that 'witnessing' reinforced feeling good about achieving children's access to and engagement with nature. Parents felt particularly positive about the experience of woodland-based activity when watching their child's evident pleasure in and enjoyment of the natural world. For example:

We've had great fun making a stick person and a stick baby, and he's enjoyed the fire haven't you? – the popcorn exploding everywhere. That was fun. [Judith, Mum with son]

This sense of deriving well-being from witnessing and being absorbed in the moments when their child makes a new discovery or a biophilic connection was perceived by the researcher during observation and clarified by reviewing the manner in which parents' answered questions.

> What have you done today?
> He's made a medallion – and he's spent most of his time looking for bugs underneath deadwood, pulling deadwood off and looking for bugs. [Kathy, Mum with son]
> What did you enjoy about your trip to? [National Trust site]
> She was really interested in all the nature and picking up all like the fir cones and leaves – different coloured leaves, she's quite outdoorsy – there's woods at the back of our house isn't there – so we're down there a lot. [Em, Mum with daughter]

Parents could answer the researcher's questions either in the first person, 'I'; in the third person as 'he/she/they' on behalf of their young child; or from a shared perspective in the first person plural 'we'. However, only occasionally did parents talk about their own experience of the day in the first person singular, such as the parenting involved or a new thing that they have learnt or done 'And what have you done today? Not a lot really just feeding her and making sure she's happy [Sam, Dad with daughter]'. Witnessing (third person 'he/she/they') and being part of their child's novel encounters (first person plural 'we') with the outdoors and natural world are how most parents explained what has happened to them.

> What have we been doing today? We had a mirror and we held the mirror so we could see the tops of the trees which was really fun, I'd never thought of doing that before [laughs] … went on a bug hunt and we found the jumping spider and a ladybird and a little black bug, and we did a listening game and we heard birds … the children made smelly cocktails – getting a whole lot of leaves and bits and pieces that they picked and then they mixed it with water and mashed it all up and smelled it, so that was a lot of fun. [Liz, Grandma with granddaughter]
> We've eaten, we've had some wild foraging … slightly confused the child by getting her to eat things in the wood. We've helped with the kettle – get the fire going. We've investigated the moss; we've investigated the big, huge rock of quartz we've just found … She's been very interested in the trees and the moss, and she's just really enjoyed. [Alan, Dad with two daughters]

'We' phraseology can be attributed in part to the parent's continued engagement with their child whilst they chat to the researcher. But this way of talking is also particularly associated with carers witnessing what are, in their eyes, significant moments for the child. These key events are most frequently novel or engaging experiences of the outdoors and natural world, as the quotes above suggest. Notably too, the moments referenced are frequently described as both sensory and sensual: employing taste, touch, hearing, smell and sight and providing gratifyingly tasty, tactile, aural, olfactory and visual experiences. As described above (*Feeling supported in meeting children's needs*), parents were conscious of a difference between extended encounters with nature that could be 'savoured' by both parent and child and more fleeting experiences they had during self-led activity outdoors.

The deconstruction of parents' purposive engagement of their children in woodland leisure may suggest a calculated experience of the woods and interpersonal bonding in that setting. Identifying the parental intent and objectives in enabling moments of family closeness perhaps suggests a less emotional, spontaneous involvement on their part. However, recordings and fieldnotes captured the mood and interactions generated through parents investing in their child's engagement with nature as warm, pleasurable and immersive. Evidence of this affective environment, combined with analysis of parents' attribution of such experiences to the first person plural or third person suggests that this balance leisure activity is contributing to creating bonded moments, where the family is the unit of perception.

In some ways these descriptions of 'witnessing' children's enjoyment suggest that the mutuality of this leisure experience may be different to the expectations of stakeholders. The aims for the activities were to create shared experiences but many parental comments suggest a more enabling and reflective role for the parents, who watch and reminisce but, for whom the principal pleasure seems frequently vicarious. This type of involvement may be indicative of parents using the National Trust organized activity as an opportunity to provide the balance leisure they feel is necessary for their children (Trussell and Shaw 2007; Shaw et al. 2008). They enjoy observing activities that they understand to be developmentally beneficial and a stimulus to family cohesion (Harrington 2002). Often in these instances, there seems to be a marrying of cultural imperatives (to be a 'good' parent) and delight in witnessing their children's pleasure in biophilic engagement (Harrington 2002; Coakley 2006). One parent observed 'he is in his element', and seeing children in this immersive connected state appeared to make parents feel good. As Harrington's (2002) research suggests parents can find satisfaction in being party to their child's successful engagement in balance leisure activity. It is possible this gratification is derived from the opportunity (through choosing to bring their children into the woods and negotiating the activity successfully) to experience themselves as competent, confident and in control caregivers; shapers of family life and history (Shaw et al. 2008). Parents associated bonding moments with children's deep absorption in natural things and these experiences may also be valued as a resource for forming positive memories that might help guide children's future attitudes and behaviours (Harrington 2002; Coakley 2006; Shaw et al. 2008).

> I suppose what we're trying to do is get her used to being outdoors and in different environments, so when she's a bit older she can, she'll understand and appreciate it. [Sam, dad with daughter]

Respondents also frequently express intentions to return with their children independently and it may be that the activity leaders' expertise is deferred to in balance leisure situations, contributing to a more passive role for parents. Certainly some literature (e.g. Waite 2007) suggests that adult memories are often of more unstructured free time outdoors rather than organized activities. Thus, as touched on above, it may be worth considering whether externally organized balance leisure is able to promote sustainable and sustained core leisure activity.

> I think it's been nice to have seen children doing their activities, getting involved in their activities and the parents maybe thinking 'I didn't really notice or know beforehand that my child would maybe want to go bug hunting and was really keen to find them bugs and getting their hands grubby' ... so it's a great thing for parents to see for themselves the development of their kids maybe in areas where they wouldn't really notice it before ... they are learning new things about their children and their development. [Marie, National Trust staff member]

Stakeholders represent the novelty of being in the outdoors and the natural world as a stimulus towards family cohesion and learning, but what they sometimes perhaps understate is parents' deliberate, purposive pursuit of this opportunity because they value these outcomes and the affirmation of their 'good' parenting through achieving them.

Conclusions

Stakeholders from the National Trust and children's centres appeared to anticipate parents' engagement in activities increasing their well-being in a range of areas. It was expected that adult participants would strengthen their feelings of competence, self-confidence and social assurance. Stakeholders also predicted that parents would feel good about their own development, through noticing the development of their children and by connecting with the natural world. Our findings generally bore out these expectations of those providing activities and those recommending families' involvement in them.

Parents' access to positive feelings of well-being often seemed to occur through being able to meet a culturally desirable aim of making 'nature' available to their children. This agenda appeared to be validated through drawing on childhood memories of good times in nature, but also through more generalized cultural references to 'nature' and idyllic settings for childhood experiences. Witnessing children's enjoyment and learning was widespread, but some uncertainty remains about the extent to which parents' sense of well-being derived directly from shared participation in activities or indirectly and vicariously through witnessing. On the whole, well-being seemed to be founded in the satisfaction of feeling like a good and competent parent via family bonding moments and the alleviation of some feelings of guilt or inadequacy through supported participation in shared outdoor activity.

There was some evidence that the woodland activities might act as a springboard to future core leisure engagement with nature or to other positive aspects of families' lives. Parents appeared to have felt competent, confident and happy as part of a group. They also described enjoying the novel and learning opportunities they encountered in the natural world, particularly in terms of their child's development and pleasure. However, the extent to which such activity led to further family-based engagement with nature and longer term impacts remains uncertain and complex. A limitation of the research was that it was not possible to arrange follow up interviews after a period of time had passed to explore the extent to which these experiences, and the confidence perhaps engendered by them, were continued and transferred into other aspects of parents' and family lives.

Notably, children's centre and National Trust staff's motivations for enrolment of families into the activity seemed to be founded on professionals' perceived benefits of engagement with nature discussed earlier and established within research such as Dillon and Dickie (2012) and evidence that lower socio-economic groups are less likely to access these benefits independently (Hunt et al. 2014). Longitudinal research would enable us to see whether externally organized balance leisure is able to promote sustainable and sustained core leisure activity of this type; where parents taking children into the natural world to engage them with nature is an everyday occurrence. On the other hand, as Ward and Zabriskie (2011) suggest, parents might attribute less value to such core leisure engagement with the outdoors and derive less family well-being from them, because adult family members perceive balance leisure activity as a stronger contributor to family cohesion and resilience. Nevertheless, this research has clearly demonstrated that family leisure in natural woodland settings can make a positive difference to parents and their children, firstly in terms of psychological and emotional well-being through meeting perceived shortfalls in their 'good' parenting and secondly, by supporting cohesion within the family through shared bonding moments.

Funding

We would like to acknowledge the support of the BIG Lottery Research programme in the UK, which provided funding for this research.

Notes

1. The National Trust is a UK charity which looks after historic property and land for public access. On its website (2014), it states: 'Every child should have the right to connect with nature. To go exploring, sploshing, climbing, and rolling in the outdoors, creating memories that'll last a lifetime.'
2. Children's centres in England were set up to improve outcomes for young children and their families, with a particular focus on those in greatest need. See Lavelle (2014) for a critique of the power relationships operating within them.

Notes on contributors

Alice Goodenough is a researcher for the Silvanus Trust, a charity working through partnerships to regenerate the woodlands in the southwest of England for economic, social and environmental benefits. Her research into people's engagement with woodlands and trees includes social, cultural and environmental impacts of tree planting, woodlands as a context for behaviour change and the well-being impacts of taking part in woodland-based activity.

Sue Waite is Associate Professor (Reader) in the Plymouth Institute of Education, Plymouth University in the southwest of England. Her research into outdoor learning includes studies of camping and education; Forest School; decline of provision of outdoor learning in schools and issues of transition; health and well-being outcomes from woodland activities; and place-based learning. She currently leads the Natural Connections Demonstration Project funded by Natural England, DEFRA and English Heritage and convenes Plymouth University's outdoor and experiential learning research network.

Jade Bartlett has worked as a freelance researcher for the National Trust. She currently farms livestock in Devon in southwest England and works with the local community in a Community Supported Agriculture (CSA) scheme. Her research interests include the benefits of CSA projects.

References

Abdallah, S., N. Steuer, N. Marks, and N. Page. 2008. "Well-Being Evaluation Tools: A Research and Development Project for the Big Lottery Fund." New Economics Foundation. Accessed May 11 2010. http://www.biglotteryfund.org.uk/wellbeing_evaluation_tools.pdf.

Bauer, J. J., D. P. Mcadams, and J. L. Pals. 2008. "Narrative Identity and Eudaimonic Well-Being." *Journal of Happiness Studies* 9: 81–104.

Bowler, D. E., L. M. Buyung-Ali, T. M. Knight, and A. S. Pullin. 2010. "A Systematic Review of Evidence for the Added Benefits to Health of Exposure to Natural Environments." *BMC Public Health* 10: 456. doi:10.1186/1471-2458-10-456.

Bragg, R., C. Wood, and J. Barton. 2013. *Ecominds Effects on Mental Wellbeing: An Evaluation for Mind.* London: Mind.

Chalquist, C. 2009. "A Look at the Ecotherapy Research Evidence." *Ecopsychology*, 1 (2): 64–74.

Chawla, L. 2006. "Learning to Love the Natural World Enough to Protect it." *Barn* 2: 57–77.

Coakley, J. 2006. "The Good Father: Parental Expectations and Youth Sports." *Leisure Studies* 25 (2): 153–163.

Coyl-Shepherd, D., and C. Hanlon. 2013. "Family Play and Leisure Activities: Correlates of Parents' and Children's Socio-emotional Well-being." *International Journal of Play* 2 (3): 254–272.

DCLG (Department for Communities and Local Government). 2007. "The New Performance Framework for Local Authorities & Local Authority Partnerships: Single Set of National Indicators." Accessed June 24. http://www.communities.gov.uk/documents/localgovernment/pdf/505713.pdf

Deci, E. L., and R. Ryan. 2004. *Handbook of Self-determination Research*. Rochester: University of Rochester Press.DEFRA (Department for Environment, Food and Rural Affairs) 2010. *Measuring Progress: Sustainable Development Indicators 2010*. London: DEFRA.

Dillon, J., and I. Dickie. 2012. *Learning in the Natural Environment: Review Of Social And Economic Benefits And Barriers*. Natural England Commissioned Reports, Number 092.

Foy-Phillips, P., and S. Lloyd-Evans. 2011. "Shaping Children's Mobilities: Expectations of Gendered Parenting in the English Rural Idyll." *Children's Geographies* 9 (3–4): 379–394.

Gittins, D. 1998. *The Child in Question*. Basingstoke: Macmillan.

Goodenough, A., and S. Waite. 2011. "Wellbeing from Woodlands." *ECOS: A Review of Conservation* 30 (3–4): 47–52.

Good from Woods. 2015. "Project Portfolio and Case Studies." www.goodfromwoods.co.uk.

Harrington, M. 2002. "Socio-Economic Differences among Families and the Meaning and Value of Family Leisure." Abstracts of Papers presented at the Tenth Canadian Congress on Leisure Research. Accessed September 1, 2014. http://lin.ca/sites/default/files/attachments/CCLR10-43.pdf.

Harrington, M. 2003. "Leisure Patterns and Purposive Leisure in Middle and Lower Income Families." Paper Presented at the 8th Australian Institute of Family Studies conference. Accessed May 20 2015. http://aifs.gov.au/conferences/aifs8/harrington.pdf.

Hendrick, H. 1997. "Constructions and Reconstruction's of British Childhood: An Interpretive Survey, 1800 to the Present." Chapter Two. In *Constructing and Reconstructing Childhood, Contemporary Issues in the Sociological Study of Childhood*, (2nd ed.), edited by A. James and A. Prout, 34–62. London: Falmer Press.

Holland, P. 1992. *What is a Child: Popular Images of Childhood*. London: Virago Press.

Humberstone, B., and I. Stan. 2009. "Well-being and Outdoor Pedagogies in Primary Schooling: The Nexus of Well-being and Safety." *Australian Journal of Outdoor Education* 13 (2): 24–32.

Hunt, A., J. Burt, and D. Stewart. 2014. *Monitor of Engagement with the Natural Environment: A Pilot for an Indicator of Visits to the Natural Environment by Children – Interim Findings from Year 1 (March 2013 to February 2014)*. Bristol: Natural England.

Jones, O. 1997. "Little Figures, Big Shadows, Country Childhood Stories." Chapter Nine. In *Contested Countryside Cultures, Otherness, Marginalisation and Rurality*, edited by P. Cloke, and J. Little, 158–180. London: Routledge.

Kellert, S., and P. Kahn, eds. 2002. *Children and Nature*. Cambridge, MA: MIT.

Kemmis, S. 2009. "Action Research as a Practice-based Practice." *Educational Action Research* 17 (3): 463–474.

Keyes, C. L. M., D. Shmotkin, and C. D. Ryff. 2002. "Optimizing Well-Being: The Empirical Encounter of Two Traditions." *Journal of Personality and Social Psychology* 82 (6): 1007–1022.

Lavelle, M. 2014. "A storm in a tea cup? Making a difference in two Sure Start Children's Centres." *Children and Society*. doi:10.1111/chso.12091.

Louv, R. 2005. *Last Child in the Woods*. New York: Workman

Lovell, R., and J. Roe. 2009. "Physical and Mental Health Benefits of Participation in Forest School." *Countryside Recreation* 17 (1): 20–23.

Matthews, H., M. Taylor, K. Sherwood, F. Tucker, and M. Limb. 2000. "Growing-Up in the Countryside: Children and the Rural Idyll." *Journal of Rural Studies* 16 (2): 141–153.

McNiff, J., and J. Whitehead. 2002. *Action Research: Principles and Practice*. 2nd ed. London: Routledge Falmer.

Mguni, N., and N. Bacon. 2010. *Taking the Temperature of Local Communities: The Wellbeing and Resilience Measure (warm)*. London: The Young Foundation.

Minnaert, L. 2012. "The Value of Social Tourism for Disadvantaged Families." In *Family Tourism: Multidisciplinary Perspectives*, edited by H. Schänzel, I. Yeoman, and E. Backer, 93–104. Bristol: Channel View.

Moles, K. 2008. "A Walk in Thirdspace: Place, Methods and Walking." *Sociological Research* 13 (4). http://www.socresonline.org.uk/13/4/2.html.

National Trust. 2014. "Natural Childhood." Accessed September 29, 2014. http://www.nationaltrust.org.uk/what-we-do/big-issues/nature-and-outdoors/natural-childhood/.

Nevill, C. 2009. *Feelings Count, Measuring Children's Subjective Well-Being for Charities and Funders*. London: New Philanthropy Capital.

ONS (Office for National Statistics). 2011. *Measuring National Well-Being, Measuring What Matters*. Accessed October 31, 2011. http://www.ons.gov.uk/ons/guide-method/user-guidance/well-being/wellbeing-knowledge-bank/understanding-wellbeing/measuring-what-matters–national-statistician-s-reflections-on-the-national-debate-on-measuring-national-well-being.pdf.

Project Wild Thing. 2014. *Take Action*. Accessed September 29, 2014. http://projectwildthing.com/take-action.

Ryan, R. 2009. "Self-determination Theory and Wellbeing." *WeD Research Review 1*. Accessed April 4, 2015. http://www.welldev.org.uk/wed-new/network/research-review/Review_1_Ryan.pdf.

Shaw, S. M., M. E. Havitz, and F. M. Delemere. 2008. "'I Decided to Invest in my Kids Memories': Family Vacations, Memories, and the Social Construction of the Family." *Tourism, Culture & Communication* 8: 13–26.

Sibley, D. 1995a. "Families and Domestic Routines, Constructing the Boundaries of Childhood." Chapter Six. In *Mapping the Subject, Geographies of Cultural Transformation*, edited by S. Pile, and N. Thrift, 123–137. London: Routledge.

Sibley, D. 1995b. *Geographies of Exclusion, Society and Difference in the West*. London: Routledge.

Swinton, A. T., P. A. Freeman, R. B. Zabriskie, and P. J. Fields. 2008. *Non-resident Fathers' Family Leisure Patterns During Parenting Time With Their Children*. Men's Studies Press. Accessed September 9, 2014. http://www.thefreelibrary.com/Nonresident+fathers%27+family+leisure+patterns+during+parenting+time ... -a0188897989.

Trussell, D. E., and S. M. Shaw. 2007. "'Daddy's Gone and He'll Be Back in October': Farm Women's Experiences of Family Leisure." *Journal of Leisure Research* 39: 366–387.

Valentine, G. 1997. "A Safe Place to Grow Up? Parenting Perceptions of Children's Safety and the Rural Idyll." *Journal of Rural Studies* 13 (2): 137–148.

Waite, S. 2007. "'Memories are made of this': Some Reflections on Outdoor Learning and Recall." *Education 3–13*, 35 (4): 333–347.

Waite, S. 2013. "'Knowing your Place in the World': How Place and Culture Support and Obstruct Educational Aims." *Cambridge Journal of Education* 43 (4): 413–433.

Ward, P. J., and R. B. Zabriskie. 2011. "Positive Youth Development within a Family Leisure Context: Youth Perspectives of Family Outcomes." *New Directions for Youth Development* 130: 29–42.

Zabriskie, R., and B. McCormick. 2001. "The Influences of Family Leisure Patterns on Perceptions of Family Functioning." *Family Relations: Interdisciplinary Journal of Applied Family Studies* 50 (3): 281–289.

Zabriskie, R. B., and B. P. McCormick. 2003. "Parent and Children Perspectives of Family Leisure Involvement and Satisfaction with Family Life." *Journal of Leisure Research* 35 (2): 163–189.

Celebrating the family abroad: the wedding tourism experience

Giovanna Bertella

School of Business and Economics, UiT The Arctic University of Norway, Tromsø, Norway

The research question on which this paper is based is as follows: How is the family celebrated at weddings that take place far from the place of residence of the involved families? This paper utilizes an experiential approach and uses the concepts of authenticity and co-creation to investigate the case of wedding tourism in Tuscany (Italy). The data collection includes primary data in the form of interviews, observations, and a survey, and secondary data that were collected online. The findings confirm the centrality of the emotional bonds that constitute the family, and suggest the coexistence of the participants' desire for togetherness and individualism. The couples and wedding professionals meticulously plan and stage the weddings, but creativity and spontaneity are not completely excluded. The collaboration between the couples and the wedding professionals has a central role of creating the event as symbolically and existentially authentic.

Introduction

Family is quite a dynamic and complex phenomenon, and it plays a central role in our society (Weigel 2008; Schänzel et al. 2012). Some demographic and cultural changes have occurred in the Western world in the last few decades that have led to a change in the understanding of the family as a horizontal unit including a couple – a man and a woman – their biological children, and their closest relatives, towards a more open, vertical, and networked idea of the family that can include adopted children, relatives living far from each other, and even friends (Yeoman et al. 2012). The study on which this paper is based adopts this emerging conceptualization of the family as a group of people, not necessarily related through blood or via legal contracts, nor characterized by their spatial vicinity. Family members are recognized on the basis of their reciprocal feelings of connectedness (Levin 1999).

This understanding of the family is focused on its relational aspect and outlines the possibility to view the concept of the family as a process. In this sense, the family can be seen as a phenomenon that is constructed through social interactions (Holtzman 2008). Both daily and extraordinary interactions contribute to form and give meaning to the family. Among the latter type of interactions, weddings are particularly important. Weddings can be seen as a ritual of passage for two individuals entering a new phase of their lives and as a social event that celebrates the family, as a centre of positive emotions and, in some cases, also as a confirmation of the individual's role in society according to the dominant view of the specific sociocultural context (Oswald 2000; Tombaugh 2009).

The focus of this paper is on weddings that are celebrated in a place where neither the bride nor the groom lives. The purpose is to investigate how such weddings are celebrated, with particular attention to those aspects that can be relevant to the conceptualization of the family. The investigation focuses on wedding tourism as a form of visiting friends and relatives tourism, and adopts the perspective of the wedding as a staged tourism experience.

Theoretical perspective

Wedding tourism

The term 'wedding tourism' usually indicates the flow of tourists generated by weddings that are celebrated in a destination where neither the bride nor the groom lives (Daniels and Loveless 2013). Wedding tourism is about travelling in order to be co-present with significant others and therefore can be qualified as a form of 'visiting friends and relatives tourism' (Daniels and Loveless 2013). Wedding tourism is not only about being in a new place, it is also about fulfilling family obligations and reproducing social networks (Olwig 2002; Larsen, Urry, and Axhausen 2007; Uriely 2010; Obrador 2012).

Some scholars have noted that any form of tourism that involves families can be seen as a search for an 'ideal home' where family members can share experiences and show their reciprocal affection, as such they are often documented by snapshots portraying family members happily spending time together when on holidays (Haldrup and Larsen 2003; Lehto et al. 2012). In this sense, family tourism is about balancing family cohesion and adaptability while striving towards an ideal of reciprocal love (Gram 2005; Backer and Schänzel 2012; Larsen Kirkegaard 2013; Schänzel and Smith 2014).

In line with these considerations, participation in a wedding celebrated abroad can be seen as a strong claim of belonging to a network of caring people as well as a display of family solidarity and loyalty. In this sense, weddings are seen as public manifestation of intimacy, and wedding tourism can be viewed as a search for a 'temporary ideal home' for the celebration of a renovated family. At the same time, the wedding as a social practice has been studied and interpreted as a form of acceptance and re-enforcement or as a form of challenge in relation to heteronormativity and traditional gender roles, and a sort of commodification of the private life (Igraham 1999; Freeman 2002; Johnston 2006; Kimport 2012). Additionally, such understandings of the wedding can be related to wedding tourism, which, ultimately, is about people acting productively and jointly, meeting, socializing and, in doing so, (re)producing the family.

The wedding tourism experience

The wedding abroad experience can be framed using the concept of staged tourism experiences. Inspired by some of the ideas expressed by Goffman in his book *The Presentation of Self in Everyday Life*, several scholars have been quite explicit in considering tourist activities as theatre-like performances that take place on more or less regulated stages (MacCannel 1973; Edensor 2001; Sheller and Urry 2004; Stuart and Tax 2004). In this perspective, the tourists are viewed as actors who follow more or less disciplined scripts, and, through their performances, communicate some values (Goffman 1959; Adler 1989; Edensor 2000, 2007).

A wedding celebrated abroad can be conceptualized as a staged tourism experience. As any other ritual, weddings tend to follow scripts that have origins in different traditions and can be adapted according to the desires and needs of the specific case. The wedding participants tend to play their roles with the result of contributing to the communication of values, such as family connectedness and traditional gender expectations.

The scenography of the wedding tourism experience can be identified in the wedding destination and venue, such as a specific castle in a particular geographical area. The choice of the wedding destination is usually based on a positive and emotionally engaging image that the couple has of the specific destination before the actual wedding and, in most cases, will be reinforced by the event (Tauer and Ryan 2005; Knudsen and Waade 2010).

At the level of the venue, drawing upon the concepts of service- and experience-scape that have been advanced in the marketing and tourism literature, a sort of wedding-scape emerges (Bitner 1992; Abubakar 2002; Tombs and McColl-Kennedy 2003; Mossberg 2007; Van der Duim 2007; Rosenbaum and Massiah 2011). The scenography of the wedding-scape can be referred to as the physical scene where the wedding experience, particularly the ceremony, takes place. This scenography is often shaped by key workers of the wedding industry, such as the florists.

Concerning the choreography, the wedding planners and the celebrants can be compared to the directors of the wedding experience (Fortezza and Del Chiappa 2012). The use of such experts for the arrangement of a wedding abroad is quite common, in part as a form of today's commercialization of the intimate life and in part for practical reasons related to the couples' generally limited knowledge about the chosen destination, in particular the local wedding procedures (Blackely 2008; Daniels and Loveless 2013).

Thus, the wedding-scape can be described as a space regulated, at least in part, by the wedding professionals and centred on the magnification of the family's values. Fully embracing the theatre-like idea of the wedding tourism experience as a staged experience, the wedding ceremony can be seen as a privileged stage where the couples and their families display their attachment to the family, presenting themselves as the characters of a tale of growing and inclusive love.

This staged approach to the wedding experience can be further described using the concepts of authenticity and co-creation.

The wedding as an authentic experience

The concept of authenticity has been extensively discussed in the tourism literature (Cohen 1988; Wang 1999; Knudsen and Waade 2010). Following the considerations presented above, everything that happens in the public sphere tends to be staged. In this sense, it lacks what is defined as objective authenticity, a form of authenticity that is related to the quality of an object or event (Olsen 2002; Steiner and Reisenger 2006a).

Some scholars have proposed the concept of constructive authenticity as an alternative and more subjective way to understand authenticity. Here, authenticity is understood as strictly related to the process of value-making that happens through the social interactions of those who are involved in the tourism experience

(Olsen 2002; Kim and Jamal 2007). The symbolic form of constructive authenticity involves those experiences that are the result of socially constructed ideas and symbols (Wang 1999). In this sense, the wedding experience can be perceived as a symbolically authentic experience as it is the projection of the ideal family.

Another form of constructive authenticity that can be relevant to the case of wedding tourism is that of existential authenticity (Wang 1999; Steiner and Reisenger 2006b). The wedding experience as a form of family tourism can be perceived as an existentially authentic experience as it can represent a context where people can feel more sincere and genuine than in everyday life (Wang 1999). The existential authenticity experienced by wedding participants can be both intra- and interpersonal. In regard to interpersonal authenticity, as mentioned above, an important element of the wedding experience is about being together: family ties among new and old members are created and reinforced through participation in a wedding. Moreover, the wedding experience can be an intrapersonal authentic experience as it is related to the 'self-making' processes of the individual participants, in particular the bride and the groom.

The aspect of authenticity can seem to be in conflict with the presentation of the wedding as a staged experience. On the one hand, the wedding is presented as a social event that follows a script. On the other hand, it is presented as an authentic experience. This apparent conflict can be resolved by adopting the concept of co-creation.

Co-creating the wedding experience

The concept of co-creation derives from the adoption of the service-dominant logic from the marketing literature, and also from the recognition of today's economy as being characterized by customers' search for experiences (Pine and Gilmore 1999; Vargo and Lusch 2004). According to such a view, the social interactions related to the customer experience, and in particular the engagement of the customer, are extremely important (Tombs and McColl-Kennedy 2003; Prahalad and Ramaswamy 2004; Grönroos 2006; Payne, Storbacka, and Frow 2008; Nilsson and Ballantyne 2014).

In tourism, the process of value creation of a tourism experience has been presented as a process centred in the interactions of the tourists with all the elements of the experience-scape (Mossberg 2007; Mehmetoglu and Engen 2011). Although physical and service aspects are important, the very essence of many forms of tourism is socially constructed (Rosenbaum and Massiah 2011; Eide and Mossberg 2013; Sfandla and Björk 2013; Prebensen, Chen, and Uysal 2014). The process of co-creation in tourism is then recognized as being embedded in the social world, and the involved subjects are viewed as acting out of their individual skills, needs, and desires and, at the same time, following and reinventing practices that acquire a special meaning in the specific context (Rihova et al. 2015).

In the wedding tourism context, the value of the experience is created by the social interactions among the couples and the guests, and also with the other central subjects involved in the celebration, such as the wedding planners and celebrants. The apparent conflict outlined above concerning the authenticity of the wedding experience is then reconciled noting that the wedding is a social practice where the participants can play an active and also a creative role and that it need not necessarily follow standard scripts. In this sense, the wedding experience can be seen as a shared and collective experience where participants construct their identities as individuals and as members of a family and of a society.

Method

This paper represents part of an ongoing research project concerning wedding tourism in Tuscany, Italy. The empirical part of this paper is based on the case of wedding tourism in Tuscany, which, initially, was investigated through the collection of secondary data available on the Internet.

The primary data collection started in winter 2014 with three deep interviews with one wedding planner and two celebrants. All of the people who were interviewed have several years' experience in providing wedding services (7, 10, and 13 years). The interview with the wedding planner was anticipated by several casual conversations during the years, and was also the trigger for the research project. The two celebrants were selected on the basis of the indication of the wedding planner as two particularly experienced and active officials working with wedding tourists.

The interviews were conducted face to face, such that the researcher met the interviewees personally (in one case through a Skype meeting). The interviews were performed in a conversational style, where the researcher probed the respondents to come up with examples and to provide their personal interpretations of the processes relevant to the wedding tourism experience, with particular attention given to those relating to the wedding ceremony, the whole travel experience, and the meaning the tourists attached to them.

Fourteen interviews with wedding planners operating in Tuscany were also performed in winter–spring 2014. The contacts with these operators are derived from the responses that the researcher had in relation to a survey conducted as part of the broader project concerning wedding tourism. The selected wedding planners were those who had several years (4 or more) experience and had shown particular interest and engagement in talking about their jobs. These interviews were conducted via telephone and were structured around the following main issues wherein the researcher posed open questions and invited the respondents to give examples: the profile of the tourists who get married in Tuscany, their relatives and friends, the requested services and products, and the related processes of development and delivery – their experiences in terms of the critical factors for the organization of a successful wedding.

Based on the indications of the 14 interviewed wedding planners and 1 of the interviewed celebrants, an online survey targeting 30 local providers of photo- and videographic wedding services was conducted. The choice of this typology of respondents was based on the central role of wedding photo-/videography in the documentation and creation of the wedding experience (Strano 2006). In addition to the question relative to the years of experience in the wedding industry, the survey contained just one other question that invited the respondents to give their personal interpretation of how the family is celebrated during weddings that are arranged for tourists. Six of the contacted providers answered the survey, giving descriptions that varied considerably in length, from a few sentences to a half page.

Finally, data were collected through the observation of three ceremonies: two as video footages and one through personal participation in a wedding celebrated in May 2014 in a village close to Florence. Two videos were provided by one of the celebrants. The videos were analysed following what has been identified by some scholars as the phases of a wedding ceremony and focused on which values were being communicated and how (Cheung 2006; Kimport 2012). These foci also proved quite useful during the observation of the wedding ceremony, which, in addition to giving the researcher a first-hand experience, allowed her to conduct some casual conversations with two wedding photographers, a florist, a celebrant and the owner of the venue where the ceremony took place.

A directed qualitative content analysis was conducted. Data were analysed solely qualitatively, without the use of statistical techniques, and already developed conceptualizations were applied (Mayring 2000; Hsieh and Shannon 2005; Kohlbacher 2006). In particular, the concepts that emerged from the literature concerning family holidays and tourism as performance were used as conceptual categories for the analysis. Figure 1 is based on the description of this deductive process by Mayring (2000), and illustrates the data analysis with an example concerning a short part of the transcript of the interview with a wedding planner.

The three key informants identified at the beginning of this section were used to validate the findings. In terms of reliability, it is important to note that both the researcher and the vast majority of the respondents have the same cultural background. This element could have influenced the collection and interpretation of the data. On one side, a sort of we (Italians)/they (tourists) way of thinking has helped the data collection. On the other hand, it could have led to some bias, especially in terms of interpretation.

Findings and discussion

The findings and discussion are organized in four sections. The first section describes briefly the context of the study, giving some background information about wedding tourism in Tuscany. The second section is about two issues that are particularly significant in terms of what type of family emerges from the way the wedding is planned and celebrated: the guests and the gender roles. These findings can be related to recent scholarly contributions concerning the 'new' family, such as Schänzel et al. (2012) and Tombaugh (2009).

The third section concerns the choice of getting married abroad and how a Tuscan wedding is considered to contribute to the family celebration. The findings of this section are discussed referring to the concept of authenticity in its objective and symbolic meaning as expressed by several scholars, in particular Wang (1999), Olsen (2002), and Steiner and Reisenger (2006a). Finally, the fourth section is about the design and the performance of the wedding. The approach used is in line with studies about tourist activities as performances comparable to theatre performances (e.g. Edensor 2001). The concept of co-creation is here used to present and discuss the wedding as an extraordinary and, especially for the bride and groom, existentially authentic social practice. This aspect is commented upon based on the considerations about the concept of authenticity in tourism by Steiner and Reisenger (2006b), Kim and Tazim (2007), and Rihova et al. (2015).

Wedding tourism in Tuscany

In the last decade, the phenomenon of wedding tourism, usually referred to as 'matrimoni per stranieri' (weddings for foreigners), has been developing quite quickly in Italy. Couples getting married in Tuscany come from several countries among which the UK and the USA are the most represented. Tuscany is among the favourite

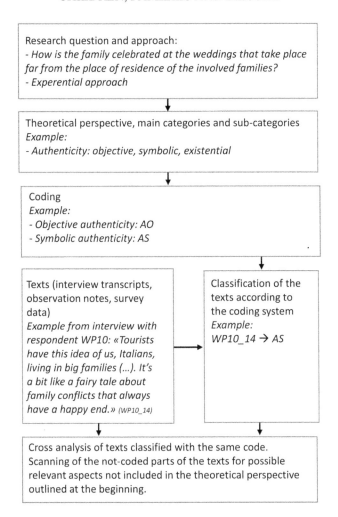

Figure 1. An example of the performed data analysis as a deductive process.

wedding destinations for lay people, wealthy people, and also show-business personalities (ANSA 2013). Celebrity events have contributed to profiling the region as a particularly attractive wedding destination, together with other factors, such as the local cultural attractions and eno-gastronomy (ANSA 2013).

The operators of the wedding industry have responded to the increasing number of tourist requests for wedding services by developing new products and packages especially tailored for foreigners. The professional figure of the wedding planner did not exist in Italy until a few years ago, but it is now becoming quite popular (Del Chiappa and Fortezza 2013). Also at the destination level, projects are developed in order to coordinate the wedding industry operators and to gain some beneficial effects in terms of regional development (Bertella 2015).

Family inclusion and gender roles

There is a broad agreement among the respondents that wedding tourism is about the celebration of the family, and this sentiment often includes families who normally live relatively close, at least in the same country, who are on this occasion combining a family event with a holiday. In some cases, there are guests who come from a country different from where the couple lives, but this is an exception to the rule.

Only when the couple is composed of two people who come from different countries, the group of people participating in the wedding tends to be international. According to some of the interviewees, this is sometimes the case for young European couples. These cases seem to correspond to the idea of a family structure that resembles the one described in the family literature: such people are networked and particularly open to people who are not blood related. One wedding planner reported the case of a couple composed of a Swede and a German who met during their participation in an exchange programme organized by their universities and the University of Florence. This wedding was characterized by the presence of many guests from all over Europe who belonged to the same group of international students to which the couple belonged.

The respondents agree that the number of the guests can vary considerably, with an average of around 35, a number confirmed by the Italian Agency of Statistics (ANSA 2013). Most of the ceremonies tend to include the couples' parents, some first-degree relatives, and a few friends. A wedding planner commented on this aspect saying that both younger and older couples tend to 'take with them a piece of their schooldays', meaning that the friends invited to the wedding are often friends from their childhood or youth.

A difference between younger and older couples noted by a wedding planner was the size and composition of the group of friends. These groups tend to be quite large and homogenous in terms of age and life-cycle phase in the case of younger couples, while they are more varied and usually limited in size in the cases of older couples, second marriages, and confirmation vows.

The respondents mentioned getting married abroad as being related to the couple's desire to have only a few guests. Limiting the guest list can be difficult when the wedding is celebrated at home, as the couple feels obligated to invite more people. Moreover, the possibility that most of the invitees actually accept is quite high when the celebration takes place close to home. One respondent commented on this aspect saying:

> When they arrange a wedding abroad they count on the fact that somebody will not be able to come, something that will lead to a celebration with fewer guests, that means lower costs and also a more family-oriented event …. In your home-country you *have to* invite your boss, your colleagues. Abroad you are freer. Choosing to get married abroad is, sometimes, a statement: we are getting married, and our wedding is going to be just for family!

The desire for an intimate celebration has been noted especially in the case of older couples and second marriages. About the latter case, one celebrant commented:

> Sometimes I have celebrated symbolic weddings where only the couple was present. They are usually older people or people getting married for the second time. They are not so much into the big celebration and the big party, meeting new relatives … Some of them have done it already! They have been through the whole process or, in the cases of older couples, they might value other things than parties.

These findings suggest that the choice of getting married abroad depends on different circumstances and could be indicative of the couples' idea of the family structure. The core of the family seems to be restricted to only a few relatives and friends. It seems that the age of the couple and their personal background in terms of previous unions and also in terms of exposure to different cultures is quite relevant. Some of the obligations that apply for weddings in general do not seem to apply to weddings abroad, and the choice of getting married abroad could also be a way to avoid such feelings of obligation.

The findings concerning the day of the wedding can help to understand the gender roles within the establishment of a new family. The respondents agree on the fact that the day of the ceremony is 'the bride's day'. This was quite evident during the observation, when most of the attention of the photographers was on the bride. Hundreds of pictures were taken during the dressing of the bride, and her rehearsing the vows. These pictures were taken spontaneously, without anyone posing, while group pictures that showed off the dress or were of the bride with the bridesmaids, her mother, and father were more formal. One of the respondent photographers reported:

> There is a common desire that the couples express, and that is to capture the process the bride goes through, often with her mom, sisters, and best girlfriends. Many brides are quite focused on these backstage pictures of a girl prepared by other women and girls to enter a new phase of her life.

Another respondent reported that in her five years of experience, only one time had the groom asked expressly to have a photographer following his preparation. He meant that some attention had to be given also to him, and not only to his wife-to-be, so he requested the photographer to document 'his last moments with his buddies before the big step'.

This focus on the bride and the other women participating in the ceremony was also noted by the wedding planners, who mentioned that the mother of the bride is sometimes involved in the planning phase.

After the ceremony, as some respondents mentioned, and as was also noted during the observation, the attention is focused on the couple, and later on, as described by one photographer, is equally distributed among all the participants, with some special attention to children, if present. A photographer also commented about the presence of children, writing about the common request to have informal pictures of the bride with the children.

Tuscan weddings: symbolic and objective authenticity

The choice of getting married abroad, and more specifically in Tuscany, can give some indications about the couples' ideals and imaginations, and can be commented upon in relation to the concept of authenticity.

Several wedding planners, when explaining the tourists' choice of getting married in Tuscany, mentioned the typical elements that attract tourists: the weather, the culture, and particularly the art cities and the eno-gastronomy. In addition to such elements, other motivations were identified as quite common. One respondent said that often the couples, or one person of the couple, have experienced Tuscany as a tourist and fell in love with the place. This might be the main motivation for choosing the wedding destination. Another motivation seems to be based on a positive word of mouth by friends who have been in Tuscany or, in some cases, have married in Tuscany. Sometimes the couples have been guests at the weddings of friends in Tuscany and decided to come back for their wedding, often choosing a location that they had visited during their first trip. Finally, a few respondents mentioned a recent book and movie (*Under the Tuscan Sun*) that had brought attention to the region, profiling it as a particularly romantic place.

The wedding planners, who are for the vast majority Italians, describe the way the wedding ceremony is planned and performed as 'the American way'. The wedding planners explained that the couples tend to ask for a ceremony as 'they have seen it in the movies'. Some wedding planners reflected on this aspect saying that for the couples coming from the USA, this way is actually their traditional way. Nevertheless, several wedding planners tend to recognize a tendency among the couples from various countries to be inspired by the American practices, probably due to the dominant position of such culture in the pop culture of Western societies. Some wedding planners also specified that although the adoption of the American practices is quite diffuse, there are couples that bring with them their own rituals and practices, often linked to their religions.

There is a broad agreement among the respondents that although these couples have decided to get married in Italy, their weddings are quite different from Italian weddings, starting from the fact that they often employed many more experts, the wedding planner *in primis*. One example is their choice of music. Quite often, the music chosen for the background at the beginning and the end of the ceremony is Italian, and the *tarantella* has become quite popular among the tourists, although it is not usual at Italian weddings, at least not in Tuscany.

Two respondents described these weddings as an 'island of foreigners in Tuscany'. According to this view, on the wedding day, unlike the days before the ceremony, the tourists want to be completely isolated: they want to have a private celebration. In regard to this aspect, a respondent remembered an episode when a venue owner's child managed to sneak into the room when the ceremony was being celebrated. The respondent described this scene as follows:

> The boy had a *schiacciata* [focaccia bread] in his hands. We were in a guest-farm. I imagine that he had been out playing in the countryside and was having his *merenda* [snack]. Well, believe me, the glances he received, especially from the mother of the bride, were everything but lovable.

This episode and the considerations presented above seem to confirm a general lack of interest in an objectively authentic experience. This might apply especially to the wedding ceremony but, at the same time, it seems likely to be part of their desire for a more general way of living the tourism experience. In regard to this, a respondent said:

> They want the Tuscany *rivista e corretta* [revised and corrected] according to their idea of what Tuscany is.

This can be also seen in the recent trend to choose a rural-chic profile for the ceremony. This aspect was reported by a decoration designer saying that the tourists seem to like the idyllic idea of big rural families living in a countryside, a setting that is simple but still elegant.

Similarly a videographer wrote:

> My experience is that the wedding is planned as a dream coming true. The dream of the couple is based on their view of Italy, and of what a family is or should be. In my job, I try to create a movie that can support this dream. I use black and white, dreamy musical

background. Details are as important as the big classical scenes. When you wake up from a dream you often remember details, but not what was going on in the dream.

Some respondents mentioned among the motivations of the couples the values that the tourists seem to associate with what they call 'the Italian lifestyle'. When asked to give some examples of what the tourists mean by this expression, several respondents mentioned the ideal concerning a life where time is spent enjoying the pleasures of eating and drinking, absorbed in magical landscapes and characterized by small villages where idyllic values related to the family dominate. The latter element was further investigated, and a wedding planner gave an answer that is quite representative of the wedding planners' perspective:

> Tourists have this idea of us, Italians, living in big families that we love each other and we quarrel and fight, but at the end, the family is always the family. It's a bit like a fairy tale about family conflicts that always have a happy end.

One respondent noted how some couples are extremely knowledgeable about Italian history and art, and, in his opinion, their choice of the wedding destination is motivated by the desire to share a cultural experience with their family, and also to affirm their identity as cultural people.

The attraction of Tuscany was also commented on in relation to same-sex marriages as such unions are not legally valid in Italy. According to the celebrants, the impossibility to celebrate legally valid weddings is not particularly relevant as the couples tend to be fascinated more by the past of the country and what it can offer in terms of cultural heritage than by the present society and its limitations.

It can be noted that in most cases, the choice of Italy and Tuscany is based on the desire of a symbolically authentic wedding experience, an experience that symbolizes the beginning of a life according to an idyllic vision of the Italian lifestyle (i.e. a combination of togetherness, passion, and culture). In some cases, the wedding experience can also be thought of as an objectively authentic experience, but, according to the empirical data, this might be true only for a minority of weddings where the people involved are particularly knowledgeable about Italian culture.

Another aspect that can be related to the concept of authenticity concerns the fact that, in some cases, the couples have already gotten married in their home country. Some respondents commented that this is not necessarily known by the guests. One celebrant commented saying:

> Sometimes guests know it [that the couple is already married], and sometimes they don't. But, at the end, what counts is that they understand that for the couple, who maybe got married in an office with no particular celebration, this is the real wedding. This is the real thing they want to share!

The wedding professionals and the couples shaping the wedding-scape and co-creating the existentially authentic wedding

Usually the couple makes contact with the wedding professionals several months before the ceremony. As observed by some wedding planners, in some cases, the mother of the bride is also involved in this planning phase.

Both celebrants commented on the importance of having a shared understanding of what the future wedding is meant to be as this is the basis for a fruitful collaboration with the couple and a successful event. Such a shared understanding concerns the meanings that the couples attach to the wedding and the value recognized in the union of two people and of two families.

For one of the celebrants, it was very important that such a shared understanding be based on a spiritual vision of the wedding. This usually implies religious ceremonies where the groom and the bride belong to the same or, sometimes, different religions. The latter case was also commented on as a challenging and exciting possibility to find unifying values concerning the union of two people and of two families belonging to different religions.

The other celebrant agreed on the importance of understanding the kind of cele-bration the couple want. At the same time, during the interview, she did not make a particularly sharp distinction between religious and non-religious celebrations, speci-fying that different views are not particularly problematic when the wedding pro-fessional is committed to delivering what the couples most want, taking for granted that is always about 'a celebration of life'. She said:

> Of course there are cases when the party after the wedding seems to have the central role, it is *the* event. But, in my opinion, if you really have developed a relatively close contact with the couple, you know also that, at least in most of the cases, what they show and what is more evident, the party, is not in reality where their hearts are. Their real focus – their emotional focus – is the commitment and making it explicit in public, and not a generic public, but your family and your new family!

Both celebrants appeared to invest a considerable time in getting to know the couple, and, although some standard rituals are usually applied, a sort of tailoring process takes place through this collaboration. In this regard, a celebrant commented on how some couples are more open than others. In the latter case, the help that the couples can get from the celebrant in the writing of their vows can contribute to the establishment of trust and can result in an easier collaboration. The importance of establishing a positive relationship with the couple has also been observed in relation to the other professionals who are involved: the wedding planners and the photo-/videographers.

The first contacts with the wedding planner are verbal, often through mail and Skype or telephone, and are followed by a first meeting at the destination. The couple takes a trip to the wedding destination with the intention to find the right atmosphere for the event. This is the time when many rituals are performed: the couple travels to Tuscany, views the possible locations, tastes the food and drinks of the catering companies, and meets the providers of the various wedding services. It is in this phase that some of the meanings and values attached to the event and that are relevant to the family become more explicit.

In the planning phase, the wedding planners are very concerned about the practical aspects of the event, including the physical elements of the wedding-scape and also the social ones, more specifically the planning of some days of holiday before or after the event. Several wedding planners reported about the importance of making clear for the couples that in most cases, the guests, including the closest relatives, are not used to living and spending so much time together. Because of this, the days the guests spend at the destination before the wedding have to be planned strategically. One wedding planner commented:

> Suddenly you have people who are used to seeing each other only for a few hours during the festivities, living together, or, in any case, spending a lot of time together. This can be the source of conflicts. Some couples are very conscious of this aspect, while others are not.

Some wedding planners tend to recommend different accommodations for the different guest groups, often identified on the basis of their age and life-phase. Some tend also to reserve the wedding venue just for the day of the ceremony and the following party, while the tourists are hosted in other locations for the rest of their stay. This is seen as a good way to organize the days before the wedding, as explained by a respondent in the following way:

> In this way the guests have their holiday. And it is a real holiday, not a stressing family reunion, all the family issues are there but … How can I explain? They are 'taken in small doses'! If well-planned, these days contribute to create a positive basis for a successful wedding celebration.

Similarly, activities such as sightseeing tours or cooking classes are arranged for the entire group or for limited groups of guests. These activities are meant to encourage the guests to 'break the ice'. At the same time, things are usually planned so that the guests also have some free time where they have the possibility to stay on their own or in the company of the relatives and friends with whom they want to spend time. One wedding planner commented quite explicitly, saying:

> To put all the guests together in the same guest-farm, for some days, with few possibilities to travel around and nothing to do is craziness!

As for the wedding planners and the celebrants, also in the case of the video-/photographers, the collaboration with the couples is considered very important. A respondent wrote about his first contacts as the moment when he understood which memories they wanted to take care of. Although he is usually left free to take pictures of what he wanted, he, as well as other respondents, indicated that the couples tend to have some ideas about what should be documented. This tends to follow a quite standard script with the following scenes: the preparation of the bride, the bride entering the room, the groom entering, the celebrant presenting the vows, the ring exchange, the kiss scene, the exit from the room, and the formal group picture.

Some respondents said that this standard script, which was also observed in the video footages, tends to be followed with few changes, but the way the pictures and videos are taken tends, most recently, to be less formal and more relaxed than it was a few years ago. One photographer wrote that on the basis of the couples' requests, there seems to be quite a common desire to capture both formal and informal aspects, with a tendency to privilege the latter, while still maintaining some of the wedding classics.

Based on these findings, one could say that the wedding professionals and the couples jointly create the premises for the wedding experience. This process of co-creation is essentially a process of understanding and sharing of the meanings attached to the event. The wedding professionals strive to create a safe platform where the tourists, each characterized by individual differences in terms of personalities and skills, can feel comfortable and can engage in the creation of his or her experience, not only physically, but also cognitively and emotionally. The result can be an experience that, as mentioned above, can be symbolically and existentially authentic.

The other participants, with the only exception of the bride's mother, seem to have a much more passive role compared to the couples. In some cases, the event seems to be planned and designed for the guests. This is illustrated by the fact that the guests are sometimes not informed about the couples being already married, as mentioned above, and also by the possible surprise effects planned and performed during the ceremony. In regard to the latter, during the observation phase, the researcher observed a 'box ritual'. The couple put two letters they had written to each other in a wooden wine box and shut it with a hammer, with the promise to open it together on a special occasion while tasting the wine and remembering the day of their wedding. This ritual came as a surprise for the guests and was a nice twist that was visibly appreciated.

Conclusions

The way the family is celebrated abroad can be indicative of several aspects related to the conceptualization of today's family. This paper's findings confirm the centrality of emotional bonds, an aspect that has been mentioned in the literature and qualified as one of the characteristics of the modern family (Levin 1999; Yeoman et al. 2012). This aspect has been found in relation to many couples' wish to be surrounded by people with whom they feel a strong emotional bond. It seems that the wedding invitations are based on such a choice more than on the desire to fulfil social obligations. These emotional bonds can be assumed to be the structural ties that form the family, and they can and do very often involve a limited group of friends with whom the couple has shared significant experiences in the past.

The findings also confirm an aspect outlined in the family literature concerning the fact that understandings of the concept of the family can vary according to which perspective is used, often depending on age and life-cycle phase (Yeoman et al. 2012).

Another factor that emerges from the findings is the coexistence of a desire for togetherness and a desire for individualism. Such elements overlap during the wedding, with a distinction between habitual practices, performed preferably alone or in small groups, and extraordinary practices. The wedding event seems to lead to the emergence of a sort of large family structure that is temporary and limited to some practices.

Staging strategies seem to be central for the success of the wedding and the identification and management of possible conflicts. This does not exclude authenticity. The findings indicate that the wedding experience is perceived as an authentic experience in terms of symbolic authenticity, with symbols coming from traditions, as well as from ideals derived from Western pop culture. In terms of existential authenticity, the experience seems to be dependent on the personality of the people involved, firstly the bride and the groom, but also the skills of the wedding professionals.

Wedding professionals set the premises for the experience and the emergence of the related value in terms of symbolic and existential authenticity. In line with this co-creation framework, wedding services providers tend, already several months before the event, to encourage dialogue and collaboration as a result of the couples' being engaged at different levels, physically, cognitively, and emotionally.

Creativity and spontaneity are not excluded from the wedding tourism experience. They are often reserved to practices that are conducted in limited groups, as mentioned above, but are not completely absent from more official practices. This is the case when the couple and the wedding professionals adapt standard procedures or when they organize part of the wedding as a surprise for the other participants. This aspect seems also to be confirmed by the trend to move away from formal and standard official wedding pictures and to instead focus on capturing informal and spontaneous scenes, including small episodes and details.

The findings also suggest that weddings are planned and performed in quite a traditional way in terms of gender roles. The study on which this paper is based did not focus on this aspect and further studies are needed to investigate how such an issue contributes to the structure of modern families, including those based on same-sex unions.

Notes on contributor

Giovanna Bertella is Associate Professor at the School of Business and Economics, UiT The Arctic University of Norway. Her research interests are small-scale tourism, food tourism, rural tourism, nature-based tourism, active tourism, event management, knowledge, and networks.

References

Abubakar, Binta. 2002. "Developing a Framework for Understanding a Tourism Service Setting." *Services Marketing Quarterly* 23 (3): 17–34.
Adler, Judith. 1989. "Travel as Performed Art." *American Journal of Sociology* 94: 1366–1391.
ANSA. 2013. "In Italia e' di Moda il Wedding Tourism", April, 19. Accessed March 11, 2014. http://www.ansa.it/web/notizie/canali/inviaggio/news/2013/04/19/Italia-moda-Wedding-Tourism-_8578881.html.
Backer, Elisa, and Heike Schänzel. 2012. "The Stress of the Family Holiday." Chap. 8 in *Family Tourism. Multidisciplinary Perspectives*, edited by Heike Schänzel, Ian Yeoman, and Elisa Backer, 105–124. Bristol: Channel View.
Bertella, Giovanna. 2015. *The Emergence of Tuscany as a Wedding Destination: The Role of Local Wedding Planners*. Working Paper. The Arctic University of Norway.
Bitner, Mary Jo. 1992. "Servicescapes: The Impact of Physical Surroundings on Customers and Employees." *Journal of Marketing* 56: 57–71.
Blackely, Kristin. 2008. "Busy Brides and the Business of Family Life: The Wedding-Planning Industry and the Commodity Frontier." *Journal of Family Issues* 29 (5): 639–662.
Cheung, Sidney C. H. 2006. "Visualizing Marriage in Hong Kong." *Visual Anthropology* 19 (1): 21–37.
Cohen, Erik. 1988. "Authenticity and Commoditization in Tourism." *Annals of Tourism Research* 15 (3): 371–386.
Daniels, Maggie, and Carrie Loveless. 2013. *Wedding Planning and Management: Consultancy for Diverse Clients*. London: Routledge.
Del Chiappa, Giacomo, and Fulvio Fortezza. 2013. "Wedding-Based Tourism Development: An Exploratory Analysis in the Context of Italy". In *Proceedings 5th Advances in Tourism Marketing Conference, Marketing Places and Spaces. Shifting Tourist Flows, October 2–4*, edited by Antonia Correia, Metin Kozak, Juergen, Gnoth, Alan Fyall, Sonja Lebe, and Luisa Andreu, 412–416. Vilamoura: Universidade do Algarve.
Edensor, Tim. 2000. "Staging Tourism. Tourists as Performers." *Annals of Tourism Research* 27 (2): 322–344.
Edensor, Tim. 2001. "Performing Tourism, Staging Tourism: (Re)producing Tourist Space and Practice." *Tourist Studies* 1 (1): 59–81.
Edensor, Tim. 2007. "Mundane Mobilities, Performances and Spaces of Tourism." *Social & Cultural Geography* 8 (2): 199–215.

Eide, Dorthe, and Lene Mossberg. 2013. "Towards More Intertwined Innovation Types: Innovation Through Experience Design Focusing on Customer Interactions." Chap. 13 in *Handbook on the Experience Economy*, edited by Jon Sundbo and Flemming Sørensen, 248–268. Cheltenham: Edward Elgar.

Fortezza, Fulvio, and Giacomo Del Chiappa. 2012. "Il Wedding-based Tourism come Leva di Valorizzazione Territoriale." In *Referred Electronic Conference Proceedings of XXIV Convegno annuale di Sinergie: Il territorio come giacimento di vitalità per l'impresa, Ottobre 18–19*, 329–342. Lecce: Università del Salento. http://www.theitalianjournalofmanagement.it/rivista/index.php/XXIV/article/view/711/491.

Freeman, Elizabeth. 2002. *The Wedding Complex*. London: Duke University Press.

Goffman, Erving. 1959. *The Presentation of Self in Everyday Life*. New York: Anchor Books.

Gram, Malene. 2005. "Family Holidays. A Qualitative Analysis of Family Holiday Experiences." *Scandinavian Journal of Hospitality and Tourism* 5 (1): 2–22.

Grönroos, Christian. 2006. "Adopting a Service Logic for Marketing." *Marketing Theory* 6 (3): 317–333.

Haldrup, Michael, and Jonas Larsen. 2003. "The Family Gaze." *Tourist Studies* 3 (1): 23–46.

Holtzman, Melissa. 2008. "Defining Family: Young Adults' Perceptions of Parent-Child Bond." *Journal of Family Communication* 8 (3): 167–185.

Hsieh, Hsiu-Fang, and Sarah E. Shannon. 2005. "Three Approaches to Qualitative Content Analysis." *Qualitative Health Research* 15 (9): 1277–1288.

Igraham, Chrys. 1999. *White Weddings: Romancing Heterosexuality in Popular Culture*. New York: Routledge.

Johnston, Linda. 2006. "'I Do Down-Under': Naturalizing Landscapes and Love Through Wedding Tourism in New Zealand." *ACME: An International E-Journal for Critical Geographies* 5 (2): 191–208.

Kim, Hyounggon, and Tazim Jamal. 2007. "Touristic Quest for Existential Authenticity." *Annals of Tourism Research* 34 (1): 181–201.

Kimport, Katrina. 2012. "Remaking the White Wedding? Same-Sex Wedding Photographs' Challenge to Symbolic Heteronormativity." *Gender & Society* 26 (6): 874–899.

Knudsen, Britta Timm, and Anna Marit Waade. 2010. "Performative Authenticity in Tourism and Spatial Experience: Rethinking the Relations Between Travel, Place and Emotion." Chap. 1 in *Re-investing Authenticity. Tourism, Place and Emotions*, edited by Britta Timm Knudsen and Anna Marit Waade, 1–19. Bristol: Channel View.

Kohlbacher, Florian. 2006. "The Use of Qualitative Content Analysis in Case Study Research." *Forum: Qualitative Social Research* 7 (21). Accessed April 11, 2014. http://www.qualitative-research.net/index.php/fqs/article/view/75/153.

Larsen, Jonas, Jon Urry, and Kay W. Axhausen. 2007. "Networks and Tourism. Mobile Social Life." *Annals of Tourism Research* 34 (1): 244–262.

Larsen Kirkegaard, Jacob R. 2013. "Family Flow: The Pleasures of 'Being Together' in a Holiday Home." *Scandinavian Journal of Hospitality and Tourism* 13 (3): 153–174.

Lehto, Xinran, Yi-Chin Lin, Yin Chen, and Soojin Choi. 2012. "Family Vacation Activities and Family Cohesion." *Journal of Travel & Tourism Marketing* 29 (8): 835–850.

Levin, Irene. 1999. "What Phenomenon Is Family?" *Marriage & Family Review* 28 (3–4): 93–104.

MacCannel, Dean. 1973. "Staged Authenticity: Arrangements of Social Space in Tourist Settings." *The American Journal of Sociology* 79 (3): 589–603.

Mayring, Philipp. 2000. "Qualitative Content Analysis." *Forum: Qualitative Social Research* 1 (2). Accessed April 11, 2014. http://www.qualitative-research.net/index.php/fqs/article/view/1089/2385.

Mehmetoglu, Mehmet, and Marit Engen. 2011. "Pine and Gilmore's Concept of Experience Economy and Its Dimensions: An Empirical Examination in Tourism." *Journal of Quality Assurance in Hospitality & Tourism* 12 (4): 237–255.

Mossberg, Lene. 2007. "A Marketing Approach to the Tourist Experience." *Scandinavian Journal of Hospitality and Tourism* 7 (1): 59–74.

Nilsson, Elin, and David Ballantyne. 2014. "Reexamining the Place of Servicescape in Marketing: A Service-Dominant Logic Perspective." *Journal of Services Marketing* 28 (5): 374–379.

Obrador, Pau. 2012. "The Place of the Family in Tourism Research: Domesticity and Thick Sociality by the Pool." *Annals of Tourism Research* 39 (1): 401–420.

Olsen, Kjell. 2002. "Authenticity as a Concept in Tourism Research: The Social Organization of the Experience of Authenticity." *Tourist Studies* 2 (2): 159–182.

Olwig, Karen Fog. 2002. "A Wedding in the Family: Home Making in a Global Kin Network." *Global Networks* 2 (3): 205–218.

Oswald, Ramona Faith. 2000. "A Member of the Wedding? Heterosexism and Family Ritual." *Journal of Social and Personal Relationships* 17 (3): 349–368.

Payne, Adrian F., Kaj Storbacka, and Pennie Frow. 2008. "Managing the Co-creation of Value." *Journal of the Academic Marketing Sciences* 36: 83–96.

Pine, James H., and James H. Gilmore. 1999. *The Experience Economy: Work is Theater.* Boston, MA: Harvard Business School Press.

Prahalad, C. K., and Venkat Ramaswamy. 2004. "Co-creation Experiences: The Next Practice in Value Creation." *Journal of Interactive Marketing* 18 (3): 5–14.

Prebensen, Nina K., Joseph S. Chen, and Muzaffer Uysal. 2014. "Co-creation of Tourist Experience: Scope, Definition and Structure." Chap. 1 in *Creating Experience Value in Tourism*, edited by Nina K. Prebensen, Joseph S. Chen, and Muzaffer Uysal, 1–10. Wallingford: Cabi.

Rihova, Ivana, Dimitris Buhalis, Miguel Moital, and Mary Beth Gouthro. 2015. "Conceptualising Customer-to-Customer Value Co-creation in Tourism." *International Journal of Tourism Research* 17 (4): 356–363. doi:10.1002/jtr.1993.

Rosenbaum, Mark S., and Carolyn Massiah. 2011. "An Expanded Servicescape Perspective." *Journal of Service Management* 22 (4): 471–490.

Schänzel, Heike A., and Karen A. Smith. 2014. "The Socialization of Families Away from Home: Group Dynamics and Family Functioning on Holiday." *Leisure Sciences: An Interdisciplinary Journal* 36 (2): 126–143.

Schänzel, Heike, Ian Yeoman, and Elisa Backer, eds. 2012. *Family Tourism: Multidisciplinary Perspectives.* Bristol: Channel View.

Sfandla, Chouki, and Peter Björk. 2013. "Tourism Experience Network: Co-creation of Experiences in Interactive Processes." *International Journal of Tourism Research* 15: 495–506.

Sheller, Mary, and Jon Urry. 2004. *Tourism Mobilities: Places to Play, Places in Play.* London: Routledge.

Steiner, Carol J., and Yvette Reisenger. 2006a. "Reconceptualising Object Authenticity." *Annals of Tourism Research* 33 (1): 65–86.

Steiner, Carol J., and Yvette Reisenger. 2006b. "Understanding Existential Authenticity." *Annals of Tourism Research* 33 (2): 299–318.

Strano, Michele M. 2006. "Ritualized Transmission of Social Norms Through Wedding Photography." *Communication Theory* 16: 31–46.

Stuart, F. Ian, and Stephen Tax. 2004. "Toward an Integrative Approach to Designing Service Experiences. Lessons Learned from the Theatre." *Journal of Operations Management* 22: 609–27.

Tauer, Birgit, and Chris Ryan. 2005. "Destination Image, Romance and Place Experience – An Application of Intimacy Theory in Tourism." *Tourism Management* 26: 481–49.

Tombaugh, Alissa. 2009. "Pretty Dresses and Privilege: Gender and Heteronormativity in Weddings." *Sociological Insights* 1: 106–123.

Tombs, Alastair, and Janet R. McColl-Kennedy. 2003. "Social-Servicescape Conceptual Model." *Marketing Theory* 3 (4): 47–475.

Uriely, Natan. 2010. "'Home' and 'Away' in VFR Tourism." *Annals of Tourism Research* 37 (3): 854–857.

Van der Duim, René. 2007. "Tourismscapes. An Actor-Network Perspective." *Annals of Tourism Research* 34 (1): 961–976.

Vargo, Stephen L., and Robert L. Lusch. 2004. "Evolving to a New Dominant Logic for Marketing." *Journal of Marketing* 68 (1): 1–17.

Wang, Ning. 1999. "Rethinking Authenticity in Tourism Experience." *Annals of Tourism Research* 26 (2): 349–370.

Weigel, Daniel J. 2008. "The Concept of Family: An Analysis of Laypeople's Views of Family." *Journal of Family Issues* 29 (11): 1426–1447.

Yeoman, Ian, Una McMahon-Beattie, Damian Lord, and Luke Parker-Hodds. 2012. "Demography and Societal Change." Chap. 3 in *Family Tourism. Multidisciplinary Perspectives*, edited by Heike Schänzel, Ian Yeoman, and Elisa, Backer, 30–49. Bristol: Channel View.

More than putting on a performance in commercial homes: merging family practices and critical hospitality studies

Julie Seymour

Hull York Medical School, University of Hull, Hull, UK

Critical hospitality studies and family studies have shown a developing theoretical convergence predicated by the 'social turn' in the study of hospitality. Recent hospitality research on 'Commercial Homes' has drawn strongly on Goffman's concept of performance to examine both guest and host behaviours. In contrast, this article introduces the family studies concept of 'displaying families'. This concept emphasises the family practices of host families as well as the commercial practices privileged in studies of hospitality. It also widens the often individualised focus on the (adult) host(s) to one that incorporates the host family. Drawing on empirical evidence, it appears that, for the hosts, displaying families in Commercial Homes is a complex and, apparently paradoxical, mix of presentation and reticence – the family has to be highly visible but not publicly privileged over guests. The inclusion of the concept of display will serve to illuminate further the arenas where family, commercial and hospitality practices intersect.

Introduction

In Lashley's (2000), opening chapter for the seminal volume *In Search of Hospitality*, he itemises the three domains of hospitality; these are the social, private and commercial. In his oft-cited Venn diagram of the three domains, these are presented as independent but overlapping arenas in which hospitality activities occur (Figure 1).

The private domain is discussed in relation to the influence of the nuclear family on the hospitable activities of the individual host and the extent to which these activities can fulfil his/her physiological and psychological needs. As a family sociologist interested in the impact on family life of owning and running a hospitality establishment or 'Commercial Home' (Lynch 2005), my focus starts within, and emerges from, this domain of the domestic setting as later articles named it (Lashley 2015). However, rather than perceiving this area as being about familial influences on individual hosts, my research focus is on all the members of the host family and in particular the strategies and practices (Morgan 1996) they employ to fulfil the multiple and potentially competing requirements of a Commercial Home[1] (Seymour 2007, 2011a). This approach then widens the focus of the private domain from the psychological influences on the host to include the sociological by considering the actual practices through which the host family can be said to be 'doing family'

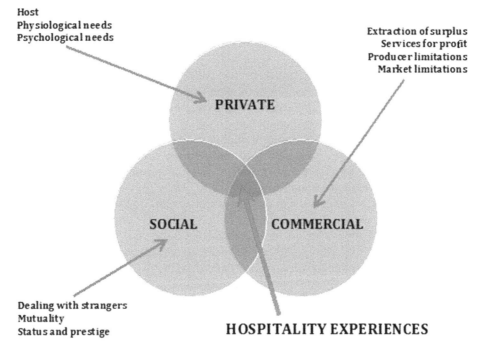

Figure 1. Hospitalityactivities.
Source: figure 1.1 in Lashley (2000).

(Morgan 1996). This focus on the family in the study of hospitality, leisure and tourism is supported by recent publications which advocate a whole family approach to both the holidaying family (Carr 2011; Orbrador 2012; Schanzel 2010; Schanzel, Yeoman, and Backer 2012) and the family that services such holidays (Getz, Carlsen, and Morrison 2004; Lynch, McIntosh, and Tucker 2009a; Seymour 2011b). Although Lashley's diagram is usually referred to as the domains of hospitality, it is important to think of these areas as sites of processes rather than fixed locations such as the home or the business. As will be shown in the development of this article, taking literally the title of the original diagram – "Hospitality Activities" – allows the consideration of the social, commercial and private/family practices which overlap to produce commercial hospitality experiences.

This article posits the question that if we start from the sociological viewpoint of the host family, how does this affect our view of hospitality processes and what might recent conceptual developments in family studies contribute to the theoretical consideration of hospitality? It will particularly review the prevalent use of Goffman's concept of performance in recent hospitality studies on Commercial Homes and propose that, to this, could be added the new concept of family display (Finch 2007). This viewpoint fits in with the integration of social sciences in the study of hospitality and the theoretical convergences between the tourism/hospitality literature and family studies in the areas of the production of social relationships and the 'doing' of everyday life/tourism (Edensor 2007).

By briefly reiterating the continuing growth of social theory in the study of hospitality in the past two decades and by outlining the gradual convergence of theory in family studies and tourism studies, this article will show why this disciplinary merging is a timely activity. It will then particularly focus on the use of the 'performance turn' (Haldrup and Larsen 2009) within the study of hospitality and outline some limitations of this approach for the study of Commercial Homes before turning to the new concept of 'Displaying Families' (Finch 2007) which has been receiving attention from family studies researchers. The article will define, explain and show the potential applications of this concept to studies of the family and hospitality providing an early in-depth interrogation of the application of this concept to the latter area. It will use as an example, Seymour's work on Commercial Homes (2005, 2007, 2011a, 2011b, 2015) where the family in focus is the one providing the hospitality for the guests. This empirical work which has been published and cited in the areas of family studies and the geographies of families now provides a relevant exemplar for new interdisciplinary conceptual dialogue about family display in hospitality research.

It therefore also feeds into the area of leisure studies by applying the focus of the whole family approach (Schanzel 2010), not to the holidaying family, but to those who facilitate such recreational activities. It provides an analysis of those families who produce and service the leisure of others. By so doing, it confirms that in the provision of hospitality, the Commercial Home is, by definition, neither a site of only domestic activities for the host family, nor a wholly work environment. This research focus then provides temporal and spatial fluidity to the work–leisure binary.

The study of hospitality in dialogue with social sciences

From 1997 onwards, the new interdisciplinary area of the study of hospitality emerged from what was seen as commercial hospitality management education. A statement outlining the new academic paradigm was aired in Lashley and Morrison's (2000) edited volume *In Search of Hospitality. Theoretical Perspectives and Debates* and included a continuing dialogue with other social sciences. The edited collection was recognised as an exploratory text, outlining early studies and understandings which would be developed in the new millennium. Within this initial volume, the application of a focus on performance was evident in the chapter by Darke and Gurney (2000) which looked at private homes, discussed hospitality as performance and outlined the inherent tensions which could occur between non-commercial hosts and guests.

In 2002, Morrison proposed a 'Pause for Reflection' on hospitality research and its relation with social sciences. Morrison reiterated that the study of hospitality was originally seen as a professional rather than an academic subject unlike tourism. She identified a need to build 'strategic alliances within the wider social science landscape towards enhancing the power of hospitality research to contribute genuine scientific value' (168). She stressed how hospitality and social sciences could be interlinked 'with [there being] a potential unity in comprehensive theory building and knowledge creation' (168). Such linkages clearly developed and within a decade of the inaugural networking meeting of hospitality researchers in Nottingham in April 1997, Lashley, Lynch and Morrison could state in their edited volume *Hospitality: A* Social Lens (2007) that the topic was being studied not just by business and management researchers but also those using the perspectives of the social sciences resulting in a less partial view. The editors confirmed that a significant element of this more comprehensive viewpoint was the increasing recognition that the focus of study was the relationship between hosts and guests and hence hospitality should interrogate the relational (2007). They refer again to the Lashley (2000) model outlined above to discuss how the social, cultural, and private or domestic socially structure the meanings, values and emotional dimensions of the commercial through relations and service inter-actions. Within this volume, Di Domenico and Lynch (2007) discuss the concept of performance to problematise the static nature of the 'stage' of the Commercial Home and to emphasise the symbolism of material artefacts in such hospitality locations.

Lashley, Lynch, and Morrison (2007) outline that, during the first decade of the twenty-first century, developments in the academic area of hospitality studies included the growth of critical hospitality studies as a distinct tranche of the research. This resulted in more links with the social sciences due to the adoption of the critical study of hospitality 'as a human phenomenon' (12) which should be viewed through 'plural social lenses' (4). They propose the adoption of critical theory as it ' ... questions imposed academic divisions that separate hospitality from social theory encapsulated in other disciplines' (4–5). This critical interdisciplinary approach was made manifest in the launching of the journal *Hospitality and Society* whose stated editorial aim is 'to transport intellectual projects across disciplinary boundaries' (Lynch et al. 2011, 13). It is in this spirit, that this article is presented to examine the extent to which a concept developed in family studies can be utilised in hospitality studies and contribute to the development of theoretical frameworks.

Tourism studies and family studies – theoretical convergences

This article also draws on the separate area of tourism studies which Morrison (2002) says was recognised as an academic area earlier than hospitality studies. It can be argued that there has been a convergence in theory in the areas of family practices/intimate relationships and tourism studies. Both are moving from a view of the family, and tourism and leisure, as a site of consumption to a focus on social relations forged through everyday practices. Gabb (2008) and Smart (2007), among others, outline these developments in family studies and the sociology of personal life. Edensor (2001, 2007) and Jacobsen (2010) develop similar themes in tourism with the former emphasising people as producers of tourism and the latter saying that twenty-first century tourism is about everyday practices, social obligations, networks at a distance and social (network) capital. Concomitantly, in leisure studies, authors such as Shaw (1997) remind us that 'Leisure is not an isolated aspect of life but is inextricably connected with social context and daily life experiences' (1).

As an example of this shift, in their tellingly entitled paper on 'The Family Gaze', Haldrup and Larsen (2003) discuss how, previously, much tourism research focused on 'how the tourism industry employs photographic images in order to script and stage places as aesthetic scenes for the consuming "tourist gaze"' (2003, 24). Now, they argue, tourist photography is viewed as '*producing* social relations rather than consuming places'. The authors state:

> While Urry's gazes are directed at extraordinary 'material worlds', the 'family gaze' is concerned with the 'extraordinary ordinariness' of intimate 'social worlds' (24) .... places become scenes for acting out and framing active and tender family life for the camera. (25)

The production of social relations involves the actions of social actors and this shift in analysis of tourist activities led to the development of the 'performance turn' in tourist studies. The next section will examine this emerging analytic lens (Haldrup and

Larsen 2009) and consider how it was applied to the hospitality activities of family hosts and Commercial Homes.

The 'performance turn' and its use in hospitality studies of the commercial home

Larsen (2008) and others (e.g. Haldrup and Larsen 2009) suggest that the theoretical focus in tourism research took a 'performance turn' from the 1990s. In doing so, it has moved on from the consuming 'Tourist Gaze' to the language of embodied doings, thick sociality, reflexivity and the performing family (Lofgren 1999). The 'performance turn' as opposed to the tourist gaze:

> *explicitly* conceptualizes tourism as intricately tied up with everyday practices, ordinary places and significant others, such as family members and friends, but co-residing and at-a distance. (Larsen 2008, 26)

This focus on doings and their siting in 'wider social discourse' (Haldrup and Larsen 2009, 4) resonated with conceptual developments in family studies which focused on active embodied agents who were 'doing' family but operating within structural constraints and ideological constructions of the family (Morgan 1996).

The 'performance turn' drew explicitly on the writings of Goffman (1959) and his dramaturgical approach outlined in *The Presentation of Self in Everyday Life*. In hospitality studies, it was developed by an inclusion of the role of material space/objects, actual rather than representational practices and the recognition that the research focus was the analysis of everyday behaviours as performance rather than an approach that said they were performances (Haldrup and Larsen 2009). Its use as an analytic lens for the study of families and hospitality and particularly those in Commercial Homes is outlined and critiqued through the examples below.

An early, and much cited, application of the performance turn in relation to hospitality and the host home was Darke and Gurney's (2000) study. This looked at private homes and host–guest relations and was not applied to Commercial Homes. Much of the focus of the chapter was on performance as a gendered process reflecting contemporary concerns at the time of publication. Within this chapter, the concept of performance was not problematised. It was described by drawing on Goffman's own definition of 'all the activity of an individual which occurs during a period marked by his continuous presence before a particular set of observers' (Goffman 1959, 32 cited in Darke and Gurney 2000). This construction hence turns the home, when visited, into a stage and the performances of the guest and host into exercises in impression management. Darke and Gurney show the number of ways in which this can lead to tension in the host–guest relationship. Their identification of these potential transgressions in the sharing of the private home with guests leads them to query whether the adoption of the term hospitality to describe similar activities in the commercial sector, and to deliberately evoke home, is wise, given that it is often hard to live up to the ideal of the perfect host in the domestic sphere.

The analytic lens of performance was later turned onto Commercial Homes with a recognition that such an approach interrogated the social interaction between all the actors under consideration, not just the performance of the commercial host. Robinson and Lynch (2007, 142) emphasise that Goffman (1959) 'analyses the structure of social encounters and focuses on the power play between two interacting "teams"'; that is, the host(s) and the guest(s). In the same volume, however, Di Domenico and

Lynch (2007) criticise Goffman's work as both failing to recognise that individuals may have more than one script and not acknowledging the performative nature of the setting. These authors remind us that Goffman's empirical work, from which the concept of performance emerged, looked at work roles, specifically those of waiters in a small hotel in Shetland. As a result, they argue that 'Goffman was concerned with exploring the presentation of the "self" within the constraints of occupational roles within organizations in the service sector, such as, the small hotel or the gambling casino' (118). This emphasis on the occupational could ignore the multiple scripts which may be enacted within Commercial Homes, and Di Domenico and Lynch recommend an approach which incorporated the more fluid approach of postmodernism. However, the multiple scripts they discuss are those of the host and guest perspectives in the 'hospitality transaction' (119). For the former, this may include the roles of host, home owner and, via identity projection through setting and artefacts, aesthete. Di Domenico and Lynch (2007) consider that the material setting of the Commercial Home has been underplayed particularly in relation to the guest's engagement with the host, the hospitality space and artefacts. They recommend that more attention is paid to the décor and the furnishings of the Commercial Home as non-verbal and symbolic parts of the performance. For Di Domenico and Lynch, 'The commercial home setting is not a static stage-set as implicit in Goffman's (1959) analysis, but an active player in the dissemination of unfolding 'scripts' (2007, 126). As a result, they suggest the Commercial Home setting is not just a prop but can be seen to perform and contribute to the transaction; in other words that it is an interactive performer itself and hence has agency. This approach fits into the material affordances approach to performance espoused by Gibson (1979 in Haldrup and Larsen 2009) which stresses that material objects have properties which influence or afford the specific embodied performance that can be enacted through them. However, Dant (1999) warns us that, while there has to be an interactive relationship between material objects and actors in order to constitute a performance, this does not necessarily afford agency to the former. While objects are drawn into relevance and constituted as meaningful by actors they do not themselves have intentions and construe meanings. Despite, this caveat, the commentary of Di Domenico and Lynch expands the range and content of performances while still employing the dramaturgical terminology of the Commercial Home as a stage. What they do not explore in their discussion of multiple scripts is that the Commercial Host and other family members will have additional family scripts – spousal, parental and child – which will also be enacted in this location.

By the end of the first decade of the twenty-first century, hospitality research on Commercial Homes was often using the term performance in a rather generic manner. Hence, Lynch, McIntosh, and Tucker (2009a) use the term uncritically as part of a list of major issues in the early pages to their volume on Commercial Homes (Preface, xvii) and again in the Introduction (2009b, 21). In the same edited collection, Benmore (2009, 118) echoes Darke and Gurney's (2000) dramaturgical approach to performance but adds the concept of emotional labour to the performances carried out by actors. The author showed how guests are the audience to the host's home-making performance which may include the hiding of 'bad' emotions. In the small UK hotels of Benmore's study, 'performance standards are self-imposed' and may be used to convey appropriate standards of behaviour such as no pyjamas, swearing or curlers in the dining room (122). Benmore does however, allow that some hosts may not be performing all the time.

So to conclude this section, Goffman's ideas of the frontstage-backstage perform-ance have exhibited remarkable staying power in the literature on Commercial Homes (and hospitality generally). Host and increasingly guest performances are recognised in these settings but not the family scripts of Commercial Home proprietors or their family members. While Benmore (2009) raises the issue of the 'authentic self' of some Commercial Hosts replacing performances, this authentic self does not include the membership of the very family which often defines the nature of the Com-mercial Home establishment. This may suggest that the 'doing' of family in Commer-cial Homes happens backstage but, as I will argue below, this also happens in the public arena of the Commercial Home (and indeed I propose that is has to). This omis-sion of the family activities of the host family seems particularly odd in light of the changing focus to everyday and relational practices, and the whole family approach in the study of hospitality which has been outlined earlier in this article. My research goes some way to redress this imbalance, but I also propose that rather than looking at performance to interrogate the actions of the Commercial Home family, this can be better achieved by the use of the family studies concept of 'displaying families'. Below I will outline this emerging concept and then go on to show ways in which it can be seen to occur in Commercial Homes.

The concept of displaying family

In 2007, Finch wrote an introductory article outlining the concept of 'displaying family' and encouraged family sociologists 'to refine the concept as well as to use it' (2007, 65). This has been started through an edited collection which interrogated and applied the concept (Dermott and Seymour 2011a) and the citation of Finch's article in over 275 subsequent publications at the time of writing. Displaying family as a concept builds on the earlier ideas of Morgan (1996) who proposed that, due to the diversity and fluidity of contemporary family groups, family studies should focus more on what families do rather than be concerned with their composition. He suggested that researchers should look at family practices, the 'doing' of family, to understand intimate lives. This work emerges from symbolic interaction but acknowledges the structural constraints in which actors may operate. Hence, as with the 'performance turn', there is a focus on both activities and discourses. Finch develops this work on practices and says that, due to this contemporary diver-sity of family members, there will be times when *families need to be 'displayed' as well as 'done''* (Finch 2007, 66, original emphasis) in order that a group of people may be recognised as a family. She defines 'display' as 'the process by which individ-uals, and groups of individuals, convey to each other and to relevant audiences that certain of their actions do constitute "doing family things" and thereby confirm that these relationships are "family" relationships' (Finch 2007, 67). Display can be done through a variety of means including activities, material objects and namings. Rel-evant audiences can vary with the settings. They may be other family members, they may be the general public (Dermott and Seymour 2011b). In Commercial Homes, they are likely to be family members, other staff and guests but may also be the State (through licencing laws). A displaying family approach then takes the Commercial Home family as the start point unlike critical hospitality studies researchers such as Benmore (2009) who start with the Commercial Home as their focus.

What is the difference between performance, performativity and display?

Doing and displaying family have the same theoretical antecedents in symbolic inter-action as do performances. Finch (2007) acknowledges that the start point for all three concepts is the same; that is, 'defining the situation to have appropriate meanings' (76). She also acknowledges that the concept of performativity, as outlined by Butler (1990), has emerged from this epistemological tradition. However, she suggests that the concepts of both performance and performativity are not adequate for understanding what is being conveyed by display and in her article, she distinguishes between performativity, performance and display (76–77).

To first briefly address performativity, Finch says that this has more to do with individual identity than with the nature of social interactions. In expanding on this difference, Heaphy (2011) says performativity is relational, it can be applied to relationships, but it focuses on power regimes. It examines how dominant frames of meaning are reflected and constituted in embodied practice; particularly the 'cultural constitution of gender practices' (Smith 2010, 181). Hence, performativity is a cultural process rather than a 'volitional enactment by an agent' (Smith 2010, 172). In contrast, display allows more for agency and change, especially change over time.

With regard to performance, Finch (2007, 76) draws on Goffman's definition of:

'performance' as the process in which an individual appears before others and therefore 'influences the definition of the situation which they will come to have'.

As a result, Finch argues that performance distinguishes between actor and audience; it is described as face-to-face interaction in which the performer remains an actor. Whereas in display, Finch suggests the identity of actors and audience are constantly shifting. The family member can be simultaneously actor and audience, both legitimating and supporting meanings as well as producing them. In addition, the family member can be an observer. Display can occur through material objects such as photographs. It does not always require face-to-face interaction in the way performance does. It does have to be questioned as to whether very young children (in Commercial Homes and elsewhere) are actively displaying, however it is entirely possible that they are being 'displayed' through opening up their family practices to public scrutiny as I will outline below. So having distinguished between performativity, performance and display, I will show how the latter is a useful transferable concept for thinking about host families in Commercial Homes.

Displaying families in commercial homes – methodology

The empirical data I will draw on to illustrate the use of the concept of displaying family in Commercial Homes come from my study of UK families in hotels, boarding houses and public houses. This study, which used in-depth qualitative interviews, was carried out in both a northern and southern seaside town in the UK in 2001. Two groups of informants were included. The first were current owners of Commercial Homes who were at present (or had very recently) combining their work and family life in one location. These interviews were carried out with at least one owner or more where this was possible. They also included children who were present and who had given their consent. This resulted in data from 15 parents and four children across 11 establishments (seven hotels, two pubs and two boarding houses). The second group of informants consisted of parents or adults who had raised their families or grown up in Commercial Homes during the 1960s and 1970s. This resulted in a further six interviews (four hotels, one pub and one boarding house). Access was negotiated first by letter through local Hotelier Associations and later by snowballing. All the interviews except two (on the interviewees' requests) were taped and transcribed. Finally, secondary data analysis was carried out on 50 oral history interviews collected for a larger Millennium project in the same northern seaside town. These transcripts included descriptions of family life in Commercial Homes (mostly Bed and Breakfast establishments) during the early and middle years of the twentieth century.[2] It was recognised that these accounts, as with those of the 1960s and 1970s proprietors and children, were based on memory and family narrative, rather than current experience (Phoenix 2009). Overall, this gave a quasi-longitudinal sample of family life in UK Commercial Homes over 50 years. All interviews were analysed using thematic analysis to identify areas of similarity and difference (Mason 2002). These were situated within the contemporary historical context of changes in the UK holiday industry.

Applying displaying families to commercial homes

As outlined above, it seemed in the analysis of host–guest interactions that performance was all, whether the location was the commercial or the domestic sphere. Then, following Finch, we can now expect family displays in the non-Commercial Home or among the non-host family in public arenas. What happens when the display of family practices and the performances of commercial hospitality intersect? First, it should be noted that some Commercial Home families kept their family life spatially and interactively separate from the commercial areas of their home so their displays would be more like those of guests/non-host families in that they happened only to other family members or to the general public outside their home. In these cases, children 'never' (Interview 2, female ex-boarding house owner) came into contact with guests as there were clear demarcation lines – either door boundaries or separate staircases (Interview 9, male ex-publican) – between the commercial areas and the private home.

For many families in the study, however, their family display occurred in the public areas of their hospitality establishment and I argue that such displays were influenced by their particular status as the Commercial Home family. As a result, they became essential rather than optional, visibly and audibly explicit and showed elements which I have labelled hypervisibility and displayed reticence (Seymour 2011b).

Commercial home family displays are essential and explicit

The 'unique selling point' of the Commercial Home in which the family live *in situ* is that it is a family enterprise (Lynch, McIntosh, and Tucker 2009b, 4–5). As a result, the host family needs to be visible and identifiable as the host family. They need to be seen to be exhibiting family-like activities, thus family display becomes essential rather than optional due to the commercial nature of the context. In addition, it must be made absolutely explicit to ensure that it is 'effective'; that is, that the audience appropriately constitute (read) the meanings they are intended to convey (Finch 2007, 66).

However, at the same time that the host family is highly visible, it must be clearly shown that they are not privileged over guests. Displaying family therefore becomes a complex and, apparently paradoxical, mix of presentation and reticence – the family has to be hypervisible while also, on certain occasions, exhibiting 'displayed reticence'. In effect, the family that live in a Commercial Home have to display themselves as a particular type of family (Morgan 2011), the Commercial Home Family, as well as showing their family relationships. This process is discussed in depth in a chapter entitled 'Family Hold Back' in Seymour (2011b) but the key points will be outlined here.

Commercial home families display hypervisibility

In a family hospitality enterprise, family members are expected to be present (or at least visible) and such Commercial Family Displays can be particularly enacted during times which can equate to Finch's 'periods of intensity' when family display is most required (2007). In Commercial Homes, this can include arrival and checking-in times, mealtimes and departures. Interviewees spoke of family members (including pets) forming a welcoming committee for guests either at registration when coaches arrived or when public houses opened:

> As people come in, you know my mum ... the landlady welcoming them in type of thing. (Interview 1, adult son of ex-publican)

Mealtimes were times of hypervisibility for the Commercial Home family. Finch reminds us that all families display in public restaurants but this is especially so for the host family as they form part of the servicescape (Carmichael and McClinchey 2009; Hall 2009; Lynch, McIntosh, and Tucker 2009c). At mealtimes, the Commercial Home families in the study who ate in the dining room were opening up their behaviour to public scrutiny (Carmichael and McClinchey 2009) showing they were capable of acting like a family in a public setting. This family however must also act as role models to convey the appropriate behaviour (Hall 2009, 69) and attire (Benmore 2009, 122) required by guests in this particular establishment. To convey this, the family display must be successful as judged by the audience and, for Commercial Home families with young children, this could not always be guaranteed. Hence as one ex-hotelier describes:

> For many years we had a table in the dining room with the guests. That began to fail after maybe a year or two, because, you know, you've got no privacy, your children wanted to have a tantrum, they'd have to do it in public. (Interview 7, female ex-hotel owner)

Commercial Home families in this setting are carrying out a complex set of practices and displays. They are attempting the basic family practice of nourishing and feeding their children; that is, they are 'doing' feeding and here family members form the audience (and participants) to these parenting activities. They are at the same time providing a family display of a family who can appropriately eat with others in a public dining room; here, the family, guests and staff form the audience as they do for all the other families who are dining. In addition though, and uniquely for the family who lives in the hospitality establishment, they must display the Commercial Home Family who set the 'tone' for dining and establish a family ambience which focuses on the display of positive emotions and the suppression of negative ones in order to display 'a (Commercial Home) Family which works' (Finch 2007, 73).

In other, less intensive times and settings, family displays could also be achieved through the use of the presence of family pets, photographs and family members acting as staff to create the 'home from home' atmosphere so central to the Commercial Home (Lynch and MacWhannell 2000). The dictates of the business however meant that there had to be boundaries as to how far public rooms in the Commercial Home reflected family life. In one case, a hotelier had to remind his son not to leave coats, pushchairs and bags in the guest lounge:

> We did use the visitors' lounge but we had people who used to complain about us using *their* lounge. (Interview 10, male hotel owner)

Simultaneously then while being readily visible, the Commercial Home Family must be seen to have no preferential access to resources and spaces that the guests have paid for; thus, they must publically carry out displayed reticence.

Commercial home families exhibit displayed reticence

In Commercial Homes, reticence by the host family is absolutely necessary and needs to be clearly shown and recognised by the guests. Hence, the Commercial Home family will need to be involved in 'displayed reticence' to counterpoint their hypervisibility as family members. Both guests and staff must be made aware that, while present, family members are not privileged over paying customers in the receipt of resources or services. Interviewees described occasions when they, or other family members, were physically visible but not involved in the guests' activities:

> She [daughter] sat there quite contentedly really all afternoon, watching everybody else. (Interview 7, female ex-hotel owner)

Dining rooms were again key locations of display. Displayed reticence could be made explicit during mealtimes through being seated at the 'worst' tables (near the kitchen or toilets), being served last or not having the choicest foods.

> Poor souls. They [the children of the hotel owner] used to get plonked on table while we were serving meals and, I [was] just saying to somebody this morning, in hindsight, we should have fed them first and then we wouldn't have had them saying 'I'm hungry Mummy, I want something to eat' and my Dad'd be saying 'Oh for goodness sake, shut up till we're finished serving the visitors', you know.

> … They were sat at the table waiting as soon as we got the pudding out then we served them with their dinner and they could get on with theirs 'cos we had a great big serving table so they used to sit at the back of the serving table. You just had to fit it in and work around things. (Interview 12, female hotel owner)

Both children and parents in the study were aware of such requirements regarding 'Family Hold Back' (and that these displays may not be carried out by non-Commercial Home families) but recognised them as a necessary family practice in such an establishment:

> I suppose sometimes I felt that the best things, whatever they were, the best cuts of meat for example, would go to the guests and, talking to other children, their parents would

always try and get the best for the family. It's such a small quantity in terms of the whole, we managed without. (Interview 4, adult son of ex-hotel owner)

If I'm talking to a guest he [son] can't come and interrupt and if I'm talking to him a guest can interrupt. He's had to learn, you know, that the work has to come first. (Interview 6, female hotel owner)

There was also a recognition that while this specific form of family display was required when the hospitality establishment was open, children and families shared in the economic benefits that such behaviour brought about. In addition, when hotels, pubs and boarding houses were closed, not only were such family displays unnecessary but the children and families enjoyed additional spaces and facilities not readily available in a private home, such as a choice of multiple bedrooms and bathrooms and commercial equipment:

Bar, drinks all the time. We've got a coke machine. (Interview 17, son of hotel owner)

Commercial family displays beyond the commercial home

As discussed earlier in this article, the atypicality of the Commercial Home as a location which is both home and work serves to contest the often held assumption that domestic and paid employment are spatially separate and that leisure and work occur in discrete places. In most families, family practices and family displays take place outside the home as well as inside (Dermott and Seymour 2011a; Morgan 2011; Seymour 2007). For families in Commercial Homes, the family displays related to their business can also take place away from the hospitality building. This could be when the children of the family are presented as representing or advertising the Commercial Home. One interviewee spoke of helping the guests with organised treasure hunts outside the hotel (which he was not allowed to win despite 'inside' knowledge) and being entered into fancy dress competitions during the annual town carnival as a representative from the family hotel rather than as an individual (Interview 4, adult son of ex-hotel owner). This was presented as an enjoyable activity unlike the next account when a woman who grew up in a Commercial Home responded to a radio programme featuring the research on which this article is based with less favourable memories. She talked about the continual hard work involved in living in the family hotel at a young age but for her the worst part was being made by her mother to wear:

ridiculous local costume to stand in the street on view to all and sundry including my peers. (Radio 4, 2009)

As these two accounts show, the audience for a Commercial Family Display outside the home includes current guests, members of the public (including peers) and potential guests. The latter audience is also reached by the use of Commercial Family Displays in advertising especially through websites for family-run hotels[3] (Seymour and Green 2009). Perhaps surprisingly, this rarely involves pictures of the family but the family is 'displayed' through accompanying personalised text in which the information and metaphorical imagery presented is focused on interpersonal relations. People's forenames are almost always used. Usually, the length of time they have run the hotel is listed, especially if this involves passing the business on from one generation to the current one. This suggests both family tradition and expertise in providing hospitality but also business acumen for maintaining a working business over this length of time. Guests are promised attention from the family members even in fairly large establishments, and the importance of 'personal touches' are stressed as the examples below illustrate:

> The Hotel is owned and has been personally run by three generations of the Newton family since 1946 when Raymond and Brenda Newton ... There is always a member of the family available to ensure your stay is comfortable and enjoyable. (Saxonville hotel, no date)

> The hotel is family run and independently owned by the Bannister family ... Inspired by the hospitality of the Bannister family, the staff at the hotel work tirelessly ... At the heart of everything we do are family values. Mr and Mrs Bannister can be seen out and about the hotel and estate every day and their son Tom, who is the hotel's managing director, is often seen serving guests their last drinks in the evening and breakfast in the morning. (The Coniston Hotel, no date)

Once again, the difference of family display from performance is emphasised in these extracts since they can be seen as a form of Commercial Home Family display through the media which does not require the face-to face interaction of performance. Throughout this section, these empirical examples of family display by the members of a Commercial Home have illustrated both the operation of this new concept and the distinctiveness of the Commercial Home Family display that is required by families who live in such hospitality establishments.

Conclusion

I have shown how the specific demands on a family living in a hospitality establishment come together in a display of the Commercial Home Family through a set of dedicated activities which are essential and explicit such as hypervisibility, reticence and normative standard setting. By suggesting there are specific forms of family display which the Commercial Home family have to carry out in the public areas of their establishments, I have drawn attention to the family activities which take place alongside business/commercial practices in hotels, pubs and boarding houses and extended the range of potential audiences for such displays. Using empirical examples, I have shown that, for some individuals, the positive focus put by Finch on family display as illustrating a 'family which works' needs to be contested. The misbehaviour of children, the awareness that for others the family would be prioritised or the embarrassment of publically advertising the business suggests that the negative aspects of (Commercial Home) family display would be a fruitful further area of research.

With regard to the study of hospitality, by taking as the start point the Commercial Home family, rather than the host or the location I have widened the form and range of interactions which can be seen to be carried out in such establishments. The multiple scripts of Commercial Home families mean they are (often simultaneously) displaying family, performing hospitality, and carrying out business practices. This then develops the study of hospitality beyond the use of performance to engage with the additional concept of displaying family. While this article has focused on the families which service leisure and hospitality, the concept is equally applicable to the new whole family approach to the study of hospitality and can be used to further interrogate the everyday production of families that occurs while they are at leisure. Morgan (2011) argues that the concept of family display needs to be

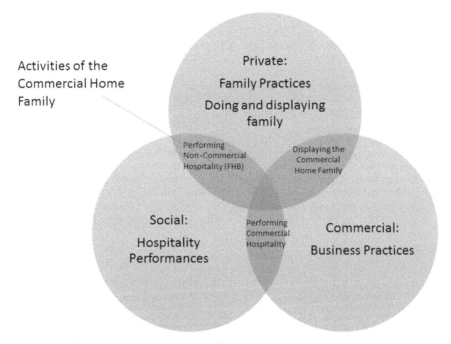

Figure 2. Activities of the commercial home family.

interrogated to establish how it can be used to display a particular type of family rather than just a family that works. This article shows the activities through which Commercial Home Families as a type of family can be successfully displayed as such. At this stage, Lashley's Venn diagram of the three domains of hospitality can be revisited to illustrate the multiple activities of the Commercial Home family. As initially outlined, if this diagram is conceived as showing activities, or practices, rather than locations then the convergence of display, performance and commercial practices can be revisualised (Figure 2). In the new three-way diagram, the Private circle illustrates the activities of family practices, that is, the doing and displaying of family which occurs in Commercial Home and non-host families alike. The Commercial circle contains the business practices carried out by staff in hospitality establishments whether family-run or otherwise. Finally, the Social circle encapsulates the performances of hospitality which take place in domestic and commercial settings. The intersections of the pairs of circles highlight family practices of hospitality (Family Hold Back), the display of the Commercial Home family and commercial hospitality: the first two of these areas are worthy of further research in their own right utilising the new displaying families concept. The central overlap of the three-way Venn diagram, the activities of the Commercial Home family, has formed the focus of this article which emphasises the families which service the holidays of other families. This topic should continue to be a key element of the emerging whole family approach to the study of hospitality. Continuing dialogue regarding the use of family practices and the additional conceptual material of displaying families developed in family studies should result in researchers from that discipline and those from the study of leisure and hospitality engaging in a fruitful collaboration.

Notes

1. While some of the hotels, pubs and boarding houses may be bigger than Lynch's (2005) consideration of homes where the hospitality revenue is secondary, these establishments have in common the fact that they are places where the home element is significant. Drawing on Di Domenico and Lynch (2007), these establishments can be labelled Commercial Homes since they are places where the home space has a dual purpose, it is not only domestic but also commercial. Focusing on these establishments provides an investigative lens to study hospitality which occurs alongside the 'doing' of family.
2. The interviews were funded by the Millennium Commission as part of the Looking Back, Looking Forward project carried out by the North Yorkshire Museums Department. I am grateful to the project's organiser, Karen Snowden, the interviewers and particularly the interviewees who allowed secondary analysis.
3. This element of the research on 'Selling the Family? Imagery and Reality in Family-Owned Hospitality Establishments' was funded by the University of Hull, Faculty of Arts and Social Sciences Strategic Research Support Fund.

Notes on contributor

Julie Seymour is Senior Lecturer in Medical Sociology at the Hull York Medical School, UK, having previously been in the Department of Social Sciences, University of Hull. She has a long-term interest in family practices and dynamics and has applied this to domestic labour, chronic illness, commercial homes and children's emotional labour. She is now looking at family practices in the area of disability, health and body donation.

References

Benmore, A. 2009. "Behaving Appropriately: Managing Expectations of Hosts and Guests in Small Hotels in the UK." In *Commercial Homes in Tourism. An International Perspective*, edited by P. A. Lynch, A. McIntosh, and H. Tucker, 115–126. London: Routledge.

Butler, J. 1990. *Gender Trouble: Feminism and the Subversion of Identity*. London: Routledge.

Carmicheal, B. A., and K. A. McClinchey. 2009. "Exploring the Importance of Setting to the Rural Tourism Experience for Rural Commercial Home Entrepreneurs and their Guests." In *Commercial Homes in Tourism. An International Perspective*, edited by P. A. Lynch, A. McIntosh, and H. Tucker, 73–86. London: Routledge.

Carr, N. 2011. *Children's and Families' Holiday Experiences*. London: Routledge.

Dant, T. 1999. *Material Culture in the Social World. Values, Activities, Lifestyles*. Buckingham: Open University Press.

Darke, J., and C. Gurney. 2000. "Putting Up? Gender, Hospitality and Performance." In *In Search of Hospitality. Theoretical Perspectives and Debates*, edited by C. Lashley, and A. Morrison, 77–99. London: Elsevier.

Dermott, E., and J. Seymour, eds. 2011a. *Displaying Families. A New Concept for the Sociology of Family Life*. Basingstoke: Palgrave Macmillan.

Dermott, E., and J. Seymour. 2011b. "Developing 'Displaying Families': A Possibility for the Future of the Sociology of Personal Life." In *Displaying Families. A New Concept for the Sociology of Family Life*, edited by E. Dermott and J. Seymour, 3–18. Basingstoke: Palgrave Macmillan.

Edensor, T. 2001. "Performing Tourism, Staging Tourism: (Re)Producing Tourist Space and Practice." *Tourist Studies* 1 (1): 59–81.

Edensor, T. 2007. "Mundane Mobilities, Performances and Spaces of Tourism." *Social and Cultural Geography* 8 (2): 199–215.

Finch, J. 2007. "Displaying Families." *Sociology* 41 (1): 65–81.

Gabb, J. 2008. *Researching Intimacy in Families*. Basingstoke: Palgrave Macmillan.

Getz, D., J. Carlsen, and A. Morrison. 2004. *The Family Business in Tourism and Hospitality*. London: CABI International.

Gibson, J. J. 1979. *The Ecological Approach to Visual Perception*. Boston, MA: Houghton Mifflin.

Goffman, E. 1959. *The Presentation of Self in Everyday Life*. Harmondsworth: Penguin.

Haldrup, M., and J. Larsen. 2003. "The Family Gaze." *Tourist Studies* 3 (1): 23–46.

Haldrup, M., and J. Larsen. 2009. *Tourism, Performance and the Everyday. Consuming the Orient.* London: Routledge.

Hall, C. M. 2009. "Sharing Space with Visitors: The Servicescape of the Commercial Exurban Home." In *Commercial Homes in Tourism. An International Perspective*, edited by P. A. Lynch, A. McIntosh, and H. Tucker, 60–72. London: Routledge.

Heaphy, B. 2011. "Critical Relational Displays." In *Displaying Families. A New Concept for the Sociology of Family Life*, edited by E. Dermott, and J. Seymour, 19–37. Basingstoke: Palgrave Macmillan.

Jacobsen, M. H., ed. 2010. *The Contemporary Goffman.* London: Routledge.

Larsen, J. 2008. "De-Exoticizing Tourist Travel: Everyday Life and Sociality on the Move." *Leisure Studies* 27 (1): 21–34.

Lashley, C. 2000. "Towards a Theoretical Understanding." In *InSearch of Hospitality. Theoretical Perspectives and Debates*, edited by C. Lashley, and A. Morrison, 1–17. London: Elsevier.

Lashley, C. 2015. "Hospitality and Hospitableness." *Research in Hospitality Management* 5 (1): 1–7.

Lashley, C., and A. Morrison, eds. 2000. *In Search of Hospitality. Theoretical Perspectives and Debates.* London: Elsevier.

Lashley, C., P. Lynch, and A. Morrison, eds. 2007. *Hospitality: A Social Lens.* London: Elsevier.

Lofgren, O. 1999. *On Holiday. A History of Vacationing.* Berkeley: University of California.

Lynch, P. A. 2005. "The Commercial Home Enterprise and Host: A United Kingdom Perspective." *International Journal of Hospitality Management* 24 (4): 533–553.

Lynch, P. A., and D. MacWhannell. 2000. "Home and Commercialized Hospitality." In *In Search of Hospitality. Theoretical Perspectives and Debates*, edited by C. Lashley, and A. Morrison, 100–117. London: Elsevier.

Lynch, P. A., A. McIntosh, and H. Tucker, eds. 2009a. *Commercial Homes in Tourism. An International Perspective.* London: Routledge.

Lynch, P. A., A. McIntosh, and H. Tucker, eds. 2009b. "Introduction." In *Commercial Homes in Tourism. An International Perspective*, edited by P. A. Lynch, A. McIntosh, and H. Tucker, 1–22. London: Routledge.

Lynch, P. A., A. McIntosh, and H. Tucker, eds. 2009c. "Conclusions and Research Considerations." In *Commercial Homes in Tourism. An International Perspective*, edited by P. A. Lynch, A. McIntosh, and H. Tucker, 204–218. London: Routledge.

Lynch, P., J. Molz, A. McIntosh, P. Lugosi, and C. Lashley. 2011. "Theorising Hospitality." *Hospitality and Society* 1 (1): 3–24.

Mason, J. 2002. *Qualitative Researching.* London: Sage.

Morgan, D. H. J. 1996. *Family Connections. An Introduction to Family Studies.* Cambridge: Polity Press.

Morgan, D. H. J. 2011. *Rethinking Family Practices.* Basingstoke: Palgrave Macmillan.

Morrison, A. 2002. "Hospitality Research: A Pause for Reflection." *Int. J.Tourism Research* 4: 161–169.

Orbrador, P. 2012. "The Place of the Family in Tourism Research: Domesticity and Thick Sociality by the Pool." *Annals of Tourism Research* 39 (1): 401–420.

Phoenix, A. 2009. "Complexities of Lived and Liveable Lives: Reconceptualising 'non-normative' Childhoods." Plenary session presented at 'Turning Personal' Conference, Morgan Centre, Manchester, September 16–17.

Robinson, M., and P. Lynch. 2007. "The Power of Hospitality: A Socioloinguistic Analysis." In *Hospitality: A Social Lens*, edited by C. Lashley, P. Lynch, and A. Morrison, 141–154. London: Elsevier.

Saxonville Hotel. no date. Accessed February 27, 2009. http://www.saxonville.co.uk/.

Schanzel, H. A. 2010. "Whole-Family Research: Towards a Methodology in Tourism for Encompassing Generation, Gender and Group Dynamic Perspectives." *Tourism Analysis* 15 (5): 555–569.

Schanzel, H. A., I. Yeoman, and E. Backer, eds. 2012. *Family Tourism: Multidisciplinary Perspectives.* Bristol, CT: Channel View Publications.

Seymour, J. 2005. "Entertaining Guests or Entertaining the Guests: Children's Emotional Labour in Hotels, Pubs and Boarding Houses." In *The Politics of Childhood: International*

Perspectives, Contemporary Developments, edited by J. Goddard, S. McNamee, A. James, and A. James, 90–106. London: Palgrave.

Seymour, J. 2007. "Treating the Hotel like a Home: The Contribution of the Single Location Home/Workplace." *Sociology* 41 (6): 1097–1114.

Seymour, J. 2011a. "On not Going Home at the End of the Day: Spatialised Discourses of Family Life in Single-Location Home/Workplaces." In *Geographies of Children, Youth and Families: An International Perspective*, edited by L. Holt, 108–120. London: Routledge.

Seymour, J. 2011b. "'Family Hold Back': Displaying Families in the Single-Location Home/ Workplace." In *Displaying Families: A New Concept for the Sociology of Family Life*, edited by E. Dermott, and J. Seymour, 160–174. Basingstoke: Palgrave Macmillan.

Seymour, J. 2015. "The Transgressive Potential of Families in Commercial Homes." In *Intimacies, Critical Consumption and Diverse Economies*, edited by E. Casey, and Y. Taylor. Basingstoke: Palgrave Macmillan.

Seymour, J., and T. Green. 2009. "Selling the Family? Family Imagery in Holiday Advertising." Paper presented at 'Turning Personal' Conference, Morgan Centre, Manchester, September 16–17, 2009.

Shaw, S. 1997. "Controversies and Contradictions in Family Leisure: An Analysis of Conflicting Paradigms." *Journal of Leisure Research* 29 (1): 98–112.

Smart, C. 2007. *Personal Life: New Directions in Sociological Thinking.* Cambridge: Polity.

Smith, G. 2010. "Reconsidering Gender Advertisements: Performativity, Framing and Display." In *The Contemporary Goffman*, edited by M. H. Jacobsen, 165–184. London: Routledge.

The Coniston Hotel. no date. Accessed February 27, 2009. http://www.theconistonhotel.com/.

Index

www.ingramcontent.com/pod-product-compliance
Ingram Content Group UK Ltd.
Pitfield, Milton Keynes, MK11 3LW, UK
UKHW010020280225
455677UK00023B/695